MECHANICS' INSTITUTE

MECHANICS'

MERCANTILE LIBRARY

A LIFE FOR WORLD PEACE

JAN WILLEM SCHULTE NORDHOLT

TRANSLATED BY HERBERT H. ROWEN

University of California Press   Berkeley   Los Angeles   Oxford

Photographs reproduced with the permission of Princeton University Library.

University of California Press
Berkeley and Los Angeles, California

University of California Press
Oxford, England

Originally published as *Woodrow Wilson: Een leven voor de wereldvrede*, © 1990 by J. W. Schulte Nordholt and Meulenhoff Informatief, Amsterdam.

Library of Congress Cataloging-in-Publication Data

Schulte Nordholt, J. W., 1920–
    [Woodrow Wilson : een leven voor de wereldvrede   English]
    Woodrow Wilson : a life for world peace / by Jan Willem Schulte Nordholt ; translated by Herbert H. Rowen.
        p.   cm.
    Translation of Woodrow Wilson : een leven voor de wereldvrede.
    Includes bibliographical references and index.
    ISBN 0-520-07444-0
    1. Wilson, Woodrow, 1856–1924.
2. Presidents—United States—Biography. 3. World War, 1914–1918—Peace. 4. United States—Politics and government—1913–1921. I. Title.
E767.S2613   1991
973.91′3′092—dc20
[B]   91-20191
                                        CIP

Printed in the United States of America

1   2   3   4   5   6   7   8   9

The paper used in this publication meets the minimum requirements of American National Standard for Information Sciences—Permanence of Paper for Printed Library Materials, ANSI Z39-48-1984 ⊛

*Een poëet mag niet alleen, maar moet in de
politiek utopist zijn.*

[In politics the poet does not have a choice
whether to be a utopian; he must.]
—*E. J. Potgieter*

*Und dann, mit einem Hochmut ohnegeleichen:
Ich und mein Haus, wir bleiben Gott vermählt.*

[And then, with matchless arrogance,
We remain, I and my House, wedded with
God.]
—*R. M. Rilke,* Josuas Landtag

I have never recognized an article about myself
in which I recognized myself.
—*Woodrow Wilson*

CONTENTS

Contents

PROLOGUE:
SEVENTY YEARS AFTERWARD

Events have become more gripping than ever. Almost every day we are inundated by dramatic news. Nineteen eighty-nine brought us huge demonstrations and then revolutions in Eastern Europe. It seemed then that all mankind had come into motion, and we imagined that we were living through the most fascinating era in history, the time of its greatest crisis. This judgment was of course distorted, because it arose out of our own particular perspective; wrong though it was, it was wholly understandable. Our perceptions are shaped after all by our own turbulent times. Yet this has always been true, for from the beginning of time there have been crises and unrest. "Why do the peoples rage?" lamented the Psalmist thousands of years ago (Psalm 2:1). We ask the same question now when we read the newspaper or watch the news on television.

This same thought must have occurred to Woodrow Wilson, a devoted student of Scripture, and when it did, it involved his entire being. What is now so striking is that the events we have been experiencing all revolve about his political concerns. Indeed, we are struggling with the questions that he grappled with and first called our attention to. Let us begin with the revolutions in Eastern Europe. There, after years of oppression by communism, nations have become free or are in the process of becoming free. There, now that the counterfeit slogans of Marxist brotherhood have proved to be lies, the old feelings of nationalism, long hidden beneath that artificial surface, are proving to be very much alive. The nations that owe their existence to Wilson are seeking to establish their true identity, while struggling with borders drawn for the most part in Paris back in 1919. Eastern Europe from one end to the other is, with all its tensions, the creation of the Peace of Versailles. In a certain sense Woodrow Wilson was the "godfather" of Poland, Czechoslovakia, Yugoslavia, and Romania. The Austrians, with their great city Vienna inside their tiny state, the Hungarians of Transylvania who have been incorporated into Romania, and the South Tirolese who form a province of Italy, all can still trace their political fate to the decisions that Wilson and his partners made seventy years ago. The Baltic states can still appeal to the principle of self-determination that Wilson preached.

Indeed, it was he who made the question of nationalism once again a matter of importance. He tried to find its solution in a grandiose vision, but failed to grasp how truly insolvable it was. It is still insolvable, but all the blame probably should not be placed upon him. As an American with a deep awareness of his country's federal tradition, he saw in the concept of self-determination the expression of the principle of "consent of the governed." He could not really comprehend the fierce emotional antagonisms within the crazy quilt of peoples—we can still call them "tribes"—that inhabit Europe. He struggled with the problem, making many enemies in the process, but also finding wise friends, like Thomas Masaryk, the Czech "father of the country." Whenever I see in the newspaper a photograph of Masaryk's successor in office and spiritual heir, Vaclav Havel, I am compelled to remember Wilson's noble aims. And I ask, why didn't Plato turn out to be right, why is the world not ruled by wise men? And I ask, too, isn't Wilson's concept of a federal solution for the problems of Europe, and specifically for the position of the great power, Germany, at its center, still the best way out of these difficulties? As 1989 came to an end, we Europeans were filled with hope for a better future.

But after 1989 came 1990. In reality we live in a world possessed by the devil, as the Dutch historian Johan Huizinga once wrote, a world that changes every day. A new crisis arose in the Middle East. And there too, as in Europe, we find the roots of the problem by going back to 1919 and the peace in which Wilson had so large but disputed a part. In 1919 the mighty Ottoman Empire ruled by Turkey collapsed and a new order was established in its place amid pains and difficulties, and most of all rampant selfishness. Able but partisan experts from France and England drew long lines upon the map, creating countries that had never existed before. The result was a new region of tensions, made still more inflammable by the Balfour Declaration, the British promise to the Jews of a national home. There too, Wilson sought for humane solutions; he even tried to guarantee the new order by American involvement, proposing an American mandate in Armenia that was rejected by the United States Senate. He hoped for a reasonable society of nations, but, as he understood only too well, the nations were not ready. For that reason he accepted compromises that at the moment seemed impossible to make work but which would be achieved in the future. He was an American optimist, a progresssive, brought up in the traditions of the nineteenth century.

He accepted compromises because he believed the problems inherent in them would be solved by international collaboration. As the founder of the League of Nations, he thought he had devised a solution to a problem we are again wrestling with so fiercely at this moment. All peoples would work together in the League, the peoples, he emphasized, not the governments, as had happened at the Congress of Vienna (the great specter at Versailles), unless the governments were really elected by the peoples themselves. He called this aim "making the world safe for democracy." This would provide a permanent guarantee of peace; for Wilson, with his pacifist inclinations and his strict conscience, this was the sole justification for the horrible war, which would be the last war, the war to end all wars.

There were, of course, several practical problems in doing this, problems so troublesome that his own country did not follow him and the Senate rejected his peace treaty and his League of Nations. Wilson preferred not to see the dark side of things; he assumed that the peoples would be happy with their newly given identities and dignity. He had a fundamentally optimistic vision of human beings. But if, within this friendly assembly of nations possessing the best of intentions, there was one that was dissatisfied, a miscreant who took up arms, what could be done? It was a question that he had to consider. In the Covenant of the new League of Nations, he tried to create guarantees against such a breach of good conduct. This was the special aim of Article X: "The Members of the League undertake to respect and preserve as against external aggression the territorial integrity and existing political independence of all Members of the League. In case of any such aggression or in case of any threat or danger of such aggression the Council shall advise upon the means by which this obligation shall be fulfilled."

This is precisely the situation that we face in the winter of 1990–1991. One country has attacked another and totally swallowed it up. It would seem to be the perfect example of what Wilson had wanted to prevent. Saddam Hussein has occupied Kuwait. What is the plain answer of the other members of the League of Nations, which is now called the United Nations? It is that they will meet their obligations. Of course there is a multitude of complications, for no historical event ever fits exactly a predetermined pattern. But that is true of all rules of law and is no reason not to enforce them. Wilson's successor in the White House today must on occasion raise his eyes to the portrait of his predecessor (or has it been taken down?) and be aware of the similarity between their situations.

Back in 1939, when the big aggressor was named Adolf Hitler (even though the United States was still not officially a member of the League of Nations), Franklin D. Roosevelt gazed upon Wilson's portrait and followed his example, if in his own way.

The problem was, of course, that the fine, strong words of the Covenant of the League were not particularly clear. The Council—now we would say the Security Council—was supposed to decide what reply would be given to this aggression. But this was the crux of the problem. What kind of force could be employed? Could the offender be deterred by the force of economic sanctions, by an embargo, or was it necessary to take up arms? The big question was, is, and remains: What force is available to meet a moral obligation? How do we link might and morality, deeds and dreams? Of course there is something called "public opinion," the general indignation of mankind. Wilson, a liberal, progressive Christian, believed very strongly in public opinion. He envisioned the outrage with which the peoples would express their judgment upon the violator of peace: "There is a great wind of moral force moving through the world and every man who opposes himself to that wind will go down in disgrace."

In our horror-filled twentieth century, ravaged by wars and mass murders, we are no longer so credulous. Public opinion is fickle: today it shouts "Hosanna!", tomorrow "Crucify him!" But we completely cancel it out: politicians must give due consideration to the attitude of their subjects, especially since the media have become so important. A balance must be found between practical politics and morality, between realism and idealism. The yearning for a better world may seem a mere chimera, but isn't it at the same time a fact of life? Human beings are not as good as Wilson hoped, but isn't it still necessary to raise constantly the question of morality in politics? Doesn't peace have a higher moral value, and isn't a war such as that now being fought in the region of the Persian Gulf a burden upon the conscience of mankind? Exactly like Wilson, we seek fervently a moral justification for our international policy and we discover it where Wilson did, however greater our realism probably is.

We are in many respects Woodrow Wilson's heirs. That is why it is of great importance to us to make out what kind of man he was, how he came to his exalted and advanced ideas, and why in the end he failed. That is my purpose in this biography. I want to examine more closely the life of a man who sought a solution to problems that are still ours, and who was therefore the first great advocate of world peace. He was, as it were, a whole peace movement all by himself.

I almost wrote "apostle of peace," but this phrase is too strong. It makes it seem that I had at least to some extent a work of hagiography in mind. Far from it! History is about people, their dreams and their failures. It would be all too easy to paint Woodrow Wilson as the great prophet who was always wiser than his fellow men. The purpose of a biography ought not to be to turn a human being into a figure of puppetry; to change the metaphor, to press him into flat uniformity. Was Wilson a prophet, an idealist, a dissembler, a practical man, a revolutionary reformer? He was to some small extent all of these. Like most great men, indeed like most people, Wilson was a bundle of contradictions. That is what makes him so fascinating. He was many things: a scholar driven by deep feelings; a poet who found his vocation in politics; a Christian consumed by his need for recognition; a lonely man who thought he understood mankind; a practical man who became fossilized in all too lofty dreams; a reasonable man full of turbulent passions. It is this paradoxical personality that I have tried to respect in this book, the irritating, moving grandeur of a self-willed man who played an immense role in history and whose importance has become extraordinarily great in our own times, even though he failed so wretchedly. That is why his life story is a dramatic tale, almost a Greek tragedy, with a catharsis at the end that still drains and raises our emotions.

J. W. Schulte Nordholt
Wassenaar, the Netherlands
January 30, 1991

ONE

You are assuredly my second edition, "revised and improved" as to content, and with a far superior letter-press and binding.
        —*Joseph Ruggles Wilson to*
            Woodrow Wilson, March 12, 1887

FATHER
AND
MOTHER

THE PARSONAGE WHERE Thomas Woodrow Wilson was born on December 28, 1856, still stands, stately and in good condition. With its high white columns front and back, it might well have been a planter's house. It was, however, the home of the minister of the Presbyterian church, Joseph Ruggles Wilson, a man of some eminence in the sleepy country town of Staunton, in the western hills of Virginia.

The story of Woodrow Wilson, his first son and third child, must begin with this imposing Presbyterian preacher. Every Woodrow Wilson biographer has engaged in the lively and even heated debate over the role that this father played in the life of his famous son. He was an impressive figure, tall and strong, with a powerful voice that carried authority. As a father, he was an overwhelming presence in the life of his children.

Sigmund Freud, Woodrow Wilson's most celebrated biographer although by no means the best, worked out an elaborate theory according to his usual pattern: the son, he held, was totally dominated by his preacher-father, to whom he owed his fears and complexes. His tension-filled life was a true and sad example of father fixation; the oppressive weight of the father's influence inhibited the son and twisted his personality. The result was that, no matter how great his successes, whatever he did turned out badly. Ultimately, Freud asserts, he was a failure because he could never emerge from under his father's enormous shadow.

For a historian such an approach is far too simple and deterministic. This historian, for one, can only strive to see, without the benefit of such high-flown theories but at least with attentiveness, what kind of man this father actually was. Was he really so dreadful? Was his son's life really so twisted? If Woodrow Wilson was indeed a failure—and that too is a matter of interpretation—was it really predetermined by his inheritance? Since the book by Freud and his American coauthor William Bullitt first appeared (it was written in 1939 but not published until 1967), much new material has come to light about the Wilson family. It is now possible to give a more nuanced picture not only of the father but also of the mother, whom Freud leaves in the shadows.[1]

The Reverend Joseph Ruggles Wilson, the son of Scotch-Irish immigrants who had settled in Ohio, was established in his pastorate in 1849, when he was twenty-seven years of age; later that same year he married Janet Woodrow, whom everybody called Jessie. She was descended from a long line of Scots preachers, and her parents, also immigrants, came from Carlisle in Cumberland.

Joseph Wilson was called to the pulpit by a number of prosperous congregations (Presbyterians were for the most part members of the upper middle class), and he also taught pastoral theology and "Sacred Rhetoric" for several years in the church's seminary in Columbia, South Carolina. The native Ohioan had moved to Virginia in 1851, and for the rest of his long life he lived and worked in such Southern states as Georgia, South and North Carolina, and Tennessee, except for the last two years before his death, which he spent with his son in New Jersey at Princeton. His son in later years boasted of being a Southerner, but he was one only by chance; nonetheless he was truly a Southerner, facing all the advantages and disadvantages of being one when he became president.

Father Wilson was a good pastor, a highly praised pulpit orator, and yet, according to his son, he was not really "meant for a pastor—despite the testimony of his splendid pulpit powers—but he is of the stuff of which the greatest teachers are made," as he wrote in 1884 in a letter to his fiancée.[2] He wrote those words about his father when Joseph Wilson had been named a professor for the second time, at Southwestern Pres-

byterian University in Clarksville, Tennessee, again with the task of train-
ing theological students in pastoral practice. Significantly, in Clarksville
as earlier in Columbia, Joseph Wilson's university career ended in failure.
There is no need to recount here all the problems and conflicts he faced;
what is striking is the strong resemblance between the course of the lives
of father and son. Both got into conflicts in which they were absolutely
certain that they were in the right and would not budge, so that in the
end they lost. In both, behind outward self-assurance lurked an inner in-
security, although they remained unflinchingly impassive. Yet they did
possess the courage—or was it stubbornness?—to stick things out to the
end. They were inflexible men who knew they were extraordinary, but
they were also true disciples of the humble man of Nazareth. This combination of inflexibility and humility was probably the source of their ethical absolutism; it made them suffer in confronting reality but also lifted
them above it.

Joseph Wilson was anything but a stern pastor, for he practiced a
mild Christianity of propitiation, in which "the blessed Jesus . . . that sum
and substance of God's completed thoughtfulness for them who hurt
Him," stood at the center.[3] He was not strict in doctrine or life; he was,
to be sure, opposed to card playing and dancing, but enjoyed pipe smok-
ing, played billiards, and was not averse to "a good nip of Presbyterian
Scotch."

Religion was for him not primarily a system of dogmatic certainties
but an inner conviction that had to express itself in daily life and was
sustained by faithful performance of religious duties, church attendance,
prayer and Bible reading at the table, kneeling together in the evening,
and singing together. Scholars without the vaguest idea of such a pious
inner life can easily caricature it, and some have done so. But Joseph Wilson's letters to his son and other evidence of their relationship tell a different story.

To prove that the child suffered under paternal oppression, it is often
argued that young Tommy did not learn to read and write until quite late;
he could not tell the letters of the alphabet apart until he was nine, and
could read easily only at twelve. This is said to have been the result of his
sense of oppression by an exacting father. But when young Tommy was
a schoolboy, the Civil War had disrupted the regular pattern of life. Probably even more important was that he inherited his mother's frail constitution, not that of his robust father. Modern medical research puts the

Father and Mother

blame for his tardy intellectual development on dyslexia, which is caused not by psychological forces but by a disturbed relationship of the two halves of the brain.[4]

The frequent letters that the father wrote to his college-bound son are a mixture of admonitions and encouragement, always permeated by intense love and warmth of feeling. From the beginning the father seemed to understand that his son was exceptional, and he therefore was all the freer with advice. His stress upon one's own experience and upon language as the means for being one's self placed a powerful stamp upon his son's character; it could be argued that it became the key theme of his life. The father saw acutely that the danger threatening his son was that he would become too vague, that he would lose himself in dreams. You can do so much, he told his son, you have talent, character, a manly carriage. "Do not allow yourself, then, to feed on dreams—daydreams though they be. The roast beef of hard industry gives blood for climbing the hills of life."[5]

Whatever psychologists may make of these exhortations, the pastor's son did not experience them as humiliating faultfinding, not to say oppression. He admired his father, was deeply grateful to him, and readily told him so:

> As you know, one of the chief things about which I feel most warranted in rejoicing is that I am your son. I realize the benefit of being your son more and more as my talent and experiences grow; I recognize the strength growing in me as of the nature of your strength.[6]

The father heard these words with deep satisfaction and was grateful to be a witness to his son's splendid career: "Ah, my son, this old heart—you fill it, and with a charm that is unspeakable."[7]

May my reader pardon me for one more quotation from the old man that is so typical of the warmth of his eloquence expressed in well-chosen metaphors, a quotation in which a father's pride reaches magnificent culmination:

> You are assuredly my second edition, "revised and improved" as to content, and with a far superior letter-press and binding. How I bless God that it is even so, and that no law of His forbids the pride your father takes in his larger son.[8]

It is easier to speak of the father than of the mother. She did not have his command of language and we have fewer letters from her. She has therefore remained in the shadow, as she would have wished. All we can say with some certainty was that she was as prudent and introverted as her husband was convivial and verbal. It was probably the introversion that a black houseservant had in mind (in the nineteenth century in the South, servants knew their bosses better than their bosses knew them) when he said, "Outside Mr. Tommy was his father's boy. But inside he was his mother all over."[9] When it came to prudence, Wilson would be his father's boy all his life.

TWO

You know my passion for original work, you know my
love for composition, my keen desire to become a master
of philosophical discourse, to become capable and apt in
instructing as great a number of persons as possible.
    —*Woodrow Wilson, May 11, 1883*

AN EXCEPTIONAL YOUNG MAN

A MYTH OF WOODROW Wilson as a lonely boy who couldn't handle reality very well but dreamed grand dreams makes too much of what actually happened. Of course Tommy had his boyish dreams, but they were the same as those of so many other boys. He was fond of sports and played baseball. Once he learned to read, he went on to read the boys' books of James Fenimore Cooper about the Indians in the American forests, and those of Frederick Marryat about English heroes on the seven seas; sometimes he played at being a little Indian, or imagined he was an admiral, "Lord Thomas W. Wilson, Duke of Eagleton, Lieutenant General, Count Schkloffe, Knight of the Garter, Knight of the Star of India, Knight of Bath, M.P."[1]

His attendance at school was irregular in those years of disrupted life after the Civil War. In Augusta, Georgia, he went to a private school for boys run by a former officer in the Confederate army, and then, in Columbia, South Carolina, to one led by a college graduate. He learned reading, writing, and arithmetic, a little Latin and less Greek, but quite a fair amount of American history. He had to memorize and recite psalms, which he enjoyed. He wrote pious songs in his notebook, which were probably his first attempts at self-expression in poetry.[2]

He did not reach his full height until 1874, which was late, but spiritual growth came more quickly. A year before, he was accepted as a member of the Presbyterian church. He continued to practice self-examination, and confessed a year later in his diary that he had already squandered seventeen years in sin and had hardly grown in grace.[3] He was away from home for the first time in the winter of 1873–1874, as a freshman at Davidson College, a Presbyterian school in North Carolina. What he himself wanted to become was not yet clear. It had been taken for granted that he would follow in his father's footsteps, but, for all the intensity of his religious feelings, this was not what he wanted to do. The decision not to follow an example that he honored must have been difficult. Feelings of remorse and uncertainty found expression not only in stereotyped words about religious shortcomings but also in extreme bewilderment. Although he was not at all a poor student, he became homesick and returned to his family in the spring of 1874. A year passed before he was ready to resume his studies.

He devoted his year away from school to reading a great deal of history, to long discussions with his father, and to learning stenography, a skill that proved useful in his later career. In the loving atmosphere of his parents' home, he got back on his feet. In the spring of 1875 he left home again to attend Princeton University, and this time everything went just as planned. Princeton is now a world-famous institution, but in 1875 it was a very provincial Presbyterian college with an old-fashioned curriculum and a strong stamp of pietistic religion.

Wilson stayed at Princeton for four years. He took the required courses, was active in sports and games, and became an enthusiastic member of debating clubs. He read and wrote a vast amount, as if to make up quickly for what he had not done earlier. As a student he was good but not outstanding. Thin of figure and awkward in movement, he was very self-conscious; yet he made close friendships, some of which he kept over the years. He was a leader in the "Whig Society," one of the two literary societies on campus, winning a prize in a debate over "The Ideal Statesman," during which he argued fervently for fair discussion without "declamation and court oratory."

He discovered that his true interest lay in history and politics, always with a very strong literary emphasis. At an age when one easily and eagerly adores great men, he devoured the great Romantic historians. Enthusiastic about Carlyle's *French Revolution*, he placed Macaulay even higher, typically admiring him for the brilliance of his imagination. He came under the spell of Macaulay's style, as can be seen clearly in the first works from his pen.[4] When, not long afterwards, John Richard Green's *Short History of the English People* came into his hands, he noted that Green combined the honesty of Carlyle, the expressive power of Gibbon, and the clarity of Macaulay.[5] All his great models were English. He read Burke, Bagehot, Bright, and Cobden with unmatched enthusiasm, and gave voice to his admiration for them in essays, making their magnificent world his own. But, in the young man's gallery of heroes, first prize went to the statesman William Ewart Gladstone, in whom Wilson found everything that he desired and admired at its peak: literary gifts, vigorous statesmanship, magnificent oratory, and deep Christian faith.

As his study of politics deepened, he came to believe that England's constitutional system was much better than America's, and this became a central theme of his studies. While still an upperclassman at Princeton, he ventured to write an essay entitled "Cabinet Government in the United States," in which he argued that the president should choose the members of his cabinet from Congress, creating a form of ministerial responsibility similar to England's. Wilson sent the piece to the monthly *International Review* and received a highly favorable response from the editor-in-chief, Henry Cabot Lodge, who was himself still an unknown. It was Wilson's first published piece, and he and his parents were proud of it. His experience with Lodge later in life would be of a wholly different character.

When the young man completed his education at Princeton in 1879, receiving a bachelor of arts degree, the need to choose a career again became pressing. He continued to reject the ministry, which his father still wanted him to enter, turning instead to politics. As he wrote a few years later, "The profession I chose was politics; the profession I entered was the law. I entered the one because I thought it would lead to the others. It was once the sure road; and Congress is still full of lawyers."[6]

With a political career in mind, he went to study law at the University of Virginia at Charlottesville in the fall of 1879. Virginia was then a small university with fewer than four hundred students. The law school had only two professors. One, John B. Minor, was a man of unusual gifts, a wise and strict teacher who was also a friend to his students. Minor invited them to his home on Sundays for conviviality and singing. But even such a model did not give Wilson any real taste for the study of law, and his choice soon proved an error. To be sure, he worked hard and read the classical works of jurisprudence, especially Blackstone's *Commentaries*, but he groaned under the requirements of precision and subtlety inherent in the field. "Law is indeed a hard task-master," he wrote to one friend, and to another, "I wish now to record the confession that I am most terribly bored by the noble study of Law sometimes."[7] To stick to dry lawbooks was simply beyond him, and he was equally repelled by the daily reality of a lawyer's life. He admitted that he was not fit for the practice of law; he could not breathe in an atmosphere of broken promises, crimes, and quarrels. He was becoming cynical, he wrote, because he was seeing only the bad side of human nature.[8] And he did not want to become a cynic; he wished to see the world from the sunny side.

He compensated for the drudgery of lawbooks with a merry student's life, and again played a leading role in the debating club—called the "Jefferson Club"—where a variety of topics, such as the gold and silver standard, ministerial responsibility, and nihilism in Russia, were discussed. Wilson rose to be president of the society and tried to introduce a new set of rules; making ideal plans was something he enjoyed. He excelled as a speaker, and an oration about the English statesman John Bright made a deep impression on his audience, which, to his delight, applauded loudly. One of his friends wrote that he "never knew a man who more keenly relished" applause.[9]

Yet it was hard for him to take losing. In a public debate over the question of whether Roman Catholics constituted a threat to American institutions, Wilson argued the negative side, but another student won the medal. Wilson was put out and reluctant to accept a consolation prize. The opponent who won the medal also beat him in a competition for the best article in the university newspaper, and again Wilson had to be satisfied with honorable mention. Again he found it hard to swallow the loss.[10]

Along with the legal studies he detested, Wilson worked hard at the things he liked. He reformulated his thoughts about the parliamentary system.[11] An article he wrote about his great hero Gladstone tells much about his own ambitions. Gladstone came "of sturdy Scotch stock," had been "a sober, thoughtful boy," was a statesman and a Christian, and his finest quality was his "poetical sensibility." The special character of a great leader like Gladstone, Wilson said, was that he instinctively embodied his country, he had the soul of a poet and the wisdom of a statesman. This theme, enunciated by Wilson when he was twenty-three years old, continued to dominate his thought as long as he lived, returning in countless variations in numerous letters and speeches. It was the theme of the true leader who feels within himself what the people feel and therefore is able to lead them with rousing words. Wilson saw this in Gladstone, who was a great man because he was a great orator, full of warmth and passion and deep conviction.[12]

Plainly unfit for the quibblings of lawyers, Wilson felt called to a mission. He was surprised, he wrote to Charles Talcott, one of his best friends from Princeton, that his vague political plans had kept him occupied every day until at last a calm confidence came over him and assured him that he was destined to do great things; but he was unsure whether it was only a figment of his imagination that arose from exaggerated vanity or something that came out of a deeply rooted strength of purpose that one day would bear fruit.[13]

Wilson never completed his studies in Charlottesville. In December 1880 he caught a bad cold that hung on, until finally, at the urging of his worried parents, he returned home. He was again utterly confused, and again he recovered in the solicitude of his parents' home. He stayed there for more than a year, completing his legal studies, as was then possible. He continued to plan a career as a lawyer, but read the orations of Cicero and closely followed political events. He was endlessly fascinated by the human drama, with its glory and its tragedy, which is played out so intensely in politics, and he continued to believe he would have a political career.

He passed his bar examination in Georgia and set up in practice with a partner, Edward I. Renick, in Atlanta. It was a city with a future, where the new industrial and commercial South was coming into its own, and he flattered himself that there, "in his native air," he could build a good career. But it all came to nothing. His partner was, like himself, a man of literary interests, and they read Virgil together, but clients did not come in.

After his failure in Atlanta, Wilson came to a firm decision that he would would try to become a "literary politician," a close observer of politics rather than a player in the game. To a friend he wrote that he hoped now to trace out a future career as a writer and speaker. But for that he needed free time: "My plain necessity, then, is some profession that will afford me a moderate leisure; what better can I be, therefore, than a professor, a lecturer upon subjects whose study most delights me."[14]

This decision embodied both disappointment and hope. Wilson preferred to believe that he was taking a detour. In a long letter to his fiancée he used the very word "disappointment"; his great ambition was still to become a statesman. He had, he wrote, a strong instinct of leadership and a clear temperament as an orator, and his greatest joy was politics. It had cost him much to be satisfied with the sober methods of the scholar and the man of letters. "I have not patience for the tedious toil of what is known as 'research'; I have a passion for interpreting great thoughts to the world; I should be complete if I could inspire a great movement of opinion."[15] It is still impressive to see how clearly the young man, hoping against hope, foretold his own future.

He had found a temporary end to his dilemma. In the spring of 1883 he left Atlanta, where he had still been financially dependent on his father, and decided to return to his studies. He was accepted as a graduate student in history and political science at Johns Hopkins University in Baltimore, and entered in September, although he did not receive the fellowship for which he had applied. It seemed he had at last found his way.

If it was not the straight way toward the world of deeds and fame, he still ventured upon graduate studies with the ardent passion and ambition so typical of him. He would also make an impression as a very exceptional young man in the world of scholarship and reflective thought, the world of the word. When the renowned historian Frederick Jackson Turner met him a few years later, he was struck by the fierceness of his personality. To an acquaintance Turner wrote: "Mr. Wilson is here. Homely, solemn, young, glum, but with that fire in his face and eye that means that its possessor is not of the common crowd."[16]

An Exceptional Young Man

THREE

Als Historiker kenne ich die Menschen nur oberhalb des Nabels; was unterhalb sich befindet, geht mich nichts an.

[As a historian I know people only above the navel; what is below does not concern me.]
—*Leopold von Ranke*

HUSBAND AND FATHER

IN WRITING THE BIOGRAPHY of a great man it is customary to stress the complexity of his personality. Yet my impression of Wilson is that he was a man of one piece, a man of fiery passion driven by ambition. Passion and ambition often go together in history. How often have the lives of men with exceptional energy been driven by these traits, sometimes leading to high success and sometimes to disaster.

The combination of passion and ambition is very striking in Wilson. Later we shall repeatedly speak of his ambition, but here it is a question of his passion. He possessed unusual warmth and strength of purpose. Passion explains his relations with women. It was said of Abraham Lincoln that he was a typical man's man, one who felt comfortable only among men, with whom he could talk politics; his marriage was no great success, not through infidelity but from inattention. Wilson, to the contrary, was a woman's man; he was happiest in female company. True, he had good and loyal men friends, but he could not exist without the deeper warmth of a relationship with women, primarily within marriage, but also outside it in a series of very intense friendships. If we know him so well, it is because he gave so completely of himself in the letters he wrote to women, in the first place to his wife, but also to many others.

He had grown up in the South, where a sultry gallantry placed the white woman on a pedestal, worshipped but not taken seriously. It was an attitude he never completely lost. He long opposed women's suffrage but declined to speak out against it in public because he thought logical arguments were not listened to; he firmly believed that women themselves did not want the vote.[1] He shuddered when he heard women speak before an audience.[2]

He enjoyed the company of women without hypocrisy; it was openly discussed at home. "Father enjoys the company of women," his daughter wrote in her memoirs, "especially when they are what he called 'charming and conversable.'" And he found beautiful women more "conversable" than "plain ones." He thought women had finer sensibilities and better understanding than most men.[3] There were boundaries, of course, that could not be crossed in these relationships, established not just by the times but, for Wilson, by his strong religious principles. They apparently kept him from the impermissible. In only one of these relationships did he go beyond what his conscience could afterward approve. Even then his marriage remained intact, the essential core of his life. Perhaps we should look at it differently. It may have been not primarily his principles but his dreams that kept him pure. He was a Romantic poet in spirit, always maintaining his distance from reality when he left the protected circle of his home. His relations with women were verbal; in the long letters he wrote to them, he could work off enough of his idyllic eroticism to keep himself happy, at least most of the time. The deeper reality of physical passion he experienced within marriage; it gave exceptional depth and brilliance to his letters to his wife, even in his later years. In short, Wilson had a happy marriage.

To be sure, he had fallen in love once before marriage. When he was twenty-four and a law student at Charlottesville, he had become infatuated for a short time with a cousin on his mother's side, Harriet Woodrow. She was a student at a college in Staunton, his own birthplace thirty-five miles to the west over the hills. He made the journey more often than was good for his studies. He seemed to live fully when he was with Harriet, but she for her part, fearful of a relationship with a close relative, rebuffed him. His last letter to her, hoping forlornly that she would relent, was signed, "Yours if you would Woodrow."[4]

His first love affair had as its only lasting result that he ceased to use his baptismal name, "Thomas," or the more familiar "Tommy." Just why is not quite clear. He may have found "Tommy" too childish and preferred the smooth alliteration of "Woodrow Wilson." Shortening his name so that it was easier to recognize and remember may have been a sign of growing ambition. He wrote to a friend that it "sticks in the mind" and was therefore a better name for a writer.[5]

His great love came two years later. It began as a typical Victorian idyll. While residing in Atlanta, he traveled on family business to the country town of Rome, Georgia. He stayed for the weekend at an uncle's home and accompanied him to church on Sunday. How much of the sermon he heard we do not know, but he saw the girl of his dreams. Though she was wearing a heavy veil, he remembered her face and her mischievous, laughing eyes.[6] One thing led to another. Ellen Louise Axson hesitated at first to accept his proposal; her mother had just died, and she was taking care of her father, the local pastor. When they met by chance not long afterwards in Asheville, North Carolina, they found the providential coincidence decisive. They began to write long, intense letters to each other.[7] He adored his beloved, of course, as was befitting a Southern gentleman. But he conceived of her after his own ideal, as neither a blue-stocking nor an innocent little goose but a woman who "had acquired a genuine love for intellectual pursuits without becoming bookish, without losing her feminine charm."[8]

They became engaged in 1885, when he had the prospect of appointment as a professor at Bryn Mawr College near Philadelphia. Their marriage took place on June 25, 1885, in Savannah, and they spent their honeymoon in the mountains of North Carolina. It was a happy marriage, all twenty-nine years that it lasted, but it was not a marriage without problems. For Ellen Axson, as for so many other women, to have a gifted and egocentric man as a husband was a tall order. Although he came first in all things, she had her own gifts. She was quite artistic and studied at an art academy in New York, learning to paint landscapes that still please the eye. She also had a romantic love of poetry, so that she could share his feelings. She soon experienced, with a half smile, the completeness of his ascendancy. It still struck her as funny, she wrote him, that she was beginning to be convinced when he said that something is thus and so, even when it is not.[9]

In a period when tradition held sway, she solved the problem of an unequal marriage by self-sacrifice. Her daughter wrote: "Mother had no jewels, Mother who had sacrificed for us, so that father might have the books he needed, the vacations; that we might study acting and singing; . . . I thought of her rigid economy, her perennial brown dress and hat."[10] Although she was satisfied to take a place in his shadow, there was more to her marriage than sacrifice. She retained her independence of judgment, gave her husband wise advice, and was a quiet source of strength that he could always fall back on. She was more skeptical than he, less trusting. Her letters are more balanced, less extreme and exuberant, than his. She had her own opinions, expressed with prudence.

Their letters to each other reveal an abiding passionate tie. The tension between romantic idealization and physical passion was, at its best, dissolved in the awareness that soul and body cannot be separated, which was quite an accomplishment for persons brought up as they were in a puritanical environment. In his letters to her there was always a tendency toward the idyllic, flowing out of character and language and the times. He called her his queen, his maid, his adored one: "I never have a vulgar thought about you, when I touch you, it is always as I were touching your soul as much as your body."[11] But he did not conceal his almost demonic passion. "Every faculty of heart and mind and body yearned for you in a way that was little less than frightful."[12] The very day that he wrote this letter, he translated a passage from Théophile Gautier's *Mademoiselle de Maupin*, describing a love scene in the most uninhibited language. He was learning French, but more than French.[13]

He tried to be frank with her. He wrote her how much he liked to look at beautiful women, how seldom he was drawn to one who was not; but it was she, his own "Eileen," who was most beautiful of all.[14] The marriage, although threatened now and then, held up not because Wilson was afraid of problems or maintained Victorian pretenses, but because he could pour out his passion to her and she understood him and gave herself to him heart and soul. He drew the best conclusion: "It is the lover that predominates in me, not the husband."[15]

These letters all date from the 1890s, when the Wilsons had already been married ten years. It is intriguing that this remained their relationship even in later years, when the great crisis came. Most of his friendships were quite innocent and his wife was always involved in them. She never showed, wrote her daughter, "a trace of jealousy. She knew there was no cause for it. She considered herself a 'grave and sober person' and often said, 'Since you married someone who is not gay, I must provide you with friends who are.' "[16]

The memories of Wilson's daughter are nevertheless a bit too rosy. One friendship became a story of pain, going beyond the bounds of his wife's trust. On vacation in Bermuda, during one of the many trips his wife permitted him without being willing to accompany him, he met a charming woman of forty-one, Mary Allen Hulbert Peck. Allen was the name she was born with, her first husband, who died young, was named Hulbert, and her second, with whom she was very unhappy, was Peck. Wilson seemed to find in her the lighthearted gaiety he missed at home. He was enraptured. She was God's gift, "so perfectly satisfying and delightful." They saw each other again in Bermuda during vacation the next winter, as part of a merry company that included the aged Mark Twain. He wrote frankly to his wife, and it is obvious that she gave him a warning, for he responded, "Of course I am seeing a great deal of Mrs. Peck. She is fine and dear. But I am remembering your injunction."[17] But his raptures went further than was proper, as he later realized. At least in his letters to Mary Peck, he revealed more of his inner self, especially of his growing political ambitions, than he did to his wife, whose loving concern he seems to have felt as obstructive. And the tone of these effusions was extraordinarily warm.

No one knows how far he went, and that is probably to the good. Ranke is right, at least to some small extent. The letters of Mary Peck to Wilson have disappeared (he may have destroyed them himself); the letters of his wife from the summer of 1908, when he was on vacation in England, are, very exceptionally, also missing. This creates a hardship for scholarly researchers, but not for the tellers of love stories who can continue to guess whether or not Wilson and Mary Peck had sexual relations, as they do in the similar cases of Jonathan Swift and his Stella, or Thomas Jefferson and Sally.

Be that as it may, the fact is that Wilson later developed a strong sense of guilt about this relationship. In 1915 he confessed his remorse to his prospective second wife (he had become a widow in 1914) in burdened words: "Surely no man was ever more deeply punished for a folly long ago. . . . May God forgive me as freely as he has punished me."[18] He declared that he had not violated the honor of the woman involved and had not been unfaithful to his wife. But still he had sinned: "None of this lessens the blame or the deep humiliating grief and shame I suffer, that

I should have so erred and forgotten the standards of honorable behavior by which I should have been bound."[19]

There is not much more to say about the affair. Wilson showed himself—and this was quite characteristic of him—to be deeply guilty over a sin committed in words. Who can say whether he concealed or repressed something more? His wife Ellen told Dr. Grayson, the White House physician, in the last year of her life, that she indeed believed that the relationship had been platonic, but that it had been "the only unhappiness" that Wilson had caused her "during their whole married life."[20]

The story of their marriage is not complete without recounting the experiences of ordinary life. There are everyday trifles even in the life of a great man. We know much about Wilson at home from his many letters as well as from various memoirs. They provide a charming portrait, in direct conflict with the well-known picture of the stiff, cold, self-important professor. At home Wilson was the good companion and happy husband. His three daughters worshiped him. They were convinced that he was infallible: "Can you imagine father failing in anything?"[21] They enjoyed his funny stories, his lilting songs, his inimitable imitations, in Scotch, Irish, or black dialect or in Oxford English. They felt his great warmth. They accepted his authority as self-evident. And all this jollity was accompanied by a heartfelt religious life, with daily Bible reading, singing, and prayer.

This picture of nineteenth-century family life is truly most attractive and exemplary. But it has also the drawback inherent in such idylls that they are not entirely true. It was not pure gain for Wilson that at home he was so admired by his wife and daughters and other members of the household (many relatives and other guests came to visit), for it made him all the more vulnerable when the evil world outside failed to fall at his feet.

FOUR

A distinct feeling of maturity—or rather maturing—has
come over me. . . . It may be all imagination, but these
are the facts of consciousness at the present moment in
one Woodrow Wilson—always a slow fellow in mental
development—long a child, longer a diffident youth, now
at last, perhaps, becoming a self-confident (mayhap a self-
assertive) man.
        —*Woodrow Wilson, March 9, 1889*

PROFESSOR AND SCHOLAR

WOODROW WILSON WAS A
late bloomer, as he himself
was well aware. He did not
want to be a lawyer, and he
could not become a statesman, so
he became a scholar, but in his own
ebullient, unscholarly way, sharply at-
tuned to the present and to a future time when his own life and that of
the nation would merge. Later he became a political observer and commentator, in the hope that his explanations of events would help bring
about a better world. It is probably a bit too harsh to say that he was
unscholarly. From the brilliant brain of the ambitious young man came
notable achievements in political science—but they were always the product of a preconceived vision, impelled more by high enthusiasm than sober reflection.

The path of true scholarship began in Johns Hopkins University,
where his ever-faithful father continued to support him. He entered a
two-year program when he was already twenty-six years of age, and some
of his teachers were only a few years older.

In the decade of the 1880s, true scholarship appeared to be making headlong progress. A lofty optimism dominated Western civilization, manifested in a presumptuous certainty about man's knowledge of himself and hence about his ability to control his fate. The human sciences seemed to be able to serve progress as concretely and exactly as technology. Historical scholarship lost its romantic, dilettantish capriciousness and found delight instead in the most fastidious precision, quantifying and systematizing. Germanic thoroughness was the fashion, and Johns Hopkins was its outpost in America. There American historians learned to do fundamental and thorough work. But all this historical scholarship was explicitly directed to the present. On the wall of the seminar room hung the motto: "History is Past Politics and Politics Present History."

One might think that all this would have had a strong appeal for young Wilson. His own ambition, after all, was "the historical explanation of the modern democratic state," and his own self was at stake: "It is a task of interpretation. Interpret the age: i.e. interpret myself."[1] Yet what was being done at Johns Hopkins was not to his taste. In the first place, Wilson himself was deeply influenced by historians in the Romantic tradition, such as Macaulay, Carlyle, and Green, and, besides, he was a poet. But, even more, he could not adapt himself to a set pattern and accept being led by others. Once again his letters to his fiancée are filled with complaints. He had to work too hard. His teachers made him read too many things at once. When the weather was good and he had to bend over his books, he felt like a fish in a darkened tank, a horse in a stall, a bird in a cage[2]—oh, how he liked metaphors!

Like so many other university students, he was vehement in his criticism of his professors. Herbert Baxter Adams, Richard Ely, the young professor of economics (who like Adams was fresh from Heidelberg), and John Franklin Jameson, an instructor, may have been scholars with reputations, but in a letter from this cheeky student we read: "Of our three Ph.D.'s one is insincere and superficial, the second a man stuffed full of information but apparently much too full to have any movement which is not an impulse from somebody else, and the third merely a satellite of the first." In his conceit he added: "I liked them at first and still do not dislike them, but I expect very little help and stimulation from them."[3] But, as so often happens, the teacher proved wiser than the student. Wilson finally found courage to complain to Professor Adams, who saw something in him and permitted him to go his own way.

Wilson at once began to make valuable contributions to the seminar.

He could work hard when he worked for himself. He was writing his first important book, *Congressional Government*, and read chapters from it to the seminar. Even then, he put his rhetorical gifts into play. A fellow student describes him in action: "Tall, slender, sinewy, wearing a drooping mustache a shade darker than his colorless hair, he spoke with an easy affability of manner and in a voice of particular charm. . . . It was clear, penetrating and flexible."[4] But he also faced criticism. It is interesting to read that Ely, who was very much the careful scholar, found Wilson's presentations "very convincing, even if they were not absolutely sincere."[5] He was obviously annoyed by what we would now call Wilson's impressionistic method.

He continued to work hard, so hard that he suffered another collapse and had to return home for rest and recovery. After a year, however, he began to ask himself what he really wished to do with all this scholarship. Would he proceed to the doctorate? He felt that pure scholarly work would not satisfy him. He had been engaged for several years and no longer wished to be alone. He understood that the passion that he suffered in loneliness had to be channeled into marriage. This meant that he would have to give up his studies and earn a living, so that writing a dissertation would have to be put off. But, as he realized a year later, that would be unfortunate, for his career would be damaged by the lack of this proof of good scholarship. In consultation with his professor, it was decided that his book would be accepted as a dissertation, along with a strong performance on written and oral examinations.

In September 1885, Wilson took his first job as a professor of history at the newly founded Bryn Mawr College for women. The college president, a Quaker, appointed him principally because he was a Christian: "He was glad to find that I believed that the hand of Providence was in all history."[6] He stayed there three years but was not particularly happy. Like every young teacher, he learned more from his teaching than did his students. He did not think that they profited much from his classes, and, with male bias, attributed it to their feminine character. To give young ladies of their age lessons in history and the principles of politics, he thought as useful as instilling in butchers knowledge of the development of fashion.[7] But the fault was probably equally his. He lectured much of the time, dictated long passages, and allowed almost no discussion. Not surprisingly, he came into conflict with his colleagues. One of them remembered years later, when Wilson was already famous, that he was "inherently a self-centered man, intensely interested in his own career."[8] But he found peace and blessing in his marriage; his first two daughters were born in Bryn Mawr.

He was glad to be able to leave in 1888. Although still bound by his contract, he broke it over a triviality, leaving bad feelings behind him. He came out unscathed, however, for he accepted a new appointment at a men's school, Wesleyan College in Middletown, Connecticut. Thus it happened that a true Southerner landed in New England and spent two happy, very crowded years there. His family grew when a third daughter was born in Middletown, but in addition the Wilsons, with the proverbial family closeness of good Southerners, took two of Ellen's brothers into their home. Concern for the family always remained a central part of Wilson's life. His mother died in 1888, and he mourned her deeply. He gave much attention to his lonely father, who came to live with them.

As a professor, Wilson gave seven or eight lectures a week, some on general historical subjects, such as a comparative history of England and France, and another a survey of the governmental institutions of various Western countries. From this course came his textbook, *The State: Elements of Historical and Practical Politics, A Sketch of Institutional History and Administration*. This work, encyclopedic in character but without depth, was very successful, because, like almost everything that he wrote, it was clear and manageable. Meanwhile, on the invitation of his old teacher H. B. Adams, he began in February 1888 a series of twenty-five lectures at Johns Hopkins University. These were such a success that over the next decade he returned for several weeks a year to give a similar series. It was there that he had become a friend of a pupil, Frederick Jackson Turner, who eventually would far surpass him as a historian. But it should be said that Turner's brilliant idea that the origin of American democracy should be sought not in Europe but in the American wilderness, was certainly influenced by Wilson. As a Southerner and a Romantic, Wilson had always been ready to place emphasis upon a native nationalism, one that had grown up on the southern and western frontiers.

The ambitious young man did not remain long in Middletown either. In 1890 he was named by his old university, Princeton, to a chair to which the title "Jurisprudence and Political Economy" was given. He received another increase in salary. At first Wilson had wanted $3,500, but in the end he was satisfied with $3,000 with the proviso that he could continue his annual lectures at Johns Hopkins, which paid $500. He had returned to his base, the place where he fit in best. Princeton was close to the South but still far enough away to be national in character. It was a college with a firmly Christian foundation but still open enough to be able to change. Wilson felt at home there at Princeton and remained for twenty years. Princeton would eventually be the starting point for his grandiose political career. He was, and remains, the only American president who built a career not as a senator or the governor of a state (although he was a governor immediately before he went to the White House), but as a professor.

Wilson found life among his learned colleagues boring indeed. He wrote to a friend in Middletown:

> The tribe I professionally belong to (historians, economists, jurists, what not!) are desperately dull fellows. They have no more *literature* in them than an ass has of beauty. They don't know anything, because they know only *one* thing; and I am terribly afraid of growing like them. I am not only not a scholar, but I don't want to be one.[9]

This was the principle by which Wilson lived. He had no desire to become a specialist. He wanted history to be all-encompassing. His students all received his full attention; he had a place in his heart for them and believed in them. He fervently defended the "honor system," which permitted students to take their examinations without proctors after giving a promise that was accepted without question. He participated in the students' daily life and was interested in their sports, was a member of the "Faculty Committee of Outdoor Sports," and cheered at their football games. He was most closely involved, however, in their debating clubs. He spoke inspiring words to them, not only in the classroom but also in chapel services, still a regular part of college life, where he called upon them as sincere Christians to serve their country. The only thing he did not want to do was read their exams and papers; these, he found, were badly written and confused in thought.

Thanks to this warm openness and universal interest, he was also active in the administration of university business. He had his own clear vision—a deep fear of technological specialization. He had prophetic words of warning: "Science has bred in us a spirit of experiment and a contempt for the past."[10] Like individual persons, the university had to stay open to the whole range of a complete life—but without becoming the slave of society. He therefore urged the continuation of requiring classical studies for university entrance, including knowledge of Greek and Latin for prospective lawyers and doctors.[11]

A university should be a world in itself, "a place removed—calm Science seated there, recluse, ascetic, like a nun, not knowing that the world passes, not caring, if the truth but come in answer to her prayer; and Literature, walking within her open doors in quiet chambers with men of olden time, storied walls about her, and calm voices infinitely sweet; here 'magic casements opening on the foam of perilous seas in fairy-lands forlorn,' there were windows straight upon the street."[12]

He was a warm person, as clearly showed in the numerous close friendships he made at Princeton. He had cordial relations with colleagues such as George McLean Harper, Bliss Perry, John Grier Hibben, and many others. There was much mutual visiting among these friends; they helped each other when in difficulty, and admired each other sincerely. The most intimate of these friendships was with the Hibbens. John Grier Hibben was a professor of philosophy and like Wilson a loyal member of the Presbyterian Church. He and his wife saw the Wilsons almost every day, and they supported each other in many ways. "How profoundly grateful I am and thankful to God for your sweet and satisfying friendship," wrote Wilson to them in 1902. "Even if you should find me out and cease to love me, I at least have the precious possession of the years that have bound us together." When the Hibbens gave him a birthday present of Thomas à Kempis's *Imitation of Christ*, he was deeply moved and promised them that he would try to be worthy of the gift.[13]

There was at the same time the most intimate circle of security, the family, in which he could be himself completely and without inhibition. The 1890s were the years of fulfillment and untroubled happiness, the years of expansion. The family remained limited to three daughters; the hoped-for son was not born. But the house was full, as we have seen, with companions of every kind, family and friends. Ellen's older brother Stockton Axson lived with them for a long time and was an intimate friend, while her younger brother Edward Axson also came to stay for a few years and was to some extent the son that Wilson wanted. Edward's tragic death with his young wife and daughter in 1905 in a ferryboat accident was a hard blow for the Wilsons.

All this life on a footing of free friendship, all this delightful conviviality, cost a lot of money. The Wilsons could afford to live on a lavish scale only because Woodrow Wilson earned so much with his lectures and books, but also because his wife was an intelligent and thrifty house-keeper. She sacrificed herself for the family; she could no longer indulge her artistic inclinations, although she did draw effective portraits in charcoal of men whom Wilson admired, notably his father and Gladstone, to put in his study. She also designed, with plans and a clay model, the house in the English timbered style which they had built in 1896. Theirs was a Christian family life, fair and fine, impressive and edifying.

Yet, when we pay closer attention, we see a shadow hanging over that happiness. There was something incomplete and unsatisfied that seemed to attack this peace and calm from within. It was present in Wilson himself, but in time it ate into the others, his wife beyond question. There was something that drove him on and permitted him no rest. What was this demon? I do not believe it was only the need to strengthen the financial basis of their life, although that was certainly a factor. There was as well something of the Calvinist imperative to live a useful life of service. But how does one draw the line between service and ambition? In any case he himself drew no such line. He never refused an invitation, gave hundreds of lectures in these years everywhere in the vast country, and wrote hundreds of articles and numerous books. He continued to teach his courses and worked prodigiously. It could not go on without another break of health and spirit.

When Freud placed him upon his short, narrow procrustean bed, Wilson became an interesting subject for psychologists, and medical doctors then also turned their attention to him. It still behooves the historian to be prudent in the matter. Physicians too do not always agree about Wilson. Because so much data have been lost, uncertainty rules what we know and understand about the serious illness that struck Wilson in 1896. He experienced severe pain in his right arm and lost the use of his right hand. Some investigators believe that he had a stroke, but the doctor who treated him did not draw this conclusion. He had none of the other symptoms, no speech difficulties and no difficulties with his right leg. Soon afterwards he enjoyed a vigorous and happy bicycle trip through England. The physician did not consider the attack serious enough to forbid this vacation journey, which was scheduled for a few days later. And, remarkably, he was soon able to train himself to write with his left hand, in a quite legible although stiffer script.

His loving wife believed too that it was good for him to go away and gave her approval. He spent two months traveling through his beloved England, mostly on a bicycle. He visited all the shrines of his romantic imagination. Most important, of course, were the landscapes that had inspired Wordsworth, the Lake District and the Wye valley with Tintern Abbey, but he also went to the graves of Adam Smith and Edmund Burke, the village where Walter Bagehot was born, and more such sites that had a sentimental value. It was a delightful trip that did him enormous good, for he lived by such poetic contemplation. He came back with his health greatly improved. But he learned nothing from what had happened. On the contrary, he threw himself into work more fiercely than ever. His brother-in-law, Stockton Axson, even remarked on a profound transformation in him, an increased seriousness and dedication, a sharpened "sense of mission." Henceforth he seemed to permit himself no more relaxation, but intensified the pace of his work. It is the opinion of a modern commentator upon Wilson's religious life that a clear integration of Wilson's religious and political ideas began from 1896.[14] Stockton later told Wilson's biographer, Ray Stannard Baker, that he had gained the impression at the time that Wilson intended "to be about my Father's business."[15] A Savior was in the making.

FIVE

The power of a nation is in its ability to purify, elevate,
and vary itself. It does not lie in the things it possesses,
but in the things it is.
— *Woodrow Wilson, December 17, 1908*

But poets read history to collect flowers not fruits—they
attend to fanciful images, not the effects of social
institutions.
— *John Adams*

HISTORIAN AND NATIONALIST

*W*OODROW WILSON'S STUDY was a model of neatness and order, "never a book or paper out of place."[1] He sat in it with all his books around him. In front of him were his pen and paper or his typewriter (he used both). He was a strict wordsmith, however rhapsodic he became about his work. When he had finished, he put everything back neatly, the pen wiped and the books returned each to its place. Then he went to the bathroom to wash his hands and brush his hair. When he came back to the dining room, he was properly groomed.

Yet he was not a bookworm. As a conscientious historian, he wrote to Ellen, one has to plunge into books, for there is nowhere else to find the past. But without experience and imagination, the past has no meaning. A person is not really made "to sit all day in a hard chair at a square table."[2] But Wilson, who made up for his shortcomings as a poet by hard work, conscientiously spent long days sitting in a hard chair at a square table and wrote what he was able to. He did not often escape into nature, most often during his extended summer visits to Wordsworth's country.

Wilson wrote almost as if he were performing some religious ritual. In all his historical work we feel the force of his imagination, sometimes to its benefit and sometimes not. His work is more spirited than solid, very typical of what present-day critics call impressionistic writing of history. Wilson himself would not have understood why the word "impressionistic" should be thought insulting in the activity of a historian.

In an article of 1895, he set forth his own method of historical work.[3] He admitted at the start that the historian has to work with facts. But he asked what facts really are. He explained that historical truth is complex using a metaphor that reminds us of Byzantine theology: historical truth consists of invisible as well as visible things. The true historian evokes truth; he gives—these are his very words, in italics!—"*an impression* of the truth." He repeats: "The true historian works always for the whole impression." This enables him to give "the true picture and not simply the theatrical matter—the manner of Rembrandt rather than of Rubens." And that true picture can be evoked only by "imagination."

Wilson was not the kind of scholar who first does his research and then draws his conclusions. He was rather the kind who first has a vision and then checks it against reality.[4] Like a poet, he was present in his work and did not keep a critical distance from it—too much so, indeed, for a historian. Most of his historical writings would probably now be forgotten if he had not later won fame in politics. Yet they are very important for understanding his life, because it is in them that we can see the growth of his ideas.

His intense nationalism appears most clearly in this historical work. He was a Southerner, a son of the region that only a short time before, when he was still a small boy, had tried to secede from the Union. But he was therefore all the more concerned with what America really meant for him. Almost all his reflections turned upon this problem. If what one of his biographers wrote is true, that for him history implied moral involvement,[5] then we must add at once that for him morality was at least as much a national as a personal task. Unremittingly he made his subject the moral content of the American nation. For him, then, the personal and the national belonged together.

Wilson's historical works were in no small degree the story of heroes. In an essay of 1893 he examined the question of the characteristics of the great men of American history.[6] The true American, he held, was one who had broken loose from the European background and dared to think not regionally but nationally. He drew up a list of heroes of American history. Benjamin Franklin and George Washington came first, then Daniel Webster and Henry Clay, the great defenders of the Union took a position of honor, culminating in Abraham Lincoln, "the supreme American of our history," in whom the whole country was summed up. This unbounded admiration for Lincoln was very typical of the growing nationalism at the end of the nineteenth century. What was unusual is that it came from a true Southerner like Wilson.

It is worthy of remark that in that same year, 1893, he published his best historical work, *Division and Reunion, 1839–1889*, which had as its subject the great conflict of North and South. He wrote it at the invitation of a colleague at Harvard, Albert Bushnell Hart, as a part of a historical series. It was a relatively moderate and balanced work, if not without Southern prejudices. Although the nation as a whole changed during the nineteenth century and moved toward greater unity, he contended, the South, which held fast to slavery, remained a supporter of the loose confederal structure of the original Constitution, bringing on the clash of 1861. Yet slavery had not been altogether bad; it had been a school for the blacks and led whites to adopt "a noble and gracious type of manhood." The great malefactors of the Civil War had been the Abolitionists.

His writings and lectures gradually made Wilson into a national celebrity. Publishers discovered him and began to harass him with proposals. He did not accept them all, but still wrote much too much. For example, he permitted himself to be persuaded to write a biography of George Washington, first in parts in *Harper's Magazine* and then as a book that became a best-seller. It was a shoddy piece of work, however, thrown together at top speed, probably primarily for the money it brought in. *Harper's* paid him $300 for each of six installments, and the book earned large royalties. But it was an unbalanced work of sentimental nationalism, which presented a portrait of a Washington almost as prissily tiresome as he had been in Parson Weems's biography.[7]

It was probably also the desire to make more money that spurred Wilson to write a work that was even bigger but not much better, a *History of the American People* in five volumes. It reached such length because the publisher printed the work in large type and with more than eight hundred excellent illustrations. It is a very readable, even an enjoyable, book. Intensely nationalist, it has many great men in it; but in contrast to Wilson's principal model, Green's *History of the English People*, it displayed no awareness of social or economic background, not to speak of the cultural. It was written in a somewhat old-fashioned and much too flowery style. It had to endure a great deal of criticism, even from friends like Charles McLean Andrews and Frederick Jackson Turner, who called attention to numerous mistakes. This did not seem to bother Wilson, who even wrote to one of his critics:

> That was an amazing blunder in dates you caught me in, but it does not embarrass me. I am not a historian: I am only a writer of history, and these little faults must be overlooked in a fellow who tries to tell a story and is not infallible on dates.[8]

Historical writing, Wilson asserted emphatically, must be concerned with the present. His present was the 1890s, a period of great change, when America was being transformed from an agricultural land existing largely apart from other countries into an industrial power with international involvements. We are accustomed to considering the year 1898, when the United States fought a brief war with Spain, as a kind of official conclusion of the nineteenth century.

The war led to a sudden spurt of national consciousness and reflection. What was to be done with the Philippines and Puerto Rico, the conquered territories ceded by Spain? America, which had once been a colony itself, could not become a colonial power like the countries of Europe—England in South Africa, France in Madagascar, Holland in Atjeh in the Netherlands East Indies, and others elsewhere—that at that very moment were so brutally subjugating the "third world," as we now call it. The outcome of this clash of interests and ideals was that Cuba became free under the protectorate of the United States and the Philippines remained a possession. In the Philippines a bitter jungle war with nationalists followed, and a furious debate resulted within America over what the nation's character should be.

Wilson followed this entire development with comments on history and current affairs. He believed that America was a unique country and at the same time a kind of vanguard of humanity. He shared fully in the typical nineteenth-century belief that what happened in America prefigured and determined what would come about in the rest of the world. Furthermore, he believed, like so many of his contemporaries (including the famed English commentator James Bryce), that providence had a special preference for the United States: "Providence has presided over our affairs with a strange indulgence."[9]

This position as the elect of God brought with it great duties, however, now that America stood on the threshold of a new time. Already in 1895 Wilson had written an interesting essay on "The Course of American History." The West was decisive in historical development, he wrote, but now the long march westward had come to an end. This meant that new tasks arose, new "frontiers" opened, for America must and would always renew itself: "Let us . . . see our history truly in its great proportions, be ourselves liberal as the great principles we profess; and so be a people who might have again the heroic adventures and do again the heroic work of the past."[10]

In these words we hear the cult of heroism so popular around 1900. It was a general hungering for great, inspiring adventures that would break the humdrum routine of daily existence. A deep need grew up for affirmation of one's manhood in the service of high ideals. Enthusiastic commitment was given to Nietzschean glorification of the dangerous life. Domestic dissension was diverted and dissolved in foreign involvements. Theodore Roosevelt emerged as the American who embodied this whole mood, and around him there was a circle of idealistic imperialists, John Hay, Henry Adams, Alfred Thayer Mahan, and others like them, who dreamed of a new task and new responsibilities for America.

It may seem somewhat strange to find Wilson in this company, because we know his later evolution toward a much more humane idealism. But the excitement of 1898 carried him along as much as it did most other Americans, and he was able to lend it historical justification. In a memorandum that he entrusted to paper in August 1898, when the "splendid little war," as Teddy Roosevelt called it, was just ending but peace had not yet been concluded, he excused the American attack as a humane action, somewhat too hasty perhaps, but this was now no time to stand still. Every nation capable of "thinking on the run and amid the whirl of events" could prove its worth. And, though the jingoes might rejoice, it had still been a just war. And, more important, America had been totally transformed by it and stood before a new future.[11]

In the next months he continued to elaborate this theme. In November he declared in a lecture that Germany and Russia were apparently becoming the major rivals of America, but it was of course plain that of the three, the Philippines should be owned by America, "inasmuch as hers was the light of day and theirs was the light of darkness."[12] To a different audience he urged that history determined the fate of America. At first, he had not been in favor of taking possession of the Philippines, but now he felt that circumstances compelled America to do so, and it was good that democracy should spread; it was America at the service of the world. He cited the arguments in favor of a life of danger that continued until 1914.

> In the first place what does the conquest of the Philippines mean? It means that this country has young men who prefer dying in the ditches of the Philippines to spending their lives behind the counters of a dry goods store in our eastern cities. I think I should prefer that myself. The Philippines offer an opportunity for the impetuous, hot-blooded young men of the country to serve their country according to the measure of their power.[13]

Such language brought him very close to the clamorous patriot Theodore Roosevelt, and Wilson too half admitted that he was an imperialist, or at least an imperialist of sorts.

When we try to analyze his imperialism, however, we meet not only the familiar components but also new elements. First, the belief that America, now that the frontier was gone, had to find new space in the Pacific Ocean. A new time was breaking out, he said, a new vision could inspire the peoples and turn them toward the Orient. Hence politics in the twentieth century was radically different from what it had been in the nineteenth.[14] And this new, surprising development was really a logical continuation of the old expansion which gave the Louisiana Territory and Florida to the United States and led to the Mexican War, brought Texas into the Union, and even made Alaska American. "Who shall say where it will end?"[15]

A second aspect of this development, according to Wilson, was that it brought isolationism to a logical conclusion. Wilson maintained that this result had actually been in George Washington's mind in his celebrated "Farewell Address" of 1796, in which he had urged his fellow countrymen to stay apart from the Old World. Isolation had been useful and wise so long as America still needed to grow to adulthood; but now it was adult and it was time to reenter the world by going still further to the west. Wilson eagerly picked up the old conception of the westward movement of civilization, as set forth in Bishop Berkeley's famous line in the eighteenth century: "Westward the course of empire takes its way." In an after-dinner speech, Wilson called enthusiastically upon his hearers: "Now, gentlemen, will you follow the Scotch-Irish across the continent and into the farther seas of the Pacific? Will you follow the Star of Empire?"[16]

Wilson saw another, third aspect of this development. Like most of his contemporaries, he had an absolute belief in the superiority of Western civilization. The Orient must be opened up and transformed, Western norms had to be imposed, peoples who had stood still for centuries (according to the current ideas, the civilizations of China and Japan had not undergone development) must be broken from their moorings and become a part of the universal world of trade and ideas, and hence progress.[17] "The Anglo-Saxon race reconstructs the affairs of the world."[18] It had the task of educating the peoples of the third world. The inhabitants of the Philippines, without the experience of authority and order, were not yet ready for independence. Freedom was "the privilege of maturity, of self-control, of self-mastery." Obedience was the foundation of all regular government. The education of that faraway people had to be conducted with wisdom, however: "We must govern as those who learn; and they must obey as those who are in tutelage. They are children and we are men in these deep matters of government and justice." Americans, Wilson held, must be not authoritarian but mild; they must not repeat the mistakes of the English colonial system. But for the time being we cannot give the colonies self-government. It is something that really cannot be given. "*Can* it be given? Is it not gained, earned, graduated into from the hard school of life?"[19]

Wilson was therefore making excuses for American colonialism. He even ridiculed "the anti-imperialist weepings and wailings that come out of Boston."[20] But—and this is the fourth aspect of the development we have been discussing—he could do this only by giving it a very emphatic ethical justification. America was not truly imperialist because it did not act out of self-interest. This was a flagrant assertion from a historian who knew all about the history of American expansion; indeed, at first he admitted that there had been a certain ambiguity in the American conduct, that there had been "an odd mixture of selfish and altruistic motives" in Florida and Mexico and in "the unpitying force with which we thrust the Indians to the wall wherever they stood in our way."[21] But this acknowledgment of guilt in the country's own history became increasingly rare in what he said and wrote. He came more and more to believe that the "moral impulse" that improved the world came from Christian nations, from America in particular. Gradually he developed a complete theory of American unselfishness. America would show to the peoples of the world "the way to liberty without plundering them or making them our tools for a selfish end." "We are a sort of pure air blowing into world politics."[22] This became one of his principal dogmas—America was in the world to serve it! This was what providence had wanted. In an election speech in 1912, he indicated how religious was his nationalism, admitting his belief in providence.

> I believe that God presided over the inception of this nation; I believe that God planted in us the vision of liberty. . . . I cannot be deprived of the hope that is in me—the hope not only that concerns myself, but the confident hope that concerns the nation—that we are chosen, to show the way to the nations of the world how they shall walk in the paths of liberty.[23]

He would not have understood or wanted to understand anyone who argued against him that self-interest still was the hallmark of every nation and of all trade and industry, for he was brought up in the liberal belief that the material and the moral follow naturally from each other. True, he looked at big business in America with doubt and mistrust; we shall see how serious he was about that once he entered politics. But he believed essentially in the goodness of humanity, in the possibility of solving problems precisely by aligning interest and morality together. When he became president, he asserted with great certitude that the interests of America coincided with those of the world. Hence America must go through a spiritual rebirth and then lead the world to a better future.[24]

It was typical of Wilson that in all that he did he was a believer, or perhaps we should say, a poet, a man who had visions and believed in them because they appeared to him as both beautiful and useful. He continually hammered on the theme of patriotism as an altruistic, poetical virtue, which lifted people above themselves. He emphasized that American patriotism implied self-criticism: "If you think the country is wrong you are no patriot if you don't stand up and say so."[25] But patriotism also meant more than criticism, it recognized itself in the symbols of unity, in the national anthem and the flag. Children should learn to salute the flag. With a labored but oft-repeated metaphor, Wilson explained the pattern of the flag: the white stripes were the "lines of parchment declaring constitutional freedom," the "red bars the blood which flowed in that declaration's victory."[26] Patriotism was poetic inspiration. Whoever fought for his country fought for something that he could not see but still was real. "He fights for a poetic idea."[27]

Finally, there is a fifth aspect of Wilson's nationalism, one that would eventually be of the highest importance for him, although he could not anticipate that when he spoke about it in 1901. He reflected then that the great role that he urged his country to take in international politics would mean a strengthening of the executive power. That had, to be sure, been true in the beginning of the country's history. The role of the president had been large when the United States had been involved internationally during the period of the Napoleonic wars (the Louisiana Territory, the embargo, the war of 1812). Only afterwards had the country withdrawn into isolation. History would repeat itself: "Once more it is our place among the nations that we think of; once more our Presidents are our leaders."[28] And it would be he who would make it true!

SIX

There is a mighty task before us and it welds us together.
It is to make the United States a mighty Christian nation,
and to christianize the world.
    —Woodrow Wilson, November 20, 1905

CHRISTIAN AND STATESMAN

F ANY THEME IN WILSON'S life was truly of fundamental importance, it was his faith. Not only was he a Christian, but he wanted to be recognized as one; indeed, that was how people saw him. He had much of a clergyman's air about him, and more than once he was "mistaken for a man of the cloth."[1] It was a mistake that probably worked in his favor, for he lived at a time when the ministry, conveying qualities of social standing and personal trustworthiness, still enjoyed great prestige. Though Wilson gave the impression of a preacher, he stood at the same time at the very center of the world of politics, which is a world of self-interest and compromises. There were some therefore who thought him a pious phrasemonger and hypocrite whose words were always prettier than reality. The picture of Wilson as a master of bloated blarney became very common after the first World War.

The question of Wilson's faith and religious activities was one that had to be discussed by the horde of historians who have written about him. Few of them, however, have had much understanding or even mere knowledge of the curious subculture that Christendom has become in the twentieth century. Their misunderstandings of Wilson in his relation to his faith were legion, and the common modern aversion to Christianity added to their errors. For Wilson's first critics in Europe, the renowned figures of Keynes and Nicolson, his faith was tantamount to hypocrisy, or at best to stupidity. "His thought and temperament were essentially theological, not intellectual," wrote the former, and the latter added: "That spiritual arrogance which seems inseparable from the harder forms of religion had eaten deep into his soul."[2]

The picture of Wilson as a strict, rigid, bigoted Calvinist became commonplace. He was said to have inherited from his father the dogmas of predestination and human inadequacy which he continued to uphold. He is supposed therefore to have had "few illusions about men and their motives" and was at the same time a good example of the Weber thesis about the relationship between morality and profit in Calvinism.[3] Such notions appear to me to be a caricature.

Wilson's most important biographer, Arthur S. Link, and his student, John M. Mulder, have both written about Wilson's religion from a position of spiritual affinity. Link certainly sees his hero as a Calvinist: "He believed in a sovereign God, just and stern; in a moral universe, the laws of which ruled nations as well as men; in the supreme revelation of Jesus Christ, and in the Bible as the incomparable word of God and the rule of life." But, says Link, while Wilson's original faith, which was very traditional, was pietist and moralist, he changed in about 1902, when he was in his mid-forties, and came to a deeper and more personal experience of faith, "a full understanding of justification by faith," and learned to live by the "guidance of the Holy Spirit." By means of this faith he became a better democrat, interpreting man's possibilities in a more positive way.

This argument seems to me to some extent a rationalization of a strange phenomenon—the Calvinist as optimist. It is true, says Link, that Wilson's faith in the goodness and reasonableness of man, in the admirable possibilities of democracy and in the inevitable triumph of justice, did lead him to harbor illusions. A much more critical European commentator, the English historian H. G. Nicolas, says it rather more clearly: Wilson had a tendency to forget the doctrine of original sin all too easily.[4]

We must ask, then, what kind of Christian Wilson was in reality. The central question remains: How was it possible that a Calvinist—and that is what Wilson is called in most of his biographies—and therefore an adherent of the doctrine of human inadequacy, could come to expect so much of mankind? Perhaps he was really a representative of typical American optimism, which cannot tolerate the old orthodox mistrust of man, as the American historian of religion Sidney Mead has argued.[5] Perhaps that was, then, the reason that the founder of the League of Nations failed so tragically in the end, like a hero in a Greek tragedy, as has been so often remarked, and not, I would add, like a sinner in an Old Testament story.

One of the reasons for the protagonist's failure in Greek drama is his personal involvement in events. This characteristic is particularly essential in Wilson's case. In everything he did, he was present with all his heart. It does not help, he told an audience of preachers, to study and know a great deal, "unless the fire burns in you, nobody will be lighted by contact with you."[6] The fire burned in him. A profound certitude was the core of his existence—a certitude won in the midst of darkness. He told his secretary, Joseph P. Tumulty:

> But I believe in a Divine Providence. If I did not have faith, I should go crazy. If I thought that the direction of the affairs of this disordered world depended upon our finite intelligence, I should not know how to reason my way to sanity.[7]

What was the passionate faith that drove this man with such fury? Was it the Presbyterian faith that he received from his home? Wilson remained all through his life true to the church of his fathers. Yet that fidelity was more a question of life-style, in which moralism and sentiment played a large role, than of doctrinal steadiness.

He was an intellectual for whom Anselm's principle of *fides quaerit intellectum* (faith requires understanding), so essential in the Calvinist tradition, remained utterly foreign. Faith was for him by definition of a different order. Although he was confronted in his immediate environment with the questions of Bible criticism and the doctrine of evolution, which were making such advances, he was not in the least shocked in his faith. He admitted: "Unorthodox in my reading of the standards of faith, I am nevertheless orthodox in my faith. I am capable, it would seem, of being satisfied spiritually without being satisfied intellectually." And, at another time: "There are people who believe only in so far as they understand— that seems to me presumptuous and sets their understanding as the standard of the universe. I am sorry for such people."[8] Feeling, not understanding, apparently defined his faith.

Still he felt at home in the Presbyterian church, although occasionally vexed by its lack of warmth and musical quality. Once, when he was thirty years old, he fled with "a sob in his heart" from a church service because the preacher was so cold and formal in his sermon and his prayer. "I fear I should take refuge in the Episcopal service, to escape preaching."[9] This was an exception, for he remained a faithful, convinced Presbyterian, and from his youth had found the liturgical service of the Episcopalians "a ridiculous way of worshiping God . . . a mere dull form."[10] But there was always present in him a tension between experience and rationality. The things that moved him in the church service were Communion and singing. He discerned the danger of too much emotion, sneered at revival meetings as "flirting made easy," yet his own faith remained all the same primarily emotional.[11] When he sang he was moved to tears. He sang often, for wherever he went to study or to live, he became a member of church choirs.

There was a delightful debate about this between him and his fiancée. Ellen Louise Axson, with her artistic interests, wrote him from New York, where she attended art school, that she had heard a series of lectures about the great hymn writers, including Keble, Faber, and Newman. How does it happen, she wondered, that these poets were all Episcopalians (Anglicans), chiefly of "high church" persuasion and some—what was worse—"indeed converts to Romanism"? In his reply Wilson explained that the Presbyterian faith was in essence intellectual, the Episcopalian contemplative and emotional. The Episcopalian church service was full of symbolism, which the Presbyterian lacked; Presbyterians had no rite between God and the heart. And he added, "They live in a sort of Lake region of religion," a quite surprising comment from a man who made repeated pilgrimages to the English Lake District, the land of Wordsworth, the poet he so admired.[12]

Wilson, who was temperamentally a poet, would probably have been more at home with a liturgical service, but, however much his temperament was that of a poet and however much it fed his piety, it was not in the end poetry but politics that was the determining force in his life. It was Wilson the politician who remained true to his Presbyterian tradition because he fitted into it so well. He was imbued with the idea of democratic church government, which is closely bound up with Calvinism and is predominant in American church history. Inspired by his Scottish origins, he started from the principle of the covenant of the fathers, the pact between God and man and between men among themselves, as defined in the Bible. It created order in society and even in personal life. Human emotion, imagination, ambition, were all tamed and kept in order by the written political pact, the Constitution. During his entire life, as a leader of student clubs, a political scientist, a reformer, the creator of a world order, he studied and drafted constitutions, and to the last and most important of those he drafted, the charter of the League of Nations, he gave the name of "Covenant."

He was thereby drawn into another stressful area. Confronted by the tension between leadership and democracy, he came into conflict with himself. This tension came to dominate his overwrought emotional life. His Presbyterian background made him a democrat, but his inclinations and his sense of special mission ran in the opposite direction. The same tension between divine omnipotence and human responsibility, between election and free will, and, still deeper, between a personal god and a moral order within nature and history, between transcendence and immanence, defined his religious imagination.

The question therefore persists: To what extent was Wilson a Calvinist? It is true that he believed in divine leadership, in his personal life as well as in history. But what kind of god was this really whose leadership he claimed to follow so unconditionally? A second, closely associated question: What was his view of man? Did he, like his fathers, admit the omnipotence of God and man's nothingness? Link describes Wilson as more than orthodox: "It is significant that his religious beliefs were not only orthodox—they were also Calvinistic, formal and stern." He refers to a remark of Stockton Axson: "The idea of an all merciful God was . . . to him a piece of soft mentality."[13] But did that mean what it had meant for the Calvinist fathers, that there was a divine election to either eternal bliss or eternal punishment? It was a matter, says Link, of moral absolutism, the duty of man to obey the eternal unchangeable moral law of the universe. Mulder correctly adds a nuance to this picture by pointing out that we should not see Wilson as a pure moralist; for him it was not man's conduct but the inspiration behind it, the love of God in the heart, that was central. There are many places in Wilson's work to support this assertion. "Christianity has liberated the world, not as a system of ethics, not as a philosophy of altruism, but by its revelation of the power of pure and unselfish love. Its vital principle is not its code but its motive."[14]

But we go back to the question: What kind of God did Wilson believe in? For Wilson, writes Mulder, God was sovereign but "shares his authority with man. God predestined man to salvation and damnation but man retained freedom." But of course such an Arminian definition does not solve anything, and the eternal dilemma remains unexplained.[15] The question that we must ask is whether Wilson's god was really a personal god or rather a force, a spiritual ectoplasm, in the universe. His innumerable spiritual talks to the students at Princeton were calls to work and love, but never or almost never did he refer to the old dogmas of redemption and eternal salvation. Christ was "the perfect image of right living, the secret of social and individual well-being." In all that he did, there was "a suggestion of divinity."[16] To be sure, the central question for every man was what he thought about Christ. He had to be the center of life, an idea that was not without mystic meaning for Wilson. He was for that reason opposed to the admission of deputies from the Unitarian church to an ecclesiastical conference. They teach "salvation by character," he said, but that is an act of desperation, for man cannot save himself.[17]

He literally felt the presence of God in his life. He heard His voice deep in his heart. What kind of god this was he explained very characteristically in a sermon to students. He drew not upon the Bible but again upon the poet Wordsworth. He had himself walked through the hills where Wordsworth had written his magnificent poem, "Lines composed a few miles above Tintern Abbey." He quoted to his listeners the lines where the poet tells of his religious experience when he heard the voice of God:

> And I have felt
> A presence that disturbs us with the joy
> Of elevated thoughts: a sense sublime
> Of something far more deeply infused
> Whose dwelling is the light of setting suns,
> And the round ocean and the living air,
> And the blue sky, and in the minds of man,
> A motion and a spirit that impels
> All thinking things, all objects of all thought,
> And rolls through all things.

There you have, said Wilson, the permanent, authentic voice of life, the voice of God, of the eternal Spirit. Such magnificent pantheism did not exclude Christ, he was "the only permanent person of history . . . the only complete and unalterable epitome of what man is and what man would be, a creature of two worlds, the world that changes and the world that changes not." He was the perfect model, "our divine kinsman . . . the only true citizen of the world."[18]

There is a sublime fascination in these words, which are typical of the world optimism of the beginning of the twentieth century, but they have little to do with Calvinism. From this positive faith Wilson moved to a cheerful vision of mankind. As early as 1884 he wrote to Ellen Axson, who had asked him whether he wasn't too cynical about people, that he was able to admire them and that there was more good than evil in human nature. He applied this to himself: "To lose faith in my fellow-men would be to make of my mental life a mere negation, would be to lose the primal element of that enthusiasm without which a man is dead while he yet lives."[19] This belief of his young years grew steadily stronger and in the long run became unrealistic. It was a belief not in any concrete person but in man as such, a belief in mankind and in the first place, of course, in American mankind.

Wilson's faith fitted smoothly into an undogmatic and optimistic, and hence typically American, complex of religion and nationalism, a trust in the American man and society, which in our time has been described as "civil religion." This is the religion that binds Americans together, a kind of extension of the Enlightenment, in which America has a very special place in God's plan of salvation for the world and is the vanguard of humanity. Faith, he said, is "a sort of enlightenment." It grows slowly but surely in the whole world. The millennium is therefore irresistible. People are moral creatures who in the end will choose the good. There is in society a "moral force," so that in the end God and man, leadership and democracy, rise together in the advance of history. That is predestined. Predestination flows over into determinism, the will of God is realized in its acceptance by men. "If I did not believe that the moral judgment would be the last and final judgment in the mind of men as well as at the tribunal of God, I would not believe in popular government."

Wilson was therefore a Christian, a democrat, and a patriot in self-evident unity. His patriotism and idealism were not merely religiously inspired, they were a part of his religion—an earthly part, as he realized. He described it well in a speech in 1902 entitled "Religion and Patriotism." Unlike an individual, he told his audience, a nation does not have eternal life and therefore cannot hope for grace after death: "A nation must save itself on this side of the grave." A nation must fulfill its mission, and the individual can play a great role in it by bringing his own future into harmony with the plans of providence and bringing others into "that great process of elevation."[20] In other words, the individual, and in this case Wilson himself, must know and in the end will know what providence wants, and he becomes totally God's fellow worker. In this address the program for the coming years is given, its complete, urgent moralism, the osmosis of personal and national mission, the colossal overextension that in the final outcome resulted in failure.

"There is a mighty task before us," said Wilson a few years later at a meeting of church youth, "and it welds us together. It is to make the United States a mighty Christian nation, and to christianize the world."[21] He repeatedly returned to this theme of national religion. He gave a long speech in Denver before no fewer than 12,000 persons about the Bible, which he called the Magna Carta of American freedoms and literature as great as Shakespeare. He concluded in the summons: "America was born a Christian nation. America was born to exemplify that devotion to the elements of righteousness which are derived from the revelations of Holy Scripture."[22] America increasingly became in Wilson's imagination the model nation for the world, the only unselfish one and hence predestined to lead the whole world to a better future.

It is not easy to understand Wilson's immense exaltation. His time, his country, his faith, were all important factors. But we still always come back to the structure of his personality. Let us say that by origin or education—and who shall say which?—he was a man of faith by character, one who had to believe in order to live. He placed inspiration above the critical sense, life above studies, nature above books, poetry above prose, faith above reality. He admitted as much in a speech of 1905, in which he set ideals and ideas, dreams and thoughts, against each other.

> The pushing things in this world are ideals, not ideas. One ideal is worth twenty ideas in propulsive force. No naked idea is fit to become an ideal until we illuminate it, dress it up, and give it a halo that properly does not belong to it. We live by poetry, not by prose, and we live only as we see visions, and not as we have discriminating minds.[23]

SEVEN

There is more of a nation's politics to be gotten out of its
poetry than of all its systematic writers upon public
affairs and constitutions.
　　　—Woodrow Wilson, June 17, 1893

POET AND SPEAKER

*W*HEN WE SAY THAT WIL-
son was a man of the word,
indeed a servant of the word,
it goes without saying that we
must write "word" with a capital:
servant of the Word, *Verbi divini
minister*. In this characteristic Wilson
was entirely his father's son. He existed through words in a way few if
any other statesmen have. He used language to make himself what he
was; he achieved greatness because he was a speaker. He believed that he
could master reality through words.

As a young man, like so many other sensitive young men, he
dreamed of more than just writing well; he wanted to be a poet. In his
college years he wrote a few verses. They are very romantic, but, as he
soon realized, he lacked true inspiration. Yet he totally retained the poetic
attitude toward reality, especially in his career as a scholar and statesman.
Therein lies, I think, the core of his special greatness but also of his final
downfall. As a poet he was confronted, first with the truth of science and
then with the reality of society. He was led in both cases to surprising
innovations as well as to tragic misunderstandings. Never renouncing his

first love for poetry, he continued to be tortured by the thought that he was a poet who could not make poetry. After he had taken his doctorate he wrote a long letter to his future wife about his aptitudes and possibilities. In this masterly document of self-contemplation, he admitted honestly his lack of ability: "I am quite aware that at my birth no poet was born; but the imagination has other spheres besides the creation of a poetic fancy and can freshen and beautify the world."[1] Although he resigned himself to the fact that he would be only a reader of poetry, it never ceased to pain him. Ten years after the confession of his poetical impotence just cited, he wrote:

> That I am idealist with the heart of a poet, I do not hesitate to avow: but that fact is not reassuring. On the contrary it is tragical. My heart fairly breaks to utter itself like a poet—and it cannot. It longs for the metrical form: its air is suffused with colour; prose seems intolerable to it. It will *die* of prose yet, I sometimes think—so galling, so intolerable are the fetters, so humiliating to an idealist.[2]

There are two remarks I wish to make about Wilson's relation to poetry. In the first place, he was an idealistic poet. He admired the poets of "elevated thoughts," as Wordsworth had called them. Poetry and indeed all art existed to exalt the human spirit, esthetically and morally; ultimately esthetics and ethics were really the same thing. It is curious to note that William Wordsworth, the poet of the English elite, became his great model, not Walt Whitman, the poet of American democracy. In the second place, I have called Wilson a poet, but, as I have also noted, he was one only in the receptive sense; he had the purity but not the originality of a true poet. Like most of us, he could experience his deepest emotions in the words of others. He borrowed his language from them and quoted them constantly. He spoke in an elevated style, much truer and better than that of most politicians, but it was still a borrowed style and not without its sentimental clichés.

Because his style could not be the language of poetry itself, it became that of rhetoric. This was the escape he discovered from his inadequacies. He followed this second path from his early years. In the letter to his fiancée just cited, he explained to her—but really to himself, of course—that "oratory," the fine art of rhetoric, could be for him the form in which he could express his poetic impulses. As a youth, he said, he had concluded a solemn pact with a friend "that we would drill ourselves in all the arts of persuasion, but especially in oratory . . . that we might have facility in leading others into our ways of thinking and enlisting them to our purposes."³

He soon earned a reputation as a good speaker, and also as one who seldom turned down an invitation. He gave many hundreds of lectures throughout the country while he was a professor, not only out of vanity and the desire to assert himself, but also to supplement his salary and to be able to pay for his fine house in Princeton. There is a wealth of testimony to the impression he made. A journalist described him as "a scholar in action, a prophet touched by fire, with unmatched strength to persuade and move the hearts of his listeners."⁴

Most listeners found Wilson an inspiring speaker, one who was less bombastic than the average politician. The great models of his speaking style were the English statesmen Burke, Cobden, and Gladstone. He learned a great deal from Gladstone, especially what he called his "passionate intensity."⁵ But Wilson could not always live up to the ideal of controlled inspiration. Sometimes it seemed that his oratory became an end in itself, with a bit of trickiness; at times it had the feel of almost erotic self-indulgence. Once, after a lecture, he wrote to his wife: "I must say that the audience seemed fooled to the top of my wish." Another time it was even more glaring: "I filled them with a glow that could not possibly help them do anything I can think of except make love! Oratory is sure an imaginative art, but who shall explore its sources?"⁶

He carried others away, but the question arises whether he also carried himself away. Did he permit himself, despite his suspicion of false rhetoric, to be tempted into words that were far too exalted for what he was saying? He certainly made that impression on some people. A thoughtful and acute critic like Herbert Croly gave a keen analysis of Wilson's oratorical style; it was a judgment influenced to some extent by political antipathy but still unforgettably penetrating. He wrote (and I quote only a few of the most salient and brilliant passages):

> Woodrow Wilson is on the side of the angels. . . . Mr. Wilson seems
> to be one of those people who shuffle off their mortal coil as soon
> as they take pen in hand. They become tremendously noble. They
> write as the monuments of great men might write. They write only
> upon brass and for nothing shorter than a millennium. They utter

nothing which might sound trivial at the Last Judgment. . . . It is the quality of Mr. Wilson's thinking to make even the most concrete things seem like abstractions. . . . His mind is like a light which destroys the outlines of what it plays upon; there is much illumination, but you see very little.[7]

It is characteristic that Wilson had a deep aversion to everything that had to do with numbers. He never was good at arithmetic and left the household finances to his wife. He did not want to count up the shortest list of numbers, his daughter tells us, and sometimes called out to his daughters, "How much is seven times eight again?"[8] Fields like economics, sociology, and other disciplines concerned with society filled him with revulsion.

Even as a teacher he was a speaker. His strength lay in his classroom lectures. He hated to review students' work, did not give his students enough leeway in his seminars, but was a very inspiring lecturer. He did not just speak, he preached. He was glad to speak in university chapel services, which were then customary, and his talks were really intended to edify his listeners. To hear them or read them, as one of his best biographers remarks, was "somewhat like going to church."[9] In the end the whole world would become his church. He based this passion for preaching upon a general philosophy. When, under the influence of the then current German scientific method, there was a threat of abolition of classroom lectures (there is nothing new under the sun!), he protested vehemently against a world that would be completely explained by science. He asked whether the gain in thoroughness was accompanied by greater depth.[10]

He seldom summarized his literary beliefs as well as in the article "Mere Literature," which he contributed in 1893 to *The Atlantic Monthly*. This fiery piece was a reaction against a philologist who had written slightingly of "mere literature." Wilson replied indignantly to such arrogance and attacked the whole of literary scholarship of his time, which, he held, reduced language to a piece of weird machinery and distorted literature with the analytic schemes of comparative method. This, he said, was the result of looking at man as the product of his circumstances.

Literature can do without exact scholarship, or any scholarship at all, though it may impoverish itself thereby; but scholarship cannot do without literature. . . . Scholarship is material, it is not life. It becomes immortal only when it is worked upon by conviction, by schooled and chastened imagination.[11]

Imagination was really the magic word for Wilson's world, and it is the key word for understanding him.

True knowledge, he held, comes from within.

> Give me a pen. Let me write a volume on the philosophy of history. True, I know precious little history; but philosophy isn't narrative. I can do some golden philosophizing with a very few facts to go upon. What the world wants is thought, and the smaller the ingredient of dull fact the purer the intellectual product.[12]

The assertion is even more flagrant in the essay "The Author Himself": "A certain amount of ignorance will insure your sincerity, will increase your boldness, and shelter that genuineness which is your hope of power." By ignorance, he said, he did not mean lack of knowledge of life, but "innocence of the sophistications of learning, its research without love, its knowledge without inspiration, its method without grace."[13] This is a truly poetic man who speaks: "The rule for every man is not to depend on the education which others prepare for him—not even to consent to it; but to strive to see things as they are, and to be himself as he is."[14]

Wilson was poetic in the romantic, exalted fashion of his time, with all its distinctive marks, its quirks, if you will. He was a man of imagination and creativity, oversensitive, passionate, and lonely in spite of all his social contacts. Above all he was a man who clung ever more tightly to the phantasm of his dreams and even identified himself with it. He found his deepest peace not in reality but in his ideal, which he sought out more and more by going from poem to poem, that is, from speech to speech, approaching the perfect truth of his dream as a poet. His lyrical impulse was strong enough to become the leavening in his scholarly career and ultimately of his politics. Or, to put it more skeptically, he remained in the grip of the tension between poetry and reality, dwelling eternally on the frontier between them.

He himself did not accept this dichotomy. Word and reality might appear very often to be at a distance from each other, he affirmed in a speech of 1890 with the meaningful title "Leaders of Men," but now and again there were great moments in history when they came together. That happened when a great cause was at stake and leaders emerged as if automatically. "Men of strenuous minds and high ideals come forward, with a sort of gentle majesty, as champions of political or moral principles." In high-flown phrases he described how such heroic leaders possess the courage to be true to themselves, so that they are abandoned by everyone, even by their best friends, but finally are understood by the people. Truth continues from triumph to triumph until the last resistance is "crushed" (a word he often used against his enemies).

Such a transformation, he continued, arises organically when the time is ripe, just as Christianity had arisen in the fullness of time.

> Great leaders do not indeed observe times and circumstances. Theirs is not a service to opportunity. They have no thought for occasion, no capacity for compromise.

These words, written in 1890, were the scenario for events thirty years later. It was all here—the noble will of mankind which crushes all resistance; the fullness of time as a gratifying period of eschatological proportions, and, of course, the leader, the chosen "deeply human man" with his "gentle majesty" who has to be himself.[15]

The true statesman, the leader par excellence, he repeated in a speech in 1903 on "The Statesmanship of Letters," is the man who joins word and reality in a lofty unity. Spiritual values prevail over material. What would America have become without the splendid words of its great leaders? America, he said, will be great if it is really understood. It will be impressive not by its wealth, its space, its power, but only by "such revealing speech as will hold the ear and command the heed of other nations and of her own people."[16]

Later, in the decisive period of the "Great Cause," the campaign for the League of Nations, he would attempt to lead the world by such "revealing speech." Everything that he had dreamed of, hoped and yearned for, seemed about to become reality everywhere in the world. The core of his being was poetic, exalted, and naive. We may apply to him the words that the English writer Elizabeth Bowen wrote about men of letters in general: "Concentration on any one writer's work almost always ends by exposing a core of naivety—a core which, once it has been laid bare, seems either infantile or august."[17]

EIGHT

The fight is on. . . . My heart is in it more than it has
been in anything else, because it is a scheme of salvation.
      —Woodrow Wilson, July 1, 1907

The beauty of a Scotch-Irishman is that he not only
thinks he is right, but knows he is right. And I have not
departed from the faith of my ancestors.
      —Woodrow Wilson, June 26, 1907

PRESIDENT OF PRINCETON

*I*N THE YEAR 1900 PRINCETON University was not the important institution of higher learning its name seemed to boast. It was a modest undergraduate college like hundreds of others in the country, constrained by the piety that went with its connection to the Presbyterian Church. Unlike a true university, it had no graduate school that prepared for advanced degrees, although plans to create one were being discussed. However, Princeton's president, Francis Patton, lacked the vigor to carry through such a change. In that period when reform was in the air in every field, Patton's diffidence and hesitations aroused deep dissatisfaction among the faculty and the trustees, and in a little "palace revolution" in 1902 he was compelled to resign. Professor Woodrow Wilson was unanimously chosen as his successor, and a graduate school was established.

Wilson entered his new post amid high expectations. His inauguration was a splendid ceremony, with a host of celebrated men present from the worlds of science, politics, and literature. They included former president of the United States Grover Cleveland, who resided in the town, J. Pierpont Morgan, the most powerful banker in the country, Booker T.

Washington, the famed black leader and president of Tuskegee Institute, the country's first black college, and two famous writers, William Dean Howells and Mark Twain. Also there was George Harvey, the editor of both *The New York World* and *Harper's Weekly*, one of the most influential journalists of the time. He wielded great influence in the Democratic party and would play a decisive role in Wilson's career in politics.

Wilson himself seemed to embody the great expectations and grand dreams that he put into words in his compelling inaugural address. Placing his ideals in the broadest framework, he gave it the title "Princeton in the Nation's Service." It was not the task of a university to prepare men for good jobs, he argued, but to make them useful to society. It had to be open for everything that moved the world, but at the same time hold its ideals high. Therefore it had to do its work in unsullied isolation and dedication. He seemed to have before his eyes the essential Christian ambivalence, being in the world but not of it. He was thankful that Princeton was not located in a big city but stood apart from the bustle of the world.

We see Wilson here within the small compass of a university with the same spiritual megalomania, the same message of total selflessness, that he later extended to the whole of his country and to the world. That is what he told the alumni:

> The objects that we seek in a university are not selfish objects. There
> is no interest served which is a personal interest. We are here to
> serve our country and mankind, and we know that we can put
> selfishness behind us.[1]

The president of a college or university in the United States has broad and important duties. He must provide leadership in scholarship and in practical affairs, but his first task is to bring in money. Princeton was not a public but a private institution, dependent on the contributions of alumni and other friends. One of Wilson's first actions as president of Princeton was to persuade Andrew Carnegie to make a gift to the university. In his letter of solicitation to Carnegie, he emphasized the genuine Scottish character of Princeton, but the King of Steel, for all his immense gifts to public libraries, was frugal with Princeton and made only a small gift.

Wilson's ideals required a great deal of money. Although he stressed the spiritual aspect of the university and resisted the rule of "science" and

Germanic meticulousness, he was quite aware of the necessity of building new laboratories, especially in biology. He began at once to raise admission standards sharply, and he drafted an improved curriculum. He desired to lift Princeton to the level of Harvard and Yale, and he therefore severed the ties to the Presbyterian Church. Yet he retained the daily chapel services, which he believed to be indispensable for the spiritual cohesion of the university, and came often to speak to the students.

A student who would later become one of his most loyal adherents, Raymond Fosdick, described him as a born leader. He was, wrote Fosdick, not a handsome man, "indeed curiously homely," with a long "horse face," but alert, lively eyes, and jaws set with determination. He was tall, slender, and walked with a vigorous pace; "the mark of leadership was on his face and bearing." We get the impression from those who described him that he became more and more impressive to the outside world, but at home—and that was now the handsome presidential house on campus—he continued to find the relaxation and conviviality that he needed. He was surrounded by many good friends, and, as we have seen, the daily companionship of Jack and Jessie Hibben was a source of warmth and joy.

His aged father, who spent his last years at his son's home, lived to enjoy these glories. He told his granddaughters that their father was the greatest man he had ever known, and they should never forget it. He died in January 1903, not quite eighty-one years of age. During his last days his son was constantly at his side, singing to him the songs they both loved.

The first great reform that Wilson pushed through at Princeton was the introduction of the so-called "preceptorial plan." It is interesting to observe that here too he was following an English example. He wanted new students to be accompanied by what were known in England as "tutors," but whom he called "preceptors" to give them their own name. They would be friends of the students in a true community of younger and older men. This would enable the university to grow without becoming a cold, impersonal place of instruction. The trustees gave their warm approval, and soon some fifty young teachers were appointed. Wilson interviewed them all and chose them himself.[2]

There was great admiration for Wilson's initiative and energy. The trustees were elated. One of the wealthiest and most influential of them, Moses Taylor Pyne, a pillar of the university, called Wilson Princeton's "most valuable asset," a man without compare. Wilson's first years as president of Princeton were a time of bliss. But after four fat years of success, things began to go awry and four lean years of bitter conflict and adversity followed. They began with illness. One morning in May 1906, Wilson awoke to discover that he could no longer see with his left eye and that his right arm was displaying the same paralytic symptoms as ten years earlier. Several medical historians speculated that he had suffered a stroke, but as before he had no difficulties in his right leg or in his speech. The first doctor whom he visited, accompanied by his faithful friend Jack Hibben, advised him to stop working at once, but another to whom he went soon afterward was more optimistic and prescribed three months of rest. The trustees of the university were as disturbed as Wilson himself, and, upon the motion of Grover Cleveland, decided that he must go on vacation until he was fully and truly recovered. What could they do without Wilson? Pyne wailed.

Once again, then, Wilson traveled to his beloved England, this time together with his wife, and found rest and relaxation in Rydal, in the heart of the Lake District, the land of his beloved Wordsworth. He seems to have possessed the gift of regeneration, for after a time he was up and about, enjoying life, and he returned refreshed to Princeton in the autumn. He learned to live with his infirmities. For a short time he could not play golf because his eyesight was too weak. He took a noontime nap every day, and even drank a glass of whiskey. But he was not able to moderate the pace of his work. Just as after the seizure of 1896, he responded to this alarming attack by becoming more intense and active than ever. Various writers find a connection between his illness and his increased animation, but it is hard to find medical proof of such a relationship of cause and effect. It is a fact, however, that he gave more and more the impression of a man with a mission, a prophet exalted to the realm of the absolute.

Restored to health, Wilson turned to a second great reform immediately upon his return, a plan that was designed to accomplish an enormous social transformation on campus. Over the previous decades there had been a development in Princeton he did not like. This was the formation of private student clubs dominated by wealthy upperclassmen. These were established in lavish buildings where the members ate their meals and enjoyed themselves. Wilson was afraid that the result would be antagonism between an elegant elite and bookworms without money. He therefore made a sweeping proposal not to abolish the clubs but to transform them into larger communities.

Once again he was following an English model. What he had in mind was the building of "colleges" around a courtyard, in which upper- and lowerclassmen would live together with members of the faculty, creating a true community. These were called "Quadrangle Colleges" because of their rectangular shape, so that Wilson's scheme was called the "quad plan." It was a revolutionary innovation, a direct assault upon the privileges of the wealthy. However, Wilson did not at first stress this strong social element in his plan but put forward rather the educational importance of intellectual exchange between faculty and students and between those of different ages. The model was not just Oxford and Cambridge, but also Jefferson's university, Virginia, where Wilson himself had been a student.

As was to be expected, this magnificent plan at once met powerful opposition. To change social habits is not something that can be done instantly. It was not only the clubs that raged against the plan, but also most of the alumni, whose gifts Princeton needed. To be sure, Wilson had put it forward in his authoritarian way, carrying along the trustees, thanks to his powers of persuasion, but failing to keep the faculty informed. He found himself in bitter conflict with a united front of opponents. The plan was expensive, they said, and would make impossible other projects that had long been in preparation. In particular there was the plan to house the newly established graduate school in an adequate building. This project had been entrusted to the dean of the graduate school, Andrew West, a professor of ancient languages who was a good organizer. Until this time West had been a loyal follower of Wilson and put his own interests aside, but little by little he found having his own plans thwarted by Wilson's new plans too much to swallow. In the conflict over the quad plan, he became one of Wilson's foremost foes. Although he was an amiable Christian scholar, he proved to be a formidable opponent.

This was probably due to the very characteristics that he shared with Wilson. West too was the son of a Presbyterian minister; he had a poetic bent, was a renowned scholar who could write witty epigrams in Latin and Greek, and furthermore was a popular speaker called upon for all sorts of occasions; last but not least he was a man full of cordiality who excelled in bringing in gifts to the university. He was a better beggar than Wilson, which would give him a decisive advantage in their contest.

Wilson's break with West was painful, but what was far worse was that Wilson's best friend, Hibben, also came out against him. Like West he found that the new plans were too great an assault on Princeton's traditional spirit, and he probably began to have enough of always walking behind Wilson, so that he was sometimes called the president's messenger boy. The break with both the Hibbens was one of the most painful experiences of Wilson's life, although in retrospect it is difficult to assign responsibility for it. Hibben, a philosopher, was a mild-mannered man, less ambitious and brilliant than Wilson, but less given to black and white opinions, and that was what mattered. It was, writes Edith Gittings Reid in her fascinating remembrances of Wilson, a question of dissimilarity in their mental outlook. Hibben was a compromiser, a tactful, diplomatic man, but Wilson could not put up with compromise and diplomacy when essential things were at stake, and in practice he found everything to be essential. Hibben had a warm, friendly personality, she wrote, but Wilson "an intensity of nature that cared for everybody and everything too much." This is a perceptive observation. Wilson had the poet's tendency to go beyond bounds, to seek the absolute. Hibben, Reid writes, was "neither a Judas nor a Jonathan," but Wilson was bitterly disappointed when the real living Hibben, not the creature of his own imagination, disagreed with him.[3] At first the two friends tried to keep their respect for each other despite their difference of opinions. But it soon came to a total break between them, for which Wilson was responsible. In the end anyone who was not with him was a traitor to the sacred cause.

And his plans were sacred causes. The quad plan, he felt, was not just a plan for Princeton alone but "an opportunity to solve a question common to all the colleges and obtain a leadership which it will not be within our choice to get again within our lifetime."[4] He treated his ideas as absolute, self-evident truths. He paid the price in his relationships with people, but he suffered deeply from the loss.

Wilson lost the battle. The trustees withdrew their approval of his plan in the autumn, for the resistance to it was too strong and the financial consequences would be more than they dared to face. Wilson was in despair and even considered resigning. Instead he did something that was typical of him. He got the idea that if the trustees left him in the lurch, the rank and file—the alumni—would back him; it was the old notion of a good people under a bad government. For, despite his bitterness against individuals, he continued to believe in mankind. He appealed over the head of the trustees to the alumni, going to different cities to speak to them, but of course it was of no use whatsoever, for it was the alumni who were most opposed to seeing traditions they loved abandoned and were unwilling to pay for changes they did not want.

Wilson's defeats—for this was only the first, others followed—present a strange, even baffling picture. What was it that brought a man of such great gifts of mind and heart, a man who believed in democracy and reason, to dig in his heels so hard? What moved him to reject so totally any of the many compromises that were proposed? And why did he do this over and over again, so that we can detect a clear pattern in his actions? A commentator who grasped what was going on in him wrote that it was both "his weakness and his strength to take a worthy cause and divert it into a personal quarrel."[5] To put it in another way, his problem—which has been that of so many great men and may well be that of every man—was that his qualities and his faults were inseparable.

His ideals were magnificent. Although Wilson at first tried to see the conflict as one only within the university, he was anything but unaware that it had political implications. He won a good name in public opinion as a champion of true democracy against the privileges of the elite, and he later used this fame with great success in his political battles. At stake, he said as early as 1908, were America's true ideals.

The struggle exhausted him, however. He was able to persist only by taking long winter and summer vacations. In January 1908, he stayed for several weeks on Bermuda, where he spent happy days with Mrs. Mary Peck, the charming friend whom we met in an earlier chapter. In the summer of the same year, he made another trip to England, traveling by bicycle from Edinburgh to the Lake District with only a few travel articles and *The Oxford Book of English Verse* in his kit. He visited Carlyle's grave and tried to find the house where his own mother was born in the city of Carlisle. But the quad plan remained firmly fixed in his thoughts. He traveled to Andrew Carnegie's country house in the Scottish Highlands to persuade him to make a contribution to Princeton, but came away empty-handed.

Nonetheless he returned home refreshed. He would indeed need all his strength, for another great crisis awaited him. This time it arose not by his initiative but that of Dean Andrew West, his old friend who was now his foe. West sat with his graduate students in a temporary building, a fine old house that the rich Moses Pyne had bought for the university, located a half mile from the main campus. There West had his own little kingdom, where he reigned amid elegance and etiquette. Prayers were recited in Latin before meals and evening wear was worn at dinner. It was an almost medieval community where American youths were transformed as if by magic into true gentlemen. For Wilson the whole show was much too elitist. Furthermore, it was beyond his control, a state within the state that began to arouse his suspicions.

The conflict that developed was inevitable. As we have seen, West had begun by helping to defeat Wilson over the quad plan, and now he went over to his own attack. He was able to do so because several sizable gifts and bequests became available specifically for a new building for the graduate school, which had grown too large for its existing home.

Wilson had no reason to oppose this expansion in itself, but a conflict arose over the location of the new building. Wilson wanted it in the center of the main campus so that it would become part of the university community and come under his direct control. West, however, wanted to keep his autonomy in a building at some distance from campus. It was no accident that the largest contributor, William C. Proctor, a soap manufacturer in Cleveland, who was a close friend of West's, made his $500,000 gift conditional on the dean's having a say in the location of the building. A bitter struggle developed, an extremely complicated affair in which there were numerous committees and lengthy meetings at which mutual accusations flew back and forth. It was total war: the best of friends turned on each other, and the atmosphere on campus turned utterly foul. It was said that the faculty wives fought even harder behind the curtains of their homes than their husbands did on campus.

It would take us too long to describe all the complications of this extraordinary struggle. It was in appearance just a tug-of-war over the location of a building but at the level of principle it was a battle over the character of American democracy between elitist separatism and egalitarian community—at least that was the way Wilson preferred to present it. In the final analysis what was actually at stake was the relative rank of two ambitious men, Wilson and West. It is significant to see how Wilson fought his battle, with idealistic words, impractical deeds, and implacable hatred. West played his hand more coolly and won the best allies for himself, the leading trustees who could no longer stand Wilson's authoritarian conduct. It tells us much that men like Grover Cleveland and Moses Taylor Pyne who once had been in Wilson's camp now turned against him.

Wilson's position was basically weak. He had originally supported West, even writing in 1902 an enthusiastic introduction for a pamphlet in which West set out his project. Then he had shown him a cold shoulder, claiming that he could not accept the spirit of West's plans. His surprised opponents asked him why he had written a favorable introduction, and he lost his balance in this critical situation. He claimed he had not even read West's pamphlet and trapped himself in contradictions. Pyne, whose support was indispensable, lost all confidence in the university president whom he had once enthusiastically supported. To a friend he wrote: "I do not think I ever saw a man in a worse position than the President has put himself in by his foolish actions, and how he can have the respect of the men who are backing him up is more than I can understand."[6]

Nonetheless it appeared that Wilson might still win out despite the opposition of the trustees. Proctor became tired of such pulling and pushing over his gift and withdrew it. At last, Wilson rejoiced, "We are free to govern the university as our judgments and consciences dictate! I have an unspeakable sense of relief." He would not resign. "The heavier the storm, the tighter I will sit."[7] He was ready to do more battle. It did not seem to bother him that the university had lost a gift of half a million dollars. He acted again as he had done in the struggle over the quad plan and went over the head of the trustees to the alumni throughout the country.

His conduct was typical. Usually he spoke with prudence and diplomacy, but on occasion he would lose his self-control and blast out with every trumpet of his sacred indignation. He raised the conflict within the university to the level of absolute truth, the eternal struggle of the common man against the elite in defense of the true equality of American democracy. This was how it was presented in the press. Wilson himself so described it to the editor of the *New York Times*, which proclaimed in an editorial that the struggle in Princeton was the same as that which had been fought in the American Revolution, a struggle on which America's whole future depended.[8]

In a speech to alumni in Pittsburgh, Wilson flung all his inhibitions aside. With the voice of a prophet, he castigated the privileged classes as such. He even seemed to have gone socialist, for he condemned Church and Capital. The churches, he said, had turned away from the masses. "They serve the classes, not the masses. . . . They have more regard for pew rents than for souls." The colleges were in the same class, "looking to the support of wealth rather than to the people." The true strength of America came not from the institutions of higher education but from "the great mass of the unknown, the unrecognized." What was really gotten from universities? asked this man who had spent thirty years in the confined world of the universities. Would Lincoln ever have become "a better instrument for the country's good if he had been put through the processes of one of our modern colleges?" Wilson surprised everyone by his radical language, wrote an amazed newspaper in Pittsburgh. According to its reporter, Wilson said that America faced a revolution if it did not reform its ways at once: "America will stagger like France through fields of blood before she again finds peace and prosperity under the leadership of men who understand her needs."[9]

He had never expressed himself so fiercely before. He became popular among reformers. Washington Gladden, a renowned social gospel preacher, asked him at once for a copy of his speech. But Wilson quickly realized that he had overstepped himself. He wrote to the New York *Evening Post*, which had criticized him in an editorial, that he realized his speech had led to misunderstanding. It was his own fault, he said, adding, with typical self-understanding, "Unfortunately, my mind is a one-track affair on which I can run only one through train at a time."[10]

Wilson seemed to have gained a victory when Proctor withdrew his gift, but his opponents did not remain still. Some were ready to accept a compromise, but Wilson was not a man for compromises. After all, he stood for absolute truth. He refused to make any concession. He could not suffer West, he declared, not even in a lesser position, as had been suggested. "It has never been possible to govern West in any respect."[11] (Note that word "govern"!) But pride came before the fall. The story took a sudden turn different from any that he or anyone else could have dreamed of, with a surprising denouement fitting for a stage play. Andrew West proved much too clever for Wilson. This canny man had discovered another source of funds, one so rich that Wilson was utterly helpless against him. An alumnus of Princeton, class of 1848, by the name of Isaac C. Wyman, had just died at an advanced age. He was a rich man, and left a pretty sum (West estimated it at between two and three million dollars, but it later turned out to be somewhat less) for a building for the graduate school. West had gone to see him during his last days, and it was West who now emerged as one of the two executors of the will. West went, of course, to the funeral, but for him it was a day not of mourning but of celebration. He wrote in triumph to Pyne: "I can hardly believe it all. It is so splendid. . . . I laid a spray of ivy from Nassau Hall on Mr. Wyman's casket and planted an ivy root from Nassau Hall at his grave. . . . Isn't it fine? TE DEUM LAUDAMUS. NON NOBIS DO-MINE." (We praise thee, Oh Lord, not ourselves.)[12]

Wilson had been beaten, and knew it. West was victorious, for Wyman's money settled the matter, and Proctor even renewed his own offer. Poor Wilson tried to face the defeat as stoically as he could manage. At this very moment, he found a splendid escape from his situation. If he had failed in Princeton, he had made his name famous throughout the country. What now happened was the accomplishment of what from his youth had been his deepest desire. The political world opened up for him. How that came about will be described in a following chapter. In the very summer when everything went wrong for him at Princeton, he became a candidate for governor of the state of New Jersey. He would have liked to remain president of the university until he was certain of his election in November, but the trustees had enough of him and demanded that he resign at once. He did so, leaving in humiliation the university for which he had done so much, and which would never have achieved such high prestige without him. But defeat was followed by victory. He was elected as governor and his name echoed throughout the country.

As was to be expected, his presidency at Princeton has often been compared to that of the United States. The similarities are striking. In each case he served eight years at the helm, with a brilliant beginning and early great successes, but ending with tragedy. Should we draw the conclusion that it is not circumstances that make history, but the man? Wilson certainly did put his own stamp on history, but in the end history overpowered him. Or did he bring on that tragic ending too?

The most painful aspect of the comparison is that on both occasions he damaged his relations with other people. The idealist believes that such breaks cannot be helped. But, although Wilson was an idealist, he suffered badly from this human weakness. An occasion arose when he had to go back to Princeton in his capacity as governor of the state. In February 1911, he was present at the unveiling of a portrait of a former professor.

He met all his old foes, notably Jack Hibben, who was acting president of the university (he was later elected as Wilson's successor). Wilson gave his account of the painful meeting to Mary Peck: "There I sat and heard discourses from men whom, for one reason or another I despise. Why will that wound not heal over in my stubborn heart? Why is it that I was blind and stupid enough to love the people who proved false to me?"[13]

NINE

Long talk with Professor Woodrow Wilson, literary in
language, but with a peculiar un-American insight into
the *actual* working of institutions as distinguished from
their nominal constitutions.
—*Beatrice Webb*, Diary, *April 25, 1898*

Government is a living thing and not a mechanical
contrivance.
—*Woodrow Wilson, March 9, 1909*

CONGRESS AND PRESIDENT

BY THE YEAR 1909, AS his splendid and tragic university career was ending, Wilson had become a man with some national reputation, but if his life had been cut off then, we would not be concerned with him here, and he would be almost forgotten by now. Neither his talents as a speaker, nor his literary essays and histories, nor his prestige as president of a distinguished university would have gotten him a place in history.

He might have a modest place in the chronicles of scholarship for his political writings about the American political system, and we must therefore pay some attention to them. During his lifetime they brought him celebrity and were of much importance for the brilliant political career that he entered in 1910, as bright and sudden as a new star of the first order of magnitude in the sky.

He had long since reconciled himself to the inescapable fact that the straight road to political fame was closed to him. But he had found solace in the thought that he would at least become the voice of his country:

"My ambition is to add something to the *statesmanship* of the country, if that something be only thought."[1]

Even as a student he had written various essays on what he considered to be the best system of government, and he had concluded his university studies in 1884 with the book that won him fame, *Congressional Government*. In it the young man set out his first sharp criticism of the political system of the United States. America, he wrote, was a country without history, without organic growth, where everything happened in too great a hurry, after too little consideration; it was not yet mature. It seemed about to outgrow its youth, but to get through this transition it needed prudent reform, for which he proposed a program.

Reform had to arise out of tradition, the English tradition. We have already observed how much the politics, culture, and heroes of England were for Wilson an example to be followed. *Congressional Government* was directly inspired by the work of the English essayist and economist Walter Bagehot, whose book *The English Constitution* had appeared in 1867. It "inspired my whole study of government," he wrote in 1884.[2] Bagehot had sought to describe how the English constitution actually worked, with stress upon the intertwining of the executive and legislative powers. He considered the whole doctrine of the separation of powers to be no more than a literary theory on which it was not possible to build an effective government. He compared the English system to the American and reached the conclusion that the American constitution had been much too distorted by this literary theory.

This argument came to Wilson as a revelation, and his own book bore its stamp. It began by making the same distinction between the English and the American systems, contrasting "Parliamentary" and "Congressional Government." It was true that the American constitution had created a "federal balance" between the national and the state governments and a system of "checks and balances" among the three powers in the national government, but this was not how it worked out in practice, for the federal government dominated the states and in Washington "the predominant and controlling force, the centre and source of all motive and of all regulative power is Congress."[3]

The work of Congress was done in committees, which made their decisions in secret. Thus there was neither true democracy nor true efficiency. The only remedy was to introduce the English system. The members of the cabinet, who were responsible only to the president but were dependent on Congress for funds, should be taken from the legislature and be responsible to it; in this way the relation of the executive and legislative branches would be improved.

It is worthy of remark that in this book Wilson displayed little confidence in the presidency. He was writing, however, in a period when that office seemed quite unpromising. After the Civil War the presidents were weak figures who could not stand up to Congress and whose position paled beside that of the "captains of industry," in less friendly terms, the "robber barons." Names like Rockefeller or Vanderbilt speak more loudly than Hayes, Garfield, or Arthur. Congress didn't trouble itself about the presidents; as Wilson wrote, "our latter-day Presidents live by proxy; they are the executive in theory, but the Secretaries are the executive in act." But they could not take initiatives because they had no fixed relationship to Congress.[4]

The president, Wilson concluded, is "part of the official rather than of the political machinery of the government."[5] Wilson did not anticipate that a total change would soon come about. He came close to seeing it when he described the developments behind the scenes, the concentration of power which made a stronger and more effective authority necessary, and he also remarked on the significance of growing American involvement abroad. But during the decade of the 1890s he still did not draw the conclusion that the executive power was about to become stronger. In the preface to the fifteenth edition of his book, he admitted that he had not foreseen the new situation; the Spanish-American War and the subsequent rise of American imperialism had suddenly given greater weight to the highest office, and his book, he admitted, was now "hopelessly out of date."

It is interesting to observe that Wilson's criticism of the American political system was really based on pure optimism. What he found lacking in the Constitution, with its balance of powers, was simple human trust. The Founding Fathers, he thought, had been too mistrustful, and therefore had divided power; but in so doing they had made it irresponsible. And "in any business, whether of government or of mere merchandising, *somebody must be trusted*." That Wilson, a conservative, became a reformer, indeed had to become one, arose, I believe, out of his optimism, his deep-rooted tendency to give a moral polish to human conduct, including government: "A sense of highest responsibility, a dignifying and elevating sense of being trusted" was the foundation for "practical, energetic and trustworthy statesmanship."[6]

This book, Wilson's first and probably his best, was received very favorably. It was a masterly work which, like so many other masterpieces, rested more on intuition than on research. Wilson drew his subject in broad lines, for he had no patience for details. Strangely, although he worked on this book in Baltimore, which is so near to Washington, he never once went to the Capitol to see how the political system he was describing actually operated. He would not take the trouble to check his arguments against the facts.

He sometimes criticized his own procedure: "The fault of my mind is that it is creative without being patient and docile in learning *how* to create." But this was to place the burden of scholarship upon the concept of creativity. Wilson the professor detracted from Wilson the poet. Yet we can defend him against himself by remarking that it was just those things that weakened his scholarship that gave him strength as a poet of a kind and as a politician. His faults were obviously the other side of his qualities. Precisely because of his powers of empathy, his subtle imagination, and most of all his immense enthusiasm, he was able before he was thirty years old to write a first-rate book.

Wilson was certainly not an original thinker. He found at least as much inspiration in the models he followed as in the subjects he chose. That too is probably typical for someone who is a poet at second hand. He resembles a translator who becomes intoxicated with someone else's words that he is putting into his own language. Wilson finally came upon a greater model than Bagehot, or at least someone who was greater for him because he was more poetic. He became engrossed in the work of the great British thinker and writer Edmund Burke. When you read Burke, he declared, you learn what is missing in Bagehot. Bagehot's strength lay in "perfect explanation," but Burke did more than explain, he inspired, he joined practical politics with the imagination of a poet.[7]

Wilson's admiration for the great conservative brings us back to the question: How conservative really was this reformer? But an answer in the abstract would assume that Wilson's thinking was a unity that can be analyzed logically, and that is only partially true. As a man of poetic temperament Wilson was diverse and variable in his thinking, and it was this that made him resemble Burke so greatly. He too believed in organic development, in natural growth and change. He identified with Burke, who was also a man of poetic temperament under strain, and a great orator. Burke too took an indirect part in politics, said Wilson in an admiring lecture in 1893, for he "had the thoughts of a great statesman, and uttered them with unapproachable nobility; but he never wielded the power of a great statesman."[8]

Wilson was most deeply impressed by Burke's famed *Reflections on the French Revolution*. It was the work that established Burke's reputation as a conservative, but Wilson, on the contrary, read it not as a defense of unswerving conservatism but as expressing a spirit of wise and moderate reform. Just as Burke hated the French Revolution—rightly, according to Wilson, for its philosophy was "radically evil and corrupting"—so Wilson turned against the radicalism of his own time.[9]

He even wished to continue in the spirit of Burke by writing a book, a *Philosophy of Politics*, that would build upon the principles of the great Irishman. Wilson repeatedly returned to this project, writing draft outlines with titles and chapter headings. But he never worked out these fine plans; he did not have the necessary patience and, as we have seen, the world did not leave him the calm he needed to write. Or was it just the other way round? Was his eager acceptance of so many administrative responsibilities a way to escape scholarship, as we see quite often in the academic world? Be that as it may, his ideas bore the stamp of Burke.

Wilson was fond of using Romanticism's magical word, "organic," meaning the opposite of "intellectual." He told a lecture audience in St. Louis: "We have been living under an impossible thing—a Newtonian system of government. A government is not a mechanism, it is an organism, because it consists of us who are organisms." He saw the turnabout, the return to the organic, taking place in his own time, and called it "as inevitable as the law of nature. Government is a living thing and not a mechanical contrivance."[10]

Wilson put his own Burkean conceptions to use in analyzing the crisis of his age. He was quite aware that he was living in a time of immense changes. As we observed in an earlier chapter, America was going through a true revolution in the years between the Civil War and the First World War, the years when Wilson went from eight to fifty-eight.

Around the turn of the century the country witnessed the spectacle of confusion and misery on the one hand and new drive and boundless optimism on the other. The feeling that they were in a crisis did not inspire the Americans to despair but rather to new analyses, practical philosophies, and splendid plans. The difficulties through which they were going, it was said, meant that America was "coming of age," that it was experiencing "the end of innocence."

Reform was the watchword in every field. The first decade of the twentieth century was dominated by the Progressives, a vague collection of assorted reformers who attacked abuses with such sincerity that Theodore Roosevelt gave them the nickname of "Muckrakers," which soon became a term of honor.

The big question was how to guide the revolution into a good path. The problem was that the interests of individuals and of society no longer coincided as they once had (or seem to have done). Individualism had led to great excesses, especially the vast differences between rich and poor. The problem was how to preserve freedom and order while correcting these abuses. It was a theme to which many gave their attention. It was given vivid formulation in the patriotic anthem, "America the Beautiful," written on the occasion of the World's Fair in Chicago in 1893:

> America, America,
> God mend thine every flaw,
> Confirm thy soul in self-control,
> Thy liberty in law.

This was a central dogma for Wilson too. He had avowed the same principle the year before: "We should not be Americans or possess liberty were we not conservative and thoughtful in reform, for we know order to be the fragile vessel which contains liberty."[11]

Even before politics swallowed him up fully, Wilson decided to put his most important ideas together in a series of lectures he gave at Columbia University in 1907, which were published as a book the next year under the title of *Constitutional Government*.[12] It is very enlightening to compare this book, Wilson's last, with his first. Both treated the same theme, the American political system; in both the theory of the balance of powers was rejected and the need for effective government argued. But where in 1884 Wilson saw salvation in cabinet responsibility along the English model, by 1908 he had come to think more fully along American lines, arguing that the presidency must be the peak and the force of American government. The office of the presidency had become more and more important owing to modern communications and the growing importance of foreign policy. The president was "the unifying force in our complex system."[13]

When Wilson gave these lectures, there was already talk of his candidacy for the presidency, which probably lay behind his plea that a president did not have to be politically experienced but should possess "particular qualities of mind and character which we are at least as likely to find outside the ranks of our public men as within them."[14] A man was required who understood his times and the country's needs. Wilson emphatically chose one side in the controversy over whether the president was only the executant of the decisions of Congress or was much more: the representative, indeed the embodiment of the nation. President Andrew Jackson had claimed back in 1834 that the president represented the whole people and Congressmen each only a small part of them; and the great statesman Daniel Webster (who never succeeded in becoming president) had protested angrily: "Now, Sir, this is not the language of the Constitution. The Constitution nowhere calls him the representative of the American people; still less, their direct representative."[15]

Wilson echoed Jackson's idea. The Constitution was deliberately vague and left room that the president could and must fill up. A president could be as great as he wished. He did not have to accept or endorse Newton's balance, he was the weightier side, "at liberty, both in law and in conscience, to be as big as man can be."[16] The president was "the only national voice in affairs"; if he won the admiration and the confidence of the people, he was irresistible. "His position takes the imagination of the country."[17] He could put Congress under pressure by means of public opinion.

These were theories that were being put into vigorous practice at that very moment by the president who sat in the White House, and we can be sure that Wilson was thinking of Theodore Roosevelt when he wrote. But, unawares, he was also describing his own future. No president in American history possessed as thorough a knowledge of the presidency as Wilson.

He also grasped to the full that the man in the White House, for all his mounting power, had to work together with Congress, in particular with the Senate, which had to ratify all foreign treaties by a two-thirds majority. He gave a precise description of such collaboration. A president must not be "stiff and offish," but maintain relations of confidence with the Senate; he must not present his plans to the Senate all wrapped up, "to be accepted or rejected," but constantly engage in "real accommodation of views instead of a final challenge and contest."[18]

We read these sage words with agreement, but also with amazement when we think of what the future held. Why did the man who knew so clearly what to do not do it, not at all, when the time to act came ten years later, when, in his own judgment, the very fate of the world depended on it? If he had, how different would have been the course of history.

TEN

I came to the office in the fulness of time.
—*Woodrow Wilson, April 23, 1911*

GOVERNOR AND PRESIDENT

FOR A DUTCHMAN LIKE myself, who lives in a land where there has been a swarm of parties for more than a century, one of the strangest aspects of American political life has been its party system, if we can call it a system. America has just two parties, never more. A third party seems to have no chance. (The Democratic party split into Northern and Southern parts in 1860, permitting the election of Abraham Lincoln, but reunited after the Civil War. I leave out of consideration the splinter parties always present on the right and left.) But if we try to define these two parties on the basis of their principles or indeed of any kind of specific content, we fall into great perplexity. What in heaven's name is the difference between these two unwieldy bodies with their glorious names? Is there really no difference? The Dutch historian Jacob Presser, who wrote a lively book about the United States, was fond of quoting two jests about the two major parties: one was that they were two bottles with different labels, but both empty; the other was that they were two hogs, a fat one with his feet in the trough, the other thin and waiting his turn. Is that all the difference there is between them? And why could a true third party never emerge, except in the one magical year of 1912?[1]

The period around 1900 was nonetheless the time when both the Democrats and the Republicans went a-hunting after their true identities by the disparate ways in which they sought to meet the rapidly changing economic and social reality of the country. We described these changes in an earlier chapter. What it came down to was this: Thanks to its industrial growth and the accompanying mass immigration, America was faced with the problem of how to combine democracy and capitalism, how to uphold Thomas Jefferson's old ideal of equality in a world where individuals were becoming so powerful. Was it possible to find a natural bond between self-interest and the interest of society, or was it inevitable that this liberal dream would come off second best when faced with the reality of "robber barons"? And, if this was true—and bit by bit this came to be believed by the whole American people, so that the Progressive movement became a hurricane—what was the best remedy?

Liberty and equality seemed to be each other's worst enemies. If so, it followed that freedom had to be curtailed if equality were to have at least a fair chance. Something had to be done about the colossal concentration of power in the big industries. Private kingdoms—the United States Steel Company, the Standard Oil Company, the great railroad companies, the New York banks—were undermining the republic. Somebody had to have the courage to stand up to the captains of industry, those pious, conscienceless, generous, and art-loving kings of capital, Andrew Carnegie, John D. Rockefeller, J. Pierpont Morgan, Henry Clay Frick, and all their fellows.

But how? And by whom? By what possible political measure? How could the trusts be attacked? For a little while there had been an experiment with antitrust legislation, but it huffed and puffed and came to naught. The Sherman Antitrust Act, which dated from 1890, was useless or worse, for it was so vague that it was used against labor unions. The problem with such blurry laws was that they usually had to be interpreted by the Supreme Court, which consisted of a majority of archconservative old men. The justices defended the sacredness of property through thick and thin, and in 1895 even found the federal income tax to be unconstitutional.[2]

One of the demands of the reformers was an amendment to the

Constitution to permit a federal income tax, which was achieved when the Sixteenth Amendment, proposed in 1909, was adopted in 1913. Connected with it was the question of import duties. Since the Civil War, industry had demanded and obtained ever higher tariffs, which provided the government with revenues taken from the common people, while the employers enjoyed the delights of protection. The result was a real political difference between the two parties, for the Republicans had systematically supported increased tariffs and the Democrats had opposed them. The Republicans could be called the party of industry, with its center in the Northeast, and the Democrats the party of agricultural interests in the South and West.

But the division was not really that simple. Both parties had the support of farmers and manufacturers, and both had conservative and progressive wings, which did not coincide with the division between the countryside and the factory owners. The great question now was what had to be done for the advancement of the nation, whether progressive or conservative. We may say that at that moment the involvement of the government with economic and social life was felt to be the most fundamental progressive principle. The state should step in and take measures, in the first place in economics, but also in politics and society. Effective opposition to the trusts, reduction of the tariffs, and introduction of direct taxation were the foremost demands. But these could be won only if there were political reforms as well, if the government became more effective, with less separation of powers at the federal level and less power for the states. There was now a general agreement with Wilson's argument in his constitutional studies that what he called the "Newtonian balance" of the Constitution had ceased to work. The Progressives screwed up their nerve to attack at last the Constitution, which had so long been viewed as sacred. Indeed, there were even historians—the most important and best known was Charles A. Beard—who argued that the American Constitution had in fact never been anything but an instrument of the ruling class to hold back democracy.[3]

In order to win, democracy had to overcome the control of politics by caucuses and cliques operating behind closed doors, both nationally and locally. Corruption was worst in the cities, where "bosses" ruled through "machines," traded jobs and improvements for votes, and often controlled economic life together with the trusts.

Public opinion began to converge against these conditions. There was a general realization that things could not go on as before. The abuses were exposed in the abundant publications of the muckrakers, for example in *The Shame of the Cities* (1904) by the journalist Lincoln Steffens (whom we shall meet again). Social injustice became the topic of the day when Upton Sinclair in his novel *The Jungle* revealed the horrors of the Chicago slaughterhouses.

Democracy became the central concern. Openness and social compassion became the watchwords. Many social laws were adopted, especially in the Western states. Female and child labor were limited, minimum wages established, along with health insurance, a shortened workday, and similar measures. One question was how to extend these improved conditions from the states to the nation as a whole. Another was which party would take the initiative in bringing it about.

Reformers were active in both parties, and in both they ran into the resistance of the established interests of industry and "bossism." At first it appeared that the Republican party might become the champion of change. To be sure, it had been the party of big capital and high tariffs since the Civil War, but it had begun as a party of idealists struggling against slavery, and the first president it had elected was no one less than Abraham Lincoln. There remained a strong strain of idealism within the Republican party, just as it exists in most Americans.

It is true that the Republicans bore the burden of governing, which meant always compromising, accommodating to reality, no matter what kind of reality it was. They had held power nationally almost without interruption since the Civil War; the presidency of Cleveland was the only exception. The Democrats were always in the opposition, so that they could be the ideal party for an idealist course of action. But they were strong and in power in many cities, where they had broad support among the immigrants, especially among the Irish, Italians, Poles, and Jews. They operated through party machines. Boss Charles Murphy was all-powerful in New York City, John Fitzgerald (President Kennedy's grandfather) in Boston, James Smith in New Jersey, and so on. Therefore the Democrats were also divided between those whom we may call, in gentle terms, realists and idealists. Among the Democrats most of the idealists were located in the West, for there is some truth to Turner's assertion that American democracy was encouraged by the frontier. In the West the Democrats had taken over many of the ideals and supporters of the Populists, an anticapitalist movement that was sincerely progressive and naively provincial. Their great leader was William Jennings Bryan, who had been the great champion of silver in 1896 and had run for the presidency three times, in 1896, 1900, and 1908, without success.

Bryan has come down in history with the reputation of a prize fool, as noble in character as he was simpleminded in his ideas, as devout as he was ambitious. But if any merit is to be granted him, it is probably that he steered the Democratic party into a progressive course so that eventually it became the majority party, the party of Woodrow Wilson and Franklin Roosevelt. But if the Democratic party was able to follow that course, it was also the result of developments in the Republican party, which we must discuss if we are to understand not only Wilson's personal success in 1912, but also the whole election campaign of that year, one of the most important in the entire history of the United States. For, although it is true, at least in part, that the Democratic party became the party of the people and the Republican party the party of wealth, this was a parting of the ways that was confirmed only in 1912.

It was in the first instance, however, the work not of Bryan, nor even of Woodrow Wilson, but of Theodore Roosevelt. We have already met this energetic, loud-spoken, restless statesman and soldier. He had stood with Wilson on the stage during a reform meeting in Baltimore in 1896, and after that they had met several times, with mutual esteem. Roosevelt was the scion of an old Dutch family in New York; as a young man he had been ambitious but impudent, playing many parts: hunter, cowboy, author, conservationist, historian, politician, popular hero—all at the same time. He won popularity during the Spanish-American War of 1898 when he led the Rough Riders in Cuba. Although he was popular among the people, he wasn't at all in the circles of politicians, least of all in his own Republican party in New York, where he became governor; they found him to be a major nuisance and kicked him upstairs by getting him nominated to run for vice-president along with President McKinley who came up for reelection in 1900. They defeated Bryan and his running mate, but within a year McKinley was dead, the victim of a fanatical assassin, and Roosevelt came to the fore again. At the age of forty-three, he was the youngest president the country had ever known. He remained in the White House for eight years and enjoyed every moment; he became more exuberant and troublesome than ever, a braggart full of life, the very embodiment of the Nietzschean belief in a life of intensity, enthusiasm, and most of all danger.

The question of how progressive his government really was is not easy to answer. He preached reform at the top of his voice. He proclaimed that government should take up the cause of a more just society. Such a program was no small thing in individualistic America. But Roosevelt did not go far beyond words. He loved words as Wilson did, but was more spontaneous and uncontrolled, even childish, his enemies said. He could not overcome the conservative forces in Congress and in his own party. He dropped the struggle against the trusts, and his social legislation was limited in its goals. His finest achievements were in the area of conservation, to which he was strongly committed. His conduct of American foreign policy was highly important. He was the first president of the United States who understood that the country had to play a major role in the world; he saw to the construction of the Panama Canal (1903-1914), was deeply involved in Central American affairs, and proclaimed the right of the United States to intervene (an extension of the Monroe Doctrine that was called the Roosevelt Doctrine); he mediated in the Russo-Japanese War (1905-1906), dispatched an American diplomat to the Algeciras Conference in Morocco in 1906, and in 1908 sent an American naval squadron with great fanfare on an expedition round the world.

Roosevelt left the White House in 1909, hoping that he had gained a place in history as a great president like Washington or Lincoln. He gave over his office to his vice-president, William Howard Taft, in the trusting belief that his "crown prince," now that he had been elected president on his own, would continue his policies. He obviously had little insight into human nature. Taft did not become a great president, did not even want to be one, first and foremost because it did not fit his tranquil, legalistic personality (he was a giant of a man, weighing at least three hundred pounds and insistent upon his comforts), but also because he believed in the principle—which seldom can be understood apart from personal dispositions—that the executive power should remain limited. When Teddy Roosevelt returned from a splendid world tour in 1910 (during which he shot lions and elephants in Africa and visited emperors and kings in Europe), a break between him and his successor soon followed.

Inspired by Herbert Croly, an original political thinker who published a book, *The Promise of American Life*, that championed a new social attitude, Roosevelt came forward with a new program that he first presented in a speech at Ossawatomie, Kansas, on August 31, 1910. The nation counted far more than the individual, he proclaimed, and labor was more important than capital. Government must become effective and rich men brought under the control of society. "The New Nationalism puts the national need before sectional or personal advantage."[4]

With such words Roosevelt constituted himself as the champion of the progressive wing of his party, and there was soon talk of his becoming a candidate for the presidency in 1912 (since he had been elected only once, it was not clear that the unwritten rule limiting the presidency to two terms applied to him). But the leadership of his party was and remained conservative and favored the reelection of Taft, who was a willing tool in their hands. Taft was not eager to run again, but he had an ambitious wife who was watchful of his interests. A break resulted in the Republican party between the conservatives and the progressives. Roosevelt won most of the primaries (1912 was the first year in which the primary system came into force), but the Republican convention in Chicago was dominated by the party bosses and nominated Taft.

Roosevelt took up arms against this "disgraceful theft." He did what is almost never done in the United States because it means political suicide, except by a man such as he: he split the party. He met with his stalwart followers a month and a half later in Chicago, where they jubilantly formed a third party, the Progressives (whose symbol was the bull moose). Their convention was more like a revival meeting than a political assembly. The "Battle Hymn of the Republic" and "Onward Christian Soldiers" resounded though the hall, and Roosevelt spoke with the voice of Judgment Day: "We stand at Armageddon and we battle for the Lord." He conducted himself as if he were the Savior, so that a newspaper in Chicago announced mockingly that the next day at 3 o'clock Mr. Roosevelt would walk upon the waters of Lake Michigan.

It was marvelous and not at all thought through. The party had an excellent social program but remained vague about tariffs and believed in government supervision of the trusts. There were two very different Republican parties now, but their Democratic opponents accused them both of being equally capitalist. Woodrow Wilson, the candidate of the Democratic party, compared them to Tweedledum and Tweedledee.[5]

Wilson had become at last the opponent of both the regular Republicans and their Bull Moose rivals. It is his story that we must tell now, after our long digression about the Republicans. He is the hero of our tale, Professor Woodrow Wilson, historian and political scientist, president of Princeton University, but a man who all his life had cherished the wanted to see which way the cat would jump. But he soon began to play up to Harvey and his friends. He drew up a sort of "credo" that included everything they wanted to hear, praise for big business and censure for the labor unions. "Great trusts and combinations are the necessary, because the most convenient and efficient, instrumentalities of modern business."[9] Naturally he had nothing good to say about Bryan in letters not intended for the public eye. Bryan, he wrote, was "the most charming and lovable of men, personally, but foolish and dangerous in his theoretical beliefs."[10]

Harvey and the gentlemen around him became enthusiastic. They spoke of Wilson's entering the election of 1908, but it was premature. Wilson was not ready to act; he spent the summer again on vacation in England, but went to Edinburgh, where he could be reached by cable, to wait for the results of the Democratic convention. 1908 was not yet his year, and he knew it. To his loyal Mary Peck he wrote that he would gladly lend his pen and his support to a reform along the well-tested principles of the Democratic party. But he added: "Certainly I do not want the presidency! The more closely I see it the less I covet it."[11]

Harvey also realized that 1908 was not their year, and he contrived a feasible detour on Wilson's route to the presidency. He wrote in 1909 in his newspaper that he expected Wilson to be elected governor of New Jersey in 1910 and then as president of the United States in 1912. He saw the support for him growing steadily.

Wilson became more and more eager. In autumn 1909 he wrote an article sharply attacking the tariffs. He admitted to Mary Peck that he was about to take part in political combat: "This is what I was meant for, anyhow, this rough and tumble of the political arena. My instincts all turn that way, and I sometimes feel rather impatiently the restraints of my academic position."[12]

Harvey mapped out his route, following to the letter the customary machinations of politics. He negotiated with the bosses of the Democratic party in New Jersey, especially with James Smith, Jr., a former senator, an archconservative and the leader of the powerful party machine in the northern districts of the state. Smith, whose sons had studied at Princeton, knew Wilson and the idea of his becoming a candidate appealed to him. Smith and his fellow party bosses were confident that they could keep their theoretical-minded professor in hand. Harvey organized a meeting secret ambition to go into politics. How did he suddenly land in this other world when he was already into his mid-fifties? It is a strange, even fantastic tale, unless we wish to believe that this man from the world of scholarship was really predestined for the high task that he coveted. That would have been the way he saw it. He himself said that he came to his high office in the fullness of time.

In any case this is the story not just of Wilson himself but also of his party. The identity of the Democratic party was decided, as it were, by his political career; his rise was directly involved with the decisive choice for his party and for himself personally between conservatism and progressivism. We have followed him in his development and seen that he believed in organic change, fully in the spirit of Burke. But in practical politics there is no such thing as natural progress, practical politics is the work of fickle persons who make a choice among the possibilities before them.

Wilson's first choice had been for very moderate change. In one of his first political speeches, given in 1904 in New York to an audience of Southerners, he had fiercely attacked the progressive wing of the party, a "noisy minority" of "populists and radical theorists, contemptuous alike of principle and of experience." What was needed, he said, was a party of "conservative reform, acting in the spirit of the law and ancient constitutions."[6]

He won attention with such language. But there was also present a "kingmaker," a typical figure in American politics, a "Warwick," so-called after the character in Shakespeare's history play. Wilson's "Warwick" was George Harvey, the journalist and publisher whom we met earlier. He made it his calling to advance Wilson's career on the highroad of grand politics. Harvey knew him as an author on the list of his publishing house and was deeply impressed by his eloquence and sound conservatism. This is the man, he thought, to keep the Democratic party and the country on the right course. As early as 1906 he began a public campaign on his behalf, lauding him at a dinner of leading Democrats as a true statesman and the best candidate for the presidency.[7] Wilson was hesitant at first to accept the role Harvey set for him. He thanked him cordially, but asked him just who these leading Democrats were who Harvey said wanted him as president of the country. The list that Harvey sent him included the names of many wealthy and influential members of the party.[8] Wilson's hesitation did not at all mean that he was not interested, but only that he between them and Wilson, who promised that if he were elected he would not attack the existing party organizations.

Such a deal with the old corrupt powers in the party was carrying things pretty far. Which, then, was the real Wilson? In that very year 1910, under the pressure of his conflict with the trustees of Princeton, he had waged a fierce attack upon the powers of conservatism, thereby gaining much approval among progressives. The strange result was that the conservative bosses of the Democratic party supported him at the same time that progressives placed their hopes upon him. He satisfied the progressives with an emphatic declaration that, once elected, he would not let himself come under "the dictation of any person or persons, special interest or organization."[13]

Wilson succeeded in remaining himself. He played the political game with masterly skill. The bosses could elect him but they could not manipulate him. They thought they were using him, but it was he who used them. Once nominated by the Democratic party convention in Trenton, he made it clear that he was not bound by the elementary political virtue of gratitude. In the speech accepting the candidacy, he proclaimed his independence: "I never sought this nomination, and if I am elected, as I expect to be, I shall be free and untrammeled to serve the people and the state. I repeat that no promises have been asked, much less exacted of me."[14]

He conducted his election campaign at a high moral level, anticipating the world-encompassing idealism of his later years. In this spirit he proclaimed in his final campaign speech of November 5, 1910, that all history was nothing else than a "slow, painful struggle forward, forward, up, up, a little at a time, along the long incline, the interminable way, which leads to the perfection of force, to the real seat of justice and of honor." He closed his address with a metaphor that gave lyric voice to his belief in progress: "Don't you see the light starting, and don't you see the light illumining all nations? Don't you see that you are coming more and more into the beauty of its radiance?"[15]

He was elected with a handsome majority and made good his words—the ones in which he spoke out for progress. Shorn of restraint, he turned against the men who had put him in the saddle and plunged into his reforms. A shock ran through the state and through the whole country when the new governor publicly opposed the candidacy of his protector, "Boss" Smith, for the Senate, because, he said, it was not in accord with the will of the people. His popularity shot up.

He went into the year 1912, when there would be another presidential election, with the reputation of a progressive reformer. His chances appeared excellent. In his letters from this period, there was some hesitation, but of course ambition won out over diffidence. In January 1911, he still was writing to Mary Peck that he absolutely did not want the office; by April he saw himself oppressed by the truly cosmic battle to which he was called:

> There is no telling what deep waters may be ahead of me. The forces of greed and the forces of justice and humanity are about to grapple for a bout in which men will spend all the life that is in them. God grant that I may have strength enough to count, to tip the balance in the unequal and tremendous struggle.

But then, a week later, he did not want to try for the presidency: "How weary I get, how *very* weary of talk of myself and of the presidency."[16]

II

1912 was for the Democrats an *annus mirabilis*, a year of the returning favor of fortune. Now, after many years of defeat, they appeared to have a chance at victory because their opponents were divided. A host of presidential hopefuls raised their heads in the Democratic party, each wanting to wear the crown. But the most outstanding man in the party, the Democrat par excellence, William Jennings Bryan, was not among them. It is the tragedy of politics that glory always comes to an end, mercilessly and totally. Bryan had been beaten three times; he had no prospect any more of becoming president. Or is that really more than we should say? Was there still a spot of sunlight somewhere deep in his warm, cavernous heart, a tiny, insubstantial seed of hope? We do not know, but it is not beyond possibility that he continued to hope that the candidates for the nomination would be deadlocked so that he could appear as a deus ex machina to capture the prize.

In any case he remained influential within the party, someone who had to be reckoned with. Wilson did not fool himself into thinking otherwise. He was not much concerned any more about his conservative friends, George Harvey and his kind, and he ostentatiously turned to the other wing of the party. After an initial meeting with Bryan, he wrote to Mary Peck that he found him "a truly captivating man."[17] On his side Bryan was no less delighted and handsomely forgave Wilson his earlier nasty remarks.

Then as now, waging an election campaign was a difficult and unpleasant business. The intellectual who ventured into its turmoil had to accustom himself to the rough and tumble, the willing recourse to malice on both sides. He must watch out, Wilson wrote to Mary Peck, that his nerves were not shaken by "the constant pursuit of me by persons of all kinds and stations, and above all, the way in which publicity is beginning to beat upon me." He had the feeling of being surrounded by vindictive men who are determined "to destroy my character, by fair means or foul. The war upon me, from this on, is to be heartless, relentless."[18]

Wilson's most important rival for the Democratic nomination was Representative James Beauchamp Clark of Missouri, usually known as "Champ" Clark. Clark was a progressive, a follower and friend of Bryan's. He enjoyed much esteem and was elected Speaker of the House of Representatives in 1911. When the Democratic convention met in late June 1912 in Baltimore, the principal contenders for the nomination were Clark and Wilson. The conservative candidates hardly counted. Nominating conventions at the time were bizarre events, competitions in absurdity, exuberant shows, while behind the scenes brazen horsetrading went on between the agents of the various candidates, who did not themselves appear (to do so would have been considered a violation of the proprieties). In the convention hall itself what mattered was who could make the loudest and the longest noise; Clark's supporters kept up their demonstration for an hour and five minutes, while Wilson's went them ten minutes better. In the back rooms the most important jobs, especially in the new cabinet, were bartered for votes. The eventual candidate solemnly declared that he was not bound by such promises, but in practice they were honored.

The odds were on Clark. By the tenth ballot he gained a majority when the large New York state delegation went over to his side. But the rules of the Democratic convention required a two-thirds majority for the nomination. Ordinarily deputies who had not committed themselves at that point began to be afraid of missing the boat and hurried to join with the candidate who had obtained more than half the votes. This was so routine that Wilson himself, who of course followed what was happening from a distance, telegraphed to his manager, William McCombs, that it was time to give up. His dream seemed at an end. Although he was still ambivalent about the presidency, he took comfort in the thought that he could go on vacation to his beloved Lake District. But McCombs hung back from conceding Clark's victory. He soon proved right, for there was no stampede in favor of the apparently predestined winner, the first time this had happened since 1844; another hour-long demonstration by Clark's supporters did not carry the day.

A long string of ballots was necessary before a decision was reached. Wilson's stock started to rise again, and in the end he was nominated on the forty-sixth ballot. Thus the "seer and philosopher of Princeton," as he was heralded to the convention, became a candidate for the highest office that the United States can bestow. It was a bestowal with a price, however; its recipient had to offer his health, his soul, and his salvation. Was Wilson ready to pay that price? Shortly before the convention he wrote to Mary Peck with a heavy heart that he was afraid of what was about to happen and hoped he could escape it. In such a career, he wrote, there was much that was fine and clean, but also much that was "distracting and exhausting and hateful without counting the excessive personal tax of a campaign. May the Lord have mercy on me."[19]

But how could the Lord show him mercy? In the end he suffered the fate described by the Dutch poet Martinus Nijhoff in the line: "despite his fear, his wish was granted." Once Wilson was nominated, the ranks of the Democratic party closed behind him. Even William Randolph Hearst instructed his newspapers to support him, although not until October, on the eve of the election.

Wilson threw himself into the campaign, or rather he was hurtled along by it. He could not go on living this way, he wrote to Mary Hulbert (as Mary Peck was now called, having at last won her long suit for divorce). It was impossible for him to continue. "Not a moment I am left free to do what I would. I thought last night that I should go crazy with the strain and confusion of it."[20]

The struggle among the three candidates (there was actually a fourth, the Socialist Eugene Debs, who was very popular among the workers) came down in fact to one between just two. It was not only Debs who had no chance, but Taft too, who was left in the lurch by a majority of his party and besides was too indolent to go on a campaign tour. Wilson was afraid only of Roosevelt. He wrote to Mary Hulbert that Roosevelt's strength was incalculable. The struggle was between Roosevelt and himself, he wrote her, and it was "guesswork" who would win. Roosevelt, he said, appeals to people's imagination, as he himself did not.

> He is a real, vivid person. . . . I am a vague, conjectural personality, more made up of opinions and academic prepossessions than of human traits and red corpuscles. We shall see what will happen. I am not eager.[21]

What resulted, then, was a struggle between two progressives. It is this that made the election campaign of 1912 so extraordinarily nebulous in character. Public opinion in the country was generally progressive; the bosses were everywhere in retreat. Wherever possible, Wilson supported progressive candidates. He proclaimed something really new, he declared, which he called the "New Freedom."

Theodore Roosevelt, no less convinced than Wilson that Americans become excited about a cause when it is presented to them as something new, proclaimed with equal force that he would take action against the bosses and their corruption, that he would be the president of all Americans, whatever their origin. But, as we have seen, he called it the "New Nationalism."

What was the difference between them, then? William Allen White, a well-known journalist of the period, used an obvious comparison from *Alice in Wonderland*: the two parties differed no more than Tweedledum and Tweedledee.[22] An astute modern historian, Robert Wiebe, holds that both candidates essentially stood for the same thing: the government, which means its administrative apparatus, keeping an eye on what was being done in the economy.[23] The only question was how far this involvement would go.

In this respect Wilson appeared more cautious than Roosevelt. He was born and brought up in the principles of nineteenth-century liberalism, and he solemnly supported free competition with as little governmental interference as possible. The trusts were the great evil force, for their monopoly threatened freedom. "The government which was designed for the people has got into the hands of the bosses and their employers, the special interests. An invisible empire has been set up above the forms of democracy."[24] It was necessary therefore to split these powerful organizations. The ideal was that there be as many small independent businessmen as possible.

Roosevelt on the contrary thought that concentration in economic life was inevitable and not harmful in itself. He was opposed only to abuses, which could be redressed by adequate governmental supervision, by turning the concentrations from serving the interests of the few to those of society.

But weren't these distinctions purely theoretical? What did they mean in practice? In one way or another the central government had to step in to regulate the economy, and Wilson did pretty much what the Progressives had always urged, if more hesitatingly and slowly. His economic reforms date from the years 1913–1914, and he turned to true social legislation only in the election year 1916. But in the end his administration was marked by social concerns that were not very far from Roosevelt's New Nationalism. One result that many of the members of Roosevelt's short-lived Progressive party finally found themselves in the Democratic party, and would one day play a major role in the New Deal. Wilson's liberalism was less bound by nineteenth-century principles than he had proclaimed.

In any case, the difference between Roosevelt and Wilson was one between two human beings who, as a newspaperman wrote, were each other's absolute opposites in body and mind. His description of Wilson seems like a negative of his portrait of Roosevelt. Wilson, he wrote, is a man who thinks for a long time before he acts, who is modest, and who is precise in his use of words. And he means what he says.[25]

Be that as it may, it is almost beyond comprehension that someone with Wilson's physical constitution could stand up to the rigors of an election campaign. He traveled everywhere in the country, gave hundreds of speeches, sometimes seven to ten in a single day, and withstood a flood of noise and nonsense (in Lincoln, Nebraska, where Bryan lived, he was greeted by nine brass bands!). He was frequently totally exhausted, lost his voice, and still had to appear before audiences of thousands. It is hard to say which was more tiring, to have to speak to them (there were no microphones then!) or to have to listen to their rejoicing for three-quarters of an hour.

The campaign had a surprising interruption in October when Roosevelt was shot by a fanatic in Milwaukee. He was hit in the chest, but was not killed because the bullet was slowed by the copy of his speech he carried in an inside pocket of his jacket. He was able to get back on his feet and refused to go to a hospital until he had spoken to his waiting audience; he gave the whole long speech, sometimes flourishing his blood-drenched handkerchief. It was grand theater, it was living dangerously and to the full. But Roosevelt really meant what he said, and he made a deep impression.

But he could not stem the tide for Wilson. The final count of votes in November gave him the victory—a majority not of the voters but of the electors chosen by the states. Wilson received 6,293,019 popular votes, Roosevelt 4,119,507, Taft 3,484,956 and Debs 901,873, a very high number for a Socialist. These numbers translated into 453 for Wilson in the electoral college, 88 for Roosevelt, and 8 for Taft. The university professor became a president, and a youthful dream became reality.

The question now was how well this outsider would be able to play the political game, how well the dreamer could confront reality. There is, of course, no simple answer. Wilson became a great president, and he failed as president. That is the tragic paradox on which this book is built. It is about how it was possible that someone could play so great a role on the political stage and yet go so far astray in his dreams, could be so down to earth and yet so like gossamer. What does a poet do in the raw world of circumstances and facts? What is his word worth in the reality around him? In politics, it has been said (and said often in my country, Holland) that nothing can be done without principle, indeed without vision. A Dutch poet, Anthonie Donker, has written:

't is nodig dat de mens een standaard heeft waarnaar hij op kan zien,
waarvoor hij leeft.

[Man must have a banner before him
That he can see and live for.]

But how far in front of the troops must the banner be carried? When does the dream turn to delirium and lose all touch with reality?

Woodrow Wilson thought that he could bring heaven and earth together because he was a democrat. In brilliant metaphors drenched with biblical force, he avowed his belief that he had his roots deep in the reality of the American people. In a campaign speech against the rich, he affirmed his vision:

A people shall be saved by the power that sleeps in its own deep bosom, or by none; shall be renewed in hope, in conscience, in strength, by waters welling up from its own sweet, perennial springs. Not from above; not by patronage of its aristocrats. The flower does not bear the root, but the root the flower. Everything that blooms in beauty in the air of heaven draws its fairness, its vigor, from its roots. . . . Up from the common soil, up from the quiet heart of the people, rise joyously to-day streams of hope and determination bound to renew the face of the earth in glory.[26]

We have already heard it said that this was all just election rhetoric. But then we must say: What an election it was in which such rhetoric was used! And we add a second, more realistic thought: If only that were true! Probably, if it had been true, dream and reality would not have grown so far apart as it happened. Woodrow Wilson is truly present in those splendid phrases. The vision grew larger and encompassed the whole world. No one, not even Wilson himself, could anticipate in 1912 how soon all America would see itself as the soul, the leader of all mankind. But the incoming president promised a wholly unselfish America at the service of mankind. This was the theme that in the coming years would grow into a dogma. It sounded clearly already in that year 1912:

What was in the writings of the men who founded America, to serve the selfish interests of America? Do you find that in their writings? No; to serve the cause of humanity, to bring liberty to mankind.[27]

ELEVEN

If he rightly interpret the national thought and boldly
insist upon it, he is irresistible.

> —*Woodrow Wilson,* Constitutional Government

THE
PRESIDENT
AS REFORMER

ON MARCH 4, 1913, THE
date set in the Constitution
for the inauguration of the
new president, Woodrow
Wilson moved to the White
House. He had been elected
back in November, and this repub-
lican interregnum was too long. That had become clear half a century
earlier, during the tragic winter of 1860–1861, when Abraham Lincoln
had to stand on the sidelines while the weak-willed president, James
Buchanan, permitted the country to slide into confusion and crisis. The
date was not changed until Franklin D. Roosevelt had it moved back to
January 20.

The year 1913 was not, however, a year of crisis, and the long interval could be useful for the selection of a cabinet. Wilson sensibly took
a vacation first, for the campaign had left him exhausted. He went with
his family to the idyllic island of Bermuda (where he had often met Mrs.
Peck) to recover. He returned in the middle of December, refreshed and
again in high spirits.

To choose a cabinet was not a straightforward task. The president-elect could not expect to be able simply to name those whom he considered best fit for office. In the first place, promises had been made at the convention, and, although he had solemnly denied that he had made any commitments, the fact was that he was bound by them. He was after all not just the head of the nation but also the leader of his party. Furthermore, this team of ministers of state and heads of departments had to constitute a reasonable representation of diverse regional interests; the cabinet was a kind of patchwork quilt of the country. The founder of Christianity, Abraham Lincoln had said, had an easier job than he did, because he could choose his disciples as he wanted without worrying about where they came from.

The most important post in the cabinet was that of the secretary of state. He was not only the country's minister of foreign affairs, but during the nineteenth century he had come to be viewed as a virtual prime minister. In any case, it was the highest prize that could be awarded by the president after the elections, and it was almost always given to the man who, from the party's point of view, most deserved it.

As an old joke put it, every boy in America had the chance to become president, but he ran the risk of becoming secretary of state. Often the number two man in the party was chosen, the man who had fallen short at the convention, or even earlier, so that the office became, as it were, a consolation prize. In the Democratic party in 1913, this of course meant William Jennings Bryan. Who deserved it more than Bryan, the great leader who had three times run for the presidency and failed each time? It was therefore purely a question of political merit, for otherwise there was no reason whatever to appoint him to this office. He came from Nebraska, out on the prairie, and knew nothing, absolutely nothing, about foreign countries. That he had no experience abroad at all did not appear a great drawback, however, at a time when the country's isolationist tradition was still very strong; but change was coming, although no one realized in that last peacetime year how close the outside world was coming to the United States.

At first Wilson did not hold a high opinion of Bryan. He found him a scatterbrain without much intelligence. He was amazed that a political leader of such importance "should have no mental rudder."[1] But, as we have seen, he had been reconciled with Bryan as the election approached, and his estimation of him went steadily upward. After all, Bryan represented the strong progressive wing of the Democratic party.

For his part Bryan had thrown himself fully into the campaign to elect Wilson. There was no escaping the necessity to reward him with the best post in the cabinet, not only because he was a three-time loser but also because of his influence in the party. Without his support, progressive legislation would hardly have had a chance of passage.

According to the recollections of Wilson's daughter Eleanor, Wilson was still hesitant, and it was his wife who pushed most strongly for Bryan's appointment. Bryan was therefore invited to come to Trenton, the state capital of New Jersey where Wilson was still a resident, and received the invitation to take over the State Department. "His naiveté is really charming—he was as delighted as a child with a new toy," Wilson told his family afterwards, not without some condescension.[2] Bryan did not hesitate at all. He set only one condition to his acceptance: he would not have to serve alcohol at diplomatic receptions, for he was a fervent teetotaler. Wilson could not turn down Bryan's stipulation, but diplomatic life in Washington became a dull affair during the next few years.

Bryan was no great acquisition for Wilson's cabinet, but it must be said that as a whole it did not sparkle with brilliant qualities. This was in part because, as was usual with American cabinets, it did not have direct responsibility to Congress and therefore worked in a kind of vacuum. But another reason was probably that Wilson was not eager to have colleagues who were his intellectual peers. To his new friend Colonel House, who helped him form the cabinet (and to whose role and importance in foreign policy we must return in the next chapter), Wilson said that there were no geniuses, thank goodness, in his team, for "geniuses were a nuisance."[3]

The cabinet therefore became an assemblage of mediocrities, fairly conservative in their views, burdened with many prejudices, especially concerning race (more than half of them came from the South), and they did not get along well with one another personally. The membership of the cabinet was not stable. Only a few held office for the full two terms. Several deserve at least some mention all the same. William McAdoo, a banker, who shortly afterwards married Wilson's younger daughter Eleanor, became the head of the Treasury Department. David F. Houston, the secretary of agriculture, wrote memoirs that are an important historical source for the period, as is the diary of Josephus Daniels, the editor-in-chief of a newspaper in Raleigh, North Carolina, who became secretary of navy (his still little-known undersecretary was Franklin D.

Roosevelt, a cousin of Theodore Roosevelt). Lindley M. Garrison ran the War Department.

Another man whom we must mention was not a member of the cabinet at all. This was Joseph P. Tumulty, Wilson's personal secretary. He was a progressive Irish politician from New Jersey, who had been converted—it was almost a religious conversion—from Wilson's enemy to his hardworking friend during the gubernatorial election in 1910. He served Wilson with heart and soul, controlled who got in to see his chief, and maintained contact with the Democratic party. With his warm directness, he repaired the relations that Wilson spoiled with his cool detachment. He was, however, impulsive, very voluble, and a Roman Catholic, a "fault" that still aroused much opposition.

Wilson was inaugurated on March 4, 1913, a day of splendid weather. He began by taking the oath of office and kissed the Bible, which lay open at Psalm 119, at the appropriate verses 43–48: "And take not the word of truth utterly out of my mouth; for I have hoped in thy judgments. . . . And I shall walk at liberty: for I seek thy precepts." And then a prediction that was not a stab in the dark: "I will speak of thy testimonies also before kings, and will not be ashamed."

His inaugural address was brief, clear, and fervent with social feeling. The growth of American industry, he said, had been immense, but at what cost in human suffering! The nation had developed too quickly; there was something raw, heartless, and unfeeling in the haste to become successful and great. Americans were now coming to their senses, said Wilson; they must redress all that injustice, put the government at the service of people, not out of compassion but of righteousness. They must protect people against the consequences of large industrial and social processes which individually they could neither change nor control.[4]

Wilson's first term of office was one of those rare periods in American history when everything appeared to work together for good. The American system of government is extremely sluggish and inefficient, but now and then it suddenly speeds up. This was to happen in 1933–1934 under Franklin D. Roosevelt and in 1964–1965 with Lyndon Johnson. It results from many causes, both of circumstances and of leadership. The circumstances in 1913 were favorable; the whole country felt the need for reform. It was also the first time in twenty years that a newly triumphant party came in with an immense majority in Congress (51 Democrats against 44 Republicans in the Senate, 290 Democrats against 127 Repub-

The President as Reformer

licans in the House of Representatives). And there was a leader who knew what he wanted, an outsider who, unlike Bryan, could retain a certain independence of his own party.

Wilson believed deeply in the solidarity of the people. It was a romantic article of faith which he proclaimed ever more fervidly. "My thinking will be effectual only in proportion as it really interprets the general thinking of the country at large."[5] The implication was that nothing whatsoever should come between the leader and the people. From the start Wilson did not trust Congress. If on the one side he willingly considered it to be the representative of the people, on the other he felt it as an encumbrance, an obstacle in his way.

He therefore made the surprising decision to revive an almost forgotten custom by appearing in person before Congress to present his State of the Union address. The first two presidents, George Washington and John Adams, had done so, but Thomas Jefferson, the principled democrat, thought it was too much like an address from the throne and abandoned the custom. (Besides, he was not a good speaker.) Since then the presidential messages had been read by a clerk amid general somnolence. It occurred to Wilson to revive the original practice. For him, of course, speaking was right down his alley. He got a quiet pleasure from the fact that it was he who had come up with the idea and not Teddy Roosevelt, who if he were in his place would have been delighted to do it. To a circle of friends, Roosevelt boasted that if Wilson had done much, the ideas were Roosevelt's. He struck his breast and said, "Wilson is merely a less virile *me*."[6]

Wilson, who was good at the kind of democracy in which he did the speaking, had restored direct contact with Congress. Nonetheless he continued to mistrust it. His grand principle that the people were good but had evil rulers, was already present as a seed in his mind. He would later repeatedly proclaim it, to his own injury. In a letter to Mary Hulbert, he asked:

> The struggle goes on down here without intermission. Why it should *be* a struggle it is hard . . . to say. Why *should* public men, senators of the United States, have to be led and stimulated to what all the country knows to be their duty? . . . To whom are they listening? Certainly not to the voice of the people. . . . They . . . exaggerate themselves in the most extraordinary degree.[7]

The presidential office probably weighed so heavily upon him because he was both oversensitive and self-assured. Wilson realized that he had to pay a high price for the intensity of his leadership.

Heavy as the burden was, Wilson was still able to govern with a strong hand and to carry through a whole series of reforms. He did what he had promised to do. First came an important revenue act that lowered tariffs on the average from 40 percent to 34 percent, the lowest figure since 1865. As was to be expected, there was strong opposition from interest groups, most of all the wool, sugar, and cotton producers, who established powerful lobbies to influence legislation. Wilson reacted with genuine indignation. It is not fair, he declared officially, "that the people at large should have no lobby and be voiceless in these matters, while great bodies of astute men seek to create an artificial opinion and to overcome the interests of the public for their private profit." And he argued, long before consumer groups had come into existence, for vigilance on the part of public opinion.[8]

The new law also provided for a revived federal income tax in order to make up for the revenues lost by the reduction in the tariffs; it was permitted by the just adopted Sixteenth Amendment to the Constitution, which overrode previous declarations of unconstitutionality by the Supreme Court. It was a progressive tax, very moderate by later standards, but it still roused a fierce political battle. Despite the opposition of an unnatural alliance of conservatives on the right and radicals on the left, the law was passed by Congress and signed by the president in October 1913.

The second major piece of legislation was also economic in character, concerning the old problem of monetary circulation. The banking system of the United States was a muddle; there was universal agreement that some kind of regulation was necessary to call a halt to the recurring crises, the last as recent as 1907. This could be done only by establishing a central supervisory agency. A national bank had existed in the early part of the nineteenth century, but it had been abolished in 1826 by ultrademocratic President Andrew Jackson; a major economic crisis had resulted at once, followed by many others since.

Throughout the country there was, however, a deep mistrust of the financial power of New York in the "crooked canyons" of Wall Street, and centralization remained controversial. Wilson himself had little expert knowledge in the question and therefore was not committed to any particular solution, but he shared the common suspicion of bankers, who he believed deliberately provoked crises. As recently as December 1912, he had warned that he would hang such criminals from gallows as high as Haman's.[9]

Senator Carter Glass of Virginia introduced a bill to establish strong federal controls over the monetary system, drawn up with the advice of Louis Brandeis. Wilson came out strongly in its favor. Another long struggle followed, but on December 23 Wilson could at last put his signature on the Federal Reserve Act, which for the first time established a central financial system for the country. It was one of the most important successes of Wilson's first term.

More such laws followed. A Federal Trade Commission was established in September 1914 to combat unfair competition. The Clayton Antitrust Act sharpened the Sherman Act of 1890 and also abolished the misuse of the law against labor unions, so that it was called the Magna Carta of Labor. But these laws looked better on paper than they actually were in action. Mostly conservatives were named to the Trade Commission, and the Clayton Act was weakened by decisions of the Supreme Court.

Wilson crossed the boundaries of the New Freedom on the way to the New Nationalism. The slogan "special privileges to none" was insufficient for social legislation. Freedom alone was inadequate to protect the weak members of society; they needed special action on their behalf. But this was a difficult step for Wilson to take. When he was pressed to act to protect minorities, he often hesitated and sought refuge behind the limits of his constitutional functions. Then, with an unusual distinction, he divided his leadership into two parts: what mattered was not what he wanted personally, but what was good for the country (which was what was wanted by the Democratic party). We find repeated instances of this hesitation. In April 1914, he vetoed a bill granting special credits to farmers. "I have a very deep conviction that it is unwise and unjustifiable to extend the credit of the Government to a single class of the community." This was a conviction, he said, that he learned "out of fire." Two years later the fire had obviously been put out, for a "rural credits" law was adopted.[10]

He also opposed a federal law restricting child labor on the grounds of its unconstitutionality; the federal government should leave such laws to the states. But constitutional convictions and emotional involvement apparently warred within him. In this matter too he later gave way, signing a law against child labor in 1916 "with real emotion."[11]

By 1916, when another presidential election would be held, Wilson had almost completely converted to supporting social legislation. The consequence was that many of the old "Bull Moosers," people such as Jane Addams, the admired founder of Hull House in Chicago, John Dewey, the philosopher of pragmatism, Lincoln Steffens, the well-known muckraker, Walter Lippmann, the brilliant young journalist, and, not to be forgotten, Herbert Croly himself, joined the Democratic party. Their support was of essential importance for a president in trouble, and for the Democratic party, which received a clear progressive stamp, enabling it to become under Franklin Roosevelt the party of major reforms in 1933 and the majority party of the country.

But the Democratic party also continued to hold the support of the Southern states. It was a strange, almost paradoxical combination. True, there was a strong progressive movement in the South, but it was precisely the radical Southerners, the "rednecks," who were the most rabid racists. And Wilson himself, although subdued on the race issue, could not succeed without the support of the Southern wing of his party. This was why the idealist president, partly out of realism and partly out of inherited prejudice, was more conservative on the issue of race relations than his predecessors had been. For the most part they had simply ignored the question, but under Wilson segregation was put into practice in the national capital.

This happened during the election campaign when blacks were being soothed with promises of equality. The promises were vague, to be sure, but in their plight they snatched at any straw. In the circles of the National Association for the Advancement of Colored People (NAACP), consisting of black intellectuals and the Northern whites with ties to blacks, Wilson had been viewed as the best candidate of the three running in 1912. Oswald Garrison Villard, a grandson of the great abolitionist William Lloyd Garrison and the white leader of the NAACP, paid a visit to Wilson in 1912 and won from him an assurance that blacks would be treated with complete equality and that he would speak out personally against lynching. It was something that "every honest man must do," Wilson said, although admitting candidly that he lacked the power to do much about the crimes that fell under the jurisdiction of the states.[12]

Young blacks who were leaning toward socialism were attracted to

Wilson by his presumed social conscience. W. E. B. Du Bois, the editor of *Crisis*, the journal of the NAACP, would rather have given his support to Eugene Debs, the Socialist candidate, but chose to be practical. He did not believe that Woodrow Wilson "admires Negroes," but he was "a cultivated scholar and he has brains." He therefore would act toward blacks with "farsighted fairness," and certainly would not enforce the offensive "Jim Crow" laws. As another pamphlet from the same circles put it, Wilson was "a Christian gentleman."[13]

These expectations were tragically disappointed. It was not that Wilson did not mean what he promised; he meant so many things in a vague, well-intentioned way. But he appointed many Southern politicians to his cabinet, and they practiced total segregation once they were in office. In one of the first meetings of the cabinet, Daniels, the new secretary of navy, proposed to remove such "abuses" as common drinking fountains and towels for blacks and whites; other members came to his support, and Wilson himself (as is reported in Daniels's diary) said that "he made no promises in particular to negroes, except to do them justice." The issue was settled without serious dispute. Wilson was for justice, but it could be denied "in particular."[14]

The introduction of segregation in the capital aroused a storm of protests. Villard wrote a bewildered letter to Wilson: "The colored men who voted and worked for you in the belief that their status as Americans was safe in your hands are deeply cast down. . . . They got from your 'New Freedom' the belief that your democracy was not limited by race or color." But Wilson replied at once that it had all been done in the interest of the blacks themselves. At the same time he wrote to the fierce racist Thomas Dixon, who had complained that a Negro had been put at the head of a group of white girls, that it was intended to bring all the Negroes in the department into a separate division.[15] Wilson, a Southerner, thought segregation was a reasonable solution, as he told other protesters.[16]

The collision between the president and blacks came to a dramatic climax at the reception of a black delegation in November 1914. They were led by William Monroe Trotter, the outspoken editor-in-chief of the *Guardian*, a newspaper for blacks in Boston. Wilson repeated his argument that segregation was a blessing for blacks themselves. Trotter replied that blacks were disappointed. Two years earlier they had considered Wilson a second Abraham Lincoln, he said, and so they had voted for him.

It was bitter for them to find that he did not think segregation was wrong. The argument raged back and forth, becoming harsher and harsher in tone. Wilson finally lost his patience. If their association wanted to get another hearing with him, he said, they must bring another spokesman. Trotter's tone was offensive. Trotter was an American citizen, as good as Wilson himself, but he was the only American citizen who had ever taken such a tone with him. Trotter had spoiled his whole case. Trotter replied, "Mr. President, I am sorry for that. Mr. President, America that professes to be Christian cannot condemn that which . . ." Wilson broke in, "I expect those who profess to be Christians to come to me in a Christian spirit." This went on for a little while, until the infuriated president showed his guests to the door.[17]

Later on he came to regret that he had spoken so freely. The affair did him no good among blacks when it was reported by Trotter. Wilson received many declarations of agreement from the South, but his liberal followers in the North were put out, and they continued to feel a degree of suspicion for this prejudiced prophet.

Woodrow Wilson, we would conclude, was not a fanatic, a "racist" in the extreme sense of that overworked word. His blindness was the blindness of his time and even more of his region. Yet it was a fault that grates unpleasantly when measured by the religious sublimity of his idealism.

TWELVE

It would be the irony of fate if my administration had to deal chiefly with foreign affairs.
    —*Woodrow Wilson, 1913*

FOREIGN POLICY

*T*HE BLISSFUL INNO-cence of these words, which are quoted in just about every book about Wilson, comes as a surprise to us because we know what was going to happen and because Wilson himself was well aware of the great changes in America's relations with the world at large. As we have seen, after some initial hesitation, he had taken a positive stand in favor of the Spanish-American War, and he had repeatedly commented that the age of American isolation was past. But he had been too busy with his scholarly work on the Constitution and with his troubles at Princeton to give much thought to the new situation. In 1913 he hoped that he could devote himself wholly to domestic reforms. This was not to be.

Problems in relations to other countries began even before the new president moved into the White House. In China, a far-off country with which America believed it was deeply involved, a great revolution had just begun that removed "the last of the emperors," a child of three, from his throne. In Mexico, which was next door, the government was overthrown at about the same time; a persistent chaos followed, which involved the United States in many different ways.

Although Wilson knew little about China or Mexico, he had to make decisions about them. This he did without delay, according to his principles, without long reflection. He at once pushed Bryan aside, taking over in person the conduct of foreign policy and reducing the secretary of state to following his instructions. "The President," wrote Houston in his diary, "was going to be his own secretary of state."[1] This did not cause the difficulties that might have occurred, because Wilson and Bryan were in fundamental agreement; both were men of principle, both idealists, and neither knew very much about the matters that they had to handle.

Bryan was essentially an old-fashioned provincial, an American from an earlier, friendlier time. As Walter Lippmann wrote, he was never able to adjust to the modern world in which he lived.

> That is why he is so irresistibly funny to sophisticated newspaper men. His virtues, his habits, his ideas are the simple, direct, shrewd qualities of early America. He is the true Don Quixote of our politics, for he moves in a world that has ceased to exist.[2]

One of his antiquated notions was that the diplomatic service was a breeding place for rich men's sons who were concerned only with the interests of their class. Another was his attachment to the "spoils system" that dated from the time of Andrew Jackson. This was the system of bestowing political office in recompense for political service, in the happy assumption that everyone was fit to hold any office. Once settled in his department—in his shirtsleeves and suspenders, with a red handkerchief tucked into his collar, "like a Hottentot chief on his tropical throne"[3]— Bryan began to replace diligent and able diplomats with political pals, whom, in a letter that unfortunately leaked out to the public, he called "deserving Democrats."[4]

Unfortunately, Wilson was not that much better than Bryan in this respect. Still bearing the scars of his struggle with the rich men's sons and their odious fathers, he shared completely Bryan's suspicion of the diplomats. In a letter to Charles W. Eliot, the celebrated retired president of Harvard, he wrote: "They have the material interests of individuals more in mind than the moral and public considerations which seems to us ought to control."[5] He too wished to make many new appointments, although, less a man of the people than Bryan, he sought his candidates primarily among idealistic professors.

In general the diplomats who were appointed in 1913 were far below their tasks. James Gerard in Berlin was a New York lawyer with good connections to Tammany Hall; Joseph Willard in Madrid a rich politician from Virginia; Thomas Nelson Dixon in Rome a savagely racist Southern novelist. They were all chosen only because they were political friends. The most competent of them was probably Wilson's old friend, Walter Hines Page, who went to London. He was a striking personality, a former editor of a number of newspapers and of *The Atlantic Monthly*, a man of vision who wrote with a sharp pen. But he soon became so enthusiastic and committed an Anglophile that he appeared to be more concerned with serving English than American interests. (It is an interesting insight into the state of the American diplomatic service that the salary of the ambassador to London was so low that Page could not make ends meet, and it was secretly supplemented by a wealthy friend of Wilson's at his express request.)[6]

The world was still at peace in the spring of 1913. A lighthearted optimism prevailed; all conflicts between nations, it was believed, could be resolved peacefully. Agreements for making such settlements were all the vogue. The Hague peace conferences of 1899 and 1907 had introduced the principle of arbitration, and America accepted it—up to a point. John Hay and Elihu Root, who had been cabinet members under Roosevelt, had concluded arbitration agreements with many countries, but these were nothing more than promises of the two parties to submit eventual points of conflict to the International Court at The Hague, provided that the disputes did not affect their national honor or vital interests. Philander Knox, Taft's secretary of state, wanted to include questions of national honor among those that could be submitted to the court, but the Senate drew out all the teeth from these agreements by a provision that it and it alone could determine what would be subject to arbitration.

Bryan continued in the tradition of his predecessors. With true evangelical zeal, he argued for "treaties for the advancement of peace." But he added a requirement for a cooling-off period during which the parties could reconsider their positions. It was a splendid idea as far it went, and Bryan was exceedingly proud of his "cooling-off treaties," which he concluded with many countries. But these treaties did not provide for a halt to increasing armed forces during the "cooling-off period."

How little they really meant was shown by the fact that England and France concluded such treaties with the United States in September 1914 after the war with Germany had already begun, obviously not out of a love of peace but in order to win the favor of the United States.

Bryan was as happy as a child with his great work for peace. He made a gift to each of his relatives of a paperweight that literally expressed the prophecy of Isaiah, for it was made from old swords contributed by the War Department, and depicted plowshares with a text from Isaiah (2:4): "They shall beat their swords into plowshares." Bryan's peace program elicited from his colleague Franklin K. Lane the comment that Bryan was one of the few men he had ever met who really believed that the Bible could be applied to everyday life.[7] Bryan's treaties had a sad fate. They obviously had no effect in the mad world of 1914. They reappeared without mention of their source in Article IX of the Covenant of the League of Nations, and their echo could still be heard in later treaties notable for their nobility of language and their ineffectuality in practice, like the Locarno treaty in 1925 and the Kellogg-Briand pact in 1928.

Wilson was very satisfied with Bryan's activities. He gave warm assent to his verbal initiatives, which anticipated the idealism of his attempts to reform the world a few years later. America, he said in a speech in Pittsburgh, had recently concluded a series of arbitration treaties providing essentially that if troubles arose anywhere, they would be put under "the light" for a year before any action was taken. He anticipated that after a year of such study, nothing would have to be done because it would have become obvious who was right and who wrong. This light is always "the moral light, the light of the man who discloses it in order that all the sweet influences of the world may go in and make it better." He spoke these lofty words on October 24, 1914. Could there have been anyone in his audience who did not wonder what he really meant by "sweet influences of the world" in that frightful moment of world history.[8] The high-principled agreement between Wilson and Bryan did not last long, soon breaking against reality.

It did not much matter, however, whether they were in agreement. Wilson conducted his foreign policy not with the cabinet member whose formal task it was (neither with Bryan nor with his successor in the office), but with a special advisor who was a special friend. Wilson was the first to follow the practice, but his advisor, Colonel Edward House, was given no official function, although his power was very great. We must learn to know him better, as much as is possible of a smooth man who deliberately worked behind the scenes. For seven years House was Wilson's faithful friend and right hand, until at last even this close relationship was severed.

House was by his own intention a man of mystery. He appeared suddenly in Wilson's life and in a short time became his bosom friend. He has come down to us as a "colonel," but the rank, conferred by states, was purely honorary and had nothing to do with soldiering. House was not a loud-voiced army officer but a quiet diplomat who crept through political problems on slippered feet. He loved manipulation. In his native state, Texas, he had helped to put many politicians in office, but Texas, large as it was, became too small for him. His ambition, although secretive, was immense. Another reason why Texas was too small and too raw for him was that he was a man of formality and good manners who had been educated at a boarding school in England and took a degree at Cornell University. He was almost too dignified for an American, it was thought in Europe. Clemenceau was astonished by his subtlety and called him "an overcivilized man who has escaped from the savagery of Texas and who sees and understands everything," the very model of a "gentleman" (*honnête homme*). In the Frenchman's opinion gratitude was owed to Wilson if only for bringing such a "good auxiliary" with him.[9] Europeans were in general enthusiastic over this natty, diligent man. Harold Nicolson found him "the best diplomatic brain that America has produced," and the renowned journalist Wickham Steed described him as "a selfless man."[10]

Others were not so favorable to House. Questions arose. Did the Europeans praise him because they thought they could use him to their advantage? What is the value of a "selfless man"? Is anyone really "selfless"? Was House too obliging, too pliant? Was there really some individuality behind that suave affability? Or was he just "a conciliator, an arranger," as Ray Stannard Baker, Wilson's friend and biographer, wrote, a dilettante, "a lover of the game"?[11]

House was a "gentleman of leisure." He had already made his fortune and therefore did not have to concern himself with the accumulation of lucre. He could be tranquilly devoted to his dreams, which we know from a utopian novel, *Philip Dru, Administrator*, he had written, in which he spells out his idealistic aspirations. The book's hero is a man who has to forego a military career because of bad health but becomes the leader of an uprising against the corrupt government of the United States at the time of the tale. Then, as an enlightened dictator, he reforms the land and finally withdraws, restoring democracy. This was a veiled self-portrait of a man who, although he deliberately remained in the shadows, had large ambitions.

A meeting with Wilson determined the course of his life, indeed the course of both their lives. It must be admitted at once that this was the most curious friendship in American history. Wilson had heard about him from Harvey, and met him for the first time in November 1911. "We talked and talked. We knew each other for congenial souls at the very beginning," House wrote. A second meeting aroused even more enthusiasm. "We found ourselves in agreement upon practically every one of the issues of the day. I never met a man whose thought was so identical with mine. . . . He seemed too good to be true." They became inseparable, gave each other their fullest confidence, and were themselves surprised how strong their brand-new friendship had become. House asked Wilson whether he realized that they had known each other only briefly. "My dear friend," replied Wilson, "we have known each other always."[12] Wilson called him his "second personality": "His thoughts and mine are one."[13] House was even more lyrical: "Almost from the first our association was intimate; almost from the first our minds vibrated in unison."[14] House was informed about everything, even Wilson's personal finances: "You are the only person in the world with whom I can discuss everything."[15]

This is all fodder for psychologists. Just what was happening? Was there really such perfect unanimity, or was House finding what he had been seeking, a man whom he could serve and influence, and to whom he therefore played up? This is the conclusion that various authors have reached, in particular the couple A. L. and J. L. George, who have written a fascinating but psychologically exaggerated book. According to them, House quite deliberately manipulated his good, great friend (as he often described him). In any case, House's letters often have a tone of flattery. One example: "You are the bravest, wisest leader, the gentlest and most gallant and the truest friend in the world."[16] Another, a few years later: Be prudent, "care for yourself, for I do not put it too strongly when I say that you are the only hope left to this torn and distracted world. Without your leadership God alone knows how long we will wander in the wilderness."[17]

The truth is that House did manipulate Wilson. It was most unfortunate, for House distorted reality. It has become usual in recent historical writings to put emphasis upon House's disastrous influence upon Wilson, and there is much truth in this judgment. But there is also a danger, I think, that this draws the contrast between Wilson and House too sharply, that as the star of the one declines, that of the other rises. Much of the blame for Wilson's failure is placed upon House's shoulders. He becomes the man who sabotaged Wilson's fine, workable plans; without him the president would have had much more success.[18] But then we must ask whether Wilson, a man of such intelligence, was really taken in by House. Did he give House his full confidence and not notice his flatteries? It is after all quite significant that Wilson allowed himself to be led. It tells something about his naïveté, but also about the obvious fact that these two men were really like each other, that House too was naive, that both overestimated their dreams. Both were figures from a novel by Henry James, innocent Americans who became entangled in the nets of the Old World. Yet they did not fit the rest of James's myth; it was not true that a noble Wilson was entrapped in the snares of a crafty House.

There exists of course a psychological explanation for Wilson's trust in the likable colonel. He had an immense need for friendship and respect. After all he met House just after he had lost his best friends at Princeton. His career in high politics had made him lonelier than ever, for the office of president was a very lonely office, at least for someone as over-sensitive and vulnerable as Wilson. And, in August 1914, he lost his beloved wife. In this situation House gave him the security which he lacked, and did so quite knowingly: "I nearly always praise at first in order to strengthen the President's confidence in himself, which, strangely enough, is often lacking." It was no wonder that Wilson thought House the "most self-effacing man" he had ever met.[19]

To this we should add that House possessed qualities that Wilson completely lacked. Wilson was an intellectual who could read and speak but could not listen, and he was quickly annoyed by the halting speech of most people. But House was by nature a talker, a negotiator, without much intellectual ballast. His primary purpose was to manipulate people.[20]

There was mutual love, that is clear. The word is not too strong. When, in 1915, half a year after his wife's death, Wilson became betrothed again, he wrote to his wife-to-be that she was for him "another such friend as Colonel House" was.[21] As was to be expected, such naïveté had disastrous consequences. Edith Bolling Galt did not appreciate the comparison. Almost at once she began to make mischief for House, and in the end she would be the cause of his downfall. He is not a strong personality, she bluntly told Wilson.[22] Wilson defended his friend in his typical fashion: House, he replied, was strong because of his unselfishness, his lack of fear and his incorruptibility; he was "noble and lovely" in character because of his loyalty and devotion. "And he is wise. . . . But you are right in thinking that intellectually he is not a great man. His mind is not of the first class. He is a counsellor, not a statesman." What a marvelous example of Woodrow Wilson's cerebral pride![23]

For the time being the situation remained unchanged. Wilson could not do without House, and the definitive break would not come until April 1919 in Paris. We have a long way to go until then.

THIRTEEN

This is the most amazing and inspiring vision—this
vision of that great sleeping nation suddenly awakened
by the voice of Christ.
    —*Woodrow Wilson on China, April 21, 1915*

Mexico has a great and enviable future before her, if only
she choose and attain the paths of honest constitutional
government.
    —*Woodrow Wilson to Congress, August 27, 1913*

TWO
REVOLUTIONS

URING A SINGLE YEAR
China and Mexico both ex-
perienced revolutions that
led to long-lasting and tragic
chaos. Wilson's government
was closely involved in both
revolutions, for the time of Ameri-
can isolation was truly past. America had long felt it had an especially
close tie with China. A myth prevailed about a special relationship between the United States and the Celestial Empire.[1] According to this
myth, China was a venerable nation with a high but ossified civilization.
The European countries had gone to China only to abuse and exploit it
for their own interests. In their yearning, the Chinese people had called
out for Christian help. "Do you hear the voice calling from afar, pleading
for help? It is a voice in pain." The only Western country that really
understood China and could help her was America. Such assistance extended to every area: trade, politics, religion. America could bring prosperity and democracy and Christianity. What a market for goods, what
unprecedented opportunities for the Kingdom of God! So went the myth.

To sketch in the background in a few lines, China had been forced by England in the so-called "Opium War" of 1839–1842 to open a number of ports for Western trade, and since then the pressure of the West had become steadily greater, leading slowly but steadily to the disintegration of the Chinese empire. This process had gone so far by 1900 that the Western powers began to establish spheres of influence along the entire coast of China—but so had Japan, which had already conquered Formosa (Taiwan) in 1895. There was talk of the "Africanization" of China. In this whole development America had taken part only halfheartedly. On the one hand, it was as eager as the European countries for the presumed immense profits to be made on the Chinese market, for that was also part of the myth; but on the other hand it wished to play the role of a disinterested third party, a spiritual role. Americans took a leading part in the idealistic invasion of China by Christian missionaries.

But light always casts a shadow. The dream of a great brotherhood between China and America soon shattered against reality. While the Americans were endeavoring to Christianize the whole Chinese nation, the Chinese who were brave enough to come to California to seek work were being exploited and even persecuted. The ambivalence of the American attitude toward China became steadily more flagrant. On the one side was the myth of the Chinese as a brother people. There was the steady stream of American missionaries who dreamed of "the Evangelization of the world in this generation," in the words of John Mott, the leader of the Student Volunteers for Foreign Missions (and a good friend of Wilson's). There was both this ideal of "China for Christ" and at the same time the unanimous dream of a boundless market for American products, such as petroleum, "oil for the lamps of China." From out of this wonderful mixture of altruism and economic interests had emerged the Open Door policy of John Hay, the secretary of state between 1898 and 1905, expressed in two notes that he sent to the astounded powers calling on them to respect the territorial integrity of China.

On the other side was the mutual incomprehension between America and China. There was the deep hatred of the humiliated Chinese people for the Westerners, culminating in the Boxer uprising of 1900, and the disgraceful treatment of the Chinese immigrants in the United States. There was above all the simple fact that American trade interests in China never amounted to more than 3.5 percent of the total American foreign trade and the investments in China more than 1.4 percent of all foreign investments.[2]

In addition, there was Japan. American policy in the years around the turn of the century constantly swung between two entities, China and Japan. The war of 1898 had brought the Far East closer; one of the slogans raised during the occupation of the Philippines was that these islands formed the key to Asia, and the Open Door policy followed logically from it. But was this policy, however idealistic it may have been (and that is open to debate), more than an empty gesture? Theodore Roosevelt did not think so. He realized that Japan had the hegemony in Asia and as a realist he put his bets on Japan, mediating in the Russo-Japanese war of 1905.

But the American relationship with Japan was also poisoned by the problem of immigration into California, where the Japanese were excluded and humiliated. Roosevelt had his hands full with the embarrassment of California's policy of segregation, but states' rights under the federal system did not give him much room to act. But his efforts at rapprochement with the land of the rising sun also aroused much opposition from the idealists who believed in China. A change of course began under Taft. There has always been considerable criticism of his dollar diplomacy, but it had a genuine idealist element. Taft and his secretary of state, Philander Knox, appealed for financial support to China, for achieving political influence by means of investments; "dollar diplomacy" was also practiced under the slogan, "Dollars instead of bullets," and described as "using Wall Street to serve our national interest and to benefit other countries."[3] Naturally these semi-idealists thought themselves true realists. They continued to bet on the future of great China and therefore remained in the tradition of "our historic policy in China."[4] They proposed that American bankers should participate in an international consortium specifically in order to create in China an American counterweight to the imperialism of other countries. In that way they became entangled in international complications that they had not foreseen. The bankers with whom they collaborated were less altruistic and demanded for their loans guarantees from the Chinese government. This constituted a clear infringement of Chinese sovereignty and integrity about which the Americans had always prated so much.

Westerners, including the Americans, in reality had hardly any understanding of China. They did not realize the humiliation imposed on China by the conditions laid down for their help. In 1905 there had been a boycott of American products in China to protest the treatment of immigrants in California. The huge, chaotic country was in ferment. National feelings, actually encouraged by Western influences, turned not only against the Manchu dynasty but also against foreigners, all foreigners. Xenophobia, after all, had a long tradition in China. One of the causes of the revolution that broke out in 1911 was indignation over the attitude of the bank consortium. It was led on the one side by ambitious realists such as General Yuan Shi-kai, who hoped to ascend the imperial throne himself, but on the other by idealists such as Sun Yat-sen, who inscribed Western ideas such as democracy and socialism in their banner.

For the time being the revolution brought little more than confusing chaos, and one of Wilson's earliest problems when he took office in March 1913 was how to respond to it. The American bankers who participated in the consortium had become unsure of their position and were afraid to go any further without the backing of the government in Washington. Wilson did not dawdle in coming to a decision. He idealistically considered the loans to be totally unacceptable. On March 18 he put out a vigorous declaration denouncing as unacceptable the complicity of the American government in the infringement of China's "administrative independence," but it painted the country's future in optimistic words: "The awakening of the people of China to a consciousness of their possibilities under free government is the most significant, if not the most momentous event of our generation." He expressed his full approval for this development, calling the Open Door "a door of friendship and mutual advantage. This is the only door we care to enter."[5]

It sounded like an honest break with the policy of self-interest and dollar diplomacy. But it rested upon the idea that China was able to save itself, that it was free to borrow without obligations and supervision, and that was not true. Wilson's abstention was of almost no help whatever to the Chinese. Indeed, it strengthened the position of Japan, which would be further enhanced when war broke out in Europe. But all the idealist forces in the United States rejoiced and praised the president. In particular the churches and the missionary movement showed themselves grateful for the moral leadership that Wilson displayed.

Wilson had acted quickly, but with little knowledge of China. As with almost all American Protestants, his relations with China were conducted through missionaries. He readily believed their optimistic reports about China's yearning for Western values. When the revolution broke out, he took it to be a breakthrough toward democracy.

The immediate question was whether to recognize the new republic. The European countries, seeing how divided China was, remained hesitant. But in this matter too Wilson was convinced that he must not let himself be at all influenced by the Europeans. He did not consult them but acted on his own, according to what he considered to be his moral obligation. John Mott immediately sent a telegram urging recognition. China was returning to calm and order, he asserted, and was rallying round Yuan Shi-kai. The Chinese hoped for American support. "American ideals prevail in China more than those of any other land. China speaking of us as the great sister republic and looking to us as to no other country."[6] This was a perfect statement of the myth, and Wilson listened to it with deepest satisfaction. He decided to recognize the new regime as soon as the first elected parliament met in Peking. It was a significant inducement.

The shrewd Yuan Shi-kai gave an extra nudge in April by asking the Christian churches in China to pray for divine intercession on behalf of the new government. Deeply moved, Bryan read the telegram to the cabinet. Wilson agreed thankfully. He did not remember ever having been so "stirred and cheered." He felt that it would be good if American churches joined in the day of prayer. Everyone in the cabinet agreed with him, with the single exception of the hardheaded secretary of commerce, William C. Redfield. He expressed doubts and wondered whether "Chinese minds" were not very different from Westerners', and whether the request was not "a play to secure the support of Christian nations." After all, there were not many Christians in China. "This did not appeal to the president," we read in Daniels's diary. He wanted prayer and recognition, word and deed, together.[7]

What is remarkable in this affair is how little attention Wilson gave to the question of the consequences of his policy. Support to Yuan Shi-kai, who soon developed into a dictator, meant denial of the more democratic wing of the revolution; its leader, Sun Yat-sen, was deeply disappointed by the recognition of Yuan. Wilson chose calm and order over increased democracy. Of course there is a risk in every choice, but Wilson did not incorporate this ambivalence in his ethical approach to the world. It remains strange therefore that in China he did exactly the opposite of what he did in Mexico.

Recognition brought with it the problem that a new ambassador had to be named. Missionary circles pressed for the appointment of Bryan himself, but he was satisfied to keep his place at the head of the State

Department and to give lectures on the Chatauqua circuit. Wilson, with his predilection for scholarly officials, thought of Charles W. Eliot, the man who as president of Harvard had made it into a modern university, but Bryan resisted that choice, because Eliot was a Unitarian and therefore a religious liberal. How could one send to the new China, "founded upon the Christian movement there," a man who did not believe in the divinity of Christ?[8] Wilson escaped the dilemma because Eliot declined the position. Wilson then thought of John Mott, but he too refused the post. Finally the president settled on another professor, a political scientist at the University of Wisconsin, Paul S. Reinsch. This turned out to be not a bad choice, for Reinsch upheld American interests in China for six long years under very difficult circumstances. He became the watchman on the sacred walls of China. He did what he could in a situation that was rapidly changing for the worse.

The problem arose from Japan's initiative. In 1914 it had seized its opportunity by joining the Allies, not out of sympathy for their cause but in order to seize the German possessions in the Pacific Ocean and on the Chinese mainland. Japanese troops entered the Shantung peninsula. China appeared helpless when, in January 1915, Japan presented a package of twenty-one far-reaching demands that added up to a protectorate, plus a demand that this be kept secret.

They failed with this last demand, for the Chinese informed Reinsch who at once cabled the news to Washington. The shaky basis on which America's ethical policy rested became clear. Bryan was inclined toward a compromise with Japan, holding that Japan's presence in Manchuria could be justified by its "contiguity" (the term always used by strong powers when they bully weak ones, as the United States itself had done in its own westward expansion). But Reinsch continued to press, and the missionaries protested vehemently. Wilson himself let the Japanese government know that its policy was unacceptable. This made an impression, but the Japanese government realized that although America was still neutral, there was not much that it could do. They backed down a little, but by an ultimatum compelled the Chinese to accept the principal demands (May 1915). The United States was able to respond only with a policy of "nonrecognition," a weak weapon in diplomatic intercourse, certainly in the middle of a world war, and especially at the moment that the Americans were fully absorbed in the crisis over the sinking of the *Lusitania*.

When it came to making a decision, however, the perpetual weakness in the American involvement with China again made its appearance. The United States was quite ready to support China morally, with good words, but not to back words with deeds. Just like Theodore Roosevelt, Wilson had to acknowledge that the Open Door could not be guaranteed, although he continued to speak in sublime phrases. In April 1915 he told a group of ministers that it was a grand spectacle to see China awaken to the voice of Christ. The country was now in turmoil and upheaval, but he asked his listeners: "Should we not see that the parts are fructified by the teachings of Christ?"[9]

In the end he had to back down. Busy as he was with the problems of relations with Germany over the Atlantic Ocean, he left the problems of the Far East in the hands of his new secretary of state, Robert Lansing, who concluded a treaty with the Japanese minister, Ishii, in which both powers solemnly avowed the principle of the Open Door, but in ambiguous language recognized that "territorial propinquity creates special relations between countries." America thereby recognized the "special relations" of Japan in China, especially where Japanese possessions were "contiguous."[10]

By then it was 1917, and it was clear that Wilson's fine policy had failed. The final seal was put upon this disappointment shortly afterward. In order to resist Japan's influence one way or another, Wilson, again with the encouragement of Reinsch, decided to offer economic opposition. Finally American bankers were invited to participate in an international consortium with a guarantee by the government of the United States. Unfortunately this was no longer effective, for meanwhile (the First World War had just ended) China had sought and found other loans on the world market.

The Far East was not an exclusive American hunting ground, far from it. China was not a special sister republic of the United States. It remained a continuing, lingering problem for American policy. In Paris Wilson would find it presented to him with an urgency he did not like, because of the Shantung question.

II

It was not only in distant China but also in nearby Latin America that the new president sought to follow a new policy based upon principles, and there too reality proved to be more resistant than he had anticipated. The announcement of his new course was inspired by the question of the Panama Canal. In October 1913 in Mobile, Alabama, on the shores of the Gulf of Mexico, he gave a speech before an international conference concerned with the consequences of the forthcoming opening of the canal for world trade. The address, intended to set out the general outlines of his policy toward Latin America, was replete with his visionary ideas. He traversed history with seven-league boots, explaining how Columbus had sailed to the west because the road to the East and its riches had been closed off by the Turks. The line from east to west, he declared, now had an additional element, a line from north to south, in the shape of the brotherhood of the United States with the countries of Latin America. The result was that these lands could free themselves from the exploitative investment of foreign countries; they could follow the good example of the United States and create a system of constitutional liberties. "Human rights, national integrity, and opportunity as against material interests—that, ladies and gentlemen, is the issue which we now have to face." For the word "America" that they all had in common was a synonym for freedom. He thereby applied his program of New Freedom to the entire Western hemisphere. He closed with a splendid paean of liberalism. He believed, he said, that the nineteenth century had brought great progress. Mankind was climbing upwards, it was near the top, almost in "the final uplands" where we at last attain a vision of "the duties of mankind. We have breasted a considerable part of that climb and shall, presently—it may be in a generation or two—come out upon those great heights where there shines, unobstructed, the light of the justice of God."[11]

Reality, alas, was not so radiantly beautiful. To be sure, one who saw paradise near at hand in 1913 could not know what a disaster would burst upon the world a year later, and Wilson was not the only optimist in this "world of yesterday." But, apart from the question of what was about to happen in the Old World, his prophecies were far from any realization in the New World either. The dream of the United States joined in honest equality with the countries of Latin America in the same constitutional freedom, was a dream that could not be made true, however readily it came to Wilson. He was encouraged in it by House, according to the colonel's diary. With his usual self-satisfaction, he noted down in November 1914 that he had exhorted Wilson to give more attention to foreign affairs, especially to "the welding together of the two western continents." He had in mind a plan for a Pan-American alliance, which could serve as a model for the lands of Europe when peace returned. And Wilson followed where House wished to lead him: "I could see that this excited his enthusiasm." In his vanity, House boasted that he had brought Wilson to his finest ideas. According to Charles Seymour, the editor of House's diary, Wilson wrote down at this time, at House's suggestion, the precise words of the famed and much debated Article X of the Covenant of the League of Nations: "Mutual guarantees of political independence under republican form of government and mutual guarantees of territorial integrity."[12]

Wilson was indeed enthusiastic. In his "State of the Union" address of December 1915, he declared that Pan-Americanism had nothing to do with imperialism, that on the contrary it was the embodiment of the spirit of "law and independence and liberty and mutual service." Shortly thereafter, he gave it an even fairer expression, calling the solidarity of the Western hemisphere a model for the world, a torch that America held high to light up the world.[13] For the moment little resulted from all these fine words about a glorious future. The Pan-American Union was not established, in the first place because Chile, which was involved in a border dispute with Peru, refused to take part, and also because most Latin American countries took fright at the American actions in Mexico (to which we shall turn in a moment). All that we can say of Wilson's high-flying plans is that they would have echoes in the future, in Franklin Roosevelt's Good Neighbor Policy and in John F. Kennedy's Alliance for Progress.

Wilson's own policies soon became a repudiation of his fine words. Once again we face the eternal Wilson riddle, which has brought to despair the best authority on Wilson, Arthur S. Link: Just what did he really mean? Wilson and Bryan, according to Link, could prattle about Pan-Americanism and absolute equality, but it was not their plan to apply these doctrines in the Caribbean region. This is the harsh judgment of a historian who greatly admires Wilson. He contrasts their conduct with the sage comment of Lansing, who had pointed out as early as 1914 that such equality could not exist, that the "primacy" of a big country like the United States was "out of harmony" with the principle of the equality of nations, no matter how fair, how altruistic, the big country attempted to be.[14]

The fact was that Wilson and Bryan in their superficial optimism believed that what was good for the United States was also good for Latin America. Lansing recognized how empty of meaning these words were. Wholly realistically, he pointed out to Wilson that the Monroe Doctrine and an eventual Pan-American Union were quite different things, and that the Panama Canal had given the United States clear interests and responsibilities in the Caribbean region. He could well believe that the Caribbean countries would probably profit from American involvement, but added pointedly, "Nevertheless the argument based on humanitarian purpose does not appeal to me, even though it may be justly urged, because too many international crimes have been committed in the name of Humanity."[15]

Wilson could not listen to such language, which disturbed his world picture and went against his grain. But, unfortunately, he had to act according to what Lansing said. The history of the involvement of Wilson and Bryan in Central America is hardly any more elevating than that of their predecessors. Probably Wilson's plan to give Colombia satisfaction in its dispute with the United States was the only one worthy of praise on ethical grounds, but it also arose out of the traditional friendship of the two countries. Colombia was the most loyal ally of the United States in South America. In 1903 Theodore Roosevelt had sponsored a revolution in Panama, which was then a part of Colombia, and then had concluded a treaty with "independent" Panama for the construction of a canal. Wilson now proposed to offer apologies to Colombia and to pay compensation of $25,000,000. Roosevelt of course was enraged, while the Senate would not accept the proposal. It ratified the treaty only in 1921.

It would take us too far from our subject to discuss the political situation of the Caribbean in all its complexity. We must be brief, but then it all comes down in the end to one familiar pattern: poverty, ambition, rivalries, revolutions, chaos, intervention, occupation by the U.S. Marines, and continuing supervision by the United States. This is what happened in Haiti in 1915, in the Dominican Republic in 1916, in Nicaragua, where Taft had sent troops in 1912, as a confirmation of the Bryan-Chamorro treaty of 1914, which gave the United States the right to an eventual canal and to a naval base, with Bryan's justification that the ultraconservative government of Nicaragua was convinced of the "disinterestedness of the United States in our dealings with Latin America." In America itself, however, the opposition, led by such redoubtable progressives as Senators

William Borah of Idaho and George Norris of Nebraska, protested that there was no difference between this policy and the old, scorned dollar diplomacy.

This was, in brief, a tale of imperialism and self-interest, with all their advantages and disadvantages, a tale—it must be emphasized—that was defined by stubborn internal factors and only secondarily by the presence nearby of the powerful and rich neighbor in the North, although that presence was certainly a factor. The Americans brought much progress and much bitterness; their protectorate was marked by paternalistic benevolence and enlightened exploitation, which were not as reprehensible as idealist opponents claimed but were still far, very far, from Wilson's glittering prattle or Bryan's unctuous certainties. The Latin American countries, said Bryan, were our "political children." The commandment that the Americans followed, he said, was: Love thy neighbor as thyself. The reality was not so pleasant.[16]

III

The two revolutions of 1911, in China and Mexico, do not fit the familiar pattern, even in the well-known analysis of revolutions by the American historian Crane Brinton. They ran a very different course than the French and Russian Revolutions; all that they had in common with these more famous events was that they too devoured their children. They have been interpreted very differently by historians, and contemporaries too did not know what to make of them. Wilson had principles but they did not help to bring about a solution, and in any case he followed one policy in China and another in Mexico. In the end his conduct was determined in both cases more by circumstances than by principles.

Mexico was the closest neighbor of the United States to the south, but it was still an unknown land for the average American. The revolution there came therefore as a great surprise. Calm, the calm of iron control and icy cruelty, had reigned in the Mexican Republic. Since 1876 the dictator Porfirio Diaz had ruled the roost, surrounded by a small group of big landowners and technocrats, the so-called "cientificos." They had contributed to the country's development by attracting foreign investors, especially British and American, but this was an economic exploitation whose benefits seeped down very slowly to the broad mass of the population. The peasants still lived in often abject circumstances, poor, ignorant, and degraded.

But in this awakening society new ideas were fermenting, stimulated by the technical changes that Diaz himself had helped to bring about. In 1911 came the explosion that brought Diaz down. The Mexican revolution probably provides a spectacle of great confusion because, as the historian John Mason Hart has written, it was not really a single revolution but actually three jumbled together.[17] It was a national, bourgeois revolution, led by men from the new middle class like Madero and Carranza; it was a peasant revolution whose goal was division of the land, under men like Zapata and Villa; and it was also an industrial revolution of the proletariat in the factories, of labor unions with modern trade unionist ideas. According to the usual pattern of revolutions, its first leader was a man from the upper classes, a big landlord with an entire family clan behind him. Francesco Madero was an idealist who believed that political reforms could bring about real improvement. But the peasants wanted social changes, land most of all. In the sublime imagination of Mexican artists and writers, the Mexican revolution became primarily an uprising of the long oppressed peasantry, often of Indian origin, against their arrogant masters. This spectacular aspect of the revolution certainly had an aspect of conservative romanticism in it as well, with Indian ideas of community playing a clear role.

Picturesque leaders came to the fore, such as the romantic Emiliano Zapata and the rude figure of Francisco ("Pancho") Villa. Then, in the North, there was the leader of the bourgeois resistance, the troublesome and ambitious governor of Coahuila province, Venustiano Carranza, who refused to recognize Madero's authority on what he called constitutional grounds.

Madero fell in February 1913, the victim of the ambition of one of his own generals, Victoriano Huerta. This sly and surly brawler, whom the gullible Madero called upon to suppress an uprising by Felix Diaz, a nephew of the old dictator, made common cause with the insurgents and was able to seize power in a bloody ten-day battle in the capital (the Decena Tragica, February 9–18, 1913). He was given support, we must note, by the ambassador of the United States, Henry Lane Wilson, an arch-conservative and active businessman. He went so far as to bring Huerta and Diaz together in his embassy, so that their conspiracy went into history as "the Pact of the Embassy." Indeed, he was a party to the slaying of Madero. When Huerta asked him what should be done with the president of Mexico, the envoy replied with indifference that the general should do "what was best for the peace of the country."[18] While on the way to prison, Madero was shot to death.

A few weeks later Woodrow Wilson became president of the United States. When he received the reports of the American ambassador, he was deeply shocked, largely out of natural sympathy for poor Madero, an intellectual and idealist like himself. After a week, he issued an official declaration about Latin America, in which he warned: "We can have no sympathy with those who seek to seize the power of government to advance their own personal interests or ambition."[19] This was the beginning of his personal vendetta against Huerta, which at once gave him the reputation of a complete idealist in foreign policy.

It was not an entirely deserved reputation. To be sure, his judgment on the events in Mexico was very stern. But, despite his hasty, peremptory declaration, he continued to be hesitant for a long while about what would be the best solution. In the beginning he even sent a fair quantity of arms to Huerta. In principle Wilson did not want to recognize Huerta, but his reaction was really personal and emotional in character. Huerta was the great malefactor to whom the traditional American policy of at least de facto recognition of any foreign government, no matter how it had come to power, did not apply. Various outbursts on Wilson's part indicate a deep moral outrage. "I will not recognize a government of butchers," he snapped at someone who urged recognition.[20]

But for the moment he followed a wait-and-see policy, which gave the impression more of uncertainty than of morality, especially to Europeans. The American government, a British diplomat remarked, is nervous; it doesn't know what it should do, but wants our support.[21] Yet there were large American interests in Mexico, even bigger than those of the British. Americans held 38 percent of all foreign investments and were dominant especially in mining and railways. But Great Britain had big interests especially in Mexican oil, which was used as a fuel by the British navy. London therefore put pressure on Wilson to recognize Huerta. However, the argument that Huerta represented the real power in Mexico lost more and more of its force. Zapata threatened him in the South, and in the North a broad coalition took shape against him under the leadership of Carranza, who received the support of Villa and of the most skillful military leader of the revolution, Alvaro Obregón. The rebels gave themselves the impressive name of "Constitutionalists," which appealed very much to Wilson.

All during the summer of 1913 Wilson continued to be unsure of himself. He was even inclined to approve a plan for provisional recognition of Huerta provided that he called an early election in which he himself would not be a candidate. But first he wanted to be better informed about the situation than was possible from the reports of ambassador Henry L. Wilson, whom in any case he soon recalled. He therefore decided upon the unusual policy of sending personal observers, men whom he could have confidence in but would also be echoes of himself. His first envoy to Mexico was William Bayard Hale, an idealistic Episcopalian minister out of the social gospel tradition who had written the election biography of Wilson. Hale's reports were extraordinarily sharp in their criticism of Huerta, "an ape-like old man," a drunkard who deserved no recognition whatsoever. We Americans, he instructed Wilson, are "the guardians of order and justice and democracy on this Continent; we are, providentially, naturally and inescapably, charged with the maintenance of humanity's interest here."[22]

No doubt these words rang sweetly in Wilson's ears, but he did not wish to rely upon a single witness. In the summer he sent another observer, the former governor of Minnesota, John Lind, a Swedish arch-Protestant and idealist who did not speak a word of Spanish, knew nothing about Mexico, and had absolutely no comprehension of the Catholic religion. He was given instructions to persuade Huerta to agree to free elections. He did not achieve very much, but nonetheless his dispatches breathed the same spirit as Hale's in favor of a positive view of the revolution. The Constitutionalists, in his opinion, deserved at the least more attention and probably support as well. Lind also warned against the machinations of British imperialism with its sordidly selfish policy in Mexico. Wilson was ready to believe Lind's charge. His idealist speech in Mobile, from which we quoted above, had also been intended as a warning to England, and he considered even making a public accusation against the English government. Fortunately events did not go that far. There was more wisdom in London than in Washington, and a special envoy, Sir William Tyrrell, was sent to the United States, to patch up the differences over Mexico. This intelligent and witty diplomat listened patiently to Wilson's long tirades, in which the notorious words were spoken: "I am going to teach the South American Republics to elect good men."[23]

England did not oppose the American policy, but Huerta continued to be stubbornly unmanageable. He refused to give way to pressure. If anything, the American pressure improved his position, and he made skillful use of the latent anti-Americanism in Mexico. From their side, the Constitutionalists were not eager for the open support of the United States. Carranza told Hale that he was against foreign interference, although he naturally hoped the American arms embargo would be lifted. But in no case would he go along with a compromise or participate in elections called by Huerta. His goal was only a military victory. Wilson was furious. He called Carranza's attitude narrow-minded and selfish. Like the others, he said, the Constitutionalists understand nothing about constitutional processes.[24]

But he reserved his greatest anger for Huerta. He seemed obsessed with this man, with whom he had a kind of love-hate relationship. To Mrs. Hulbert, to whom he continued to pour out his heart, he wrote with artificial airiness: Huerta "is a diverting brute! He is always so perfectly in character: so false, so sly, so full of bravado . . . and yet so courageous, too, and determined—such a mixture of weak and strong, of ridiculous and respectable." One moment you are ready to drink his blood, and then you feel "a sneaking admiration for his nerve."[25]

In November Wilson began to abandon his policy of "watchful waiting." In a note to the powers, he threatened American intervention, "less peaceful means," if Huerta did not depart voluntarily. In February 1914 he lifted the arms embargo, which was of course welcome news for the Constitutionalists. Lind, who spent the entire winter in Vera Cruz waiting for further instructions from Washington, meanwhile sent Wilson a stream of letters. They are virulent against Huerta, whose position he imagined to be stronger than it was, and full of praise for Villa, whom he called cruel but intrepid and resourceful, and especially for Carranza: he was honest, had convictions, was intelligent, and was a man of his word. In any case, he said, American help was urgently needed. In biblical language that Wilson understood well, he urged that the United States from now on be for poor Mexico the pillar of cloud by day and the pillar of fire by night.[26]

He was spoiling to intervene, and got his chance in April. He seized upon a minor incident—the arrest of two American sailors in the port of Tampico, an error for which apologies were quickly offered—in order to demand full satisfaction, punishment of the guilty parties, a twenty-one-gun salute, and other humiliations. It was an inflated incident put to classically imperialist use. Wilson did not at all anticipate the consequences. Huerta did not consider capitulating, for he hoped that anti-American feeling could still save him. Wilson directed his retaliatory action not against Tampico but against Vera Cruz, further south, because a German ship with a cargo of arms was due there. That would be killing two birds with one stone, he thought. He gave orders to occupy the customhouse of the city, so that the arms could not be delivered.

But things did not run as smoothly as he had expected. The Mexicans fought back bravely in a full-scale battle, with many killed and wounded, before the Marines could occupy the city. What would happen now, no one knew. The German ship sailed to another port and unloaded its deadly cargo. Wilson neither wished nor was able to push further into Mexico, for in the United States public opinion, apart from a few jingo voices, remained very cool. To wage war seemed going much too far. He therefore sat still: he now had a little army in the port city that could neither advance nor retreat. To show their good intentions, the troops spent their time cleaning away the rubble, introducing a number of health measures such as forbidding spitting and urinating in public, the eradication of mosquitoes, medical inspection of all prostitutes, and the like. But Huerta did not fall, and even the Constitutionalists condemned the invasion (except the shrewd Villa, who at this time was still betting on the American card).

Wilson was saved from his awkward position by an offer of mediation from the South American A.B.C. powers (Argentina, Brazil, and Chile). In May 1915 delegates of the different parties met in Niagara Falls; the conference achieved little, but enabled Wilson to save face. Vera Cruz was evacuated in the fall. Shortly afterwards Huerta fell from power anyway, not because of Wilson's zeal against him, but because the combined strength of his enemies became too great for him. The revolution was still in full course. Carranza, who had emphatically rejected American help, entered Mexico City in triumph, and in October 1915 his government was recognized de facto by the United States and most of Latin America. He too had to struggle with continuing resistance, however, in which social aspirations as well as personal ambitions played a part. The poor peasants passionately wanted land and followed any savior who appeared on the scene. The warlords (to use the Chinese expression) marched with their armies through the country. Villa and Zapata, the principal ones, joined forces against Carranza and were able even to occupy the capital briefly.

The notable factor in this situation was that Wilson, just because he came to understand the social forces behind the revolution, did not really know what he should do. It is certainly true, as the English historian Alan Knight observes, that Wilson showed more insight than the European statesmen, who were realists concerned only with their own countries' interests.[27] There is probably among all Americans, North and South, a certain affinity in idealism. Many liberal Mexicans recognized Wilson's dream but were at the same time suspicious of the means of force he employed.

What Wilson desired was harmony between interests and ideals. In his Fourth of July address in 1914, he had Mexico in mind when he described the limits of the commercial interests of the United States. He too, he said, was glad to see American businessmen show themselves throughout the world. But there were limits to this expansion. "If American enterprise in foreign countries, particularly in those foreign countries which are not strong enough to resist us, takes the shape of imposing upon and exploiting the mass of the people of that country, it ought to be checked and not encouraged."[28] He harped upon the same string in an interview that he gave to a newspaperman at the end of April 1914. He emphatically chose the side of the "great mass of the population" against the "aristocrats, the vested interests . . . the overlords, the hidalgos, the men who have exploited that rich country for their own selfish purposes." He pounded on the table with his fist. He asked for an example, a single example, in the whole history of mankind when freedom was handed down from above. Liberty always came from below, from the people moved by "the sense of wrong and oppression and injustice." And he formulated a maxim that he would later apply to Europe as well: America "has no quarrel with the Mexican people," but only with those in power. America was unselfish. This was how he applied the Monroe Doctrine. And to those who said that the Mexican people were not ready for self-government, he readily replied that every people "when properly directed" was fit to govern itself.[29]

The question remained, of course, where this "proper direction" would come from. What could Wilson do in practice? Because his insights still rested upon little knowledge, he put his bet for the time being on Villa. The Robin Hood of the revolution, Villa was an ambitious, cruel, totally amoral bully, described by an American who knew him well as a man who hunted men and was hunted by them, a man with "a daring, cunning, animal craftiness and alertness." Ishmael comes to mind: his hand was against all, and the hand of all was against him. But Wilson, as credulous as his observers, permitted himself to be told that Villa was, to be sure, "a crude and cruel barbarian," but honorable and "the greatest Mexican of his generation." The president sent to Page in London with his strong approval an article in the magazine *Outlook* in which Villa was described as a true reformer.[30]

Villa's attempt together with Zapata to overthrow Carranza failed completely. His cruelty and capriciousness resulted in most of the generals, including the able Obregón, turning against him, and he soon had to slink off to the North. There he continued to make trouble for the Americans, and when they ceased to back him, he swore revenge. In January 1916 he had eighteen American engineers on their way to their jobs in the mines taken from a train and shot in cold blood (only one escaped). A full month later, at the beginning of March, he crossed the border with his forces and left a trail of killing and burning in the frontier town of Columbus, New Mexico. Wilson had to take action. With the agreement of the Mexican government, a punitive expedition under the command of General John J. Pershing was sent against the bandit. But Pershing was not able to find Villa in the wild mountains of North Mexico. Early in 1917 the expedition was recalled; the Mexican government could no longer tolerate the presence of so many foreign troops (Pershing's small force had meanwhile grown to 6,000 men), and the European war was occupying the full attention of Washington. Shortly afterwards in 1917, Carranza was able to introduce a new constitution and his government was recognized de jure by the United States. But only a few years' respite was given him. The revolution really came to an end with the coup d'état of General Alvaro Obregón in 1920.

This also brought an end to a confused and bitter period in American-Mexican relations. In retrospect, the question remains what Wilson's half-intervention had meant. There are several cautious observations to be made. First of all, by approaching the question from the position of the United States, we can easily make the error of thinking that the history of Mexico (as of all Latin America) was decided by the powerful country in the North. That was the miscalculation of Marx and Engels when in the name of progress they rejoiced that the United States defeated Mexico in 1848. And of course it is true that there were large American interests in Mexico, as we have seen. The pressure of the American owners (men such as William Randolph Hearst and the oil magnate Albert B. Fall) on Wilson to act more forcefully in Mexico was persistent and strong. But Wilson had no intention of giving in to them and conducted a clearly moderate policy. To see the Mexican revolution as a war of national liberation against the United States is a distortion of the truth, a misunderstanding of the movement's own character. But it is a common illusion, neatly formulated in a famous observation attributed to various Mexican leaders, particularly Diaz: Poor Mexico, so far from God and so close to the United States. Although there may be an element of truth in it, it still fails to appreciate the internal forces of Mexican society. Huerta did not fall because of Wilson's actions, although this is often asserted, and Villa did not owe his rise and fall to the bizarre support given to him by Wilson and Bryan.

But it is Wilson who concerns us, and we must confine ourselves therefore to the question of the significance of his involvement in the Mexican events. He is often accused of a rigid moralism, and his own language gives much reason for doing so. But the Mexican question makes it clear that ethical and realistic policies cannot be separated as clearly as seemed to occur in Wilson's exalted parlance. It was not his intention to neglect the interests of his country; he was ready enough to talk of unselfishness, but he was after all a liberal who believed that self-interest and ideals were not in conflict but rather coincided. He applied his New Freedom to Mexico.

His moralism promoted the revolution, although he did not know clearly what he should do. He learned from developments, as he observed with some self-satisfaction: "I learned the truth about Mexico by hearing a multitude of liars talk about it."[31] What he was really learning was that he could not act as paternalistically in Mexico, a big country, as in the little lands of Central America. No matter how many mistakes he made, in retrospect his involvement promoted the Mexican revolution more than it hindered it.

His own conclusion was that his principles had stood the test in Mexico. Whether or not that was good for Mexico the future would show, but at least America had proved that it upheld the "high doctrine" of a government "for the common benefit, protection and security of the people." "We have unhesitatingly applied that heroic principle to the case of Mexico, and now await the rebirth of the troubled Republic." In brief, he was personally not dissatisfied with his conduct, and history may share his judgment at least a little.[32]

FOURTEEN

The world itself seems gone mad, and there is a sort of
grim pleasure, and stern compulsion to keep sane and
self-possessed amid the general wreck and distemper.
    —*Woodrow Wilson, September 6, 1914*

1914

*F*OR MOST PEOPLE IN
the Western, civilized world before 1914, war seemed to have
become an antiquated absurdity. Only a
few spoke up to warn of the darkness that
lay ahead. Optimism ruled, forecasting that
peace would last forever. This eagerly cher-
ished illusion gleamed all the more brightly in the United States because
the country lay faraway on the other side of the ocean.

But the war did come. The European nations stumbled blindly,
foolishly, as Lloyd George would later say, into the horrible catastrophe.
It may be, though, that this is not what really happened. Was World War
I deliberately started by the military authorities in Germany in a "grab
for world power" (*Griff nach der Weltmacht*), as has been argued by the
German historian Fritz Fischer in his celebrated book of that title?
Whether this was true or not is the subject of a vehement historical debate
that we must keep in mind in this study, for the whole problem of war
guilt, which played an immense role in 1919 and notably in the mind of
Woodrow Wilson, is involved.

Whatever the answer, when war came in 1914 in the frightful month of August, Europeans greeted it with a shudder and a sigh of relief. The Dutch poet Albert Verwey described the infatuation in unforgettable words:

Knapen met bebloemde helmen
Reizen lachend naar de grenzen,
Sterven zalig voor de leuzen
Dat zij van hun ouders leerden.
Dat is oorlog! In hun harten
Openden zich diepe sluizen
En de donkre dammen braken.
Vloeden van gemeenzaam voelen
Overstromen de genoten.

[Lads with flowers on their helmets
Laugh loudly on the way to the front,
Die gloriously for the slogans
They had learned from their parents.
That's war! In their hearts
The floodgates opened
And the dark dams broke.
Floodwaters of shared feelings
Swept over the comrades in arms.]

Only here and there was there comprehension of this strange irrational force that the poet felt so clearly present in that mood of excitement. Scarcely anyone in the United States understood it; Americans, although alarmed by events in Europe, were relieved not to be involved in them. We find a good example in the memoirs of David Houston, Wilson's secretary of agriculture. He described his dismay: "I had a feeling that the end of things had come. Figuratively speaking I stopped in my tracks, dazed and horror-stricken." Yet he thought he understood why war had come. European nations were unfortunately ruled by governments that sought not so much the welfare of their people as territorial expansion, prestige, and power under the leadership of the princely dynasties and aristocratic military cliques.[1]

This theme of the great separation between the good people and their evil rulers was a typical dogma of nineteenth-century romantic liberalism, and it would play a large role in Wilson's thinking. It forms an important element in the first American reactions to the outbreak of the

European war. Small groups of princes and generals, or, in one variant, of bankers and manufacturers, had pressed for war against the desires of their peace-loving subjects. It was the fault of the three emperors of Russia, Germany, and Austria, *The Nation* asserted.[2] "Do you want to know the cause of the war?" wrote the incredibly naive Henry Ford: "It is capitalism, greed, the dirty hunger for dollars. . . . Take away the capitalist, and you will sweep war from the earth."[3]

Americans found comfort and reassurance in knowing that they, in any case, were not so foolish and blind. Never before were Americans so grateful to their forefathers for having left the Old World, wrote a newspaper in Indiana. This had been a favorite theme since the days of Jefferson and Adams: the old, corrupt Europe doomed to go under, as contrasted to the bright New World, innocent America. Henry James put the theme to subtle use in his finely wrought novels. Such ideas became prevalent again and remained so for the duration of the war, and they became even stronger in 1919 when Wilson set foot among his crafty counterparts in Paris. We hear it trumpeted in every key in 1914. "It is the genius of our people to live in peace," according to William Allen White, the renowned editor-in-chief of the *Emporia Gazette*. "We care little for glory and conquest. . . . The flag with the stars and stripes stands for the civilization that exalts the spirit of Jesus Christ." But not everyone was so complacent. The reform weekly, *The Independent*, sang a different tune: "We sit undisturbed in happy peace, and we thank God Americans are not like people in other countries." But are they really less rapacious, asked the paper, or do they just have less opportunity because they are separated from them by a wide ocean?[4]

For all the affirmations of isolation on the far side of the ocean, it was by no means as total as these complacent commentators thought. Americans (that is, white Americans) all were or were descended from immigrants who came from the Old World; emotionally most of them were still very tied to their motherlands. It was only in this new situation that the phenomenon of "hyphenated Americans" was discovered. A hyphen joined the names of their "motherlands" across the ocean and their present American identity; but "hyphenated Americans" was an invidious distinction accorded primarily to the supporters of the Central Powers. The most important were German-Americans and Irish-Americans. Although the large majority of the American people were bound to England by origin, language, and culture, there were also some eight million

German-Americans and four million Irish-Americans who made no bones about their sympathy for England's foes. This was also true of most American Jews, who were skeptical about the Entente cause because one of the Allies was Russia, from which they or their fathers had fled to escape atrocious pogroms. These divisions within the American people added to the importance of maintaining neutrality, but at the same time they were also a good argument for making an attempt to mediate sooner or later. America could bring an understanding of both sides, as Wilson repeatedly affirmed.

One way or another, public opinion counted heavily in the United States. In the land of democracy, no government could exist that stood as distant from the people as European rulers. At least this was what Americans liked to think. America, wrote *The Public* (the newspaper of the supporters of the celebrated reformer Henry George), stood out among the nations of the world as Saul had stood out above his brothers ("from his shoulders and upward he was higher than any of the people," 1 Samuel 9:2), not because it was stronger, bigger, or richer than they, but because it had an ideal, democracy, and because, at that moment, they were led "by a man who is trying to live up to that ideal."[5]

We must still ask where Wilson himself really stood. What kind of role could the president of this exceptional nation play? How neutral was he in actuality? In August 1914 Wilson was suddenly confronted by problems he had never expected but which an ironic fate imposed on him. Arthur Link, who is his outstanding biographer but also his apologist, has been bold enough to claim that Wilson, with his thorough command of international law, modern history, and comparative government, was the best-informed president in foreign affairs since John Quincy Adams. Furthermore, ever since 1898, he had urged his country to take a larger role in the world, and in his book *Constitutional Government* he had emphatically assigned to the president the role of carrying out such a policy![6] Unfortunately, Link's argument is not persuasive. The matters that Link has in mind were still vague. In international affairs Wilson possessed principles but hardly any knowledge of the real situation in Europe. True, he had read a great deal about the government in many countries, but, except for England, he was almost totally ignorant of their political and historical background. At least we find not a single sensible word about them in all his extensive writings. He was at home in phrases, abstractions, ideas, not in raw reality.

House, who always thought himself wiser than his good friend and in his vanity was wont to imagine that it was he who had guided Wilson into his international role, wrote with self-satisfaction: "I find the President singularly lacking in appreciation of this European crisis. He seems more interested in domestic affairs and I find it difficult to get his attention centered upon the one big question."[7]

But, however vain House may have been, he was probably right in this judgment. Wilson was a stranger in world affairs; he had never been a member of any of the numerous organizations involved in international studies. He was a man of domestic affairs. Only the war changed him, as an expert in the field like Edward Buehrig remarks.[8]

The outbreak of the war affected the president deeply. It shocked his sensitive nature. We read for example in a letter to House in August: "I feel the burden of the thing almost intolerably from day to day."[9] Two months later he wrote in the same vein but at greater length to Walter Page, the ambassador in London:

> The whole thing is vivid in my mind, painfully vivid, and has been almost ever since the struggle began. I think my thought and imagination contain the picture and perceive its significance from every point of view. I have to force myself not to dwell upon it to avoid the sort of numbness that comes from deep apprehension and dwelling upon elements too vast to be yet comprehended or in any way controlled by counsel.[10]

Here we see once again in Wilson the tension between feeling and detachment.

This only emphasizes the importance of the question of how neutral he really was or wanted to be. His first personal reactions were emotionally favorable to the Allies. He was, after all, imbued with English values and ideals. The French ambassador to Washington, Jules Jusserand, wondered what "the great doctrinaire" in the White House was thinking, but the president soon gave his answer, as it were, to the English ambassador, Sir Cecil Spring-Rice. Spring-Rice informed Sir Edward Grey, the English foreign secretary, that Wilson had admitted to him that everything he held dear was now at stake. The president, he added, spoke with deep emotion. The ambassador, who knew the man he was dealing with, quoted a few lines from Wordsworth's sonnets about English freedom written during the Napoleonic wars. He knew them by heart, Wilson said with tears in his eyes. (Spring-Rice, as it happened, was also playing up to Grey, who, like Wilson, was passionately fond of Wordsworth.)[11]

In his personal feelings Wilson was not in the slightest neutral. House heard him inveigh against everything German—government and people and what he called abstract German philosophy, which lacked spirituality![12] But he was quite able to separate his personal opinions and his official duties. In the first place, he understood that neutrality was necessary, that the American people were totally set against intervention. But he was also moved by the great goal that he had glimpsed since the beginning of the war, a possibility that fitted his character like a glove. It makes its appearance in his call for neutrality, for he did not merely issue a scrupulously formal official declaration, as any other president would have done. He did more, accompanying this declaration with a personal call to the people to remain truly neutral in thought and words. America, he reminded them, was composed of many peoples and too great sympathy for one or the other side could bring division among them.

Unity was even more necessary for another reason as well. This was the grand ideal that he now made public officially for the first time and which henceforth would inspire him and more and more involve him in international complications. America, he announced, was chosen to mediate, as only America could, just because it was neutral. He spoke in an exalted, religious tone, as he liked to do on so many other occasions. It was as if the war at last made possible things that all his life he had dreamed of—his country as the model and the very leader of the whole world, and himself called and chosen as the leader of his country and the maker of the future.

We have already observed frequent anticipations and premonitions of this theme in his thoughts. The ideals of the American Revolution, he had said in a speech back in 1909, "the golden accents of that creative age in which we were born as a nation," would reecho over the whole world, "so that America might again have the distinction of showing men the way, the certain way of achievement and of confident hope." If there were only a single great speaker, he had said in an act of self-revelation, who could arouse the peoples, "make men drunk with this spirit of self-sacrifice," what would that not mean for the future![13]

Now the time he had in mind had come. The old theme became brighter than ever. It was the hope that began to bloom in him; through storms and defeats and changes of front, it would ripen in the strange ruined harvest of 1919. He ended his call to true neutrality in thought with an affirmation of this dream. He hoped, he declared, that America, his beloved America, "should show herself in this time of peculiar trial a nation fit beyond others to exhibit the fine poise of undisturbed judgment, the dignity of self-control, the efficiency of dispassionate action."[14]

Wilson *was* neutral, therefore. He was able to distance himself realistically from his own pro-English feelings. In some of his conversations during the first months of the war, especially with House, he expressed opinions that show this split between his judgment of fact and his feelings. During the evening of August 30, he talked over the situation with his friend at his summer home in Cornish, New Hampshire. How, they wondered, would power in the world be divided once the war was over, even "some centuries hence"? Wilson put forward the idea that "eventually" only two great powers would remain, Russia and America. House added China, which would rule Asia, while Russia would rule Europe and America the Western continent and the English colonies.[15] On another occasion, he explained that he did not see what good it would do "to destroy Germany politically and economically, so that France and Russia might divide the dictatorship of the continent and Great Britain be rid of German naval and commercial competition."[16] This sounds as if Wilson was able to think in the realistic terms of balance of power. But what he really had in mind was more a balance of forces within the war, a deadlock that would give America an ideal position for mediation. Neutrality then became a natural position for him to adopt.

When voices arose crying out against the German invasion and atrocities in Belgium—which were of course painted in the blackest colors by British propaganda—Wilson was prompt in his opposition to the protesters. He wrote to Bryan that it would be wrong to begin with protests, for then each side could constantly seek to elicit them against the other. His goal remained what it had been: "I think the time for clearing up all these matters will come when the war is over and the nations gather in sober counsel again."[17]

Wilson's deliberately neutral attitude was not shared by most of his collaborators, certainly not by the officials of the State Department. Only Bryan agreed wholeheartedly with him. The secretary of state, the British ambassador wrote home, was distributing his plowshares "adorned with quotations from Isaiah and himself. He sighs for the Nobel Prize."[18] But

House, Robert Lansing, a counselor in the State Department, ambassadors like Page and Gerard, indeed, the whole top stratum of American diplomacy, were inclined toward the Allied side.

In the long run Wilson certainly was influenced by them, however much he tried to be neutral. Furthermore, his own ideas about constitutional government made it harder for him to maintain his disposition toward neutrality. How could he be neutral while he tried to act so strongly on principle in his approach to foreign countries? We observed in the Mexican situation how much he tried to maintain a principled policy. Try as he might to act as if there were no differences between the belligerents, in his heart he knew better. The tension between his liberal sympathies and his deliberate neutrality made his position more and more difficult.

The summer of 1914 was a difficult time for Wilson, not only because he was suddenly confronted with political problems of such immensity, but also because, in that bewildering month of August, he was also put to the test in a different way in his personal life. In March his wife, the quiet, modest woman to whom he he had been married for twenty-nine years, began to show the first symptoms of serious illness. Wilson lived between hope and fear, as his letters reveal. To Mary Hulbert he wrote in June:

> I am very, very blue and out of heart to-day. My dear one absolutely
> wore herself out last winter and this spring and has not even started
> to come up hill again yet. She can eat and retain almost nothing
> and grows weaker and weaker, with a pathetic patience and sweetness
> all the while which makes it all the more nearly heart-breaking for
> those of us who love her.

But the doctors had assured him that there was nothing organically wrong.[19] It remains surprising that the serious kidney disease from which Ellen Wilson suffered was not diagnosed earlier.

The doctors remained uncertain right to the end. Late in July Wilson repeated to a friend that it seemed certain that nothing organic was involved, and only the bad weather prevented her recovery.[20] But the end was in fact very near. At the beginning of August, it became clear that Ellen Wilson's condition was hopeless. The doctor told Wilson that he must let the children know. On August 6, they were all by the deathbed.

Wilson was holding his wife's hand when she died. On August 11, she was buried in Rome, Georgia, the little town from which she came. In a driving rain, the choir sang the hymn, "For All the Saints Who from Their Labour Rest."

Wilson's recovery from the blow was slow and difficult. At first he could not speak about it. To Mary Hulbert he wrote only a few words: "God has stricken me almost beyond what I can bear." He told his niece, Mary Eloise Hoyt, that it was all his fault, that his career had demanded too much of Ellen.[21] At the end of August, he was finally able to voice his feelings to the faithful House: "Tears came into his eyes, and he said he felt like a machine that had run down, and there was nothing left in him worth while." House comforted him with wise words of solace: "I spoke of the great work there was to do for humanity in the readjustment of the wreckage that would come from the European war. . . . But few men had been given the opportunity to serve as he would have."[22]

It took time before Wilson was emotionally back on his feet. In a long letter to Mary Hulbert in November, he tried to give her a picture of how he felt, with the subtle insight and self-understanding typical of him. It seems as if his personal life was blotted out or rather swallowed up, he wrote; he existed only in the events around him, in "the day's work." He played some golf every day in order to keep alive. He wrote not to complain, which would be "silly and wicked besides," but only to describe how someone in such circumstances feels that his personal life is in suspense and does not count any more, even to himself:

> But here I must stay for a little while; and the less I analyze my feelings the better. They are wholly irrelevant, and only mess and belittle matters when they intrude. Woodrow Wilson does not matter, but the United States does and all that it may accomplish for its own people and the people of the world outside of it. It is a mighty fine thing to be part of a great endeavour, whether I personally enjoy it or not.[23]

The consolation House had offered had obviously helped. Wilson recovered his courage as he returned to his great dream, using the familiar words of unselfishness and self-sacrifice.

He possessed a life force that enabled him despite everything to go forward bravely. He wanted to live and came through the difficult winter.

In the spring of 1915, he was in love again. He was a man who could not exist without the care of a woman. As House wrote in his diary: "His loneliness since her death has oppressed him, and if he does not marry, and marry quickly, I believe he will go into a decline."[24]

Surprisingly, Wilson did not turn to his old friend Mary Hulbert, for their friendship was no longer as intense as it had once been. In any case marriage to a divorced woman would not help the president's prestige. One day his niece, Helen Woodrow Bones, who after Ellen's death took her place in the White House as mistress of the household and hostess, brought a friend with her to lunch, a widow of forty-three years, Edith Bolling Galt. She was a charming, self-assured, intelligent Virginian, and Wilson soon fell in love with her. When he proposed marriage, she was at first hesitant. He hardly knew her, she protested, and it was not a year since his wife died. Furthermore, she did not want to marry him out of pity, and certainly not because he was president. But Wilson became young and poetic again. In the very midst of his heavy duties, he wrote long love letters almost every day, full of fire and impatience, sometimes twenty pages long, with many poems and the constant confession: "My love is so much greater than anything I can write," he wrote at seven o'-clock one early June morning, or, two days later, "I love you beyond all words."[25]

As the German poet Theodor Storm has written,

Noch einmal fällt in meinen Schoss
Die rote Rose Leidenschaft.

[The red rose of passion falls
Once more into my lap.]

And now House complained that the president was so absorbed in his love affair that he neglected everything else.

There were inevitable political complications, of course. House and Tumulty feared that a marriage so soon after the death of his first wife would harm the president's reputation in the country, while there would be another election that year. Worse still, there were rumors in the country about his relationship with Mary Hulbert. Was the $15,000 that Wilson had given her in financial assistance really hush money? McAdoo came to him with a story that he had received an anonymous letter from California, where Mrs. Hulbert now resided, which indicated that she had permitted other people to read Wilson's letters to her. It was in fact utterly untrue. She had indeed been approached but had flatly refused to enter into such shady business. It is not clear whether something really was up or McAdoo exaggerated what he had heard in order to prevent Wilson from marrying. Whatever it may have been, Wilson would not be intimidated. Mrs. Galt, to whom he guiltily confessed his past life, easily forgave him. His courtship went well. As was proper, the couple waited a while before their wedding. It was celebrated in December 1915, and they spent their honeymoon in their beloved Virginia.

Edith Bolling Wilson was a socially acceptable wife. She took well to life in the White House. She enjoyed her life as the First Lady, as we can read in her generally vapid memoirs. Unfortunately, she loved intrigue. She ran down the men around Wilson—Bryan, House, Lansing, Tumulty—in her letters to her husband, and she played a part in their downfall, as we shall see.

FIFTEEN

For my own part, I cannot consent to any abridgement of
the rights of American citizens in any respect. The honor
and self-respect of the nation is involved. We covet peace,
and shall preserve it at any price but the loss of honor.
    —*Woodrow Wilson, February 14, 1916*

WAR
AT
SEA

*L*IKE IT OR NOT, AMERICA HAD
become a part of an old, sad world on
which, in its headstrong youth, it had
happily turned its back. But once the
country had reached its full growth
around 1900—"America's coming
of age," it has been called—it could
not persist in its innocent isolation. It had built up worldwide interests
that it had to protect.

Like it or not, this was one reason the United States adhered to neutrality. The war in Europe placed it in an ambiguous situation. On the
one hand, the United States wanted to make the fullest possible use of
the profitable position of a neutral power amid the belligerents, and therefore it upheld the most sacred rights of neutrality—once again the duality
of interest and principle. On the other, the more it appealed to those
rights, the more it became involved in the struggle at sea, which had become for the United States a vital artery.

As we have seen, Wilson himself had much more in view in a policy
of neutrality than just the country's commercial interests, although he did
not lose sight of them. He believed that America must remain neutral so

that it could act as mediator. But that too created a dilemma. Was it really true that a country that stood aloof from the conflict was the best mediator? Wasn't it a fact that the very moral superiority that Wilson derived from America's political purity in the long run exasperated the belligerents? Whenever that happened, it would present a fundamental problem for the role of umpire. But at the moment Wilson continued to believe that America had to remain impartial. He therefore insisted that the warring powers observe the agreements on neutrality which had been entered into at international conferences before the war.

Like most most rules laid down in advance of the events to which they are to apply, these agreements were out of date and inadequate; they did not fit the unforeseen circumstances of a modern war at sea. In the main, the rules still in effect had been adopted by the Congress of Paris in 1856, after the Crimean War, amplified by the rules drawn up in London in 1908–1909. But the London treaty had never gone into force thanks to England's refusal to ratify it.

Once war came, England, which ruled the sea, sought to enforce a total blockade of Germany. It did not proclaim it, however, thus getting around the legal problems, but it treated as contraband just about everything shipped to Germany. Such products as copper, rubber, and cotton were placed upon the list of articles whose shipment was absolutely forbidden. This ban was damaging to American interests, particularly those of the cotton growers in the South, who lost an important market.

But England, although believing that it had to do what it was doing, nonetheless was as prudent as possible. It was dependent upon arms shipments from the United States, which soon became very large, and therefore it tried to avoid offending American sensibilities too bluntly. The experienced English foreign secretary, Sir Edward Grey, defined the goal of British diplomacy succinctly: "The object of diplomacy, therefore, was to secure the maximum of blockade that could be enforced without a rupture with the United States."[1]

It did not help much that the Americans pressed the English government to abide by the agreements of the London Conference. During the first months of the war, Ambassador Page was repeatedly sent to the Foreign Office to present protests against their violation, but England had never ratified them and had of course no intention of yielding on this point. Furthermore, Page presented his messages with little conviction. This fervid diplomat had not been in England very long before he became more English than the English themselves; he soon seemed more like a defender of English interests in America than the other way around. Even before the war, he had put forward the idea that Wilson should go to London so that England and the United States could together guarantee world peace: "Such a visit might possibly prevent an Anglo-German war, which seems almost certain at some time, and an American-Japanese war, which is at least conceivable a decade or so hence."[2] Page might indulge in prophetic fantasies, but Wilson was not yet ready to do as he proposed. A president should not leave the country, Wilson thought: "It might be the beginning of a practice of visiting foreign countries which would lead Presidents rather far afield." How ironic is the sound of these words to those in whose ears the future rings. Nonetheless he found Page's proposal "a most attractive idea."[3]

No sooner had the war broken out than Page took sides. In his lively letters, which give an excellent picture of the excitement in London in August 1914, he did not mince words. To Wilson he wrote that the Prussian military system must be cut out like a tumor.[4] He had the greatest admiration for Grey, whom he considered a profound and great man. More and more he allowed himself to be taken in tow by the able Englishman. In his memoirs, Grey tells how Page came to him with an American protest, read it, and then said: "I have now read the despatch, but do not agree with it; let us consider how it should be answered."[5] After a while he almost refused outright to knock at the door of the English government with protests about international agreements. He even wrote to House that he could no longer stand Lansing's drivel about them. "If Lansing again brings up the Declaration of London—after four flat and reasonable rejections—I shall resign. I will not be the instrument of a perfectly gratuitous and ineffective insult to this patient and fair and friendly government and people."[6]

You may drive a horse to water, but you can't make him drink. Page was Lansing's "horse," but he could get away with his recalcitrance because there was not much that America could do about it when the English snapped their fingers at the London agreements. Finally Washington let the matter rest, and expressed the more modest hope that the British would conform to the general rules of "traditional international law." The British violation of neutral rights was embarrassing and even painful, but for their part the Americans did not want to press the issue to the point of conflict. That was the last thing Wilson wanted, for it would shatter his aspiration to be a mediator. He told House that as a historian he had learned from the past. The War of 1812, when under very similar circumstances the dispute between England and the United States had led to war, stuck in his memory. He read over again the relevant part of his own *History of the American People*: President Madison, a peace-loving man, had been forced into war. He and Madison, Wilson said, were the only presidents who had studied at Princeton. These parallels were striking : "I sincerely hope they will not go further."[7]

This situation continued in the years that followed. The relationship with England would be difficult, irritation might rise high on occasion, but in principle the United States did not want and could not risk a conflict with the British Empire. For most Americans war with the mother country was unthinkable. Emotion and sentiment were certainly involved, but also practical considerations. There prevailed in leading circles a general feeling that the Anglo-Saxon countries were together the high point of Western civilization and its guarantee. Furthermore the Americans began very soon to make large shipments of arms and munitions to the Allies. The deliveries became so voluminous that they had to be supported by loans. England and France were in distress, not least financially. American prosperity came to be totally dependent upon this immense arms trade; exports to Europe rose from $500,000,000 in 1914 to three and a half billion dollars in 1917. But didn't these "golden chains" inevitably pull America into the maelstrom of the war? Its interest in an Allied victory became so great that it was later often asserted that it had no choice but to enter the war in order to protect its investments.

The problem with this accusation is that this argument is nowhere to be found in the documents that tell how Wilson and his advisors formed their decisions. It was very far from Wilson's thoughts. No material interests could force him into war. That he finally went to war was the result of a whole set of circumstances and principles and the conflicts among them. Of course support for the Allies was one factor, if not the decisive one. In this regard circumstances determined the situation. England and France, which were open to the seas, had access to the American arsenal, while Germany, enclosed in Central Europe, did not. It was completely in agreement with international law that private persons could trade with the belligerents, in arms as with other goods. But was it really neutral to help the Allies so exclusively? There were of course voices in America which opposed such a policy. It was primarily the Irish-

Americans and the German-Americans who formed pressure groups and attempted to push through an arms embargo, as provided in proposals in Congress in December 1914. But an embargo—as historians remembered from the events of 1807—was not neutral either. As *The New Republic* correctly observed, it would at one stroke provide Germany with a total blockade of the Atlantic Ocean: "The proposal is a piece of thoughtless morality, a bit of good intention with unconsidered consequences. As a method of warring against war it belongs with incantations, spells, and the sacrificing of goats."[8]

Wilson himself felt the helplessness of his position. Whatever he did, he would inevitably help one or the other side. To a New York banker he wrote: "My lack of power is so evident that I have felt that I could do nothing else than leave the matter to settle itself."[9]

One thing led to another. The arms shipments led to loans. Bryan, the pacifist-minded secretary of state, doubted that this flow of funds, which went almost entirely to the Entente, was really neutral. In good biblical fashion, he saw money as the root of all evil. Was it not written in Scripture that where one's treasure was, one's heart was too?[10] He was able to convince Wilson that steps had to be taken against these loans, and American bankers were therefore warned on August 15, 1914, that such credits were "inconsistent with the true spirit of neutrality." But such a splendid position could not be maintained in the long run. Arms deliveries continued to grow, and the American economy could not do without them. In the spring of 1915 Bryan's idealistic approach was abandoned and one loan after another was floated in the United States. When America entered the war in 1917, the loans to the Allies had risen to more than two billion dollars, while those to the Central Powers amounted to no more than $27,000,000.

Although it is not correct to say that America went to war to protect its interests, it must be added that it was not fully neutral either. The majority of the people were favorable to the Allies, and so was their government. Wilson himself tried to be neutral, but his closest collaborators very soon were of the opinion that it was to America's interest that the Allies win the war. Furthermore, the majority of the Republican opposition in Congress was very pro-English, especially the old, influential, and experienced elite from New England. They soon came into conflict with Wilson's policy of neutrality. Theodore Roosevelt was the initiator and the central organizer of the opposition to the president, and alongside him stood powerful men, such as Elihu Root, the "grand old man" of the Republican party, a former secretary of war and of state, and Henry Cabot Lodge, a senator from Massachusetts. Both Root and Lodge were brilliant men and bitter foes of the Southern intellectual who had deprived them of their traditional positions of power.

By the end of 1914 they were in conflict with Wilson. It was the first painful encounter about a matter that was in itself not terribly important but became the prelude to a colossal, stubbornly fought struggle whose ultimate consequences would be fatal. At issue was the difficult position of American shipping as a result of the outbreak of the war. Too few merchant vessels were American-owned, so that freight prices rose alarmingly. The U.S. government then came up with the idea of buying the idle German ships in American ports that did not venture out to face the British. It would be a risky step, however, as a possible violation of neutrality. As soon as the British government heard of the plans, it sent a warning and placed conditions: in no case would these ships, even under American ownership, be permitted to sail to Germany or even to neutral countries bordering on Germany. Wilson at first waved aside these difficulties, assuming that England was not very serious about them. When a ship purchase bill was introduced in Congress, a storm broke out at once. Root and Lodge, the Republican leaders in the Senate, considered that buying these ships would be an unfriendly act toward England and a threat to American neutrality, and they found much support on both sides of the aisle, among Democrats as well as Republicans. Suddenly Wilson faced a full-scale revolt in Congress and in his own party. With his usual truculence he attacked his opponents in person. His trusted weapon was speech. On Jackson Day, the traditional holiday of the Democratic party, January 8, 1915, he gave an address to the party faithful in Indianapolis in defense of his position. He spoke again with the tone of irritating self-assurance that got under the skin of his opponents. He hammered on his favorite theme—that he, and he alone, understood what the people were feeling. The newspapers, he said sarcastically, wrote against him in furious rage, but "Woodrow sat back in his chair and chuckled knowing that he laughs best who laughs last, knowing, in short, what were the temper and the principles of the American people."[11] He would say such things in the heat of a speech and later regret them, in this case the very next day; but they still reveal the depth of his rancor.

He also attacked, of course, the members of Congress who dared to resist the will of the nation and did not understand what a magnificent task America now had: "Only America is using her great character and her great strength in the interest of peace and prosperity." And, once more, he was smugly certain that time would prove that he was right. Eventually the whole world would turn to America and admit, "You were right, and we were wrong. You kept your heads when we lost ours."[12]

Such speeches had an effect opposite to what was intended. The "gentlemen" were not persuaded, quite the contrary. Lodge in particular was infuriated by Wilson's disdain. He wrote to Theodore Roosevelt that the speech was "not only angry but cheap," that the "natural cheapness of the man has come out." Root's primary objection was that the purchase of the ships by the government was "socialism." Wilson reacted in kind. To his friend Nancy Saunders Toy, he confided that he had always thought that Root and Lodge at least possessed a conscience, but now he discovered that they did not. He had to fight them therefore with every weapon: "We must hit them and hit them straight in the face, and not mind if the blood comes." Everything was at stake. This was a new battle of society against private interests: "God only knows what will come of it. Only reform can prevent revolution."[13]

The battle became extremely fierce. Wilson's proposal was accepted in the House, but the Senate rejected it and in the end the whole plan fell through. The only lasting result was the personal embitterment on both sides. No human understanding was possible any longer between Wilson and Lodge. They continued to mistrust and hate each other. Lodge wrote to Roosevelt: "I never expected to hate any one in politics with the hatred I feel towards Wilson."[14] This animosity would have disastrous consequences in the future.

The American relationship with England continued to be one of persistent irritation and argument, but neither side really wanted a conflict and none happened. The English attitude was often arrogant, the Americans thought, and sometimes the tensions rose high. Especially in 1916, when the threat from U-boats seemed to be declining, the problems with England became more difficult. In the spring the British government published a so-called "black list," with the names of a considerable number of American firms that were barred from all relations with England because they traded with Germany. The indignation in the United States mounted. Wilson himself was upset. He wrote to House that his patience with England was coming to an end. The "black list" was the last straw;

he was seriously considering proposing to Congress to bar loans and exports to England.[15]

This step was not actually taken, but the relations with the British Empire came into serious danger. It was primarily circumstances that made Germany the enemy rather than England. While the English were an irritating problem for America, the Germans were a threat. From England the Americans faced unpleasant troubles, ship halting and seizures, black lists. But Germany, which was blockaded, used very different weapons that cost human lives. It was the difference between a gang of thieves and a gang of murderers, wrote an American newspaper. To seize ships at sea and bring them into port was one thing, but to sink them on the high seas was an assault upon the deeper emotions of public opinion.

II

War brings all international agreements into question, for war is unpredictable and full of surprises, always different from what anyone could have imagined. This was never so painfully evident as in the question of submarine warfare, since submarines were a weapon without equal, but operated effectively only by surprise. A multitude of notes discussed and debated the question of their surprise attacks. What was the status of the fine agreements about merchant ships in wartime? The answer was clear: a warship might halt, search, seize, and even sink a merchantman, but only after prior warning and giving civilian travelers the opportunity to leave safely. But a submarine that adhered to such rules would of course become defenseless and useless.

When the war broke out, German ships were swept off the seas, Germany was blockaded, and the Germans desperately turned to the submarine as a means of breaking the Allied stranglehold. The initial successes of the U-boats in the autumn of 1914 brought a sudden resurgence of hope, and the German military command slowly realized what a powerful weapon it had in its hands. On February 4, 1915, the German government published an official declaration putting a blockade around the British islands: in a zone around Great Britain, all enemy ships, including merchant vessels, would be attacked without warning. Neutral ships were advised to avoid these regions, since the Allied ships could always be disguised with neutral flags.

It was a risky weapon, the most blatant violation of international standards of conduct. The Germans were aware of that difficulty, but war seldom leaves intact much of standards and morality. The German fleet commander, Admiral Friedrich von Ingenohl, had his argument ready. Since England disregarded international law by its hunger blockade, Germany had the right to act without regard to the treaty agreements. More important than the moral question, however, was whether the weapon was as effective as the Kaiser's admirals wanted to believe. From the beginning the question had to be faced of how America would react to such drastic measures of naval warfare. Political leaders in Germany, with Chancellor Theobald von Bethmann-Hollweg in the forefront, were hesitant, and a bitter controversy arose between the German political and military leaders.

The submarine weapon made it much more difficult for the United States, like all nonbelligerents, to remain neutral. Neutrality became a dilemma as never before. Was it neutral to waive fundamental rights of free navigation? Wasn't this itself a serious breach of international law, a grave derogation of morality in a world where morality seemed more and more on the wane?

Wilson, a man of principle, protested, but in so doing he reduced his chances for mediation. A sharp note was sent to Berlin, declaring that the policy set forth in the German note was "so unprecedented in naval warfare that this Government is reluctant to believe that the Imperial Government of Germany in this case contemplates it as possible." The American government would hold the German government fully responsible for the consequences.[16] This seemed like plain talk, but what would happen if American rights were really challenged could not be foreseen. It was nonetheless probable that once such a stand on principle was taken, a conflict would result. The German U-boat commanders sat looking through their periscopes with gruesome orders. The moment of truth appeared near.

It seemed at hand in March 1915 when a British passenger ship, the *Falaba*, was sunk by a submarine. One of the victims was an American, and America was therefore concerned. Discussion began at once in Washington about how to react. Should the affair be viewed from the legal side and insistence be placed upon the right of Americans to travel on belligerent ships? Or would it be better to take a stand on the basis of the highest moral principles? And how sharp should the note to Germany be? How much risk should be run? Bryan argued for caution, considering that it would be exaggerated and even absurd to place peace itself in danger for the sake of the rights of individual citizens. If a ship on which an American was traveling had munitions or other contraband aboard, then allowing the presence of neutral citizens was equivalent to putting women and children in front of an army.[17] In a moving letter he implored the president not to permit the affair to be driven to a head:

> The loss of one American, who might have avoided death, is as nothing compared with the tens of thousands who are dying daily in this "causeless war." Is it not better to try to bring peace for the benefit of the whole world than to risk the provoking of war on account of one man.[18]

But Lansing, the State Department counselor, was in favor of a sharp note, based upon American rights. Wilson himself did not want to approach the question too legalistically; the scuffling over the rules of international law could be interminable. No, what was involved were higher principles, morality was at stake. He answered Bryan: "My idea, as you will see, is to put the whole note on very high grounds—not on the loss of this single man's life, but on the interests of mankind which are involved and which Germany always had stood for."[19]

But, while the debate was still going on in Washington about a proper, decisive reaction to the killing of a single harmless American, more than a hundred others became victims. The British passenger ship, the *Lusitania*, the pride of the Cunard Line (30,396 tons), which had sailed from New York on May 1, was sunk without warning by a German torpedo on May 7, in broad daylight in the Irish Sea. The great majority of the crew and passengers, almost 1,200 persons, were drowned, including 128 Americans.

The shock created by this brutal attack was enormous, not least in the United States. House, who was in England at the moment, relates in his diary that he had a talk with Sir Edward Grey that very morning, and "the possibility of an ocean-liner being sunk" came up (this remark later provided revisionist historians with reason to smell a conspiracy). He told Grey, House wrote, that in that event "a flame of indignation would sweep across America, which would probably carry us into the war."[20] He was right about the indignation, but war did not immediately result. Angry commentaries in the press lashed at the German action as senseless murder of defenseless civilians. There were many who cried out that they now saw what the war in Europe was really about. It was a struggle between barbarism and humanity. The question began to be put whether America could remain neutral. Public opinion became strongly anti-German. The German ambassador reported to Berlin that German propaganda had been totally defeated by the "*Lusitania* incident." There were two persons present in the American character, he asserted: one was a "cool, calculating businessman," but once his passions—"here they are called 'emotions'—took over, he became a hysterical woman. Then talk was of no avail."[21]

Wilson did not let himself be carried along by this agitation. Like everyone else, he was completely surprised that Friday noontime by the frightful news. In Link's biography of Wilson, his reactions are recounted in complete detail but also with the hagiographic tone of admiration and respect that characterize this work. It was more than Wilson could bear, writes Link. He went outside alone, did not even notice that it was raining, wrestled desperately with the problem of what should be done, but then became himself more than ever: "Now as never before did his true character manifest itself in word and deed."[22]

Wilson, we learn from Link's edition of his *Papers*, was really busy with quite different matters in these days. His love affair with Edith Bolling Galt had reached a high point. He wrote her long, lyrical letters every day, full of passion and romance, with sonnets from Shakespeare and passages from Wordsworth, and even a sonnet from his own hand. "These are the supreme years of my life. Minutes count with me now more than days will some time—and my *need* is supreme."[23] And of course he experienced his love as a religious experience; it was the "wonderful love God has given us,"[24] he wrote on May 7. The very evening of the day when according to Link he had walked alone and noble in the rain, he bent over another long letter. And she was his equal in ardor, writing him that same evening that she felt like the Virgin Mary during the Annunciation: "The wonder of it is as gracious as the shining presence of the Angel when he came in gleaming whiteness to the Virgin. Why should I be chosen among all women to help you in your masterful strength to serve—and serve so worthily, so unselfishly a great nation?"[25]

The first dispatches came in on Sunday. House cabled that high demands must be placed upon Germany to assure that it would never happen again. Otherwise it would be better to go to war, for "our intervention shall save rather than increase the loss of life."[26] Bryan saw things from the other side: the sunk ship had had contraband aboard, and the conclusion should therefore be that such ships "should not be permitted to carry passengers."[27] Wilson went to church that Sunday morning as he always did, wrote two long letters to his beloved and explained to her that she was his only light in those dark days. And meanwhile he attempted to keep calm and not permit himself to be carried along by the momentary agitation. He was quite able to do it, he could keep his distance from the emotions of the moment, and, furthermore, he realized his responsibility and did not talk lightly about war. One of the telegrams that flooded the White House in these days exhorted him: "In the name of God and humanity, declare war on Germany"; on it he commented, "War isn't declared in the name of God; it is a human affair entirely."[28] These were words in the tradition of Abraham Lincoln.

But emotions did in fact play a role in his detachment, as came out when he made his first comments in public. On the evening of Monday, May 10, he gave a speech to a large group of immigrants, recently naturalized Americans, in which he made a number of remarks that became all too famous, that would go on to have a life of their own and would be used to the full against him by his enemies.

> The example of America must be the example, not merely of peace
> because it will not fight, but of peace because peace is the healing and
> elevating influence of the world, and strife is not. There is such a
> thing as a man being too proud to fight. There is such a thing as a
> nation being so right that it does not need to convince others by force
> that it is right.[29]

Too proud to fight! Just what did that mean? Could it not be interpreted as cowardice pretending to moral greatness? Or was it a brilliant instance of self-control, of biblical peace of mind? According to Tumulty, Wilson suffered intolerably during these days and explained to his trusted secretary how deep feelings were concealed behind his cold and apparently indifferent exterior:

> I have spent many sleepless hours thinking about this tragedy. It has
> hung over me like a terrible nightmare. In God's name, how could
> a nation calling itself civilized purpose so horrible a thing?[30]

But he controlled himself and declared that he was "too proud to fight." His enemies employed these words with grim pleasure, like the boisterous Theodore Roosevelt, who accused him of "mean timidity and mean commercial opportunism." He was "the demagogue, adroit, tricky, false, without one spark of loftiness in him, without a touch of the heroic in his cold, selfish and timid soul."[31] That was a caricature of Wilson, but the president was himself embarrassed by Roosevelt's remark. He told a journalist that he was making it a habit to think aloud, and he scrapped the offending sentence in a later version of the speech.

But was it really as thoughtless as it seemed? Did not Wilson express pretty well in these haughty words the real feelings of the American people? They were almost identical with words that he had used earlier. In a speech to newspapermen in New York a few weeks before, he had expounded his favorite theme that America was a nation of many nations and therefore fit to mediate. But to do so it of course had to remain neutral:

> I am interested in neutrality because there is something so much greater to do than fight: there is a distinction waiting for this nation that no nation has ever yet got. That is the distinction of absolute self-control and self-mastery.[32]

Wilson therefore was holding fast to his great ideal of being the founder of peace.

But not peace at any price. That was the dilemma that was considerably sharpened by the crisis of May 1915. There had to be a response, a clear response, to the German action. On May 13, a note was sent to Berlin emphatically affirming the right of American civilians to travel on belligerent ships and demanding that the German government disavow the sinking of the *Lusitania*, pay reparations, and take measures against a repetition. But this strong language did not make much of an impression in Berlin, in part because of a misunderstanding. The Germans thought that the note was not seriously meant, that it was intended only for domestic effect, to calm public opinion. The story was heard in Berlin that Bryan had said something to that effect to the Austrian ambassador, Konstantin Dumba. The German reply of May 28 declared that the *Lusitania* had had arms and munitions on board (which was true), and that

Germany therefore was not bound by the rules of identification and search.

This raised the affair to a serious diplomatic crisis. Bryan swore that he had not uttered that remark, but something of the kind could easily have come from his lips. He continued to believe that travel upon belligerent ships had to be prohibited; he could not in honor and conscience support a policy of national honor, certainly not when a second, sharper note to Germany was being prepared. After several sleepless nights, he decided to submit his resignation, feeling passed over and superfluous. He confessed to Wilson with "a quiver in his voice and of his lips: Colonel House has been Secretary of State, not I, and I have never had your full confidence."[33]

Bryan's resignation caused great excitement, but if the poor man had hoped to win sympathy by it and even to unleash a kind of peace movement, he was disappointed. Most press comments were devastating to him, and a sigh of relief went up in government circles in Washington. Some even described his departure as desertion or betrayal. Wilson himself understood clearly why the break had come; it was difficult to reconcile national honor and neutrality. He wrote to Bryan how difficult it was to satisfy the double wish of the people to stand firm toward Germany and yet do nothing that would endanger peace.[34] But he confided to his beloved, whom he continued to inundate with ardent letters, that he felt insulted by Bryan's resignation (although in fact he had long hoped that Bryan would step down, as he had told House back in December!).[35] He even expressed a suspicion that something sinister lay behind it. The widow Galt agreed eagerly and fed his suspicions. She even wrote Wilson that she could kill the traitor Bryan with her own hands. Wilson echoed everything she wrote. She was such a good hater! And she was right, "For he is a traitor, though I can say so, as yet, only to you."[36]

Although Edith Galt did not want to marry Wilson because he was the president, she was ready now to interfere in everything. She had the arrogance that came from making her way successfully to the top. When Wilson told her that he was thinking of Lansing as Bryan's successor, her first reaction was, "But he is only a clerk in the State Department, isn't he?" and Wilson had to explain to her that Lansing was a "counsellor" and he wanted him in particular because he was under the influence of his father-in-law, John W. Foster, a wise, experienced man "for whom I have great respect."[37] (Foster had been secretary of state under President

Benjamin Harrison and had written several important books on foreign policy. Interest in diplomacy belonged to the family. Not only did his son-in-law Lansing follow in Foster's footsteps, but also his grandson John Foster Dulles, who would hold the same post under Eisenhower.)

Wilson wrote to Mrs. Galt only about the personal aspects of the appointment. He discussed it more fundamentally with House. The vacancy had to be filled without delay, the president thought. Lansing had a great deal of experience, although of course House himself was more capable, but did not want to appear in the foreground. House, haughty as always, replied that Lansing was very competent, and it was important "to get a man with not too many ideas of his own and one that would be entirely guided by you without unnecessary argument, and this, it seems to me, you would find in Lansing."[38] In the final analysis Wilson would always be his own secretary of state and Lansing "would not be troublesome by obtruding or injecting his own views."[39] Wilson therefore did not have to worry that Lansing was "not big enough," it was actually an advantage.[40]

Yet it remains surprising that Wilson named Lansing to the most important post in his government. After all, he was the opposite of Wilson in every respect and things would not go as smoothly as House predicted. Robert Lansing, eight years younger than Wilson, had had a brilliant career as a lawyer in New York. He had become interested in international problems after his marriage to Eleanor Foster, the daughter of John W. Foster, but he approached them with the exacting methods of a lawyer. He was precise as Wilson had never wanted to be, a meticulous, clear, logical legal scholar, as analytical and sober as Wilson was intuitive and romantic. This could be seen even in his outer appearance; he was a short, gray, impeccably dressed gentleman, who lived a very regular life (he suffered from diabetes and had to be careful), and recorded the events of the day in a tiny hand. Ray Stannard Baker described him as an indefatigable diarist and a man who had the habit of "doodling" at meetings, drawing portraits that were sometimes distorted to the point of caricature.[41] The doodling annoyed Wilson, although the sketches were unusually charming and striking. Over time the relationship between Wilson and the leading member of his cabinet became very strained. Lansing, Wilson told House, has no imagination, no constructive ability, really no ability whatever. He had "a wooden mind," couldn't write a clear report, and so on.[42] For his part, Lansing in his diary gave a razor-edged portrait of Wilson as a man who relied on his intuition, unable to listen to reasonable arguments. "Even established facts were ignored if they did not fit in with his intuitive sense, this semi-divine power to select the right. Such an attitude of mind is essentially feminine." This was why Wilson thought himself so superior, believing that he was always right and his judgments correct. "How did he know they were right? Why, he *knew* it, and that was the best reason in the world. . . . When reason clashed with his intuition, reason had to give way."[43]

It was not only incompatibility of temperaments that separated the two men. They also had diametrically opposite views about foreign policy. Often Wilson and Roosevelt are set in contrast to each other as perfect representatives of idealism and realism, but it was only half true, for Roosevelt too was a man of intuitions and whims. A better contrast may be found between Wilson and Lansing. Lansing, a true Calvinist (much more so, actually, than Wilson), was as pessimistic about human nature as Wilson was optimistic. Lansing did not believe that nations can be held to the same morality as individuals. They could not be held to their promises when these conflicted with their interests; they never allowed obligations of morality, law, or humanity to prevail when they battled for their bare existence. "I do not recall a case in history in which a nation surrendered its sovereignty for the sole purpose of being right."[44] He wrote this sentence in his diary on May 25, 1915, obviously in reaction to Wilson's words of two weeks before about "a nation being so right that it does not need to convince others by force that it is right."

This does not mean that Lansing had no principles. Far from it. He was at least as much a convinced democrat as Wilson, and he adapted this conviction more consistently from the beginning to his conduct of foreign policy. He saw the war in Europe as being fought between autocracy and democracy. He was sure that America would have to choose sides in it, especially after the destruction of the *Lusitania*. But he understood that public opinion was nowhere near ready to go so far and therefore supported Wilson's policy of neutrality, although he saw no chance for his mediation efforts. Germany had to be totally defeated, "not be permitted to win this war or to break even."[45] His notes to Germany were precise and sharp while those to England were deliberately prolix. He admitted it in his memoirs: "Short and emphatic notes were dangerous. Everything was submerged in verbosity. It was done with deliberate purpose. It ensured continuance of the controversies and left the questions unsettled."[46] Diplomats can still learn a lot from Lansing.

Lansing became a member of the cabinet. This is what the historian John Milton Cooper wrote about him:

> Lansing turned out to be the worst appointment Wilson ever made. At his best, he lived up to the president's misgivings about his smallness of mind and character. At his worst he believed House's assurances about his docility and lack of ideas.[47]

If someone is not too large for his boots, say that he is too small; you can cut anyone down to size that way.

The British historian Patrick Devlin is almost as negative. He describes Lansing as vain, small-minded, self-important, and stingy, with "the label of a second-class lawyer stuck so plainly upon him" that it was easy to forget that he was "a good second-class" man and had a lawyer's virtues, "a sound and balanced judgment and a deep sense of fairness."[48]

Others have defended him. George Kennan calls him a man with "powers of insight."[49] Whoever is right about Lansing, at the beginning his collaboration with Wilson went reasonably well. They were in agreement during the *Lusitania* crisis, although from differing motives. The second note to the German government was even sharper than the first, with even more emphasis upon the "high and sacred rights of humanity" and the repeated demand for a German promise to prevent any repetition.[50]

This was far from being the end of the affair. The German government on the one hand did not want to look weak to its own public opinion, but on the other hand it was afraid of a conflict with the United States. Temporarily, therefore, secret orders were sent to U-boat commanders not to attack any more passenger ships, a warning that came in any case too late for the British ship *Arabic*, which was torpedoed on August 19, with more American lives to be mourned. After this repetition of U-boat attacks, there did not appear to be much that Wilson could do other than break diplomatic relations; warnings were not enough. But Wilson did not want to take that step; he was convinced that the American people still did not want war and he continued to dream stubbornly about playing the role of neutral mediator. He wrote to House: "It would be a calamity to the world at large if we would be drawn actively into the conflict and so deprived of all disinterested influence over the settlement."[51] Was there no middle path to be followed? Perhaps England might be admonished to be more pliable in its policy on contraband and blockade? But House warned him, with shrewd flattery, that he must act vigorously:

> Your first note to Germany after the sinking of the *Lusitania* has made you not only the first citizen of America, but the first citizen of the world. If by any word or act you should hurt our pride of nationality you would lose your commanding position over night.[52]

Wilson now openly threatened a break of diplomatic relations. Germany again drew in its horns, or at least the German ambassador in Washington, Johann von Bernstorff—who probably went beyond his government's instructions—promised that no more unarmed passenger ships would be attacked. This was a victory for Wilson's diplomacy, if only a temporary one. The *Lusitania* conflict continued for a time, and only ended officially with a German note of February 4, 1916, promising nonrepetition and reparations, and including a veiled admission of guilt. The Germans continued to avoid using the word "illegal," but conceded that "retaliation must not aim at other than enemy subjects."[53]

Fundamentally, of course, the crisis in the Atlantic Ocean was unsolvable. America stood upon its rights, German could not abandon its best weapon, and England could not lift its blockade. Every settlement was temporary, every promise vain in the long run. The next crisis came soon, in March. The German U-boats went to work with a will in firing upon targets, including two Dutch ships, the *Tubantia* and the *Palembang*, which went down on March 16 and 18. The French ship *Sussex* was the victim on March 24. It was en route to Folkestone when it was hit; it did not sink, but an explosion cost eighty lives; four Americans were wounded. The whole debate was resumed in Washington. What in heaven's name was the right response? When would the moment come when patience would be lost and only deeds, not words, would be effective? Lansing was ready for such a decision, and he drafted a sharp note including the breaking of relations. House was for it, and so was Mrs. Wilson (as Edith Galt was by this time), who obviously had a taste for politics. But Wilson remained cautious. He wrote a note that was sharp and even threatened Germany, but gave it a chance to restrain itself. His demands and the tone in which it was written made an impression. The debate flared up again in Germany between the chancellor and the generals. The Kaiser himself fumed and fretted, and wrote a bitter comment on Wilson's note: his humanity applied only to American interests. The American president obviously did not think it inhumane to starve out a whole people by a hunger blockade, but when Germany defended itself and a few Americans died who had no right whatsoever to be on those ships, then it was suddenly horribly inhumane![54]

But it did not yet come to a break. Once again Bethmann Hollweg was able to calm his Supreme War Lord, thanks to a memorandum from the commander of the navy, Admiral Henning von Holtzendorff, warning that America was too wealthy and too unassailable to be made into an enemy. Wilhelm was ready to be convinced, and he even received the American ambassador, James W. Gerard, very cordially in his headquarters in occupied North France, and a few days later Gerard received the surprising German reply: Germany promised to attack no more merchant ships without warning, and the safety of the passengers would be assured. It added a paragraph unashamedly asking the United States to press England too to observe international rules.[55]

The German promise, called the "Sussex Pledge," was a striking victory for Wilson. He had insisted upon America's absolute rights and had gained his point; he had been able to preserve both national honor and peace. And this time his success seemed to be more permanent than in earlier cases. In the summer there were no more incidents. Nothing could be better in a year in which presidential elections were coming up.

SIXTEEN

Therefore, is it not likely that the nations of the world
will some day turn to us for the cooler assessment of the
elements engaged?
    —*Woodrow Wilson, April 20, 1915*

What a dust we raise, said the fly to the chariot wheel.
    —*John Adams, February 21, 1782*

MEDIATION

THE HISTORY OF THE involvement first of Colonel House and then, in his footsteps, of President Wilson with European tensions and conflicts begins well before the war. The tale begins with the contrast of American optimism and European pessimism, with belief in the future as against entanglement in the past, with the cleavage between good intentions and obdurate self-interest. In short, it is a myth in the shape of a story, with its grand theme of American innocence (read: simple-mindedness) against European wisdom (read: cynicism), it is material for a novelist of the stature of Henry James. And we cannot read this tale, or even tell it, without wondering if something else was present on the American side besides pure humanity, pure idealism.

House went ahead and Wilson, the leader, followed him. It was House who developed the first plans. His conceptions were typical of the Anglo-Saxon feeling of superiority in England and America at the beginning of this century. The rich countries, he held, should work together for development of the rest of the world. England, Germany, and the United States (sometimes France or Japan was added) should learn to trust one another; they should disarm and invest the money saved in "proper development of the waste places, besides maintaining an open door and equal opportunity to every one everywhere."[1]

In the summer of 1913 House visited London, where he met Sir Edward Grey and discussed his ideas with Ambassador Walter Page, who responded to them with enthusiasm. How intensely American House's optimism sounds! He looked ahead: "If the great world forces could, by fortunate events and fortunate combinations, be united and led to clean up the tropics, the great armies might gradually become sanitary police, so in Panama, and finally gradually forget the fighting idea and at last dissolve."[2]

House went beyond letters full of excitement, however. He came up with the notion that as President Wilson's personal envoy he should and probably even could forestall the threatening war. He first sought information from those he visited about the European situation, for instance, how best to approach and soothe the German emperor. He came up with a proposal to give Germany a zone of influence in Asia Minor and Persia, and he continued to hold stubbornly to this fantastic notion.[3] In May 1914 he went to Berlin, where he was given a friendly reception. He spoke with many persons in high places, including Admiral Von Tirpitz and the minister of foreign affairs, Von Jagow ("Neither has ability of the highest order").[4] He was startled by the martial fervor in Germany, which he described in a letter to Wilson. One passage became famous:

> The situation is extraordinary. It is jingoism run stark mad. Unless some one acting for you can bring about an understanding, there is some day to be an awful cataclysm.[5]

It was not difficult to guess who that "some one" should be, but a solution would bring eternal honor to "your administration and our American civilization." It was a tall order, as even the eternally optimistic House realized, but he believed he could fill it. He even received an audience with the emperor. He at once compared him with Theodore Roosevelt, as did every other American, and found him charming but less forceful than the former American president. Wilhelm II asserted that Germany, England, and America were related nations and ought to work together. But the English were fools to join hands with Latin and Slavic peoples, who were unreliable allies and "semi-barbarous." The conversation went on and on, but little was said that was new. Of course Germany did not want war, said the emperor, and it built a fleet only in order to inspire respect. It was quite an experience for House. He wrote to Wilson: "I have been as successful as I anticipated." Now he went at once back to London to finish off the business. Who knows, he might be in Kiel next month with both the emperor and Grey for the naval review and they could discuss reconciliation further. He told this to the affable Grey, who was "visibly impressed," but, added House, "this was not gone into further."[6]

Yet House gained the impression that the emperor as well as the British were ready to continue to talk with him. Soon each of the governments would have to respond in some way to "the moves we are making and every human being may be concerned in the decisions reached from day to day."[7] A delighted Wilson thanked House from his heart for the fine work he did so quietly and tactfully. "I could not have done the thing nearly so well."[8] Three weeks later, he wrote: "It is perfectly delightful to read your letters and to realize what you are accomplishing. I have no comments except praise and self-congratulation that I have such a friend."[9] But, before we conclude that all this is just a sturdy specimen of American naïveté towards old Europe, it is worth remembering the unexpected comment of Sir Cecil Spring-Rice, the British ambassador in Washington. This thoughtful and intelligent Briton saw a very specific cause-and-effect relationship at work in House's mission. He thought that House had brought general peace so palpably near that the Austrians, who were hot for war, took fright and quickly took advantage of the assassination of Archduke Ferdinand in Serajevo. For them it was war now or never, and they forced matters to a head.[10]

In actuality, of course, House's mission had accomplished nothing. It makes us think of the equally pedantic and delighted enthusiasm of another American diplomat in Europe, John Adams, who really thought that the memorial he submitted to the States General of the Dutch Republic in 1782 requesting diplomatic recognition of the United States, could influence the whole course of European politics. But Adams was a man who at least could doubt himself and who, at the end of a long letter on his own triumphs, concluded with an ironic phrase: "What a dust we raise, said the fly to the chariot wheel." House, like Adams but without his sublime irony, was nothing more than a fly on the chariot wheel of European politics, and his appearance did not prevent war. If only that had been true! All the naïve bustle that he so enjoyed signified absolutely nothing in the atrocious drama of confusion and blindness of that disastrous summer, and his exertions are not mentioned in any of the vast number of books devoted to the causes of the war. Only in the history of Wilson and of House himself do they deserve a modest place.

Even then, their only importance is that they were the prelude to a long tale of even greater naïveté and optimism. It was another display of mythological—or should we say, theological?—thinking. House, and Wilson with him, learned little from their first failure. To the contrary, starting not from reality but from noble and exalted principles, they went joyously ahead. Their theology was rooted in an unshakable dogmatism, total acceptance of notions that were for them self-evident (to use a classical American adjective), and which in Wilson had developed from a robust nationalism around 1898 to a more humane internationalism.

The first tenet of this dogmatism, which was already present in Jefferson's Declaration of Independence of 1776, was that America was a special, indeed a unique country, a land (to use a phrase of the evangelists) with "a word for the world." The "word" was that all mankind, not just Americans, had a right to "life, liberty, and the pursuit of happiness." It established, Wilson believed, America's place as a model, a vanguard, a representative of mankind. America was the country that was not based upon its history and origin but upon an idea. As Richard Hofstadter put it so pithily: "It has been our fate as a nation, not to have ideologies but to be one."[11] Wilson had been imbued with this thought long before the war. Examples from his speeches are legion. Here is one from 1907: "This is the one country which has founded its polity upon dreams, which has seen and told the world that it saw visions that were to come to pass through its instrumentality."[12] And, very appropriately on July 4, 1914, an unconscious preface to what was about to happen:

> My dream is that, as the years go on and the world knows more and
> more of America, it will also drink of these foundations of youth and
> renewal; that it will also turn to America for these moral inspirations
> which lie at the basis of all freedom . . . and that America will come
> into the full light of the day when all shall know that she puts
> human rights above all other rights, and that her flag is the flag, not
> only of America, but of humanity.[13]

America was unique because it was selfless. Wilson repeatedly gave voice to this notion, although of course as a historian he knew that it was not at all true. He was brought up with the Christian ethic of unselfishness, of overcoming one's self—and he cited it so many times! And just as an individual ought to be unselfish, so should a country, or at least the chosen nation. This was a Jewish conception transferred to the New World, although it was not unknown in the Old as well. My own country, the Netherlands, thought of itself as a "chosen land," "another Israel" in the West during the period of the Dutch Republic, when one writer boasted it was "the only Power which risked blood and wealth in order to stay faithful to its alliances, without thought of conquests."[14] Wilson said the same later about America. He asked what the founders of America had intended. Was it to "serve the selfish interests of America? Do you find that in their writings? No; to serve the cause of humanity, to bring liberty to mankind."[15] America must become "the justest, most honorable, the most enlightened Nation in the world."[16]

Of course Wilson was deeply committed to these magnificent ideals. Some of Americans' "finer passions" were, he hoped, ensconced in his own heart. He was the leader who would bring about their dreams.[17]

During the war he shifted his stress. America was able to serve the world so well because it was a nation composed of many nations. It was neutral for that reason, not in the sense of being impartial and uninvolved, but because it had sympathy for all humanity. America was "the mediating nation of the world. . . . We are, therefore, able to understand all nations."[18]

The entire period of American neutrality continued in this vein. Its great leader sang the sweet tune of impartiality, chosenness, selflessness; of America's service as "a great spiritual conception," a "moral force of great and triumphant convictions"; of America as the country that "does not want any selfish advantage"; of America that "in the Providence of God" had remained a continent "unused and waiting for a peaceful people who loved liberty and the rights of men more than they loved anything else" (oh, the poor Indians!), of America as the first nation in the whole history of the world that chose to be selfless in its foreign policy.[19]

We could continue with this list of quotations, but, the longer we listen to this unworldly voice, this unhistorical lyricism, the stranger it sounds. It is good to hear it completely, it has its own puzzling fascination. But, however characteristic it was for Wilson himself, this language was still rooted in an authentic American feeling of spiritual and material superiority, which in the isolation of the nineteenth century had been able to deny reality. What is interesting, however, is that Wilson, in breaking out of this isolation, became even more vehement and exalted in applying this timeless language to the outer world. He was an angel in the wilderness.

Mediation, however, turned out to be less than simple. The parties clashing in Europe were certainly not ready for it; each side had confidence in its own victory. Wilson therefore realized that he would have a chance of succeeding only when the battling parties had become exhausted. From the beginning this was the hope he built on. The best chance, he said in an interview in December 1914, was a "deadlock." All the seeds of Wilson's later peace program were present in this conversation. A true peace, he averred, could only come if neither of the parties won, for the misery of history was that, time after time, the winner humiliated the loser, who then in turn took his revenge. It was better not to place the responsibility on one of the parties, not on Germany alone. And, most important of all: the peace must be made not by the governments but by the peoples. Here we have expressed Wilson's three principles that would play a great role in his endeavors to mediate, but were difficult to sustain over the long run. First, peace without victory; second, no raising of the war guilt question; third, the peace to be decided not by governments but by the peoples.[20]

He began therefore to think about a peace of the peoples. As early as August 1914 he told his brother-in-law, Stockton Axson, that they should unite in "an association of nations, all bound together for the protection of the integrity of each, so that any one nation breaking from this bond will bring upon herself war; that is to say, punishment automatically."[21]

Such an association of the peoples was very far away, however, and for the moment only the first cautious steps could be taken in its direction. The words with which he set forth his plans to Stockton Axson sound almost too fair, too fixed, too complete. In general Wilson's actions were still naïve, hesitant, and uncertain. It was no wonder, for he was suddenly confronted with a host of strange new facts.

In this situation House was, from the beginning, his advisor and representative, not Bryan, who was Secretary of State. True, Bryan also favored mediation and urged it fervidly upon Wilson. But he wanted to act out in the open. He wanted to make an appeal to the battling countries to discuss their differences frankly. As Christian nations, they must be ready to do so, he thought.[22]

House, the man who was pulling the wires behind the scenes, believed only in secret diplomacy and thought himself much more wily than the simpleminded Bryan. In his fancies he constructed a plan of action. First, and importantly, Germany must be pushed back within its own borders, for House was much less neutral than Wilson. When that had been done, he wrote in his diary, "I thought it would be advisable for me to go there and see the Kaiser and endeavor to get his consent to two conditions. One being the indemnity of Belgium, and the other such a reduction of armaments as would insure lasting peace in Europe." He presented these simpleminded ideas to Wilson, who was somewhat more realistic, thinking that it would be pretty hard to persuade the Kaiser. But House was incorrigibly optimistic: the Kaiser would see that he must choose peace.[23]

Wilson was a bit more realistic. In order to avoid Bryan's naïveté, Wilson accepted House's naïveté, although it was concealed by his velvety charm. He let himself be won over by the silly House in order to avoid the silly Bryan. He got rid of the good by insisting on the better. Together Wilson and House considered how they could keep Bryan totally out of the affair. Wilson was a bit ashamed of his secretiveness toward his secretary of state, and when he finally informed him, Bryan was quite pained. He would have been ready to go to Germany himself, he said, in order to talk about the so-called "cooling-off treaty," which had never been signed, and so "bring about a general discussion of mediation and peace parleys."[24]

It was House who went, however, all by himself, practicing his customary deep diplomacy. Not surprisingly, Wilson entrusted the whole matter to him. House knew how to use fine words to placate his friend and master: "The world expects you to play the big part in this tragedy, and so indeed you will, for God has given you the power to see things as they are."[25] House thought he saw them the same way. Deeply convinced of his superiority in wielding the instrument of diplomacy, he went ahead with the phantasmagoria of his plans. He was fascinated with his technique as a diplomat. To his diary he confided: "It is certainly original as far as I know, but I thoroughly believe in it."[26]

House began with a plan to bring together in Washington the ambassadors of the hostile parties. The German envoy, Johann von Berns-

torff, who thought that any overtures would offer the possibility of shifting the odium of failure to the opponent, was willing. The Englishman,
Sir Cecil Spring-Rice could do nothing without his allies and therefore
refused. House also developed his own program for peace, in which
France would get Alsace back but Germany would retain Lorraine, and
other similarly unrealistic terms for settlement.[27]

The German government was more responsive than the British, although with many reservations. The German deputy minister of foreign
affairs, Arthur Zimmermann, wrote to House at the beginning of December that he appreciated his unselfish services. House, happy with even
an extended finger, hurried with this letter to Washington (he lived in
New York), and Wilson was just as pleased, and asked him to go to Europe as soon as possible as a mediator.[28]

In January 1915 he sailed again for Europe, now in the grip of war.
He descended upon the warring countries like an angel of peace. Wilson
sensibly advised him to tell all those with whom he conferred that the
United States was not suggesting terms and conditions of peace, but was
trying only to bring the parties together, offering its services as mediator.[29]
The president was committed heart and soul to the splendid undertaking.
He brought his friend to the train in Washington, and on the platform
thanked him with moist eyes for his unselfish and intelligent friendship.
House reminded him how they had become friends three and a half years
earlier, and Wilson replied that they had always known each other, but
had just come "in touch" then. House told his friend that he had given
meaning to his life at a time when it was "more or less a failure." How
idyllic![30]

House's reception in Europe was less heartwarming. Naturally he
was shown full deference; after all he was the alter ego of the president
of the powerful United States. The English, who wondered what he really
wanted, dreaded his visit. They soon saw through him, however, and realized that they had nothing to fear from him. Or anything to expect
either. He talked indeed about a peace conference to be held in the summer if peace had not come by that time.[31] But when Grey asked him
whether in that case the United States would be ready to share responsibility for the peace, he retreated into isolationism: America would never
take that step, he said, for it would violate the unwritten law of nonen-
tanglement in European affairs.[32]

Grey grasped at once how harmless and pro-English House really was, and he praised him later in his memoirs as a man of exceptional wisdom and understanding, with whom it was a pleasure to talk.[33] The self-confident Englishman took him in as easily as he had Page. House was flattered "beyond measure, that he has such confidence in my discretion and integrity."[34]

House became practically an English pawn. He was even willing to let the English decide whether and when he should go to Germany. This was too much for Wilson, who warned him not to let the English government prescribe for him what he should do.[35] House cabled back how difficult his position was; several Russian and French ministers who had just come to London did not want to see him at all. The Allies wanted to fight on until Germany was defeated, and he really did not think that was so foolish, for whatever else happened, militarism had to be destroyed.[36]

Finally, in March, Asquith and Grey acquiesced in his departure for Berlin. He traveled by way of Paris, where he met the French leaders both on his way to the German capital and on his way back. Delcassé, the French foreign minister, tolerated him ironically, but made it quite clear that House's trip would not have any results. House was not perturbed; he was glad that they had received him so cordially, and he drew the conclusion that he had really accomplished a lot. Most important, he informed Wilson, was that "France has at least tentatively accepted you as mediator, and that, I think, is much."[37] House's optimism was indestructible. He ascribed his difficulties to the lack of a dominating figure in London and Berlin: "If there were a Palmerston or a Chatham here, and a Bismarck in Germany, it would be easier." House's superficiality and self-satisfaction were not shaken.

The Germans were forewarned as to what to expect. Bethmann Hollweg wrote to the Austrian minister of foreign affairs that the Central Powers should avoid the appearance of wanting to wage war to the bitter end, although obviously the American offer of mediation had no chance of success. "As to the individual points of House's offer," he wrote, "they seem to me all to be dictated by such an impractical enthusiasm for peace that it would be difficult for a *Realpolitiker* to give them a precise answer. . . . However . . . it seems to me necessary to find a form for the answer that will . . . give the impression of a sympathetic reception."[38]

Bethman Hollweg succeeded, for House was open to a friendly reception. The American understood that he must not speak at length about peace, but, inventive as always, he tried another tack. He argued to the

Germans that the best chance for a better world lay in the principle of freedom of the seas. He informed Wilson that he had talked with them about what Americans and Germans shared and thought he had accomplished a great deal, although the Germans were not willing to buy peace at the price of evacuation of France and Belgium. Yet he was returning home "fairly satisfied" because there was "something definite to work on, and the warring nations have tacitly accepted you as their Mediator."[39] Note the capital letter—it meant that tacitly and tentatively a Mediator was in the making.

House now saw his task as persuading the English government that freedom of the seas was a satisfactory condition for peace. If they accepted it, and he thought it probable they would, then the German government could inform its subjects that the major aim of the war had been attained and it was no longer necessary to continue to occupy the Belgian coast.[40] On arriving back in Paris, House wrote at once to Grey that the Germans were not willing to enter peace negotiations, but that his visit had had great value, and freedom of the seas was a good starting point for further talks. Grey was not impressed by this argument. Freedom of the land, he said, seemed to him at least as important and he wrote back to House that he could not favor freedom of the seas in wartime, and that in peacetime the seas were free "anyhow."[41]

Practical politicians did not see much use in the term "freedom of the seas." What was its meaning in the actual situation? Did it forbid the British blockade or the German submarine campaign? Lansing, as strongly pro-Allied as House but infinitely more realistic, admitted that the term could be used to initiate anything; he could never learn from the president, however, what he specifically meant by it.[42] But for Wilson it remained one of the great principles of his policy; he later made it the second of his Fourteen Points. Yet it remained vague and met much resistance from England.

House, a diplomat fond of double meanings, had always had deeper intentions. He believed in his own subtlety. With discussion of freedom of the seas, at least a "paper campaign" could be begun, he wrote to Wilson. He had to write about it to Grey and Grey back to him, and then the correspondence could include the German chancellor and Zimmermann. "This will necessitate replies, and we may have them talking to one another before they realize it." Thus, imperceptibly, with open minds, the belligerents would suddenly be led by House's sly diplomacy toward one another. The greatness of Wilson would do the rest: "I feel sure that your thoughts upon the subject and the felicity with which you express them, will help beyond measure to convince these warring peoples."[43]

Wilson was in complete agreement with him, for House was doing the preparatory work for his great task.[44] Behind the scenes, House loved secrecy. We are keeping this great endeavor secret, he wrote to Wilson, "between yourself, Sir Edward and myself, and even the men I shall discuss these things with will not know the full purposes."[45] The artless guile of House had of course almost no effect or importance upon the course of events. Who besides Wilson believed in him? And what does it say about Wilson that he allowed him to be taken in tow by such a complete amateur in politics? Just when House was about to leave London to return home, the whole relationship between America and Europe entered a new phase with the torpedoing of the *Lusitania*. But House in Berlin had not once spoken about the burning question of submarine attacks! Page, observing with growing suspicion all these secret doings of House, wrote in his diary: "Peace-talk, therefore, is yet mere moonshine—House has been to Berlin, from London, thence to Paris, thence back to London again—from Nowhere (as far as peace is concerned) to Nowhere again."[46] ("Nowhere" is of course English for "Utopia.") Just as damning a judgment upon the activities of the apostle of peace came from the English prime minister, Asquith, who called it "the twittering of a sparrow in the tumult that shakes the world."[47]

II

Germany's intensification of the U-boat campaign only made Wilson even more certain of the urgency of his mediation efforts. After the torpedoing of the *Lusitania*, he made a personal appeal to the German government through the German envoy in Washington to accept the principle of the free sea; it was one of the key conditions for peace. At the end of May he suggested a peace conference to von Bernstorff, naming as terms for discussion the status quo, freedom of the seas, and a general settlement of the colonial question. Three days later he received the ambassador "in an extraordinarily friendly conversation," and proposed that Germany give up submarine warfare, while he would press England to raise the blockade.[48]

The idea of a definitive settlement concerning the sea continued to inspire the American leaders. It seemed the panacea for keeping the country out of the war and to enable it to mediate. It remained Wilson's ideal. In August 1915 he wrote to House that the American people did not want war. It would be a disaster "if we should be drawn actively into the conflict and so deprived of all disinterested influence over the settlement."[49]

Because mediation through the channel of von Bernstorff offered little hope of success, House went on another mission to Europe in the winter of 1915–1916. The American pressure brought Grey in the autumn to declare in several vaguely phrased letters that mediation would not be unwelcome, provided—and this was the issue at stake—that in an eventual peace the United States would be a guarantor of the new international order. This would be a central issue in relations between America and Europe, the most important stumbling block.

Grey was driven by very humane motives. He suffered more than most of his colleagues from the insanity of war; he was, like Lincoln, a man who recognized the sadness of the human enterprise. He believed, like the later Wilson, that the horrendous sacrifices of the war ought not to be in vain, that they should serve to bring a better world into being. He was therefore very prudent in putting out feelers, and very alone in his prudence. But he set out a sensible precondition, that America must be a coguarantor of a new international order. If Europe were to be left to itself, he wrote to House, we will repeat these disasters every century. The pearl of great price to be found, if possible, was "some League of Nations."[50] House had declared to him a year earlier, as we have seen, that the United States could never make a permanent guarantee, but Wilson now realized that the country would have to go down this path. And House wanted to figure out schemes for getting to the goal.

Encouraged by Grey's letters, House developed an ingenious plan. America must take action, first "unofficially" sounding out the Allies whether they would assent to America's mediation. If they consented, the government of the United States would make an official demarche to both sides to accept such mediation. If Germany also consented, "we would then have accomplished a master stroke of diplomacy." If it refused, America could make demands, break diplomatic relations, and "the whole force of our Government might be brought against them." The president, wrote House, "was startled by this plan. He seemed to acquiesce by silence."[51]

House's whole scheme was based upon the expectation that Germany would then play the role of scapegoat. A great deal depended upon seizing the right moment for taking this step favorable to the Allies.

These fantasies began a whole history of misunderstandings and confusion between America and the Allies, but also between Wilson and House. Although it seemed to be their common plan, Wilson placed the emphasis very differently. He really wanted to mediate, and he wanted a conference over which he would preside. He was willing therefore to exert pressure, but only prudently, within certain bounds, and not with the automatic sanction of U.S. participation in the struggle. The United States would "probably" participate. The word "probably" became the key term in Wilson's diplomacy and the heart of the first misunderstanding between him and House.

Wilson still trusted House, however, and began to believe in the idea of an honorable peace. In December 1915 just when House dangled his fine plans before him, Wilson declared in a speech before a chamber of commerce that the war would be followed by a real peace, not a "patched-up peace." A peace with guarantees, a peace in which law, not power, would rule. America would participate in it by "spiritual mediation."[52]

House, on the contrary, wanted unlimited pressure because he did not fear its consequences. His second trip took place about a year after the first. It was prepared by a letter to Grey in which he expounded his plan in vague phrases: America would quickly come between the belligerents (the ambiguous term that he used was "intervene") and demand peace negotiatons "upon the broad basis of the elimination of militarism and navalism."[53] Wilson went through this letter with House and approved it with a few changes. Where House spoke of the necessity of joining the Allied side, Wilson added the word "probably." As usual, House overwhelmed Wilson with the flattering prospect of world leadership: "This is the part I think you are destined to play in this world tragedy, and it is the noblest part that has ever come to a son of man."[54] But in the meantime our John the Baptist obstinately followed his own ideas in preparing the way for his Son of Man.

Wilson at first continued to hesitate, House reported in his diary. There was misunderstanding. The president, he wrote, was less bellicose; he seemed to think that the United States could still stay out of the war. But House wanted "action," which as yet did not mean participation but only letting the Allies know that America stood on their side and would not permit Germany to win.[55] In the end Wilson gave his assent to

House's plans, but upon the basis of his own assumptions. In a letter the president expounded his own general ideals of how a definitive peace should look: first, disarmament on land and at sea; second, a league of nations to protect every country against aggression and to guarantee absolute freedom of the seas. For the rest, he wrote, he did not want to give House any instructions; he knew what was at stake and in any case would maintain constant contact. But, Wilson again stressed, just as he had done a year earlier, that he and House were agreed that America should have nothing to do with "local settlements—territorial questions, indemnities and the like." It was a question only of guaranteeing future world peace. And he added with warmth: "I am sure that you know how fully my heart goes with you and how deeply grateful I am for the incomparable and inestimable services you are rendering the country and me, your friend."[56]

Wilson therefore began his mediation by adopting a very ambiguous position, one that in the long run was impossible. He wanted America to play a great role in the international order, but without it having anything to do with the conflict of interests in Europe. America would participate and still remain unique, it would stay pure and yet bear responsibility. It would participate in the wicked world and yet keep its hands clean. That curious paradox continued to define his position for a long time; indeed it can be said that he never really broke away from it, and it was this that made his relations with the Old World so complex.

This presented at once a difficult starting point for House, who would have to talk in Europe about peace but not the conditions for peace. He did not adhere to this position. In the beginning of January 1916 House journeyed to London on the *Rotterdam* of the Holland-America Line. He began anew a long series of discussions with statesmen in London, Paris, and Berlin, with hidden meanings and corresponding expectations and disappointments. House even gained the impression that Grey wanted to end the food blockade if Germany halted its submarine campaign.[57] Grey wanted to know precisely what House meant by his promise that the United States "wanted the British Government to do what would enable the United States to do what was necessary for the Allies to win the war." But House had no answer to give and remained vague.[58]

David Lloyd George, the minister of munitions in the English cabinet and already clearly the coming man, told House that England would first win a major victory during the summer and then the time would be ripe for American mediation, for public opinion would compel the Allied governments to take the step. Then the peace terms could be dictated by Wilson, but otherwise nothing would succeed. But these terms had to include: evacuation of Belgium, the return of Alsace-Lorraine to France, the independence of Poland, with compensation to Germany in Asia Minor. England would refuse to discuss only one issue, he added, and that was the German conception of freedom of the seas.

House was deeply impressed by the charm of the whimsical statesman from Wales, who added the comment that America must take care to remain as strong as possible. Lloyd George was obviously playing up to the American; it was just at this time that preparedness was under discussion, as we shall see. And he flattered Wilson too by saying that there never had been a man in history with his opportunities, "and that if the world went on for untold centuries, history would record this as the greatest individual act of which it had record."[59]

From London House went to Berlin, where there were more lunches and dinners (he was impressed by the quantity of beer that Bethmann Hollweg could down), but also a great deal of bitterness against England, as well as terms for peace that he knew would not be acceptable to the Allies, even including a demand for indemnity for the costs of occupation in France. The attitude was so negative that House could not even present his splendid plan of mediation. He was disappointed, feeling that the Germans did not want peace. The chancellor was the most unreasonable of all those he met, although he was a pleasant, well-intentioned man with admittedly, in House's judgment, a "limited ability." The most intelligent of the Germans was Zimmermann.[60]

Next came Paris, where he talked with Aristide Briand, then the premier, and Jules Cambon, the secretary general of the foreign ministry. The French still did not believe in mediation. But House, subtle as he was, did not talk about it; on the contrary he gave Cambon assurance that America would soon choose the Allied side. The Frenchmen couldn't believe what they heard and asked him to repeat what he said, wrote it down, and had him read what they put down. It is correct, he said.[61] In his diary House noted: "In the event the Allies are successful during the next few months I promised that the President would not intervene. In the event they were losing ground I promised the President would intervene." But what did "intervene" mean? Cambon heard it as meaning military help, but House in his letters to Wilson intended it only as mediation. And he was aware that America could not unconditionally commit itself to come to the aid of the losing side.[62]

Back in London in the second week of February, House at once fell into a bitter clash with ambassador Page, who still thought the whole mediation proposal "moonshine" and wanted the United States to speed to the aid of the Allies as soon as possible. He refused to support House in his peace plan.[63] But House went forward without tiring. He cabled Wilson with enthusiasm that the Allies "will agree to the Conference, and if Germany does not, I have promised for you that we will throw in all our weight in order to bring her to terms." Did Wilson grasp what House meant by those words? It was in any case not a correct presentation of the facts. Neither the French nor most of the English favored House's plans. But, optimistic as always, House minimized the difficulties. The English leaders also heard from him that at an eventual peace conference Wilson "would throw the weight of the United States on the side of the Allies," which according to House meant "on the side of those wanting a just settlement."[64] This was vague enough; what Wilson would eventually do was not clear pending the meeting. Prime minister Asquith asked what the president would do in the event the Allies proposed a settlement that he found unjust? Then, said House, he would "probably withdraw and leave them to their own devices."[65] It was a disappointing reply, meaning that Wilson would come to dictate peace or drop it. House too said "probably," a word typical of his activities.

But Grey, prudent and very worried, decided nonetheless to come to a provisional agreement with House, which meant putting down with him on paper "as precisely as could be done in advance the action that President Wilson would be prepared to take."[66] That was how the famed House-Grey Memorandum came about. Wilson, according to its terms, would make a proposal for convening a peace conference as soon as he heard from England and France that the moment was favorable. If the Allies accepted the proposal and Germany did not, then America would "probably enter the war against Germany." And then came the notorious sentence: "Colonel House expressed the opinion that, if such a Conference met, it would secure peace on terms not unfavourable to the Allies; and, if it failed to secure peace, the United States would leave the Conference as a belligerent on the side of the Allies, if Germany was unreasonable."[67]

What a fantastic construction! The French did not want to hear a word of it, nor did most Englishmen. Grey himself drew back fearfully when he heard the reaction. Paul Cambon, the French ambassador in London (he was the brother of Jules Cambon), told him that neither French nor English public opinion would swallow America's dictating the peace. Wasn't this an election stunt of Wilson, the Puritan and professor, who was supposed to be selfless?[68]

Europeans understood Americans for the most part as little as Americans understood Europeans. Wilson was not aiming at a political success. His dream was deeper. He meant what he said he wanted, and for European realists that itself was puzzling enough. But the problem here was that House did not present his intentions accurately. He first gave a wrong impression of Wilson's opinions in the European capitals, and when he returned he gave Wilson an incorrect report on the chances of success. Did he mislead him? Or did he believe himself in his boundless optimism that he had achieved something?

We could almost believe this when we read the elated pages in his diary about the matter. He showed Wilson the memorandum, "the substance of my understanding with France and Great Britain" (as if the French had approved it). And Wilson, he wrote, was enthusiastic; he accepted it in toto, only suggesting that the word "probably" be inserted precisely between the words "would" and "leave" in the phrase, "the United States would leave the Conference as a belligerent." House obviously considered it a trifle. He described furthermore how grateful Wilson was to him. He imagined with pride seeing the president sitting soon at the head of the conference table, in The Hague, where it should be held. And Wilson said, "My dear friend, you should be proud of yourself and not of me, since you have done it all."[69] The question remains whether Wilson was actually as glad and naïve as House and was satisfied with such a perfect castle in the air. In any case he was more cautious.

Nonetheless House went ahead. In a subsequent conversation he had considered how the conference would have to be organized, with two representatives from each of the belligerent countries and one from every neutral. Wilson asked why that should be, since in any event the United States would only mediate and have nothing to do with the organization of the conference itself. Leave that to me, said the brave colonel, I will arrange it. For the United States, Wilson himself should of course be the only delegate; none other was necessary. What about House himself? Yes, he had concluded that the president would have a staff of expert advisors, informed about "proper solutions," who would urge "this country to give way here and that country to give way there. I have this force pretty well picked out in my mind now." House was truly inexhaustible, foreseeing everything. The "force" of which he spoke we will meet again in 1918.[70]

What an idyll, what success! But that additional word "probably" of course completely destroyed whatever pleasure the not overly eager Allies had in the whole plan. They ceased to pay much attention to it. At a meeting of the British cabinet the vote against it was unanimous, including even those upon whom House had placed his hopes, Lloyd George and Balfour. Grey himself did not even bother to defend the memorandum any more. He permitted the French to see it, but they were all agreed that the time was not suitable, and when Asquith and Grey visited Paris in March, it was not even discussed. In May, Grey wrote to House that mediation was premature, but that he continued to be favorable to Wilson's plans for a League of Nations. House was deeply disappointed. "Now that we have informed them that we are ready to involve ourselves," he wrote in his diary, "they begin to hesitate and stammer."[71]

Thus nothing came out of the whole affair. But the whole tale leaves a strange aftertaste. How was it really possible that Wilson and House could take on such an enterprise, believe in it, and hold on to it so stubbornly? To speak of House first, he was a visionary, admittedly an intelligent and persistent visionary, but no more. The British historian Devlin, in his detailed examination of the case, observes that the British leaders esteemed House highly and calls upon Lloyd George as his chief witness.[72] But it was just Lloyd George, in the passage that Devlin quotes only in part, who described House as a friendly man, "a well-balanced but not a powerful mind," by far not on Wilson's intellectual level, but rather adroit and superficial, and he comes to a devastating conclusion: "It is perhaps to his credit that he was not nearly as cunning as he thought he was."[73] House, we can conclude, came to his plans upon the basis of a mixture of vanity and typical American ignorance of Europe.

But Wilson? The great Wilson himself? How is it possible that he permitted all of this to go on? Why did he let himself be led by House in that way? What would have happened if the House-Grey Memorandum had ever become public? Hadn't he perceived the far from subtle difference between himself and House? Was this all a cunning game of

Wilson's? Was he thinking primarily of the elections and therefore keeping all roads to peace open?

At a deeper level there was the yearning of the president to be a great peacemaker. This ambition was already present in him in embryo in 1914 and stirred him more and more. But, just like House, he knew little about Europe. He knew the various constitutions, but he had little idea about European history, European mentality. Worse indeed, probably, was that he knew little about human mentality. He was an optimist, he saw people as he wanted to see them. An idealist, he believed in mankind. And as an American he thought he could find an adequate, total, final solution for human suffering, a panacea for all pain. All alone, with only the loyal flatterer House at his side, he had to improve the world. That was his great tragedy.

We can also wonder what would have happened if the impossible had just turned out to be possible. Various participants in the strange drama speculated about it afterwards. The most that could have been hoped for, wrote the realist Lloyd George in his memoirs, was that the Americans would have become involved earlier in the war.[74] Grey, the philosopher, attempted, years after the war and deeply disappointed about its results, to imagine what might have happened had both the Allies and the Germans responded positively to Wilson's proposals. Of course it would have been totally impossible in view of Prussian militarism. But on the other hand, "if a Wilson peace in 1916 had brought real disillusionment about militarism, it would have been far better than what actually happened." The war went on for two more long years, and totally exhausted Europe. How much better the world would have looked if House had succeeded, if there had been a peace without harmful secret thoughts of revenge.

That is very close to the thinking of Wilson himself, who suffered so gravely from the horror of the war. Yes, wrote Grey in 1925, so disappointing is what has happened since 1917, so dark is the present situation (and he was not writing in 1935, not to speak of 1945!) "that we are tempted to find some relief in building castles in the air; and, if the future is too clouded for this, we build them in the past."[75]

SEVENTEEN

There is nothing that the United States wants for itself
that any other nation has.
—*Woodrow Wilson*

The President's great talents and imposing character fit
him to play a great part. He feels it and knows it. He is
already a mysterious, rather Olympian personage, and
shrouded in darkness from which issue occasional
thunderbolts. He sees nobody who could be remotely
suspected of being his equal, should any such exist in
point of intellect or character.
—*Sir Cecil Spring-Rice, January 26, 1917*

1916

THE POSSIBILITY OF AN invasion of England has tempted the imagination of continental rulers since 1066, but they have all been deterred by the Channel. It is and remains a tremendous barrier. How much more improbable, then, is an invasion of America, whose barrier is an entire ocean. If England could for centuries bask in "splendid isolation," how much more did America have to thank the Almighty for the Atlantic Ocean, a prayer of thanks it has sent up to heaven without interruption ever since. But does "splendid isolation" still hold true in modern times? Theodore Roosevelt, who played such a great part in breaking out of that isolation, wrote to his friend Rudyard Kipling that the English were indeed shortsighted isolationists, but not as shortsighted as the Americans. The difference was about as large as that between the width of the Channel and of the Atlantic Ocean. Because it is so large, the American people think that they are safe and have no responsibility for what happens in Europe.[1]

There were, however, Americans who were beginning to realize that this safety was no longer as reliable as it had been. Yet, although such understanding still required great force of imagination, in December 1914, the important magazine *Harper's Weekly* could print an elaborate report of an invasion of New York. In great detail it told how a hostile force approached the coast, defeated the American fleet, and landed 150,000 men on the Connecticut shore, and then rapidly occupied New York City. The hoax was not pointless, however, for in the Northeast, which means New England and New York State, a region with large maritime interests in the Atlantic, there were many who were already bold enough to think internationally.

In New York a National Security League was established in December 1914 with the aim of shaking the people out of their slumber and preparing the country for eventual war. A stream of propaganda was disseminated throughout the nation. Books and pamphlets appeared with such titles as *Defenseless America*, *The Invasion of America*, *America Fallen*, *The Sequence of the European War*, and the like. An important shock effect was produced by the translation of the pre-1914 book of the German general Friedrich von Bernhardi, *Deutschland und der nächste Krieg* (Germany and the Next War). This was a typical product of German super-nationalism mixed with Social-Darwinian ideas; it was typical of Germany and typical also of the period, full of heroic fantasies, with the famed national historian Heinrich von Treitschke as its chief source. It included chapters on war as a right and a duty, "War as a Biological Necessity" and "Peace Efforts Which Poison the Soul of the German People." The Christian religion was in fact a real "religion of battle," and pacifism an immoral endeavor. The book was very hostile to England but not to the United States; it even voiced a hope that Germany and the United States would work together, for they had no interests in conflict. But Germany had to become a world power or perish.[2]

The book did not appear on the American market by accident. The English propaganda service discovered what a striking proof it provided of German mentality. The National Security League, for which Germany was the real enemy imperiling American security, gleefully put it to use. That the real enemy of American security was Germany was a familiar idea in the circles around Theodore Roosevelt: America must stand by England in defense of the balance of power, which was being endangered worldwide by German expansion. In 1914 the idea became more timely than ever.

The big question now became whether America was ready. As early as October 1914, Representative Augustus P. Gardner, a son-in-law of Lodge, expressed serious anxiety about the state of the army and navy. America, he maintained, would not be ready if danger threatened. What he feared was not so much a direct attack upon the United States as that the country would not be strong enough to maintain the Monroe Doctrine against German and Japanese threats.

The new battle cry that became fashionable thanks to all these activities was the word "preparedness." It was not simply a plank in a political platform, but, as happens so often in America, a popular sentiment expressed with excitement and enthusiasm. For the time being Wilson stood aside from all this warlike bustle. His patriotism was not the martial kind. He could not believe, he declared in a discussion with House in November 1914, that Germany could present a threat to America. Even if it won the war, it would never be in a position to attack the United States. House warned him that Germany could call up a huge military force, but Wilson remained skeptical. He said that if it ever came to war, there would be time though to take the necessary preparations. "He talks as innocently as my little grandchild, Jane Tucker," wrote House in his diary.[3]

In his annual message to Congress of December 8, 1914, Wilson replied to his critics on defense. He used the classic argument: America was a peace-loving country and feared a standing army could become a danger to democracy. And no one could maintain that American independence was in danger. He believed in neutrality; he would not allow himself to be thrown off balance because some "nervous and excited" persons reacted so strongly to the war in Europe.[4]

Slowly, however, his opinions changed. In the course of the year 1915 public opinion became rapidly grimmer. War and rumors of war became a growing reality for the American public. Even in more moderate circles, there was talk of "preparedness." To be strong for peace became the American variant of the old dictum, *si vis pacem, para bellum* (If you want peace, prepare for war). "To have begun to prepare is on the whole a symptom of confidence," wrote Herbert Croly in *The New Republic*. And Lippmann in the same journal called for cool and defensible self-assurance.[5]

Wilson read *The New Republic*, but he was slow to be persuaded. House continued to press him. Just by being unready America exposed itself to German aggression, he said. House believed that a full eighty percent of the population now realized how dangerous the situation was.[6] In August 1915 Wilson was persuaded by these arguments, and he asked his secretaries of war and navy for reports and plans for defense. In October, he received these reports: the army had to be doubled and in addition a reserve army formed of 400,000 men. The fleet should be expanded by ten battleships, six battle-cruisers, a hundred submarines, and a vast number of smaller ships so that within a reasonable time it would be the equal of the British navy. Wilson approved the program, a bill was introduced, and a bitter struggle ensued in Congress. For, while the Northeast was ready for preparedness, a strong isolationism continued to be dominant in the rest of the country, particularly in the West.

In reality a struggle was being waged for the soul of America. Although Lippmann in his haughty way might talk of a strong but peace-loving America, and Wilson himself, by a strange paradox, might be becoming a pacifist advocate of preparedness, the question remained whether such a position was in fact possible. Could the national passions be held in check? Again the perpetual question arose: Can one be at the same time pure and responsible? Was Wilson aware of the paradox of his position? So a problem began, of which preparedness was only the first phase, but which would grow to much greater dimensions in 1917.

He began to expound and defend his changed viewpoint, and one can still feel the tension in his words in a speech in New York in November 1915: "We have it in mind to be prepared, but not for war, but only for defense, and with the thought constantly in our minds that the principles we hold most dear can be achieved by the slow processes of history only in the kindly and wholesome atmosphere of peace." He continued to be cautious, warning against panic: America was not threatened. He repeated the theme in his annual message of December 7. America was peace-loving, the great democracies were peace-loving and sought no conquests. But America had to protect its trade, and hence reinforcement of the army and navy were necessary. But, again, no panic: "I am sorry to say that the gravest threats against our national peace and safety have been uttered within our borders."[7]

But, however cautious Wilson continued to be, his turnabout caused nonetheless a flood of excitement. For the authentic realists in the Northeast, he did not go far enough, although they held off their criticism. But the great head wind of opposition came from the side of the pacifists, from the large number of those who believed in the tradition of neutrality and isolation. Pacifism fitted America; it was the sign and seal that the New World was specially chosen by providence. The war in Europe stimulated the pacifists' exertions. For them, America should not concern itself with the world but preach peace. This was a paradox that did not bother them. In the autumn of 1915 endeavors of many kinds were undertaken to reconcile the sides in conflict. As was to be expected, women took a leading part, for this was the time when the first feminist movements were on the march. The renowned feminist Jane Addams, who began social work in the slums of Chicago, traveled to Europe and attended the Women's Peace Congress in The Hague, which had been organized by the famed Dutch feminist Aletta Jacobs. Together the two friends traveled to the European capitals to present the resolutions of their congress to the men who still stood everywhere alone in power. Jacobs then accompanied Addams to America, where they had a long and difficult conversation with Lansing, who found their ideas impracticable. Jacobs was finally able to get to see Wilson. "He was very kind and manlike [it is not clear whether this was meant as a compliment] and gentlemanlike," she wrote in her Dutch-tinged English to Jane Addams. Later, in her memoirs, she told how she got the impression that he was a man who "cherished high ideals but would lack the force to achieve them if great obstacles ever arose." Furthermore, he knew much too little about Europe. But this was in fact wisdom after the event.[8]

Peace was the everyday topic of conversation in the autumn of 1915. Peace, peace, and there is no peace, to speak with the prophet Jeremiah. The oddest American peace enterprise was the pilgrimage of the famed automobile manufacturer Henry Ford. With an assemblage of all kinds of innocent folk, including many of the women peace activists, he sailed to Europe on a rented liner to put an end to the war: "We are going to try to get the boys out of their trenches and back to their homes by Christmas Day." There was not much in the way of results. The ship (soon nicknamed the "Ship of Fools") got no further than Scandinavia. Ford learned something from the episode, for he was a practical man. On his return to New York, he said that he had thought that the bankers and munitions manufacturers had been responsible, but now he saw that it was the peoples themselves who wanted to slaughter each other. If this remark had come to Wilson's attention, he might have found it sobering.[9]

But American pacifism, as we have said, was not merely the hobby of individuals; it rested upon deeper forces in society and had important adherents in Congress. Members of Congress from the South and the West, populists in their origin and inspired by suspicions of the capitalist Northeast, began to turn against Wilson once he began to preach preparedness. Bryan became their principal spokesman, and he trumpeted everywhere that the army reform was a capitalist plan directed against the people. Bryan continued to have great influence, which Wilson had to take into account.[10]

Wilson believed that he could continue to dream his dream of a peace undefiled by the pressures of preparedness. Obviously this drew upon him a great deal of criticism from the idealists who did not have to carry any responsibility. The preachers were in the lead among them. A preacher in Chicago wrote that the time had come for the followers of the Prince of Peace to remain true and cease their hypocrisy. Fortunately for Wilson, he too knew his Bible, which has many things to say. He found a fitting reply in Ezekiel 33:6: "But if the watchman see the sword come, and blow not the trumpet, and the people be not warned, if the sword come, and take any person from among them . . . his blood will I require at the watchman's hand."[11]

But the watchman had something quite different on his mind at this time. Just then, in December 1915, he was busy with his wedding and honeymoon. This meant that he was absent for weeks at a time, just when the struggle over preparedness broke out in full fury. Senator Lodge, who hated Wilson from the bottom of his heart, wrote to his friend Roosevelt that Congress now had a peaceful vacation because the president's "vulgar" marriage meant no public business could be conducted for a fortnight.[12] The opposition, left and right, gloated over the supposed weakness of Wilson, who gave no leadership.

But, by the beginning of January, Wilson was again at his post and discovered that immense resistance had grown in Congress against the plans for rearmament. In this critical situation, Wilson again decided to go over the heads of the members of Congress to the people. It was a step very typical of him. He was by character the man in charge, a democrat in words but one who was quickly annoyed when the legislature opposed him. He had therefore developed the myth of the good people whose rulers are evil. It was a myth that he repeatedly called upon, as we shall see. It was a theory more democratic in appearance than in reality, however, for it was Wilson, not the people, who decided what the people should want.

At the end of January he began a speaking tour through the Midwest, where the resistance was strongest. In nine days he gave eleven speeches to explain his views. He enjoyed such oratorical activity, for a crowd is not as ready to contradict as a legislature. In his speeches we meet again the familiar themes of America's glory in service and her calling to mediate. "Our chief interest is not in the rights of property, but in the rights of man." The people would understand him, because the peoples are more peace-loving than governments.[13]

But, however fine it all sounded, he was not promising peace at any price. He recognized his dilemma and repeatedly explained it. People say to him, he told his audiences: "We are relying on you, Mr. President, to keep us out of this war, but we are relying upon you, Mr. President, to keep the honor of the nation unstained." Wilson warned that a time might come when it would be impossible for him to do both.[14] He hoped that it would not come to that, for there was no immediate danger. But it could arise at any moment, and then America must be ready.

For all his love of peace, Wilson had to face the fact of war. He was ensnared in his dilemma, and therefore, despite all his humanity, he could not escape stirring up nationalist feelings. Yet, complex of personality as he was, what he did was not wholly against his character. He was half a pacifist, true, but he also had martial traits. He readily employed national symbols. He would point to the brilliant colors of the American flag and declaim that the red symbolized the warm blood of each hero over whom it waved, and the pure white the peace of his soul. Above them the blue field of stars: "Those stars which exemplify for us that glorious galaxy of the Union—bodies of free men banded together to vindicate the rights of mankind."[15]

Indeed, Wilson did want to serve the world, the whole wide world, but not without making distinctions, not without American self-exaltation. America was great in its humility, a sort of *servus servorum Dei*, "servant of the servants of God," like the emperors in the Middle Ages. Its power was used in the service of mankind, but, it must be noted, he added that its power must be the greatest of any nation. In St. Louis, he told his hearers in the American heartland that the American navy must become "incomparably the greatest in the world."[16] No wonder that in Great Britain suspicion continued regarding what he meant by freedom of the seas.

Wilson's tour apparently strengthened his political position, although this is difficult to establish exactly. But opposition in Congress remained strong, and if the rearmament bill became law, it was due not so much to his oratory as to the fact that on an important point he climbed down a peg. The states did not want the National Guard to be totally absorbed in a new Continental Army, and he met them halfway on this issue. This compromise caused a break between Wilson and his secretary of war, Lindley M. Garrison, who submitted his resignation at the beginning of February. As his successor the president named the former mayor of Cleveland, Newton D. Baker, a man from the ranks of the reformers.

The proposals were adopted during the summer after long discussions. The army was more than doubled, and whole squadrons were added to the fleet. In addition another law was passed to increase the merchant marine sizably under the supervision of a United States Shipping Board. America had to be strong in order to remain neutral, and probably also so as to be able to mediate.

II

Wilson emerged with greater strength from the struggle over preparedness. For the moment, in fact, he seemed in a position to maintain a balance between peace and national honor, saving both for his neutral country. At the same time he offered prospects to those who continued to hope for a better world after the war. In the same spring of 1916, in a speech at the end of May before the most influential peace organization, the League to Enforce Peace, he came out officially for a postwar international organization.

This League was not at all an assemblage of abstract, muddleheaded idealists out of touch with reality. To the contrary, the most important leaders of the country were members, statesmen and politicians, even at first the dyed-in-the-wool realists like Henry Cabot Lodge, whom we have slowly come to know as a vehement supporter of the Allied cause. The League's chairman was former president William Howard Taft, a practical man of great integrity.

The League was able to bring so many people under its banner because it had emphatically separated the ideal of an international peace organization from current political goals. It did not exist in order to stimulate mediation, but only made plans for the future. What it proposed was to consolidate international arbitration, which before the war had been discussed incidentally and bilaterally, in a permanent organization, with a court and a Council of Conciliation, and also certainly with the possibility of economic and military sanctions to protect peace effectively. These were ideas that sounded bold enough, but remained quite vague. The big question was and remained who would guarantee the peace by power, and how far America, when it came to the point of acting, would in fact be ready to join in guaranteeing an international order.

What was at stake, the more militant realists asserted, was more than peace by itself. Peace without law—which meant international "law and order"—was not real peace. Theodore Roosevelt had contended as much when he received the Nobel Prize in 1910 in Oslo. He had on that occasion spoken out strongly for a League of Peace, which he argued could not exist without the use of the force of one or another "international police power." For the time being, what was needed was a combination "of those great nations which sincerely desire peace." It calls to mind the ideas of his cousin, Franklin Roosevelt, about the "four policemen," the great powers.[17]

Such a vision expressed a clear-cut realism, even pessimism. Lodge, who was Roosevelt's best friend and Wilson's worst foe, thought in the same terms. He gave a very interesting speech in June 1915 on the theme "Force and Peace." Peace, he contended, cannot be brought about by fine words from those who stand on the side and bear no responsibility. Peace was a cause of the democratic countries acting together, and could be guaranteed only by the force that the united nations were ready to devote to it.

It is important to pay close attention to these ideas of Roosevelt and Lodge, which contributed in a fundamental way to the debate over the future. The former president and the senator had a much more realistic vision of mankind than Wilson; their league of nations would not rest upon human goodness but upon human selfishness. The speech that Lodge gave in June 1915 seems to have been aimed particularly at Wilson, certainly at the end when he defended his idea of peace through strength as far better than the idea "that war can be stopped by language, by speech-making, by denunciations of war and laudations of peace, in which all men agree. . . . We cannot possibly succeed in any measure if we mix up plans for future peace with attempts to end the war now raging."[18] Since he also used the word "utopia," some historians have accused him of later reversing his ideas, wrongly, we see, because the issue for him was a different one.[19]

The difference between the thinking of Lodge and of Wilson went very deep. Lodge was in the first place a man who always put American interests in the forefront and made all the country's international responsibilities subordinate to them. Deeper still, his idealism—for it was certainly a kind of idealism too—was the idealism not of the future but of tradition, not of human rights and reconciliation but of duty and loyalty. It was a fundamentally different cast of mind than Wilson's optimism.

Realists prefer to distinguish things, to separate the present and the future, the real and the ideal. Idealists see them instead in their interconnection. But, so far as the difference of mind between Lodge and Wilson went, it was only emerging in the the spring of 1916. It was therefore possible for them to sit amicably together on a single stage on May 27, 1916, at a meeting of the League to Enforce Peace. Taft had invited his successor in the White House to speak, and Wilson had gladly accepted, for he wanted very much to make an official declaration of his ideas about this point. Many different things were demanding his attention at the same time that spring: House was receiving fewer replies from the Allies to his efforts to bring about mediation, but Wilson and House continued to believe in it stubbornly. The *Sussex* crisis had just passed. Relations with England were becoming more and more difficult. The struggle over preparedness was still raging furiously. The presidential elections in the autumn were casting their shadow before them. Wilson therefore placed considerable importance on his speech; he even had the feeling, as he wrote House, that it was the most important he would ever give. What suggestions could his faithful friend make to help him?[20] House sent him some material, a few quotations from English statesmen about a future world order, and then his own draft in which he laid down the principle of the necessity of openness in international relations. Had the nations openly said in 1914 what they planned to do, then war would not have resulted. He urged that nations, like individuals, should be bound by moral norms.[21]

Lansing also contributed some advice, which was more cautious than House's. His legal mind saw many difficulties in an undertaking that had not even yet been mapped out. He was afraid of permanent involvement of the United States, and he could not imagine how "force" could be legally regulated. Yet he did believe in something like the outlawing of an "offending nation."[22]

Wilson gave his big speech on May 27 before an audience of some two thousand persons. Traces of House's advice are to be found in it, but he was a man of greater vision than House. Its argument was an example of Wilson's own oratorical rhetoric and his own idealism. Unlike Lodge, he could not distinguish present and future. He began with a discussion of what gripped everyone's mind, the great war in Europe. He still remained impartial with regard to it, he said. "With its causes and objects we are not concerned. The obscure fountains from which its stupendous flood has burst forth we are not interested to search or explore."

Idealists do not wish to separate but to bring together, from top to bottom. Wilson had an understanding of the dark, irrational element in war, what he called "the obscure fountains." That was precisely why he could not choose sides and angered both sides at once. And, it must be added, he made his own position in the future a difficult one.

The war was an ordeal, he continued, but probably also a chastening, a lesson that henceforth law and not one's own self-interest must prevail. The nations must work together to this end. He developed three large but still vague principles to be followed. In the first place, the right of the peoples to self-determination. Second, the principle that small states have as much right to respect for their sovereignty as large countries. Third, that the world had the right to be freed from any disturbance of the peace arising from aggression.

For this reason, he went on, the United States was ready to take part in an association of the peoples. America would collaborate by mediating, he promised. "Our interest is only in peace and its future guarantees." For this reason there had to be a league of nations with two great goals: freedom of the seas and the prevention of aggression. But instead of speaking of "force" in this regard, as Roosevelt and Lodge had done, he held the view that the best means to prevent war from arising out of disputes lay in "full submission of the causes to the opinion of the world."[23]

In principle Wilson's ideas about a new world order were already present in this speech, even if in their infancy. He began to believe that there existed something like a world public opinion which would be "a virtual guarantee of territorial integrity and political independence."

Thus, for the first time the old principle of isolation was officially abandoned by the head of the American government. It sounded incredible, certainly to European ears. Spring-Rice reported at this time to his minister about the League. There was a great deal of talk about American participation in the League, he wrote, but when the time comes to take action, everyone will hesitate. The president can promise everything, but Congress will never support him if no American interests are at stake.[24]

Wilson, who could so easily soar above reality with words, was able, however, to give a new twist to the problem. On the same day, May 30, that the English ambassador sent his highly skeptical report, the president gave a Memorial Day speech in which he took up the question. He was remaining true to Washington's warning against "entangling alliances," he said. But what he was now proposing was a "disentangling alliance," which he defined as "an alliance which would disentangle the peoples of the world from those combinations in which they seek their own separate and private interests and unite the people of the world to preserve the peace of the world upon a basis of common right and justice. There is liberty there, not limitation."[25]

Wilson's speech called forth a variety of reactions. In progressive circles he earned a great deal of approval and even praise. The man who had preached preparedness had remained true to high principles. Walter Lippmann, still young and much more optimistic than he became in later years, lauded the president exuberantly in *The New Republic*; he found it very inspiring that Americans were giving up their isolationism not in order to participate in the intrigues of diplomats but in order to internationalize world politics. This was the greatest step forward "ever made in the development of international morality." Wilson and House were "considerable men," filled with courage and imagination.[26]

But among conservative Republicans there was far less enthusiasm. Wilson's coupling of mediation and the league of nations aroused strong opposition, and it would remain so until the bitter end. The leaders of the Allies admitted that they were upset. How did Wilson ever think he was going to mediate if he was so insensitive to the moral implications of their struggle for democracy? What pride was it that inspired him? Spring-Rice wrote in a tone of contempt: the good Samaritan did not cross to the other side in order then to place before the authorities in Jericho a plan for better protection of the public highway.[27]

III

The year 1916 was an election year, as we must not forget. Wilson himself certainly did not forget it, even though it would be a quite wrong evaluation of the man to call his peace dreams an election maneuver. But, let me repeat, idealists do not make distinctions, their world is essentially not split but whole, everything involves everything else. Wilson was not against practical politics, he was not against being in business and making money, and he could even play the game of politics with considerable skill, but they were all just material things, mundane necessities in a world in which the spiritual principle was dominant, the apex of such activity.

In 1916 he engaged in practical politics and hoped for reelection. But it was and remained emphatically progressive politics, even more so than before. Wilson now went much further than befitted his original liberal ideals of the New Freedom. He approached very closely the New Nationalism of Roosevelt and Croly. This was not at all an accident. The former supporters of the Progressive party of 1912 were a group of voters worth having; they had been left out in the cold after Roosevelt returned to the Republican party. Wilson clearly adapted his policy to this new situation.

A whole range of reform measures in which the government concerned itself with society were now adopted, as we have seen. The nomination of the humane judge, Louis D. Brandeis, "the people's lawyer," to the Supreme Court, where he would be the first Jewish justice, was well received by many, although opposition from the conservative side was so strong that the Senate gave its approval only after months of furious debate, marred by occasional anti-Semitic insults.

The Progressives of 1912 ended up for the most part in Wilson's camp and thereby finally in the Democratic party. The "great swap" of 1912 was complete: the Democrats became the party of government involvement and social legislation, the Republicans came out for "free enterprise" and individualism. This development would be crowned by the New Deal of Franklin Roosevelt, in whose brain trust a considerable number of former Progressives played a part.

Theodore Roosevelt was the man who was largely responsible for the crippling of the Republican party in 1916. He had split the party in 1912, and now he thought he could return to its ranks not as a prodigal son but as a victor, a candidate for the presidency. At the same time he organized a second convention of his old Progressive party, not with the intention of falling back into separatism but in order to exert the greatest pressure upon the Republicans. This sly game went completely awry. The old bosses would not forgive Roosevelt's betrayal of 1912, and they also understood that his noisy bellicosity was not popular with the voters, the large majority of whom stood behind Wilson's policy of neutrality. Essentially the American people do not like running risks or going to extremes. Down to our own time this has led to the defeat of far-out candidates, such as Goldwater on the right and McGovern on the left. The Republicans in 1916 sought a candidate in the middle and found him in the person of a Supreme Court justice, Charles Evans Hughes. Hughes, who was five years younger than Wilson, had become well known as a good governor of the state of New York. He was very much like Wilson himself—a hardworking intellectual, a moderate reformer, an incorruptible moralist. He was outwardly quite different, however, a heavyset, bearded, and dignified man of stately bearing. But he was different in more than bearing. Hughes totally lacked Wilson's charisma, his poetic impulse. In contrast to the president, he was an authentic lawyer, a man who preferred meticulous analysis to wide-ranging dreams.

At the Republican convention in Chicago, Hughes was nominated after three roll calls. Roosevelt had not had any chance of winning the nomination, although he maneuvered with his Progressive convention, which met simultaneously in the same city. He tried to talk his old supporters into supporting the candidacy of his archconservative friend Lodge, but they did not buy it. They wanted Roosevelt himself, but it was obvious that he could not run, and finally he asked them to join ranks behind Hughes. That was the end of the Progressive party, which broke apart in sobs of pain and easily fell into the comforting and welcoming arms of the new Nationalist, Woodrow Wilson. The Democratic platform, which was written by Wilson in person, was filled with social programs and emphasized neutrality and the demand for a league of nations.

How popular the policy of neutrality was became clear at the Democratic convention, which was held in St. Louis. Wilson had recommended making "Americanism" the theme of the campaign, but the delegates had applauded the loudest when neutrality was mentioned. The whole convention was another magnificent example of American political culture, as an almost erotic intertwining of rhetoric and emotion, with several daily episodes of orgasms of acclamation, bringing a whole crowd into ecstasy. Wilson himself was not present, as it was not at that period considered proper for candidates to come in person to push their cause. Others did their glorifying for them.

The convention began with the keynote address of a former governor of New York, Martin H. Glynn. He realized he was touching a responsive chord when he first mentioned neutrality, and he played upon it in masterly fashion. His speech became a crass recital of questions and answers: "What did we do? What did we do? We didn't go to war!" This went on for minutes at a time. Fragments of meaningless oratory floated upward like large and empty balloons.

A following speaker, Senator Ollie M. James of Kentucky, a true hero of the oratorical craft, continued in the same vein. He sang the praises of Wilson's policy of neutrality; without making a single American child an orphan or a single American mother a widow, without the firing of a single rifle, or the spilling of a single drop of blood, it had extracted recognition of American rights from the most warlike country in the world. A demonstration followed lasting at least twenty minutes. Wilson was sanctified as the apostle of peace. James described the president arriving in heaven on Judgment Day with the "accusing picture" of Henri Danger, "Christ on the Battlefield," in his hand: "I can see him with the white light streaming upon his head and hear the Master say 'Blessed are the peacemakers, for they shall be called the children of God.'" Wilson was then nominated by unanimous vote. The demonstration that followed lasted three-quarters of an hour.[28]

The prospects of Wilson's reelection were not very bad in the summer. The *Sussex* crisis had been brought to a favorable end. In the conflict with England over the blacklist of American companies doing business with Germany, the president had stuck to his guns. Social legislation brought him the support of the Progressives. The only shadow on his path was a serious labor conflict that broke out in June on the railroads. The workers demanded an eight-hour working day with the same wage that they had been receiving for a ten-hour day and extra pay for overtime. The presidents of the railroads refused point-blank to meet these demands, so that a general strike threatened. The labor union set it for September 4. It would be an immense catastrophe at a time when almost all traffic was handled by rail, and it would also damage Wilson's chances of election.

The president attempted to mediate. During August he held long, intense discussions with the managers and the unions. The compromise that he proposed—introduction of the eight-hour day, but establishment of a commission to examine the other demands—was accepted by the unions but not by the companies. Wilson turned then to Congress, which supported the president by a large majority and speedily adopted a law (the Adams Act) introducing the eight-hour working day as of January 1, 1917. Wilson signed it almost at once, on September 2, so that a strike was averted.

Wilson thereby demonstrated that he could be not only an idealist but also a very practical and hard-nosed political negotiator. His action certainly won him a great deal of support among the workers but brought the business world into opposition. The elections took on more of the appearance of a conflict of principle between labor and capital, between progressives and conservatives. After Wilson signed the eight-hour day law, almost all contributions to his election campaign from the business world ceased. But he received more and more support from intellectuals. An influential journal like *The New Republic*, which originally had been friendly toward Roosevelt, now came out openly in favor of Wilson. Editor Walter Lippmann was invited by Wilson to advise him. Lippmann and many other progressives pressed the president to lead a campaign of principles, to run as a liberal against conservatives. It did not have to be said twice. Principles were Wilson's meat and potatoes.

In his speeches Wilson presented himself as a strong progressive, who in four years had "come very near carrying out the platform of the Progressive party as well as our own; for we are also Progressives."[29] Two major points dominated his campaign: "Progressivism and Peace." The issue was between the elite and the people, he said. "The United States has now to choose whether it will have a government for the people or a government for the special interests."[30]

This was probably not completely fair to the Republican party, whose problem was that it did not know itself what it was and what it wanted. There were still some former Progressives who had returned to the Republican ranks, and the quarrels between the two wings of the party sometimes became very bitter. Hughes, caught between them in a position to which he was not accustomed, made what were probably inevitable errors. He was won over by the "bosses" in California, angering the former Progressives. This did him great harm, for their leader, Hiram Johnson, running for a seat in the United States Senate, was a redoubtable politician who was not to be trifled with (as Wilson too would find out later). Hughes lost California and with it the election.

Hughes was a weak candidate, a man who did not live up to the great expectations for him. To be sure, he was incorruptible and clear-headed, but he lacked warmth and enthusiasm. He spoke so badly that Wilson never replied to his attacks, saying that it was a good rule not to murder someone who has committed suicide. Wilson campaigned with the skill that came from experience. He knew exactly whom he should hate and whom he should love. When the venomous Irish agitator Jeremiah O'Leary sent him a telegram containing the most ugly accusations, Wilson happily made it public along with his reply: "Your telegram received. I would feel deeply mortified to have you or anybody like you vote for me. Since you have access to many disloyal Americans and I have not I will ask you to convey this message to them."[31] It was an imaginative political stroke.

But in the end it was Wilson's stress upon neutrality that was decisive beyond question. He returned constantly to it, accusing the Republicans of seeking war. He was smart enough not to mention Roosevelt by name, but dropped hints in his direction and thus saddled the Republicans with the Rough Rider's noisy bellicosity.

Wilson promised peace. He was in the same situation as Franklin Roosevelt twenty-four years later. He promised peace so far as it was in his power, but not unconditionally. He preferred to describe the European war as a foreign conflict with obscure causes and obscure goals, a distinctively European affair that America should stay out of. America wanted to fight only if it knew what it was fighting for, and that was not for "the rights of property or of national ambition, but for the rights of mankind."[32] The time would certainly come when America would be involved in a world order, but he hoped that it would happen only after the war.

The peace visions of the president were broad and vague. They were therefore vigorously supported by Bryan. Not one to hold a grudge, he sallied forth to support the president. His backing was of essential importance because his voice carried authority in the West. In the Northeast and Midwest, in the great industrial states like New York, Pennsylvania, Ohio, and Michigan, the Republicans were dominant, so that only one of them, Ohio, in the end fell to Wilson.

The hatred of the Republican leaders for Wilson was intense. Even levelheaded and honorable leaders like Taft and Root gave signs of their deep scorn for the Democratic candidate. In private correspondence, Taft called him "a reckless hypocrite" and an opportunist "who has no convictions that he would not barter at once for votes." Root claimed he was disgusted by the hypocrisy and humbug of this government; he had never seen such an "unscrupulous and dishonest president" as Wilson. If this was the reaction of such sober persons as Taft and Root, it is easy to understand how men such as Roosevelt and Lodge, inflamed by hatred, denounced the hypocrite in the White House. Wilson's administration, wrote Lodge, had "debauched public sentiment, lowered and disintegrated the American spirit." Another four years of Wilson would be a disaster! To vote for him meant moral degradation.[33] Roosevelt carried off the prize for denunciation. He found Wilson "far more dangerous than poor, silly, emotionally sincere Bryan." Wilson was "as insincere and cold-blooded an opportunist as we have ever had in the Presidency."[34]

Hatred and slander belong to politics and to democracy, which is a system of unvarnished humanity; and they belong of course to elections. The campaign of slanders that was unleashed against Wilson in 1916 was fierce and widespread. Naturally the question of Mrs. Peck turned up once more. Adultery was a delightful subject for gossipers, although the gutter press had not yet sunk to its present levels of insinuation. According to these accounts, the first Mrs. Wilson had died of a broken heart, or her husband had thrown her downstairs, and so on. Newspaper reporters who wanted to go after the private lives of their victims stopped at nothing. It is difficult, however, to say how much damage was done by this nonsense.

Shortly before the end of the campaign, an ugly encounter took place between Wilson and Lodge. They had become gamecocks facing each other, less and less ready for reconciliation. Lodge accused Wilson of having added a postscript to the second *Lusitania* note that had deprived it of its character as an ultimatum by offering Germany the prospect of arbitration. Wilson denied this, and he was literally correct, but not in reality. Under pressure from Bryan, he had in fact left open in a postscript to the *first* (not the second) *Lusitania* note the possibility of discussion. He sidestepped Lodge's accusation with a piece of obfuscatory subterfuge, but Lodge had been really correct in his accusation. From that moment it was barely possible for them to meet face to face. Shortly afterwards, Wilson refused to attend a ceremony for no other reason than that Lodge would also be there. The enmity boiling up then would have great consequences a few years later.[35]

The election was very tense, a neck-and-neck race. In that period it took somewhat longer than now before the results came in, especially from the West. During the evening Hughes seemed to have won, for almost all the large cities in the East had voted for him. The newspapers reported his election. Wilson did not officially concede, although he had little hope left when he went early to bed. But the loyal Tumulty remained awake, and even when he heard that Hughes had won, he declared quietly that Wilson would still come out ahead, for the West had not yet been heard from.[36] The next day he turned out to have been right. It was the West, the traditionally Republican region, which had voted for Wilson. The fusion of Populists and Progressives there had carried the day, although the majority for Wilson was very thin. The final count showed the president with 9,129,606 votes and 8,538,221 for Hughes, that is, 49.3 percent to 46 percent; in electoral votes, Wilson had 277 to Hughes's 254.

In retrospect the picture was surprising. Hughes won the entire Northeast, including all the big cities. This was probably due to the votes of the Irish, who were bitter over Wilson's pro-British policies, especially when the Irish question became urgent after the Easter uprising in Dublin, and the votes of most Catholic immigrants, who could not forgive Wilson his support of the Mexican revolution. But Wilson won the whole of the traditionally Democratic South and most of the western states. He had reestablished the old agrarian coalition directed against the financial and industrial Northeast that dated back to before the Civil War. His victory embodied therefore a nostalgic element of resistance to modern times. This was an ironic fact, for at the same time his coalition was the basis for the renewed Democratic party of Franklin Roosevelt, which fifteen years later would lead the country into the modern era.

All political analysts are agreed in any case that the principal reason for Wilson's victory was his neutrality policy. "He kept us out of war." This was an even more ironic fact, for he would not continue the policy for long. He personally felt the obligations that flowed from it, and held stubbornly to his peace policy. The old attempts at mediation, which House had sought with his missions to the belligerent capitals, seemed to have failed. But, if the Allies did not want to cooperate, then he would engage in mediation on his own. This became his great task during the coming months.

Hughes, who had been so close to victory, was deeply disappointed. Only fourteen days afterwards could he bring himself to admit his defeat officially. The telegram that he sent to Wilson was, the recipient quipped, "a little moth-eaten when it got here but quite legible."[37]

EIGHTEEN

Even so doth God protect us if we be Virtuous and wise
. . . by the Soul Only the nations shall be great and free.
    —William Wordsworth, September 1802

THE FINAL MEDIATION

IN 1916 EUROPE STILL SEEMED far away to Americans. It was still possible for them to keep busy with their own concerns, such as the elections in November. All the while the Old World was in the grip of a death struggle worse than any it had ever known. At the end of 1916 the madness had been going on for more than two years and there was no prospect of its ending. There had been fighting all spring and summer, at Verdun, on the Somme, in Galicia, and in Romania, at the cost of millions of young lives. In this disastrous third year of the "Great War," which was not yet called the "First World War," neither side had gotten any closer to victory. New generals, new ministers in government, swore more doggedly than ever that the struggle had to be fought to the bitter end. In what we may call "self-fulfilling profanation," it was proclaimed that such immense sacrifices would not be in vain!

In Germany at the end of August the supreme commander, General Von Falkenhayn, was replaced by General Von Hindenburg, the hero of the Eastern Front, who was the model of steadfast self-assurance and German fidelity. At his side was General Von Ludendorff, a strategist whose brilliance was matched by his insolence. Von Hindenburg and Von Ludendorff had been put in their new posts by Chancellor Von Bethmann Hollweg, but they soon used their military authority to dominate the whole range of German policy. From the start their plan was to conduct *"rücksichtslos"* warfare, literally "reckless" warfare, which we may loosely translate as "victory at any price." They began at once to press for the use of the perilous strategy of unlimited submarine warfare. Bethmann's argument that it would bring America into the war made no impression on their foolhardy determination, and they shrugged their shoulders at the possibility that other neutrals might come into the war. In December, when Romania was defeated in a swift campaign, they declared that they now had enough divisions left over to handle the Dutch and Danish armies. They did not want to wait any longer, and the cautious chancellor could obtain no more than a delay.

The Allied leaders were at least as determined to play all-or-nothing. There were some politicians who began to be troubled and suffered under the responsibilities they bore, but the generals argued that it made sense to continue the war. Sir William Robertson, the British commander, declared that the campaign of the coming spring would be begun with increased knowledge and prestige and a definite moral superiority on the Allied side. The General Staff, wrote Sir Maurice Hankey, is so intolerably complacent that it will not listen to any outside opinion, and meanwhile they are bleeding the country to death.[1]

> Yes . . . and the War won't end for at least two years;
> But we 've got stacks of men . . . I'm blind with tears,
>   Staring into the dark.[2]

This protesting voice was that of the poet Siegfried Sassoon, but he was only one person. Did he speak in the name of the people? It was not only the politicians, it turned out, who swore to hold out to the end. It is a melancholy mistake, but one made not only by President Wilson, to believe that the peoples were more peace-loving than the governments, or that democracies are more peace-loving than dictatorships. To be sure, there were those in every country who began to come to their senses; they came especially from among the left parties, the Liberals and Socialists. In England even the old Conservative statesman Lord Lansdowne, who had lost a son at the front, raised his voice against the madness. He wondered how long it could go on: "We are slowly but surely killing off the best of the male population of these islands."[3]

The English government was as deaf to such protests, however, as was the German, for otherwise it would fall from office. That happened toward the end of the year to the Asquith government because it was accused of not conducting the war vigorously enough. David Lloyd George, who was called the wizard of Wales, was named the new prime minister of Great Britain. Capricious and elusive in character, he was probably the most gifted and most perverse politician England possessed in these years. It is uncertain how much he was driven by conviction and how much by ambition. According to his foes, he was totally untrustworthy and irresponsible, but he had an infallible sense of the people's mood and played on it with a masterly touch; he was characterized by Beatrice Webb as a man of "heroic demagogy."[4] He did not believe in peace, although in the spring he had given the naïve Colonel House the impression that he was very favorable to Wilson's mediation proposal. He spoke with the voice of the British people when in the autumn he declared in an interview that the war had to be fought "to the finish—to a knock-out." Neutrals with good intentions and "humanitarians" with fine motives must realize that in the present state of the war, there could be no consideration of interference from outside.[5] This language—and the sharpest intrigues—opened his way to power. In December he became the head of a war cabinet that included many of his old Conservative opponents and few of his Liberal friends. It had only one aim—to win the war.

Erratic, elusive gambler with men and power that he was, Lloyd George was nonetheless convinced that the war was going badly and that every resource had to be committed to it. His greatness rested on the his being not only a visionary but also a realist. England, he understood, could not go on as things stood; even in purely economic terms, the sacrifices called for could not be sustained. The German submarine campaign was becoming steadily more effective. In the late months of 1916, an average of 350,000 tons of shipping was sunk each month. Supplies were running dangerously short, warned Admiral Jellicoe. The costs were prohibitive, five million pounds a day! The country was becoming more and more dependent on American loans. The economist John Maynard Keynes warned in a report: "It is hardly an exaggeration to say that in a few months the American executive and the American public will be in a position to dictate to this country on matters that affect us more nearly than them."[6]

This was no idle threat, for Wilson was playing with the idea. What did he want more than to be able to dictate terms, especially to dictate a good peace? And American financial circles began to watch anxiously how their risky and gruesome investments were going. The director of the Federal Reserve Bank asked whether the United States had the bull by the horns, or the bull the country. He replied with a pun: "In this case, it is John Bull who would have us by the tail."[7] Americans began to fear they were too deeply involved in the Allied cause, and at the end of November the Federal Reserve Board with Wilson's approval issued a warning against investment in inadequately covered war loans. The result was a serious drop in English shares on the New York Stock Exchange and great alarm in England and France. But this did not mean that Wilson could now compel the belligerents to accept his mediation. American diplomacy was too weak and uncertain to be able to exploit successfully their country's strong economic position. In the end America did what the English wanted; it shipped arms, it gave up export to the Central Powers, and it entered the war, but, as a Dutch historian has written, "all *without* gaining anything for its money in the form of guarantees about eventual disarmament and the nature of the future peace."[8]

It was Wilson's opportunity and his misfortune that he was an outsider, who sought to keep detached and yet constantly involved himself in the great conflict by his mediation efforts. He wanted to make peace, out of humane considerations that were probably not entirely free of personal vanity, but how was it possible to speak of peace initiatives without mentioning specific terms?

As we have seen, Wilson waited until after the elections to come to grips with the problem. He told House that he wanted to send a note to the belligerents "demanding that the war cease." If he did nothing now, America would inevitably be drawn into the conflict by the German submarine campaign.[9] House was critical of the idea, for he was not actually opposed to war with Germany. A mediation proposal, he feared, would be an insult to the Allies. And he did not want to to undertake another journey, as Wilson suggested; he would rather go to Hades, he said.[10]

Wilson would not be diverted from his resolution, however. At the end of November he put his ideas down on paper. First he wrote a kind of preamble for a peace note; it is probably one of the most interesting pieces Wilson ever wrote. It was conceived in the first instance for himself and was so frank that he decided not to make it public by either speech or writing. In it he gave voice to all his personal conceptions. War, he thought, used to be an exercise in heroism, a "national excursion . . . to vary the monotony of a lazy, tranquil existence . . . with brilliant battles lost and won." But in the "contest of systematical destruction" that had been waged for the past two years, no one gained glory and the imagination struggled to comprehend "untold human suffering."

Both sides were in the right, which meant that they were more truly in the wrong. Both German militarism and British "navalism" had to be abolished. The greatest danger would follow if one side gained a victory; this would lead as always to humiliation, and humiliation to revenge. The best example was the Franco-Prussian War of 1870–1871, in which Germany had taken Alsace-Lorraine from France, which thereupon was impelled to seek revenge. "We see it abundantly demonstrated in the pages of history that the decisive victories and defeats are seldom the conclusive ones. One Sedan brings on another, and victory is an intoxicant that fires the national brain and leaves a craving for more."

A lasting peace could only be brought about after both sides were exhausted. "The present war, with its unprecedented human waste and suffering and its drain of material resources presents an unparalleled opportunity for the statesmen of the world to make such a peace possible." Only if both sides understood the uselessness of their sacrifices would there be a psychological basis for such a peace. "Deprived of glory, war loses all its charm; when the only attribute of it is suffering, then it is something to be detested." After Verdun, what did glory mean? This worst war in history should serve "far-sighted statesmen" as an object lesson for the future, "by bringing it to a close with the objects of each group of belligerents still unaccomplished and all the magnificent sacrifices on both sides gone for naught."[11]

We have here a full-length self-portrait of Wilson, the complete outsider. All his traits are present: the greatness, the humanity, the naïveté; the wisdom, the clear and simple insight; and the utter lack of comprehension of the real situation or of insight into people's deepest impulses. Not a word about the causes of the war, either in general or specifically. German militarism and British "navalism" are equated as the two great evils. The peoples involved in struggle and gripped by emotions are urged to remain calm so that they can understand that all their "magnificent sacrifices" (his very words!) will have been for naught. We dare not think about the immense storm this piece would have caused had Wilson made it public.

Immediately afterward Wilson drafted a note to be sent to the warring powers. Its central concept remained the same: "Upon a triumph which overwhelms and humiliates cannot be laid the foundations of peace and equality and good will." Now, however, he prudently prefaced this argument with others. The neutrals were falling into an increasingly intolerable position, from which they derived a right to participate in discussions. What was really at stake? What were the war aims of the belligerents? The leaders of both sides had declared that they were not trying to destroy their opponents, that they were not seeking conquests, even that they were fighting for the rights of small and weak nations.

Wilson thus returned to the argument that there was little difference between the two sides, so that the United States had a right to play a part. After all, America had the same aims and was ready to become a member of a league of nations to guarantee these aims. Finally, he suggested a conference with representatives of both the belligerents and the neutrals in order to achieve peace before it was too late.[12]

It was the same old story, then, provided we understand that, after a summer in which German submarine warfare spared Americans but the British acted with increasing insolence, Wilson now took a much more neutral stand than in the spring. He would mediate, nothing more. He could not think about anything else. He told House to come at once, and his friend arrived in Washington two days later. Wilson read the statement he had prepared, not the first one, which he kept for himself, but the second one. But House again had difficulty with Wilson's attitude of neutrality. The Allies would be outraged, he said, when they read that the causes of the war were trifling and that the aims of both sides were similar. He advised a delay before acting.[13]

Lansing was even more critical. He believed that the plan would go nowhere, nor, for that matter, did he want it to go anywhere. America must take part on the good side, the Allied, "for we are a democracy." But if Germany accepted Wilson's proposal and the Allies did not, he foresaw a danger that America might end up on the wrong side.

Wilson agreed to amend his plans a bit, but remained steadfast on their principle. At the beginning of December he even told House that he was in a hurry. He had heard that Bryan—yes, Bryan!—had got the idea of undertaking a peace mission to Berlin on his own. How likely this mission was and how seriously Wilson took it are not quite clear. House wrote Wilson that he should make light of it.[14] At that very moment the English cabinet crisis on December 6 made delay necessary in any case. House now lost his direct contact with Grey, and he did not know much about his successor Balfour. But he did know the new prime minister, Lloyd George, who he thought was not averse to mediation. He had spoken favorably about the House-Grey memorandum and even said that Wilson could dictate peace. House in his letter of congratulations to Lloyd George took the opportunity to remind him of what he had said.[15] He hoped to be able to revive the stillborn plan, but Wilson did not like the idea very much, preferring his own much more neutral position.

The new English government turned out to be less open to mediation than its predecessor. Lloyd George found his support more among the Conservatives than among his own Liberals. The prospects of mediation worsened even more when several days later, on December 12, the Germans came out with their own peace proposal. The imperial chancellor, Theobald von Bethmann Hollweg, was given, as we have noted, one more chance by the commanding generals at supreme headquarters.

The question arises whether Bethmann actually wanted peace. Since the appearance of Fritz Fischer's sensational book on Germany's war aims, the figure of Bethmann Hollweg has become very controversial. Was he in fact, as Fischer contends, a Machiavellian character whose aims were really the same as those of the generals? Or was he a timid, Hamlet-like dawdler, noble and humane but too weak to cope with hard reality?[16] The able American chargé d'affaires, Joseph C. Grew, who spoke to him in November 1916, was deeply impressed by his genuine concern: "I can only remember the man as he seemed to me that day . . . sitting at his desk, speaking slowly, deliberately and sadly of the horrors of the war. He seemed to me like a man broken in spirit, his face deeply furrowed, his manner sad beyond words." If he were playing a role, Grew thought, then he was a consummate actor.[17]

Bethmann desired mediation. He saw that the war could no longer be won and felt its sufferings personally, but he was probably too unsure of himself, too weak and tired, to be able to hold out against the generals. The peace note was his last chance, and he received it only because the generals saw in it a way to keep the home front quiet and to arouse the antiwar feeling in the Allied country. That was all the O.H.L. (*Oberste Heeresleitung*, the usual name at the time for the supreme command of Hindenburg and Ludendorff) saw in it, but they thought that any mediation, whether on Germany's initiative or Wilson's, could serve to shift the guilt for failure to the Allies and thereby probably keep the United States out of the war. That was a consideration that would hold weight with Bethmann too, although his aims went much further.[18]

The chancellor had also thought of the possibility of help from Wilson, and in October and November he swung back and forth between the possibilities. The idea of mediation aroused strong opposition in Germany, where deep suspicion reigned in government circles over "the mediation of a statesman like President Wilson, who was so naive in all his conceptions and so inclined toward the English standpoint."[19] Wilhelm II was personally very opposed and let it be known "that the Emperor declined to accept Mr. Wilson as a peace mediator and the participation of America in a peace congress."[20] Finally, therefore, the chancellor acted on his own and by himself. The generals thought that the victory over Romania, clinched by the occupation of Bucharest on December 6, was a good starting point. On December 12 a German peace note was issued offering to begin peace talks. Bethmann let Wilson know through a variety of channels that he wanted what the president wanted, and he hoped they could work together for peace.

Wilson hoped, of course, that his initiative would be considered separately from Bethmann's. His own note was issued on December 18. In it he did not talk about an eventual conference, nor did he propose peace or even mediation. He pointed with stirring words to the hopelessness of the struggle. He took the liberty of reminding the belligerents that their aims on both sides were "virtually the same." Would it not make sense, therefore, "that soundings be taken in order that we may learn, the neutral nations with the belligerent, how near the haven of peace we may be for which all mankind longs with an intense and increasing longing"?[21]

That was all it came down to, a request to the belligerents to say just what they wanted. It was typical Wilson diplomacy, vague, lofty, and full of feeling. What did he really mean by his question about war aims? He asked for "precise objects" and regretted that the world could only guess "what definite results, what actual exchange of guarantees, what political or territorial changes or readjustments, what stage of military success even, would bring the war to an end." But did he really believe

The Final Mediation

that such queries could stimulate the holding of peace talks? And then did they not mean that the United States, which meant Wilson personally, had to play the role of mediator?

The note was doomed to failure even before it was issued. First it was sabotaged by sullen Lansing, who gave a statement to the press in which he asserted that the note was intended only to vindicate American rights, because the country was moving steadily "nearer the verge of war." "Neither the President nor myself regard this note as a peace note; it is merely an effort to get the belligerents to define the end for which they are fighting."[22] It was a defiant declaration that Wilson found hard to swallow. Angrily he demanded a correction from Lansing, who at once issued a second statement in which he regretted "eventual misunderstandings." But he continued to follow an opposite policy; at this very time he discussed with the English and French ambassadors the terms of peace which he thought they should include in their reply. He hinted that Wilson stood alone, that the American government was of course favorable to the Entente, and that they did not need to concern themselves very much about a league of nations.

Various historians have sharply faulted Lansing for his attitude. Link calls him a vain saboteur who committed "one of the most egregious acts of treachery in American history."[23] There is much truth in this accusation, for Lansing did act in an underhanded way. But a host of questions must also be asked about Wilson's conduct. Was Wilson without fault? Why did he keep Lansing as secretary of state? Why didn't he dismiss him? How does that all fit with Wilson's desire for peace? Did he want to do everything himself? And there are further questions to be asked in extenuation of Lansing's behavior. What could he do when he perceived the reality of the situation? He was responsible for the conduct of foreign policy, yet what could he say about all the froth and foam of the president's emotional and ineffectual verbiage? The source of the problem was the entire situation, Wilson's solitary exaltation no less than Lansing's impotent troublemaking. These two men did not belong together.

Wilson's relationship with House was infinitely better, yet it also was filled with frustrations. House too worked against the note. In his diary he complained that Wilson seemed obsessed with the idea of objectivity, which made him unpopular among the Allies. In utter conceit he added: "I find the President has nearly destroyed all the work I have done in

Europe."[24] House contradicted Wilson quite sharply, but the president did not gladly listen to criticism. This clash between the two bosom friends was the first blow to their relationship. No break came for a long time because Wilson could not do without House, but there was a beginning of mistrust. Some of the former cordiality begins to be lacking in his letters to House. "Dearest Friend" becomes "my dear House."

In the Allied capitals Wilson's note aroused suspicion and anger, just as Lansing and House had anticipated. The Entente leaders worried that Wilson was playing into the hands of the Central Powers, perhaps unawares but perhaps deliberately. Wilson's remarks at this time, Page wrote to House, are seen as tantamount to treating both sides alike. A guest at Buckingham Palace told Page that the king wept when he heard about the note.[25] But the English and French were really not too concerned. Spring-Rice and Jusserand were able to report from Washington what Lansing had told them. That gave hope that the Americans wanted nothing more than a fine statement that accorded with their ideas. After much deliberation an extended reply was drafted in which the terms set for peace corresponded very neatly with Lansing's suggestions: restoration of Belgium, Serbia, and Montenegro; evacuation of the occupied territories in France, Russia, and Romania; liberation of the oppressed Italians, Romanians, Czechs, and Slovaks; expulsion of Turkey from Europe; and reasonable reparations.

The big question was and remained how waging war and making peace could be reconciled. The English leaders repeated what Roosevelt and Lodge had maintained in the United States, that there could be no peace upon the basis of equality, or conditional upon establishment of an international order. In the discussions in London, Balfour put his finger on the sore spot: Did Wilson really believe, he wanted to know, that an international order had nothing to do with the course of the war? Lloyd George said the same thing more emphatically in the House of Commons: "We accepted this war for an object, and a worthy object, and the war will end when that object is attained. Under God, I hope it will never end until that time."

The Germans on their side were no more conciliatory. They had initiated the affair, but for their own purposes. Only the ambassador to Washington, Johann von Bernstorff, seemed to realize how dangerous the game actually was and did everything he could to make the mediation succeed. Ludendorff later reproached him. "You wanted to make peace in America. You thought we had come to our end!" Bernstorff defended himself: "Not at all. I wanted to make peace before we came to our end." Ludendorff replied: "But we didn't want it."[26] The Germans had hardly any understanding of Wilson. Such innocence escaped them or they made fun of it. There is an interesting comment in this regard by Max Weber: "Wilson, in his pedantry which was so fatal to us, remained absolutely true to himself." But people in Germany, were incredulous that someone could engage in politics with all the formality of a law professor giving a lecture or a doctoral examination; even his note concludes with a sentence that he took straight from a college lecture on responsibility in international law.[27]

Wilson was logical, and Professor Weber thought he recognized his mania, but he was profoundly mistaken. Indeed, so was the German government. It did not plan to make a precise statement of its war aims, which would lead to disastrous controversy between right and left. Instead the German reply to Wilson's note contained only compliments to Wilson. Germany, it said, was grateful to him for his noble initiative, but the Imperial government found that the splendid operation of banning war could begin only when the present war was over. Then it would gladly cooperate in this sublime task. Even the German realists did not plan to link war and peace, the present and the future.

At that very moment the Germans had decided to play their last card. When the German leaders met at Pless castle at the beginning of January, the generals, who had been relentlessly demanding the initiation of unlimited submarine warfare, won out. Ludendorff and Holtzendorff reported that there was no reason to be afraid of America; within six months England would be on its knees and not a single American soldier could put a foot on French soil before then. The chancellor was not happy about it, but, with his power of resistance gone, he had no choice but to give in. The Imperial command to begin unlimited submarine warfare was sent to the navy amid the most profound secrecy.

Meanwhile Wilson continued lightheartedly with his peace initiative. Obviously he could not know what was happening in Europe behind the scenes, but still the reports were not promising. Nonetheless he went ahead, doggedly optimistic. He was spurred to act by the German ambassador Bernstorff, who, with the courage of desperation, kept urging continued discussions. At the invitation of Wilson and House, Bernstorff sent a message to Bethmann Hollweg on December 29, again asking whether he wanted to state terms for peace.

At once Wilson and House turned enthusiastic. Wilson told House that he believed peace was probably close. He was considering making public his own ideas for a general settlement, "making the keystone of the settlement arch the future security of the world against wars, and letting territorial adjustments be subordinate to the main purpose." It was the very position that he would later adopt in Paris. Wilson stubbornly went on dreaming. He discussed with House the grand principle, the right of self-determination of the peoples. It applied to Poland, Belgium, and Serbia, but they were not as sure about Alsace-Lorraine, wrote House in his diary, although "we agreed that Turkey should cease to exist."[28]

Their idea was that Wilson should announce his plans in a speech to the Senate. But before he could do that, a halfhearted reply about peace terms came from Germany, sent by Zimmermann, who had become the new minister of foreign affairs in Berlin. He suggested that the terms were "very moderate and remain within wholly reasonable limits, in contrast to those of the Entente." He promised that Germany would not annex Belgium and held out the further prospect that the German Empire was willing to conclude a cooling-off treaty on the pattern of Bryan's prewar proposal.[29] This reply aroused some hope in the American leaders, principally because Bernstorff made it somewhat more acceptable by his own interpretation. House believed that Germany was agreeing to everything "that liberal opinion in democratic countries have demanded."[30] But the reply meant absolutely nothing. A few days later Bernstorff received a secret cablegram informing him of what was about to happen in the war at sea. He was advised to take measures in the event that America broke diplomatic relations. He could not obviously communicate the full truth to House, but he did write him that the unfavorable reply given by the Entente to the German peace offer had changed the situation. Germany was compelled to take strong measures and no "Bryan treaty" could restrain the U-boats; their eventual activity would be the legitimate reply to the British hunger blockade.

This was a bitter disappointment for Wilson and House on the very eve of the president's scheduled major peace address to the Senate on January 22. Yet House was not completely daunted. He sent Bernstorff's disappointing message to Wilson with his own comments. What he understood was that the Germans intended to shift all guilt to the Allies "and justify Germany in the eyes of the neutrals in resorting to extreme measures." But if Germany could be gotten to the conference table, much would be won, since once the conference was under way, "it can never break up without peace."[31]

It is probably too easy, with the retrospective wisdom of the historian, to condemn the naïveté of Wilson and House. They could not know what we know; they could not size up the complicated German scene, which we historians still debate. But they were also still deeply rooted in an optimism that in part belongs to the nineteenth century and in part is typically American. It is an attitude which, unfortunately, has become very distant for us. Unfortunately? Yes, unfortunately, for let us imagine that they had been right and that the Germans had been persuaded. How infinitely better it would have been for the world, for the United States, for Germany. The German Supreme Command—whether out of desperation over the irreconcilability of the Allies, as Link says,[32] or out of blind self-overestimation—committed one of its greatest blunders. It put its trust in a weapon that was faulty because an effective reply—convoying of merchant ships—was soon found.[33] It compelled Wilson, who had done almost everything to remain neutral, even forgetting the *Sussex* promise, to take sides. This blotted out the last hope for a reasonable end to the war, which was mediation. The war now entered a stage of total grimness "to the bitter end." Perhaps it was inevitable, but how inevitable is destiny?

Idealists do not believe in inevitability; for them hope may not die. Wilson's speech about peace without victory became the magnificent expression of this hope.

II

There is a poem by Paul Verlaine in which he speaks of the *"tendre bonheur d'une paix sans victoire"* (the gentle happiness of peace without victory). These wise words are spoken by a woman, and she has reconciliation with her beloved in mind. Wilson would not have known these verses, for he did not read French poetry and the fact that he made these very words world-famous is therefore pure coincidence. There has been a great deal of investigation of just where he found the resounding term "peace without victory." In the magazine *The New Republic*, which counted Wilson among its faithful readers, an article appeared on December 23 with these very words, "Peace Without Victory." But in the article the author, Walter Lippmann, had warned *against* a peace without victory that would humiliate the Allies and leave Prussia a free hand in Europe. For that reason, wrote Lippmann, the Allies should not accept the German peace offer. The editorial board of *The New Republic* was divided about whether to favor mediation or war. Herbert Croly stood much closer to Wilson's position, which the president acknowledged with gratitude.[34]

Wherever the inspiration for the phrase came from, the address that the president made to the Senate on January 22 was genuine Wilson from beginning to end. It was a plea, splendid, grandiose, and vague, for America's involvement in a future world order. That order—an organization of the peoples with its own force—had to come, he said. The question was, what kind of force? This was and remained the point of difficulty. For Wilson, the moralist who knew that without human inspiration and dedication the finest promises are empty, had in mind a "force" that was greater than the force of any country or alliance, which was "the organized major force of mankind." The nations must come to an agreement and then the old system of the "balance of power" would give way to a "community of power." And that could happen only if there was true reconciliation, upon the basis of a "peace without victory," a peace among equals.

That did not bring pleasure to everyone's ears, he realized. But he had to say it, for his intention was "only to face realities and to face them without soft concealments." Dreamers want so much to be taken for realists!

"Peace without victory." At stake were the peoples. Nothing could be brought to pass in the world if the peoples did not believe in it. It was not the governments but the peoples who had to be brought together. Behind this lay a great American principle: "the consent of the governed." It was this principle that made America the model for the world. America was what the other nations still had to become, a land that, in Wordsworth's words, was made "great and free" by its soul. In the name of the United States he spoke to the whole world. He was defending, he said, American principles, and so he sought to disarm the criticism from the far right. His solution for world peace was not denial of the Monroe Doctrine but its application to the whole world. It was the best means to avoid for all time the "entangling alliances" against which George Washington had warned: "There is no entangling alliance in a concert of power." What he proposed, "consent of the governed," freedom of the seas, arms limitation, were the true American principles. He concluded:

> These are American principles, American policies. We could stand for no others. And they are also the principles and policies of forward looking men and women everywhere, of every modern nation, of every enlightened community. They are the principles of mankind and must prevail.[35]

That was the purest essence of Woodrow Wilson. He spoke in the name of the United States of America, the unique and superior country, as he himself liked to call it, forward-looking and in the lead in the service of mankind. All liberal-thinking people everywhere, in Europe and in America, rejoiced at his words. But conservatives (must we call them the realists?) on both sides of the ocean shook their heads over such empty phrases. Among the first of these, as we know, were persons in Wilson's own backyard, his closest advisers. Lansing had warned against the term "peace without victory." What did it really mean? And, most of all, how would these words be taken in the Allied countries? But, Lansing tells us, Wilson did not want to listen. "I did not argue the matter, especially as I knew his fondness for phrasemaking and was sure that it would be useless to attempt to dissuade him."[36]

Wilson consulted collaborators but was loath to listen to them. Certainly not to Page, whose far from foolish suggestion was to write not "peace without victory" but "peace without conquest."[37] Wilson listened when he heard words of agreement, not of criticism. He preferred to read letters from his enraptured friends and partisans, like those from Senator John F. Schafroth, who declared that the speech was "the greatest message of the century," or that from Senator Robert La Follette, who called it "a very important hour in the life of the nation."[38]

All progressives responded with enthusiasm. Wilson's strange special envoy in Europe, George D. Herron, rejoiced that Utopia was near: "It is Utopia or perdition that awaits the human race in the end; it is the kingdom of heaven or yet deeper hells than the one through which the world is now wading."[39] And Ray Stannard Baker, who had developed from a doubter into a total and choice admirer of Wilson's, wrote in his diary that the speech was "the very quintessence of the American ideals applied to world affairs" and "the greatest and most daring act of statesmanship." Even Croly, a critical man, thought the speech the greatest event of his life, and Lippmann, deeply moved, agreed with him.[40]

On the other side of the political spectrum stood the critics, the isolationists, the realists, the nationalists. Senator William E. Borah of Idaho, who was beginning to develop into one of Wilson's most picturesque and redoubtable foes, replied to the speech with a special motion in the Senate demanding maintenance of American isolation and the Monroe Doctrine. Theodore Roosevelt opened all the stops of his wrath in an article in the *New York Times*: "Peace without victory is the natural ideal of the man who is too proud to fight." Wilson proved again that he was a coward and a hypocrite. Roosevelt applied to him a text from the Bible (Judges 5:23): "Curse ye, Meroz, said the angel of the Lord, curse ye bitterly the inhabitants thereof, because they came not to the help of the Lord against the wrongdoings of the mighty."[41]

As was to be expected, Lodge surpassed all the others in his hostility to Wilson. In an angry speech to the Senate he wielded the full resources of his logic to tear apart the arguments of his enemy. What did it mean to say that America had no interest in the peace terms but only in the peace? How can men be required to wage war not to win, so that all their sacrifices were in vain, "a criminal and hideous futility"? How could the Monroe Doctrine be given worldwide application when it had nothing to do with the rights of small or great nations as such but applied only to the Western Hemisphere? How could the "organized major force of mankind" be applied? Voluntarily, or automatically, or compulsorily? When the idea of a league was broached two years earlier, he had been greatly attracted to it, but the more he thought about it, the more problems he saw. It could not be made effective by "high-sounding phrases, which fall so agreeably upon the ear, when there is no thought behind it." Does it mean that the small nations can, by majority vote, involve the large nations in war? "Are we prepared to commit ourselves to a purely general proposition without knowing where we are going or what is to be demanded of us, except that we shall be compelled to furnish our quota of military and naval forces to the service of a league in which we shall have but one voice?" A league for peace meant readiness to wage war against any country that did not obey its decisions. What if it decided that Japan and China should have the right of migration anywhere, and Canada,

Australia, and New Zealand declined to accept the decision? Or California, for that matter?[42]

The points made by Lodge were fundamental, which is why I present them at such length. Already at this time, in January 1917, the lines of division were drawn which would define the great debate and the great tragedy of 1919. On one side stood the idealist, on the other the realist, and on both sides more than personal animosity was involved. Furthermore, a political alliance was beginning to take shape that slackened during the war years but operated with full force in 1919; it brought together the Republican isolationists from the West, who were also idealists, for the most part from the Progressive camp, and the Republican internationalist realists, Borah on the one side and Lodge on the other. It was an alliance that would bring disaster to Wilson, but in 1917 he could not foresee that.

The reactions in Europe were as divided as those in the United States. The Pope praised the speech, and it gave joy to Liberals and Socialists in every country. But the Allied governments and their supporters were aghast. What in heaven's name did Wilson want, asked the *Times* of London, perpetual peace on earth? Lord Bryce asked whether he thought he could achieve it by returning to the status quo ante. The editor of the *Times*, Geoffrey Dawson, thought "peace without victory" would end up as meaningless as "too proud to fight."[43]

But however people responded to Wilson's grandiose mirage, it did not matter very much. In the end bitter reality went far beyond his dreams. In point of fact, we may ask to whom his speech was really addressed. Literally, of course, to the Congress of the United States and not to the belligerent powers. There was no reason therefore to expect official replies. Yet Wilson continued to press the Germans. Through House he put Bernstorff under pressure, and the ambassador sent a cablegram to Bethmann Hollweg urging him to trust Wilson's mediation and not to begin unlimited submarine warfare, for Wilson would "treat it as a blow to his face" and it would certainly bring America into the war.[44] The cablegram was sent on January 27, four days before the submarines were let loose. The German chancellor apparently had a last spark of hope, for he rushed to general headquarters and explained to the generals what an opportunity was being offered. It did not help, for there was no real desire for peace among the German leaders. On January 29 Bernstorff received a cablegram in reply stating new German conditions. Part of Alsace would be returned to France, and Belgium would have to make concessions if it wanted to be independent again. Furthermore, the submarine war once begun could not be halted, if only for technical reasons. These terms yielded so little that they offered small opportunity for opening discussion.

Wilson's hope was in vain, how vain it became clear only a few days later. On January 31 Bernstorff went to the State Department to inform them that the submarine war would break out in full force the next day. There were tears in his eyes. Lansing told Wilson at once and urged an end to delay; it was time to do what had been threatened in so many notes, to break diplomatic relations. But Wilson could not bring himself to do it. In this time of crisis it became particularly clear how complete Wilson's neutrality was. He understood Lansing's arguments well enough, and he did not wish to throw away the country's honor. He therefore asked Lansing to draft at once a note for an eventual diplomatic break.

What held him back? It is extraordinarily fascinating to inquire into the reasons for his profound resistance to breaking with Germany. Another factor was at work besides his undoubted and honest horror of war. His first reactions revealed a different threshold. He had been brought up in the nineteenth-century belief in the essential superiority of white civilization, which should be a blessing for the whole world. He did not want to see America, the last bulwark of this civilization to remain at peace, caught up in the maelstrom of destruction. He told this to all and sundry during these days. Already in January he told House that the United States would not go to war. It was the only great white nation that was still at peace, and it would be "a crime against civilization" for the country to go in.[45] He declared to Lansing that he "had been more and more impressed with the idea that 'white civilization' and its domination over the world rested largely on our ability to keep this country intact, as we would have to build up the nations ravaged by the war."[46]

Wilson was at his wit's end. He told House he had the feeling that everything was going wrong, the world no longer turned from east to west but just the other way round. What in heaven's name should he do? While waiting for Lansing, should he play some golf? House advised him not to, for it would give an impression of frivolity. Instead he played billiards, safely indoors.

At noon Lansing arrived with a draft, but Wilson continued to hesitate. He wanted to meet his full cabinet first, but when they assembled, he presented them with the same considerations. He asked them point-blank whether or not he should break diplomatic relations with Germany, and continued philosophically: "He would say frankly that, if he felt that, in order to keep the white race or part of it strong to meet the yellow race—Japan for instance, in alliance with Russia, dominating China—it was wise to do nothing, he would do nothing." He would then be able to carry the blame.[47] These considerations found little support in the ranks of the cabinet, however, although one Southerner, Josephus Daniels, candidly agreed with him. Most of those present, Lansing and Houston in the lead, strongly urged a quick decision, and even called for a declaration of war.

Wilson did not want to do anything without consulting Congress. That same day he spoke to a number of Senators, and they too in their large majority favored a break in diplomatic relations. This was done on February 3. The president informed the assembled Congress that all diplomatic relations between the United States and the German Empire were being broken. Even then he left the door ajar; he hoped, he said, that war would not follow, and that Germany would not go to the extreme and attack American ships.

Thus Wilson's neutrality policy finally came to a halfhearted end. He was unable to believe it had happened. What could the peacemaker do in a world of anger and violence? His disappointment meant that he retained a deep resentment against the country that had robbed him of his beautiful dream. "He sees red when he thinks of the Imperial government," Bernstorff maintained, and he was probably right that this was the earliest beginning of Wilson's changed attitude toward Germany, which ended with the tragedy of the Versailles peace.[48]

NINETEEN

When the road changes, so does the inn.
    —*Spanish proverb*

WAR

"I DO NOT BELIEVE WILSON WILL go to war unless Germany literally kicks him into it," wrote an irate Theodore Roosevelt to his friend Lodge.[1] For the tempestuous Rough Rider, it was a mystery how Wilson could sit waiting, with folded arms, while Germany had already gone over to open aggression. He asked why Wilson did nothing and wondered whether he was afraid. Lodge replied that Wilson was indeed afraid, plain afraid, physically and morally.[2]

But Wilson was waiting not because he was afraid but because he took his responsibilities so heavily. He endeavored to escape his disappointment and perplexity by analyzing his motives, both for and against. In a conversation with the philosopher Henri Bergson (an envoy of the French government, which probably thought another professor could help persuade Wilson), he explained that the American people were divided. But that was not really the principal reason. He was personally still uncertain and considered that both parties were in the wrong. England was fighting only for "commercial preponderance" and the German people were not too evil, but were, he thought, hostile to their own government.[3]

Wilson continued to become steadily more insecure, and therefore he clung to any straw that seemed to promise peace. The assertion of revisionist historians in later years that America went into the war because it was tied to the Allies by the "golden chains" of loans and deliveries is complete nonsense, at least so far as Wilson is concerned. He was not a hypocrite; he did not want war in the slightest; he did everything he could to remain neutral. At most one can say that his extreme emphasis upon the rights of neutrals led him into a position from which he could not retreat. It was the situation Bryan had anticipated.

Wilson was unable to change course. Vague suggestions of mediation—such as a request from the Austro-Hungarian minister Czernin (the Dual Monarchy was by this time suffering from severe war exhaustion) and also an attempt by the Swiss envoy—at once aroused his pleased interest. Who knew, perhaps a miracle might still happen? As long as the Germans did not carry through on their threat and their submarines did not literally aim their weapons at Americans, he would do nothing. Roosevelt was right about that.

In this dogged conviction he stood practically alone, at least in government circles in Washington. He found almost no support within his immediate circle, for even House was in fundamental disagreement with him. The members of his cabinet believed that war was the only way out. In a cabinet meeting on February 23, there was renewed discussion of the hopelessness of the situation; American citizens were mistreated in Germany, and there were food riots in New York, where half of the merchant fleet lay idle in harbor. Things could not go on this way. The people did not want to take any risks, said Wilson. He was then asked why he wasn't angry about the indignities to which American women in Germany were being subjected. Various members of the cabinet pressed upon him that public opinion seemed to be shifting. The president became angry with them. They wanted war, and the arms manufacturers and the Republicans were behind them. Franklin K. Lane, the secretary of the interior, commented that he did not know whether the president was an internationalist or a pacifist; in any case his patriotism was "covered over with a film of philanthropic humanitarianism."[4]

Wilson shrank from taking the final step, not out of fear, not out of unsullied pacifism, but because his whole conception of mediating between the belligerents (and thereby saving white civilization) would be shattered. This was the principal reason for his hesitation. And so he talked during these weeks in almost pacifist terms about war and imperialism, spoke out in anger against the support for war from right-wing circles, which he described as "Junkerthum trying to creep in under the cover of the patriotic feeling of the moment." Something similar was happening in England, for the so-called "coalition cabinet" of the Liberal Lloyd George was in actuality a Tory government. That's what Lloyd George is good for, he wrote to House.[5] But he, Wilson, wanted peace, and he waited.

Was no middle way possible? Did neutrals have to become the victims of the belligerents? Wasn't it possible to create a defensible neutrality by providing one's own vessels with light cannon for defensive use? It was a measure that offered some hope to Wilson; it seemed a reasonable solution, if not an ideal one, a solution halfway between war and peace. It was preferable that it be taken in consultation with the other neutrals, but they were not enthusiastic about participating in a League of Armed Neutrality, such as Catherine the Great of Russia had organized in 1780 for defense against British violations of freedom of the seas. The Dutch envoy, Van Rappard, told House that for two years the small countries had asked the United States in vain for its cooperation. He suggested that a conference of neutrals in Washington would offer prospects of a settlement. This proposal might well have been prompted by Bernstorff, House thought (Van Rappard was known in Washington to be pro-German).[6]

The United States had to act on its own. As early as February 26 Wilson appeared before Congress to present his plan. He asked for support without delay (the session of Congress would conclude on March 4) for "armed neutrality" and arming of the merchant fleet. He went no further, not wanting to speak of war. "War can come only by the wilful acts and aggressions of others." He was discussing only measures of self-protection, "defensive arms."[7]

It sounded reasonable and moderate. But the United States in these months found itself in a strange transitional mood, uncertain and divided. The great majority stood behind the president, certainly in Congress as well as among the people; but there were also pacifists who did not want to go along and decided to resist tooth and nail. A small group of senators snatched at the most extreme measure available under the remarkable rules of procedure of the upper house of Congress, the filibuster. The result was that Wilson's proposal was accepted with a huge majority in the House of Representatives but was blocked in the Senate by a few recalcitrant idealists, among them such renowned progressive leaders as Senator Robert La Follette of Wisconsin and Senator George Norris of Nebraska. Their filibuster began on Saturday, March 3, and continued until noon of the next day, when the vice-president, who was chairman of the Senate, had to close the session. The proposal was shelved.

This happened on the day Wilson was to begin his second term of office. The official day for the inauguration was at the time March 4, which in 1917 was a Sunday. Wilson took the oath of office on Sunday, but did not give his inaugural address until the next day. At noon on Sunday, House recorded in his diary, Wilson was so resentful and emotional that he burst out in angry denunciation of the filibustering senators. House suggested that Wilson write down what he had just said, and the president did so straight off. His declaration therefore became a bitter, unbalanced piece that showed how deeply he had been offended. What kind of impression must it make in the world, he asked, when the government of such a mighty country is made so powerless; the Senate of the United States seemed to be the only legislative body in the world that was not able to act. And then the notorious sentence: "A little group of wilful men, representing no opinion but their own, have rendered the great Government of the United States helpless and contemptible."[8]

Wilson's statement was understandable, unfair, and superfluous. It was understandable because the national interest was, he thought, seriously damaged. Unfair, because in the first place it was his own procrastination that had delayed the decision, and in the second place because not all of the eleven senators who had opposed the measure had taken part in the filibuster. Superfluous, and this is what is the strangest part of the affair, because Wilson's legal advisers at once explained to him that he did not at all need the approval of Congress, for there were precedents for going ahead on his own. This is what he did, taking steps on his own hook in mid-March for arming of the American merchantmen.

Wilson's outburst received a great deal of support in the press and from the public. In the uncertain state of public opinion, there was readiness to place trust in the strong leader in the White House; he would know what needed to be done. But the great majority were also convinced that the danger was not very great; in the minds of most Americans the European war was still far away and the German threat not very real.

This feeling of satisfaction was suddenly undermined by a blunder of the first order committed by the Germans themselves. This was the so-called "Zimmermann telegram." Arthur Zimmermann had succeeded Gottlieb von Jagow as foreign minister in Berlin in November, which well-informed Americans considered a good thing in view of his reputation as more conciliatory and pro-American than his predecessor. A blond, mustachioed giant of a man, cordial and charming, "with a sunny smile" and great ambition, was how he was described by Joseph Grew, the American chargé d'affaires.[9] But Zimmermann had a most unusual surprise up his sleeve. In the most profound secrecy he sent a telegram to ambassador von Bernstorff in mid-January to be retransmitted to his colleague in Mexico City. In it Germany's foreign minister informed the German diplomats that the submarine war would begin on February 1 and that he hoped the United States could be kept out of the war. But if this could not be done, then Germany would propose to Mexico an alliance against the United States, and would help it to regain the territories lost to the United States—Texas, New Mexico, and Arizona. Even wilder was the proposal that Japan (which, it should be noted, was an ally of the Allies) should be involved.[10]

This weird plan ran afoul of British intelligence. The secret service in London, led by the very shrewd Sir William Reginald Hall (who, according to the admiring Page, "can look through you and see the very muscular movements of your immortal soul while he is talking to you"),[11] had been for some time in possession of the German codes and readily deciphered all German dispatches that came into its hands. Thus the government in London was able to read what Zimmermann proposed.

Obviously the British in this crisis gladly made effective use of this spectacular information. Balfour called in Page and with visible pleasure handed to him the text of the telegram. The Americans could see what they had to expect from Germany. Page immediately sent the document to Washington, and Wilson saw it on February 23. He was appalled, especially when Lansing told him that the telegram had been sent to Bernstorff in mid-January over the cable line that had been made available to the Germans by the American government especially for the communication of peace discussions. He had been deceived and his good will misused. "Good Lord!" he exclaimed repeatedly in his bafflement.[12]

The telegram was so improbable that at first there was some doubt whether it was authentic. But it was. When it was published on March 1, there were many, especially in pacifist and pro-German circles, who considered it to be a hoax of British propaganda. But truth soon overcame disbelief, for Zimmermann himself officially admitted the authenticity of the telegram. This was a crucial blunder, Lansing thought, because he could easily have left the burden of proof to the Allies. If he had been in Zimmermann's place, Lansing later wrote, he would have challenged the American government to prove its case.[13]

The importance of the Zimmermann telegram was considerable, but not because it changed Wilson, who was still full of doubts and continued to cling to armed neutrality. But what the telegram did do was to shake the American people out of their slumbers and make it clear to them that the time of their self-satisfied isolation was past and that Germany could literally be a threat to the Western Hemisphere, which in fact was its aim. Public opinion changed, therefore, but still Wilson did not take the last, decisive step.

In his inaugural address on Monday, March 5, Wilson held stubbornly to his position, but without committing himself. The United States had nothing to do with the war; it had been shamefully attacked in its rights but did not wish to take revenge; it hoped to remain neutral by arming its merchant ships. But "we may even be drawn on, by circumstances, not by our own purpose and desire, to a more active assertion of our rights as we see them and a more immediate association with the great struggle itself." But his aim remained what it had been, peace, an honorable peace among equals, a peace that did not rest upon a balance of power, a peace through democracy, peace and freedom of the seas, peace and disarmament. And he gave that splendid program—God's providence, the nation chastened into unity, dedication to the well-being of the world—the brilliance of his splendid rhetoric. Its apotheosis was his favorite metaphor of the light in the future: "The shadows that now lie dark upon our path will soon be dispelled and we shall walk with the light all about us if we be but true to ourselves."[14]

Thus he began his second term of office with many cares and many problems. At table, in the always small circle of his family and House, there was a great deal of talk about them; the atmosphere was peaceful, for the marriage was an idyll of closeness. House describes the intimate "all-in-the-family" effect of the following evening, when the city of Washington was celebrating the inauguration:

> The President and Mrs. Wilson sat by a side window, curtained off, and asked me to join them. The President was holding Mrs. Wilson's hand and leaning with his face against hers. We talked quietly of the happenings of the day and I spoke of my joy that we three, rather than the Hughes family, were looking at the fire works from the White House windows.[15]

The idyll would not last.

Meanwhile the pressure on Wilson increased. The strange calm before the storm that seemed to protect the American ships in February was grimly disturbed at the end of the month. On February 25 the British ship *Laconia* was sunk; among the victims were Americans, including a mother and a daughter, and the dramatic manner of their deaths made a deep impression upon the American public. On March 12, the American ship *Algonquin* was torpedoed without warning by a U-boat; fortunately the crew was saved. That was the beginning. Soon the bad news began to come in more and more rapidly. On March 18, three American ships were the victim of the *furor teutonicus*, and this time there were many victims. The situation seemed untenable. Roosevelt wrote to Lodge that he was restraining himself, "but if he does not go to war with Germany I shall skin him alive."[16]

Surprisingly, it was to Lansing and not to House that Wilson listened most closely during these days. On March 19, the secretary of state talked to him for at least an hour in order to persuade him that war was inevitable; that same evening, he wrote a long report for him repeating the same arguments, but adding an appeal to Wilson as a peacemaker: "It is my belief that the longer we delay in declaring against the military absolutism which menaces the rule of liberty and justice in the world, so much the less will be our own influence in the days when Germany will need a merciful and unselfish foe."[17]

Wilson was truly in a moral dilemma. He wrestled, as we know from his remarks, with the problem of war in general. He was the Puritan on whom responsibility weighed heavily. He was a "liberal," born and raised with a belief in progress in which war was an atavism. He was the American who had always looked with flabbergasted scorn at the primitive European society in which war, in Clausewitz's words, was the continuation of politics with other means. He could approve and accept such means only if it was the last effective way to bring all strife to an end.

It is true that the slogan "the war to end all wars" had been thought up at the beginning of the war by a European, the English utopian H. G. Wells, who later, on the basis of still more radical ideas, would regret his own enthusiasm of 1914. But in America the idea was much older; it had been present during the American Revolution.[18] During the Civil War it had been very popular among the idealists in the North.[19]

Wilson, although a Southerner, stood in this tradition. He could not accept war as something to be taken for granted. But it must be added that he was not a pacifist. If in his imagination, at the level of the ideal, he could set the issue straight, then he could excuse war. After initial hesitation, he had greeted the war of 1898 as a necessary act and had even seen an exalted purpose in it. He was not free of romantic admiration for readiness for self-sacrifice and devotion to an ideal. In a curious statement at the commemoration of the dead who had fallen during the attack on Vera Cruz in the spring of 1914, which had been made on his responsibility, he asserted that, besides a "war of aggression," which was to be condemned, there was also a "war of service." And he at once applied this idea with exaggerated poetic sensibility to himself:

> War, gentlemen, is only a sort of dramatic representation, a sort of dramatic symbol, of a thousand forms of duty. I never went into battle. I never was under fire, but I fancy that there are some things just as hard to do as to go under fire. I fancy that it is just as hard to do your duty when men are sneering at you as when they are shooting at you. When they shoot at you, they can only take your natural life, when they sneer at you, they can wound your living heart.[20]

Once carried away by his stream of poetic language, he could go even further. Already in 1911 he held forth about holy war: "When men take up arms to set other men free, there is something sacred and holy in the warfare." (In these words we hear an echo of the "Battle Hymn of the Republic": "As He died to make men holy, let us die to make men free.") In his election tour of 1916 he repeated, again with nicety of imagination:

in extreme necessity, for the sake of a league of nations for peace, there was a

> cause in which it seems a glory to shed human blood, if it be necessary,
> so that all the common compacts of liberty may be sealed with the
> blood of free men. Every man has to die. It is done only once,
> and being a single and distinguished act, it ought to be done for a
> single and distinguished purpose. It ought to be thrilled through with
> the purposes of life, so that, as a man lived and loved, so he may die,
> striving for the things which put all the corpuscles of his blood into
> shouting shape whenever great things were proposed.[21]

This was the Wilsonian version of war as a positive good. "Oh Lord, give each his own death!" wrote the German poet Rilke. How much of those words of Wilson come out of poetic excitement and how much out of actual experience?

But, when the time for action came in 1917, Wilson shrank back. He weighed the pros and cons of a decision against each other. Did not war mean, as he had increasingly learned, an end to the drive for reform? Wouldn't the national interests be sacrificed to big business? Wouldn't the army become a state within the state? How much he hesitated is most apparent in the well-known conversation he had at this time with the newspaperman Frank Cobb. It was a dramatic interview, so unusual that historians have doubted its authenticity. Cobb, it happens, did not write it down at the time but told it later to two friends, and he certainly did not remember the right date, for it did not take place on April 2, on the eve of the war, as he maintained, but in all probability on March 19.[22]

Wilson had just felt the full blast of Lansing's arguments, and he was more uncertain than ever. He confided his deepest motives to Cobb.

> I'd never seen him so worn down [wrote Cobb]. He looked as if he
> hadn't slept, and he said he hadn't. . . . For nights, he said, he had
> been lying awake. . . . He said he couldn't see any alternative. . . . It
> would mean that we should lose our heads along with the rest and
> stop weighing right and wrong. . . . The President said a declaration
> of war would mean that Germany would be beaten and so badly
> beaten that there would be a dictated peace, a victorious peace.

On the home front it would mean hysteria. "Once lead this people into war and they'll forget there ever was such a thing as tolerance. To fight you must be brutal and ruthless." What would remain, then, of American constitutional liberties?[23]

Wilson, writes his biographer Link, went through Gethsemane during this week of March 12 to 20.[24] The image can be found in use at the time, but nowadays it rings a bit ponderously in our ears. Yet I believe that it is then that we see our hero at his best and greatest. He suffered from the responsibility that he had to bear; it is a theme that resounds over and over in his words. Walter Lippmann, who looked at him with cool rationality and was among those bitterly disappointed with him after 1919, draws for us nonetheless a portrait of Wilson in his book *Men of Destiny*, showing the orator of light learning about darkness. He gazed in March 1917, says Lippmann, "in the bottomless pit." He was "an anguished prophet," full of compassion and doubt, a man who experienced the tragedy of his time and therefore was able, with overwrought absoluteness, to see the league of nations as the only justification of his action.[25]

With this as his justification he went into the war, not out of economic interest, not because of the violation of the neutral rights of the United States, although these played a part, but in order to bring about genuine peace. Only if America took part could it have a voice in the peace. Mediation through participation would be more effective than neutrality, he now believed. To a delegation of pacifists led by Jane Addams, he said on February 28 that "as head of a nation participating in the war, the President of the United States would have a seat at the Peace Table, but that if he remained the representative of a neutral country he could at best only 'call through a crack in the door.'" Personal ambition and general interest concurred in what we may call a mission. The man and his times seemed to fit each other like the two halves of a piece of fruit.

With these grand dreams he could pull himself over his own fears and anxieties. At last he took the final step, the decision, with pain but determination. There was another event that had some influence upon this decision. In this very month of March, so replete with tension and drama, the Russian Revolution broke out on the other side of the world, an event that would fill the whole world with hope and terror—for the moment, with hope more than terror.

In the United States Russia was pretty much an unknown country; most Americans had heard of it only because of the hideous pogroms at the beginning of this century. Wilson personally knew little about Russia; virtually nothing about the country is to be found in his papers. When he began to hold hopes of the presidency, he had spoken in New York in December 1911 to a meeting protesting the discrimination against American Jews, who could not obtain visas for Russia.[26] That is the sum total of what can be found. But the Russian Revolution awakened great expectations in him, as in most other Americans. He obtained information through Lansing from the Slavic studies scholar at the University of Chicago, Samuel N. Harper. His informant was a true American optimist, who assured him that real democracy had come to Russia. House, who shared his optimism, saw an excellent opportunity to flatter his friend: "I am not so sure that the present outcome in Russia is not due largely to your influence," and urged him to grant swift recognition to the new Russian government. Wilson did so with pleasure on March 22. But it is difficult to determine how much influence the Russian Revolution had upon his decision to enter the war. He told the cabinet that it was in any case not a decisive factor.[27] But public opinion believed that a stumbling block had been removed from his path.

The decision seems to have been clinched in the cabinet meeting of March 20. We have a fascinating account of that meeting in Lansing's hand. Wilson came in calm and controlled: "Nothing ruffles the calmness of his manner or address." He put two questions to the members: Should he call Congress into session before its scheduled return on April 16? And what should he say then? All the members, from the resolute McAdoo, Houston, and Lansing to the hesitant half-pacifist Daniels, declared unanimously that they were for the war. War had actually begun, some said; the fact had to be accepted, armed neutrality was not working. Lansing brought in the revolution in Russia, which meant that the war had become one between absolutism and democracy. The hope of a league of democratic nations was now realistic. At the close Wilson thanked them cordially for their clear advice, but did not tell them what he planned to do.[28]

Daniels, the pious Southerner, also thought of Gethsemane: "I had hoped and prayed this cup would pass." But there was no escape. "If Germany wins, we must be a military nation."[29] After the end of the meeting, the president detained Lansing and Burleson, the postmaster general, and asked them how much time was needed to recall Congress. They estimated a week. On March 21 Wilson called Congress into special session on April 2 "to receive a communication concerning grave matters of national policy."

Wilson took his decision by himself. Even House did not share in it, and was told what it was only when he was brash enough to ask. His conversation with Wilson was quite remarkable. Through the pages of House's diary we glimpse that the two friends no longer fully understood each other. House told Wilson—or at least he wrote that he told him—that he (Wilson) was not fully fit for the harshness of events.

> He admitted this and said he did not believe he was fitted for the Presidency under such conditions. I thought he was too refined, too civilized, too intellectual, too cultivated not to see the incongruity and absurdity of war. It needed a man of coarser fiber and one less a philosopher than the President to conduct a brutal, vigorous and successful war. I made him feel, as Mrs. Wilson told me later, that he was not up against so difficult a proposition as he had imagined.

Would House have understood how badly his words were taken, not least by Mrs. Wilson? The next day they discussed more fully what Wilson should say. According to House, it was he who pressed for making a clear distinction between the German government and the German people in order to "break down the German Government by 'building a fire' bath of it within Germany." In any case that was a point that Wilson welcomed; it fit his own ideas.[30]

The entire speech of April 2 was Wilson's own work. "He does not indicate in any way," wrote House in a huff a few days later, "that he is conscious that I had any part in it." Wilson was his own inspirer; he could get along without House and without ghost writers. He worked hard on his speech during the weekend of March 31. On the evening of April 2 he stepped before the House chamber, which was filled with members of both houses, guests, and newspapermen, while outside a crowd of curious persons and demonstrators clustered tightly. When Senator Lodge appeared, a demonstrator, a pacifist according to Lodge, denounced him as a dirty liar and Lodge, a pugnacious little man of sixty-seven years, responded with his fists.

This was the only untoward incident of an impressive evening. Wilson, according to all reports, made a deep impression. He began with the horrors of the German submarine war, which caused not only economic losses but the loss of women and children; it was a weapon directed not only against the United States but against mankind. He had hoped that armed neutrality would provide sufficient protection, but it had proved "ineffectual." Worse, "it is likely to produce what it was meant to prevent," leading to war unless the United States yielded. But "we will not choose the path of submission." These words unleashed the first storm of applause. The orator had his audience under his spell.

War, he continued, was therefore the logical conclusion. It had become a fact that had to be recognized, and it had to be waged with the full commitment of the nation. But that did not mean that his (he said, America's) ideals were changing. What he had said on January 22 retained its full force; the same principles of peace and law were at stake. It was not a war against the German people, for whom he and all Americans felt only sympathy and friendship; it was against the German autocratic government, which aimed only at the maintenance of its power. In Wilson's vision the people were always good, even democratic. He next turned to Russia; the situation there was the same, with a small group of powerful persons having the country in their grip. But those who knew Russia knew that it was at its heart democratic. The autocracy which had ruled there had not been Russian and fortunately had now been shaken off by the people, who had risen in revolt in their simple majesty: "Here is a fit partner for a League of Honor."

Germany was now everywhere recognized as the last great foe of a better world. Americans could now face the facts and fight for the "ultimate peace" of the world, for the liberation of all peoples, including the German. And then the famous words: "The world must be made safe for democracy." America, unselfish America, wished to help and serve. Wilson ended his address by noting how heavy his decision had been, and how great was the ordeal that he faced. But right was costlier than peace, the struggle was being waged for democracy, for a "concert of free peoples."

> To such a task we can dedicate our lives and our fortunes, everything
> that we are and everything that we have, with the pride of those
> who know that the day has come when America is privileged to
> spend her blood and her might for the principles that gave her birth
> and happiness and the peace which she has treasured. God helping
> her, she can do no other.[31]

He had ended with Luther's words, suitably modified. His address had lasted exactly thirty-six minutes. It was greeted with heavy and sustained applause. The audience was swept along by the orator. What could he do better than this—inspired, erect, alone, and proud to be himself, yes, better than himself in the majesty of his words? Even his archenemy Lodge was moved; he did the handsome thing, went up and shook his hand, saying, "Mr. President, you have expressed in the loftiest way possible the sentiments of the American people."[32]

Letters of support flooded in. Lippmann wrote that only a statesman could have acted as he had done. From Page: "Your speech cheers the whole enlightened world and marks the beginning of a new international era." From his friend from college, Cleveland H. Dodge: "You at last have the united American people with you." From his son-in-law McAdoo: "You have done a great thing nobly! I firmly believe that it is god's will that America should do this transcendent service for humanity throughout the world and that you are his chosen instrument."[33]

But Wilson's own mood was not one of elation. He felt the tragedy of the whole situation. That tragic aspect also could be clearly seen in his address. He spoke of "a profound sense of the solemn and even tragical character of the step I am taking," of a "distressing and oppressive duty," of a "fearful thing to lead this great peaceful people into war, into the most terrible and disastrous of all wars, civilization itself seeming to be in the balance." This was no blast of the triumphant trumpet. The historian Cooper, who has dubbed this speech a "work of somber beauty," is right in a way.[34] Wilson suffered under the weight of his decision because he grasped its scope. Tumulty, his faithful but exuberant secretary, even maintains that Wilson, speaking about his responsibility, broke out in tears and "then laying his head on the Cabinet table, sobbed as if he had been a child."[35] The episode seems too good to be completely true, too melodramatic for Wilson's character. But his tragedy was not less in any case. It was as if at that moment he suddenly realized that in politics the choice lies not been good and evil, but that in order to achieve the great good in which he believed he had to dirty his hands. That is why his address was so masterly, says Devlin: "He had been given a sudden revelation of the tragedy at the fount of all human endeavour," and that was why it was as simple as Lincoln's Gettysburg address.[36] This is why, Cooper asserts, he ended with the words that recalled Luther, and he cites Luther's *pecca fortiter* in support. But this is a misunderstanding, a secularist application of Luther's ideas to Wilson.[37]

We must be cautious about an overly philosophical explanation of

Wilson's ethics. He thought not in abstract concepts but in images of reality. What he found literally agonizing, as we have said, was the realization of the responsibility on his shoulders. "It wrings my heart," he wrote to Arthur Sidney Burleson, the postmaster general, "when I think of the thousands of American boys that we are going to send to their death. There is nothing I wouldn't do to avoid such a catastrophe." And House told Bergson, the visiting French philosopher, that when Wilson declared war, he felt that "God would hold him accountable for every American soldier killed."[38]

Yet, if the dilemma was to be overcome, it had to be acknowledged. Wilson might be aware of the tragic element, as Lippmann wrote, but essentially his sense of life was not tragic but optimistic. In order to take the guilt upon himself, he had to believe totally in the end that sanctified—literally—the means. As Devlin wrote, "justification" had to become "sanctification."[39] He had to maintain steadfastly that there was no difference between his ideal of peace without victory and his commitment to the war; he had to want to win without wanting to triumph. Obviously this was impossible, and it created a dilemma that he never overcame, not even during the peace negotiations in Paris in 1919. It was the old dilemma of purity versus involvement. Now, in the elegant phrases of Golo Mann, "the good President" had to be on guard lest "the immense weight of America on the one side of the balance scale drive up too suddenly and swiftly the German side on the other. That would mean Germany would in the end be defeated, and the goal of a just peace without hatred or revenge would be missed."[40]

As the Spanish proverb at the beginning of this chapter says, when the road changes, so does the inn. Wilson slipped into an impossible position. The difference between his thoughts before 1917 and afterward was too fundamental. A war that until then had been unclear in its causes and purposes now suddenly became a struggle for true democracy; guilt, which formerly had been so tragically borne by both sides, now was forced upon Germany.[41]

As was to be expected, there was criticism of this change from right and left. Lodge wrote to a friend that the gap between Wilson's standpoint earlier and now was too great to be bridged. And Roosevelt, as always a man of extremes, thought it "really nauseous hypocrisy" to declare in April that Americans were fighting to make the world safe for democracy when sixty days before there had been talk of a peace without victory.[42]

Realists easily pass judgment upon the efforts of idealists to adapt to reality. Many liberals went through the same crisis as Wilson. Most of them followed their master and believed with the same ardor as he that the great step taken made sense. But then how close did they come to the well-known phenomenon—which had also been so common in Europe in 1914—that the war was turned into a positive good, a new meaning for the uncertainties of existence? War freed people from the desire for ease and prosperity. An "uneasy people," a "discouraged and ashamed" people, felt itself taken up into a greater bond.[43]

Wilson, with his great vision of a better world, gave the liberals an alibi to soothe their consciences. It is now quite certain, wrote *The New Republic*, that the war that began "as a clash of empires in the Balkans will dissolve into democratic revolution the world over," and William Allen White, the renowned editor from Kansas, proclaimed that Americans now knew that they were shedding their blood in a holy war for a democratic peace upon earth.[44] One member of Congress declared that just Americans could do it, because they went into the war not for dollars or selfish interests. "Could any nation enter a war so completely without selfishness and guile?"[45]

TWENTY

No one was himself just then and patriotism (in peace-time an attitude best left to politicians, publicists and fools, but in the dark days of war an emotion that can wring the heart-strings), patriotism made one do odd things.
　　　　—*W. Somerset Maugham,* Miss King

Let's make these Bolshewiks our Bolshewiks.
　　　　—*William Boyce Thompson*

PATRIOTISM AND BOLSHEVISM

AMERICA IN ITS HISTORY moves by fits and starts, for it is a young country unsure of itself. It has a rich pacifist tradition but also a past filled with aggression and violence. It has conducted innumerable small expeditions and half-wars; just on its own soil it has been in conflict with the Indians for a century and a half. But it was never ready for a big war; it always became involved suddenly, and it had no adequate army ready in 1861, 1917, or 1941, which were the decisive years.

It is true that Wilson had waged a campaign for "preparedness," and there were major plans for reorganizing the armed forces, most of which had yet to be put into practice in April 1917. The big work was still to be done; an entire country had to be suddenly converted from production for peace to production for war. It was a task in which Wilson personally could provide little leadership; he gave no attention to military affairs and did not understand them; he could not follow the technical talk of the generals. The only thing that interested him—and this was very typical of him—was the spirit that dominated the army, the welfare and hardships of the common soldiers. He wanted an army, as he wrote, that was "mentally, morally and physically" at a high level. His secretary of war, Newton Baker, agreed with him wholeheartedly about this; he was no more a military expert than the president, but an even more fervent reformer. Together they hoped to create an army of noble heroes. "Let it be your pride, therefore," he told the troops, "to show all men everywhere not only what good soldiers you are, but also what good men you are, keeping yourselves fit and straight in everything and pure and clean through and through."[1]

Wilson believed in an army without drunkards and whores, a vanguard of unselfish America and really of all humanity. He took deeply to heart the fate of the young men whom he was sending overseas; it was, as we have seen and shall see again, a responsibility that seared his conscience.

Wilson's belief in an army as the representative of the nation, in a word a "people's army," fitted in well with his whole conception of democratic nationalism; it was a component of his notion of self-determination. The war was, after all, a war of the peoples, not of the governments. He therefore wanted no part of the old system of volunteer corps organized by individuals or regions, which had been so popular during the Civil War. This was the principal reason he rejected a proposal that came from Theodore Roosevelt. This pugnacious, restless man saw the glory days of 1898 returning, and proposed to lead a host of heroes into battle; but for this he needed to seek the permission of his personal enemy, Woodrow Wilson. After some hesitation (for he knew what this fire-eater thought of him) the president received him and was charmed by the effusive geniality of his guest, but nonetheless refused on principle to grant him the permission he requested. There must be no special elite units in a people's army, which should be called up on the basis of a completely fair system. Congress passed a conscription law to which the pleasant name of Selective Service Act was given. All men from twenty-one to thirty years of age (later from eighteen to forty-five) were called up and examined and their status determined by local boards. Under this rational system a total of five million men were brought under arms.

In this way the old ideal of a people's army, in contrast to a standing army, was achieved. Wilson boasted about it: "It is then not an army that we must shape and train for war, it is a nation. . . . The whole nation must be a team in which each man shall play the part for which he is best fitted."[2]

An army was called up, a navy was built, and, what was probably most necessary, hundreds of new freighters were laid down. England was gripped by great hardships; the U-boats were exacting a heavy toll, and in April alone 875,000 tons were lost. The United States came to the rescue; and once again it displayed the amazing energy that enabled it to raise whole armies and fleets from scratch. It was also able to pay for the enormous exertions; a first Liberty Loan of two billion dollars issued on May 14 was swiftly oversubscribed by a billion dollars. And, of course, taxes were sharply increased at a very progressive rate.

It was impressive, but still not quick enough for the Allies, whose situation was becoming desperate. During the spring of 1917 they were losing an immense number of lives in fruitless offensives, and they had a crying need for reinforcements. American help had to come. And it came! General John J. Pershing, who had just proved his ability in the expedition against Pancho Villa in Mexico, became the supreme commander of the American Expeditionary Force (AEF). In October the first American troops appeared at the front, and in the spring of 1918 there were sufficient numbers to shift the military balance. In June and July 1918, they played an important part in stopping the final German offensive at Château Thierry.

Still, theirs was a small share in the bitter conflict. It is difficult to answer the question of how far the American participation was of decisive importance. To do so, it would be necessary to weigh factors that are in fact immeasurable. The United States not only helped England to overcome the blockade, it not only filled the gaps in the French lines, but by its enthusiastic help it gave new courage to the Allies and by its superiority in strength it provided the certainty that the war could no longer be lost. The losses suffered were not comparable with the millions of French and English dead, but the approximately 50,000 dead and 193,000 wounded of the AEF were still a considerable sacrifice on the American side and a heavy burden for Woodrow Wilson's conscience.

War was a huge commitment. America itself was deeply affected and changed by it. Conversion to war meant not only an economic effort beyond measure; it also required a spiritual readiness that after so many years of peace was not easy to achieve. A new mentality had to be created.

Patriotism and Bolshevism

America had to become militant and intolerant. Very deliberately Wilson had to take personal part in arousing an attitude against which he had warned in his interview with Frank Cobb. It is not possible to arouse the enthusiasm of the masses with a goal that cannot be achieved, with the aim of a peace without victory. The idea that one does not have to succeed in order to persevere (a remark that is incorrectly attributed to the Dutch "father of the country," William the Silent) is wasted on the people. It is too subtle for their enthusiasm.

War feeling was very much a deliberate product. Already in April a special body was established with the task of selling the war to the people. It became a typically American operation. War was just one more product to be advertised; the committee began "a vast enterprise in salesmanship, the world's greatest adventure in advertising." This was the characterization given by the fiery chairman of the Committee on Public Information, George Creel, a man who equaled Wilson in idealism and excelled him in enthusiasm. The war, he proclaimed, was "a Crusade not merely to re-win the tomb of Christ, but to bring back to earth the rule of right, the peace, goodwill to men and gentleness he taught."[3] Soon the Committee flooded all America and even Europe with its propaganda, through pamphlets, books, lectures, and films; it was a gigantic work of evangelism, possessing its own savior, Woodrow Wilson.

A mood of great agitation made itself master of the susceptible American people, as propaganda engendered a witch-hunt. Holiness and fanaticism border closely on each other: woe to anyone who dares to speak out in opposition. For the moment there was no sign of "gentleness." Congress collaborated valiantly; freedom of the press was limited by laws on censorship and espionage. Some 1,500 opponents of the war, including the Socialist leader Eugene V. Debs, vanished into the prisons, and the post office refused to handle pacifist newspapers. Whoever appealed to the country's old humane values was likely to get into trouble. "They give you ninety days for quoting the Declaration of Independence, six months for quoting the Bible, and pretty soon somebody is going to get a life sentence for quoting Woodrow Wilson in the wrong connection," was the sardonic comment of the then Socialist Max Eastman.[4]

Hysteria knew no bounds. The campaign against everything German grew to ridiculous proportions. Symphony orchestras no longer dared to play German music, and the German language and German philosophy were struck from the curriculum of a number of colleges. It was permitted to look at Germany only with the eyes of a caricaturist. Typical in this respect was the great success of the Dutch artist Louis Raemaekers, who portrayed the German Emperor and his government as barbaric beasts in his drawings for the newspaper *De Telegraaf*, which was then anti-German. Wilson admired Raemaekers's simplifications and received him at the White House when he visited the United States in 1917.[5]

It was as if the long summer of progressive idealism broke up in the fierce storm of this militant crusade. The formal prohibitions rained down everywhere, but what was really ravaged was the whole national heritage of tolerance, humaneness, and impartiality. The American people were suddenly taken over by bigotry and fanaticism of devastating intensity. When peace came in 1918, they were not able to shift back at once to gentle moderation. It became almost automatically impossible to think of fighting for the peace without victory that had recently been so solemnly proclaimed as the aim of the war.

Wilson himself kept the goal in sight as long as he could. He did this in the first place by maintaining distance from his new allies. Not long before he had declared that he neither understood nor approved of their goals, and now he could not fall into their arms. He was ready to support them for the sake of victory, and did so in fact, but he still did not know and did not understand whether the Allies and he were seeking the same victory. For that reason he would not take the term "Ally" for the United States, but came up with the name "Associate" in a letter to House. He told the English officer and diplomat Sir William Wiseman that he was playing "a lone hand."[6]

The differences of opinions and intentions between the Allies and the United States ran very deep. The Allies fought their war for very realistic ends; they wanted to win and to safeguard their victory; and they were determined to make their enemies pay with territorial cessions and reparations. To that end they had already concluded a number of secret treaties with each other. Wilson on the contrary did not believe in such classical power politics, most assuredly of its opposite. He continued to believe in a fair peace.

This brings us to one of the most remarkable puzzles about Wilson's policy. In the summer of 1919, a year after the war ended, he declared very emphatically at a public hearing of the Senate that during the war he had not known anything about the secret agreements of his European "Associates." It was a strange declaration over which contemporaries and historians have racked their brains.

How could he have not known? How could he, the leader of mighty America, not have been aware of such essential matters? An answer to this puzzle is important because it concerns the key question of the whole conduct of the war, the meaning of the drama. More than ever after April, all of Wilson's activities had been concerned with it. Before the United States entered the war, we will recall, he had asked the belligerents for a statement of their war aims. Now the Allies were his cobelligerents. Didn't he want to know what they wanted? They came in person to tell him their intentions, and they sent him their statements in writing.

But for Wilson these declarations were anathema; they were unthinkable and therefore impossible propositions (for that is the way his mind worked, "what shouldn't be can't be"), horrible examples of the old system of a balance of forces and spheres of influence. He did not know about them, he asserted in July 1919, before he was confronted with them in Paris.

We must ask whether he was deliberately lying. Or did he push out of mind the reality he loathed? Or had he only been negligent, so that he did not know what he could have known, and what his opponents said he should have known? As soon as America entered the war, an important British delegation came to Washington headed by the new foreign secretary, the phlegmatic philosopher Arthur James, Lord Balfour. In lengthy discussions between the British and the American leaders, many things of importance were spoken of, including the war aims. At first—and this is what is curious—Wilson and House did not want to discuss them in detail, as if they wanted to avoid defilement. It would only lead to disunity, while later England and America together would be able to dictate "broad and generous terms" that could bring about "permanent peace."[7] As for agreements among the Allies themselves, Wilson at once informed House, the United States would not be bound by them.[8]

House, who kept in the forefront of the discussions, nonetheless at once took up the question of peace terms with Balfour. With a map on the table, they examined everything: Alsace-Lorraine, Belgium, Poland, the Italian *irredenta* (Italy is very greedy, said Balfour). House asked what treaties existed between the Allies. Balfour sorrowfully replied that the Allies had divided up the bearskin before the bear had been killed. House then inquired whether it would not have been proper to provide the president with copies. A reasonable request, Balfour thought, but he was not sure that he had them with him or not. In any case, House went on, it would be better if the United States did not enter these treaties, so that at the peace conferencce it could be a counterweight against all that greed. America must remain free of "petty, selfish thoughts." Balfour was enthusiastic about the idea, he said, and he continued: "I like to confer with you. I like your mind. It is clear and direct." House, pleased at the flattering words, recorded them in his diary.[9]

Two days later the discussion was renewed, this time with Wilson present.[10] And on May 18 Balfour sent the various treaties to the president; they were no small number.[11] Wilson therefore heard about the secret treaties and received them at his home. Did he fail to read them? From a letter a few months later to House, it appears that he knew about them. England and France, he wrote, do not share our ideas about the peace. He consoled himself with the thought that when the war would be coming to an end, it would be possible to do something about it, for then the Allies would be "financially in our hands."[12] He continued, however, to brood about the agreements. Late in the year, while he was busy with the Fourteen Points, he asked Balfour specifically what agreements England had made with Italy. Balfour replied that the treaty of London had indeed conceded a great deal to the Italians; whole areas along the Dalmatian coast that were not Italian but Slavic in population were promised to Italy. This settlement was "justified not on grounds of nationality but on grounds of strategy."[13] Wilson must have read this with horror.

Wilson received the secret treaties, and if he did not read them word for word, he must have been aware of what they were about. He did not know all the details, says Link in defense. Yet he was familiar with the essentials, and in any case he was able to read the text of the treaties in the newspapers later in the year, which reprinted them when they were revealed by the Bolsheviks in November. But it remains possible, strange though it may sound, that in July 1919 Wilson totally forgot them, because so many things had happened in the meantime.[14]

It remains a queer business, probably a superb instance of repression of memory. The course of events may well have been that Wilson received the treaties, glanced at them but did not read them attentively (his copy lacks the usual underlinings and marginal comments he made when reading). He understood that they concerned agreements that he did not like;

he therefore wanted to keep his own hands as clean as possible and thus maintained his distance as if to avoid contagion. Two years later he had become so immune that he no longer remembered them.

II

President Wilson made a deep impression upon many of his visitors from abroad. They often found him the prototype of the American man. A Frenchman (a French mission had followed right upon the heels of the British, and they too had many questions) described him vividly as "a very Anglo-Saxon type, thin, a long, bony face, a calm and piercing eye behind his pince-nez, and measured in his gestures." But behind that cool exterior hid "a sensitive soul" with "an interior flame that enlivens him only on rare occasions."[15]

From the same period we have a description by someone who was very close to him but detested him, Senator Lodge. He too looked at the thin face and saw there "a curious mixture of acuteness, intelligence and extreme underlying timidity—a shifty, furtive sinister expression can always be detected by a good observer."[16]

People can see each other in very different ways. Most did not find Wilson as ugly as Lodge did, quite the contrary. Admiration was predominant. He was of course most impressive as a speaker, when he was in his own element. In the first months after the declaration of war he often appeared on the lecture platform. He seems to have been compelled to present his dilemma candidly; when he spoke, as often happens with persons of poetic temperament, he discovered his own truth. But there remained a certain ambivalence in these speeches. Wilson continued to talk to his hearers about the great goal of peace, but no longer of peace without victory. And the man who not long before had maintained that the causes of the war were vague was now convinced that the whole guilt lay upon the ruling caste in Germany. This now became his great simplification: the guilt of the German government. Henceforth the grand theme of his addresses became that everything would come out well if the German government, the last bulwark of autocracy, were swept away. On the occasion of Flag Day, he sketched a picture of Germany's "grab for world power" that Fritz Fischer forty years later could hardly improve on.[17]

What it came down to for him was that the real antagonists in the war were American democracy and German autocracy. Germans were too thorough, too professional. America, he told naval officers in another speech, was "the prime amateur nation of the world," always inventive and surprising, but Germany was "the prize professional nation of the world." This idea was characteristic of the poetic person who preferred to think of himself as an amateur, an outsider among lawyers, historians, and politicians.[18]

It was just because the Germans were so thorough, he explained at another time, that they had become so ambitious for power. They were not satisfied with their excellent position on the world market. Their government wanted more: "All the while, there was lying behind its thoughts and in its dreams of the future a political control which could enable it in the long run to dominate the labor and industry of the world."[19] One can feel in such statements that he was beginning to absorb into his judgment the German people, whom in April he had still absolved of all guilt. In his annual message in December, he returned to this theme. Germany wanted military and political hegemony, but the world could not accept it.[20]

The world would no longer permit that. Here we come again to a key theme in Wilson's philosophy, which we ought rather to call his theology. There was in his mind such a thing as a world will, the will of common people in every country. This will coincided with the will of providence and was therefore irresistible. All history proved it. He applied this idea skillfully when he spoke to a reunion of Confederate veterans of the Civil War (a good number still remained). The United States had remained one country, a strong country; no wise heart could see anything in it but divine intentions, a majestic plan. Within their own times Americans had been too shortsighted to see this, but now they understood what God had in mind for them, for He worked in his mysterious providence. This was the true piety of Woodrow Wilson.

The very first person to be convinced of this theology by Wilson was himself. He could not help but respond positively to his world. He justified his great change of policy, stressing that it was made in heaven. He also convinced most of his progressive followers. Pacifists and idealists like Jane Addams, Upton Sinclair, Lincoln Steffens, and Ray Stannard Baker, along with many others, experienced with him how war became the great purification, the great gift of meaning to the world, because what was at stake was a new world. Their experience was later recalled

Family portrait taken around 1890 at the home of Dr. George Howe in Columbia, South Carolina. Woodrow Wilson is the first on the left in the third row. In the middle of the same row is his father, Joseph Ruggles Wilson, and next to him are Marian and Joseph Wilson (in uniform), sister and brother of Woodrow Wilson.

Woodrow Wilson in 1879 as a student at Princeton and member of a dining club called the Alligators. Wilson is the third from the right, holding his hat in his hand.

Woodrow Wilson and his family in September 1910. The daughters are, from the left, Eleanor, Jessie, and Margaret. This was the first picture of Wilson taken for political use and was published at the time of his candidacy for the governorship of New Jersey.

President Wilson and former president William Howard Taft.

President Wilson opening a World Series game.

President Wilson with his cabinet in 1913. Clockwise from the left are
W. G. McAdoo, J. C. McReynolds, J. Daniels, D. F. Houston, W. B. Wilson,
W. C. Redfield, F. K. Lane, A. S. Burleson, L. M. Garrison, and W. J. Bryan.

J. Bryan   D. F. Houston   A. S. Burleson   W. B. Wilson

Lindley M. Garrison   Franklin K. Lane

Colonel House and President Wilson, September 1917.

Wilson's welcome to Paris in 1917.

President Wilson and Captain McCauley on the bridge of the S. S. George Washington, en route to Europe in December 1918.

*President Wilson and Raymond Poincairé, president of France. Taken
during Wilson's arrival in Paris in December 1918.*

*President Wilson and Vittorio Emanuele, king of Italy. Taken during
Wilson's arrival in Rome in January 1919.*

President Wilson and General John J. Pershing in France, saluting while the national anthem is played.

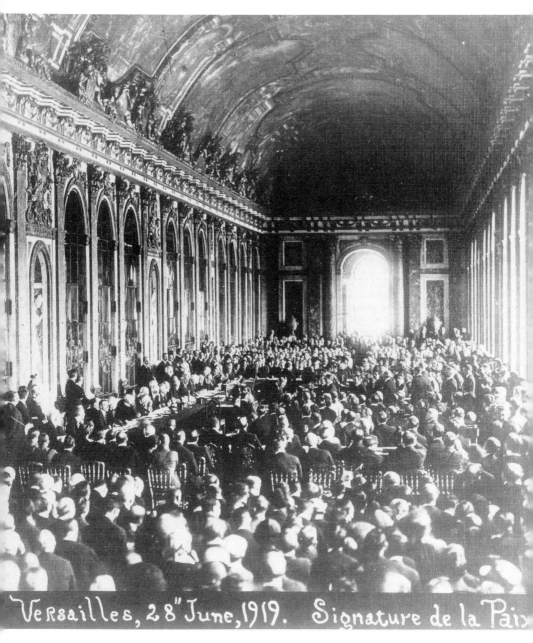

Signing of the treaty of Versailles, which formally ended World War I in June 1919.

This photograph, taken in 1920, was requested by Mrs. Wilson to reassure the U.S. public that President Wilson was in good health despite his stroke. The photographer took the picture from Wilson's right side since the president's face sagged on the left and his left arm dangled, requiring Mrs. Wilson to hold the letters he is signing.

President Wilson leaving the presidential mansion for an Armistice Day celebration in 1923. He is supported by his valet.

by the historian Carl L. Becker, when he looked back in disappointment upon his youthful enthusiasm.

> Having been long engaged in destroying what we are pleased to call civilization, a genuine emotion welled up within us when Mr. Wilson beautifully and positively assured us that war is an abomination, but that this war was different from all other wars because in this war we were fighting to end war and to bring in a New Order of peace and just dealing. The emotion was pleasant and necessary because it enabled us to believe that it was right, in this one case alone, to force millions of young men to go out to kill and be killed.[21]

Millions were indeed sacrificed in the ever more insane holocaust. The year 1917, "the year of troubles," was a year of great changes—the revolution in Russia, the entry of the United States into the war—but in the summer the war was going into its fourth year and no end was in sight. The colossal offensives in East and West, Brusilov in Galicia, the British at Passchendaele, the Austrians at Caporetto, changed the situation a little but made no essential difference. Many in desperation sought to find a meaning in the unending madness. Many then and many later, statesmen then and historians in our times, have wrestled with the horrifying drama of this gigantic mass murder. Wasn't the war, it was asked, a world revolution? Didn't this bitter conflict crystallize the deeper contrast between old and new, between autocracy and democracy. Wasn't all Europe divided, therefore, into two parties, on the one side the party of tradition, stagnation, and imperialism, and opposing it the party of change, progress, and a diplomacy in the service of ideas?[22]

Wilson himself was more and more inclined to think in these terms, and many progressives in Europe sought to explain the significance of the war in similar ways. Liberals and Socialists in the warring countries began to present demands that expressed their understanding of the conflict. This has been truly called "the Americanization of war aims." Everywhere demands were made that the coming peace should embody these noble ideals: no annexations, no reparations, no balance of power, but open diplomacy, international administration of the colonies, a League of Nations.

The call for peace became ever louder. In brutal fact, however, it remained a one-sided process. The yearning it embodied for a better world could be heard. One may believe with Wilson that there was a "moral force" responding to the great destruction in this way. But it is very much a question whether it was also really a "major force," as he believed. The cry for peace became louder, but on the other side leaders from all the belligerent countries came to the fore who would have nothing to do with mediation, who wanted a "peace with victory." Lloyd George in England, Clemenceau in France, Orlando in Italy, and not least the Supreme Army Command in Germany, all wanted war to the bitter end. They found the support they needed for their program among their peoples. War arouses not only a yearning for peace but also rage and vengefulness.

In the summer of 1917 the yearning for peace found expression in a number of political declarations. In Germany the army command was able to bring down Chancellor Von Bethmann Hollweg with the help of the Reichstag, but a week later a majority of the same Reichstag (Center, Liberals, and Socialists) under the leadership of Matthias Erzberger, adopted a resolution demanding a "peace of understanding" (*Verständigung*). It had little effect, for the generals and the new chancellor, their puppet Michaelis, paid little attention to it.[23]

It was followed on August 1 by the peace message of Pope Benedict XV. It resembled quite closely the calls for peace that Wilson had made before he became a participant in the war. The pope enunciated the principle of peace without victory. He pleaded that the moral force of right be permitted to prevail over the material force of arms. He even examined various territorial questions, asking for the evacuation of Belgium and French territory (but without mentioning Alsace-Lorraine), spoke of the restoration of Germany's colonies, and held that a spirit of fairness and right could solve the other problems.[24]

The leaders of Europe merely shrugged their shoulders. Of course they wanted peace, but not at the moment and not in this way. Wilson became more perplexed. Did he have to reject what he had been pleading for only a half year before? His advisers were divided. House saw a new chance for peace. He wrote Wilson that he could take the peace negotiations out of the hands of the pope "and hold them in your own." Germany would then understand that only the president of the United States was in a position to attain peace, and the Allies would have to follow him.[25] Lansing gave opposite advice. Behind the pope's message lay Austria, he said. The proposal in any case went no further than the German declaration in December. Wilson listened to Lansing. It was incredible, House commented in his diary; he was sure he had given a much more complete survey of the situation than the president or Lansing.[26]

At the end of August Lansing sent the American reply to Rome. It was drawn up by Wilson personally. He agreed with the pope that the war was horrible, but he had to proceed upon the basis of hard facts. The world must first be freed from German militarism. The word of the present rulers of Germany could not be trusted; it guaranteed nothing.[27]

Wilson could no longer approve what he himself had said earlier, which was being repeated not only by the pope but also by the Socialists. At the initiative of leaders in neutral countries such as the Dutchman Troelstra and the Dane Stauning, the Socialists convened a peace congress in Stockholm, in which Russian Socialists from Petrograd soon took an active part. But their efforts failed because of the recalcitrance of the Allies. London and Paris refused to give British and French delegates the necessary passports, so that the meeting became a narrow affair of the Socialists from Germany, Austria, and the neutral countries, plus the Russians. Wilson accepted information about the conference from American Socialists, but they assured him that it was a dangerous conspiracy of the German emperor, and therefore he too refused passports to those Socialist party leaders who were more pacifistically inclined.[28] It was a misunderstanding, complained the Socialist leaders at Stockholm, and they informed him by cable that their conference was based on the very principles that he had expounded in his address to the Senate.[29]

But was it in fact a misunderstanding on Wilson's part? He was caught in his persisting dilemma. He had to win the war, but he was in difficulty with himself. His whole nature was focused on the unity and interconnection between dream and deed, on moral certitude. And now he stood in a position of opposition to his own principles, he had to work with nuances and be cautious. Nowhere was he confronted with so much simple radicalism as in the new Russia. We have seen that Wilson enthusiastically had greeted the first revolution in the spring, welcoming Russia as a democratic ally. There was no enemy left anywhere in the whole world except Germany (and its allies, Austria-Hungary and Turkey).

Americans knew very little about Russia, however. They began very characteristically to see Russian conditions as if somehow they were like America's. They thought they recognized American progressives in the persons of Russian liberals, and in the revolution itself they saw the

American principle of "consent of the governed." They honestly believed that their recognition of the new government would have "a stupendous moral effect."[30] In the motley assemblage of Americans in St. Petersburg, inspired by a variety of commercial and idealistic aims, there were only a few who showed greater understanding.[31] The majority believed that Russia in its muddled state provided an ideal place for application of their ideas. Picturesque reformers like Raymond Robins and Edgar Sisson worked for the Committee on Public Information and translated and distributed Wilson's speeches in large editions.

Everything turned of course on the question of whether the Russians were still willing to continue fighting. The Russian leaders Miliukov and Kerensky made large promises, but were the Russian people still ready or even able to continue? The Petrograd Soviet issued a declaration in May that peace must be made without delay, upon the basis of principles that were as alike to Wilson's as two peas in a pod: no annexations, no reparations, peace without victory. The president was being overtaken from the left, it seemed, and he was bothered, as appears from the message that he sent to the first American mission to Russia at the end of May.

Like all the Allied countries, the United States did its best to keep Russia in the war, and this was the assignment of the official mission, a varied band of well-wishers and businessmen with the conservative old statesman Elihu Root as chairman. In the message that Wilson gave them for the Russian government, the emphasis lay not upon the great ideals of selflessness and self-determination, although they were mentioned, but upon the necessity for holding out. The great rhetorician declared that it would be fine if "statements of principle" were formulated "that will have a pleasing and sonorous sound," but that "practical questions can be settled only by practical means. Phrases will not accomplish the result." Thus, with a touch of the tragicomic, the idealist tried to be a realist, the talker a doer. Russia had to continue fighting, whether it wanted to or not: "If we stand together, victory is certain." That was a different sound than talk about peace without victory.[32]

The mission accomplished nothing. The members of the mission were fêted by their Russian hosts, but their warning, "No fight, no loan," was ineffectual. They saw, if they wanted, the festering spread of chaos around them. One man who did see hope because as a pure-blooded reformer that is what he was eager to see, was the renowned journalist Lincoln Steffens. This intense and colorful American optimist had become famed by his revelations of corruption in American cities at the beginning of the century, set down in his book *The Shame of the Cities*, and he would later enter the literary pantheon in America with his *Autobiography*. Steffens was a true muckraker. He saw with razor sharpness the evil in his own decaying capitalist country and was very keen on finding the good in another, faraway land. For this purpose Russia was ideal. Steffens came, saw, and was conquered by the sight of a nation that was, he thought, by its nature democratic and willing. "Some of us who lived with the Russians in their joy will never again lose our belief in the possibilities of human nature in the mob; of man in the mass."[33]

With such an attitude he could give clear and strong advice to Wilson. He wrote to House that the Allies must proclaim a peace without punishment, without compensation, without territorial aggrandizement, but with self-determination for all peoples; then Russia would fight on.[34] Returning to Washington during the summer, Steffens went to the president to tell him this in person, as Kerensky had asked him to do, he said. Let Wilson and his allies openly disavow the secret treaties, and then the Russian people would persevere. But, Steffens tells us in his *Autobiography*, which is not wholly reliable, Wilson had to reply that he was not acquainted with these treaties and therefore could not do anything about them. But the tone in which he responded made his feelings clear to Steffens. "He was disturbed. He got up, walked to the window, and forgot me in his reflections."[35]

III

It is a deep human dream to be able truly to begin history anew, to do creation over again, to do better than ever before. And then there is the feeling of being young, that everything lies open before you, that everything is possible. Wordsworth, who was in France in the opening years of the French Revolution, described that feeling in famous words:

> Bliss was it in that dawn to be alive
> But to be young was very heaven.

Young Americans in Russia in October 1917 experienced the same ecstasy when the Bolsheviks seized power; everything was changing, everything was new. One of them, William C. Bullitt, in his enthusiasm quoted

Wordsworth's lines and rejoiced: A new dawn was rising, not of political machinery but in the hearts of men. The peoples would come to a spiritual conversion. It was beginning in Russia, where the nation was becoming "brotherly, open hearted, free from convention and unafraid of life." Wouldn't such a "state of grace" (those are his very words) break through as well in the rest of Europe and in America?[36] And his friend Lincoln Steffens found his vision in the Bible: the revolution in Russia would establish the kingdom of heaven upon earth, so that Christ could soon return and rule forever. "Forever and ever, everywhere."[37]

That was the feeling of many, even of eyewitnesses. They were sure it must be possible to work with the new rulers, who were idealists too. "Let's make these Bolshewiks our Bolshewiks; don't let the Germans make them their Bolshewiks," said one of the Americans in Petrograd.[38]

It soon was evident that this would not be easy. The Bolsheviks revealed themselves as ruthless radicals who aroused fierce hostility in more conservative circles in the West, and they adopted an unorthodox (to put it mildly) foreign policy. They apparently realized the dilemma in which Wilson was trapped, and they ostentatiously inscribed his liberal slogans, somewhat sharpened, on their red banners. On the first full day they were in power (November 8), they issued a peace decree drawn up by Lenin personally, which called for a peace without annexations and reparations and for open diplomacy. Their intention in this document was not only to call their Marxist kindred spirits in the West to revolution, but certainly also to influence American public opinion. The peace decree, writes E. H. Carr, was a forerunner of Wilson's address of two months later.[39]

In other declarations as well they formulated their ideals, which amounted essentially to peace without victory. In these documents there was also some ambiguity; they spoke of the right of self-determination of the peoples (not only for the Belgians and Czechs, but also for the Irish and Indians), but they were also internationalists who thought in terms not of nations but of classes, and this became their dilemma in their foreign policy. At the end of 1917, however, they were in such desperate straits that they could not worry about principles and had to be very flexible.

They did make good at once upon their principle of open diplomacy. Digging into the archives, they published the secret treaties that they found there. At the end of November the first of these were published in *Izvestia*, and in the course of the winter all the treaties were made public in a series of pamphlets. The treaties soon found their way to the West; the *Manchester Guardian* published them in English translation on December 12, and the *New York Evening Post* followed immediately. Did Wilson not read them now either? They certainly had a definite influence upon the Fourteen-Points speech in January.

Americans had very different reactions to the Bolshevik action. A traditional diplomat like Lansing was dismayed and at once wrote a "statement" in which he forthrightly called the Bolshevik revolution a coup d'etat that did not at all represent the Russian people. The violation of treaties, he asserted, was a proof of unreliability. Didn't the new Russian leaders threaten, if they were not recognized, to go over the heads of the Allied governments to their peoples?[40] But Lansing, at Wilson's insistence, did not make his statement public. Why did Wilson restrain him? After all, he too was angry at the publication of the secret treaties and called it, in a talk with Wiseman, "outrageous conduct."[41] Did he feel that the Russian action put him in a bind? Their stated war ends were strikingly similar to his. And he himself, after all, was also fond of going over the heads to speak directly to the peoples, and he would soon do it again.

The similarity was noted by many observers. Arthur Bullard, a discerning American journalist in Petrograd (as the city was renamed), wrote that it was Wilson who should be able to understand the Bolshevik ideas; both he and Trotsky, who was the first commissar for foreign affairs in the new regime, hoped for a new anti-imperialist Germany, and in any case both wanted the Allies to disavow their expansion plans.[42] Trotsky's book, *The Bolshewiki and the World Peace*, was published in New York at this time, and the advertisements for it reported that the author "tells in this book how he would make the world safe for democracy."[43] If Wilson would only tell Trotsky that he meant what he said, Lincoln Steffens told Walter Lippmann, it would "make a great difference in Trotsky's behavior."[44] Trotsky, Bullitt maintained, "is a good deal ahead of us in the march toward world liberalism, but he is marching in our direction."[45] And the well-known journalist Lincoln Colcord explained in a long letter to Wilson that the Bolsheviks were not as bad as they were painted, that they had brought order, not chaos, to Russia, and that Trotsky's publication of the secret diplomatic correspondence fitted perfectly into the American diplomatic tradition.[46]

Wilson himself wisely did not dream these vain dreams. He received so much contradictory information that he became more skeptical. Ambassador Francis sent him in November the speech in which Trotsky had denounced the United States as a capitalist, hypocritical, and greedy country. Wilson read it to his cabinet, called it shameless and scorned the actions of Lenin and Trotsky as a kind of "opera bouffe."[47] It was his opinion that the similarity between his policy and that of the Bolsheviks was more external than real. He came to see the new Russian leaders as muddled idealists who allowed themselves to be taken in by the Germans. He became cautious, and decided not to recognize the new Russian regime for the time being.

Lansing attempted to persuade him to give support to the rightist regime of the Cossack hetman Kaledin, which had its base in the Don district. According to Lansing, Kaledin was very much like General U. S. Grant.[48] But that went too far for Wilson; he did not want to give up the dream of a new, democratic Russia. In his annual message of December 4 he spoke with great sympathy for the Russian people. Had they only heard from the beginning of the revolution a clear statement from the Allies that this was only a war for the self-determination of the peoples, things would not have gone so badly in Russia. But unfortunately they had become the prey of the German generals; they were poisoned with the same lies that had kept the German people in ignorance "and the poison has been administered by the very same hands. The only possible antidote is the truth."[49]

Did he himself still believe this? In meetings of the cabinet he expressed himself in more somber terms. All propaganda in Russia, he said, was like pouring water into a bottomless well.[50] But in any case he had to do something; he agreed with his collaborators that the second Russian revolution in any case required a response.

This became even more urgent as a result of further developments in Russia. At the end of the year a Russian delegation went to Brest-Litovsk to make peace with the Germans. The Russian delegates proposed to make these discussions into a propaganda battle, going over the heads of their German enemies to the world. Trotsky described himself as a prosecuting attorney![51] For this reason a message was sent to the peoples and governments (in that order) of the Allied countries, in which all the Bolshevik peace demands were repeated and the nations were called upon to come together to make peace.[52] Shortly thereafter, on January 3, a cablegram came from Ambassador Francis suggesting that Wilson address himself to the Russian people, restating the noble ideals that he had set forth in his Senate speech (the speech of January 22, 1917, on "peace without victory").[53]

Various other advisers also urged an appeal to the Russian people. It was not necessary to recognize the new government, wrote William Boyce Thompson, a rich American idealist in Russia, Wilson could speak directly to the people; the Bolshevik rulers would recognize and value such action, for most of them were "kindly, earnest men, heartily desiring to live in peace with their fellow men," and ninety percent of the Russian people thought the same way.[54] The Russian ambassador Boris Bakhmetyev, who had been in Washington for only half a year and was now unemployed, came with the same suggestion, which fitted well with Wilson's idea of good peoples suppressed by evil governments.

Wilson saw himself placed before the difficult task of responding to the Russian revolution. What he had to make clear was both points of agreement and disagreement. Was there more than an external similarity? When two persons say the same thing, they don't have to mean the same thing. Idealists, then and later, liked to stress the agreement; they readily affirmed that Lenin and Wilson were the two prophets of the future. Lenin's final goal, declares one historian, was as utopian as Wilson's, although his road to it was admittedly more destructive.[55] Idealists readily see similarities, as we have already observed; they live for the goal and not for the means.

The reality was of course that Wilson and Lenin were poles apart in their means and their ends. An abyss separated them. Although some Americans talked gullibly about Lenin, on the other side the Bolsheviks deeply distrusted Wilson. Lenin personally told an American visitor, the anarchist (and later Communist) Robert Minor, that the League of Nations was a league of imperialists intended to strangle the peoples. "President Wilson is a shrewd man."[56] Wilson as a hypocrite! This was a characterization that would put down roots, not only in Russia but also among many disappointed idealists in the West.

A comparison between Wilson and Lenin was made in another, quite different way as well. Western Socialists in particular, shocked by the Bolshevik terror, bitterly opposed the new Russian regime. They felt themselves forced to make a choice. The French Socialist Albert Thomas expressed their attitude strongly in *L'Humanité*, their newspaper: "Either Wilson or Lenin. Either the democracy born of the French Revolution, strengthened by a whole century of struggle, further developed by the great Republic of the United States; or the primitive, incoherent, brutal forms of Russian fanaticism. We must choose."[57]

Wilson or Lenin—it was essentially the difference between evolution and revolution, between organic thinking in the tradition of Burke or idealistic thinking in the tradition of Marx, the difference between liberalism and Communism. As the American historian Whittle Johnson formulated it in words pregnant with meaning: "What Wilson saw as the fulfillment of progressive history, Lenin saw as the critical stage in the degeneration of the old order and as the prelude of its violent overthrow. And what Lenin saw as the inevitable course of the progressive revolution, was for Wilson a tyrannical derailing of normal constitutional development. Wilson's point of rest was Lenin's point of attack."[58]

But, precisely because the contrast was so great, Wilson was driven all the more to clarify what the difference was and to explain why his idealism was better and truer than Lenin's. He could not allow the wind to be taken out of his own sails.

TWENTY-ONE

You do not know and cannot appreciate the anxieties I
have experienced as a result of many millions of people
having their hopes raised by what I have said.
—*Woodrow Wilson*

FOURTEEN POINTS

ILSON HAD TO RESPOND
to the new and strange threat
in Eastern Europe, but he was
an idealist whose attitude was
too positive to be only a reaction.
His Fourteen Points were in a certain sense a response to the challenge
of Bolshevism, but they were also something much more, a program for
peace that he was developing long before the Bolsheviks took over Russia.
It is a dangerous historical distortion to see Wilson's peace efforts in the
years 1918–1919 as only a reaction to something else. The man was more
than his circumstances. If we want to see him in his time, we must recognize that his peace program was an attempt to express the deepest
dreams of the whole eighteenth and nineteenth centuries, the culmination
of two centuries of belief in progress.

If the Fourteen Points were also a response, it was in the very first
place to his own dilemma as a belligerent who was seeking peace. He
wanted to present a program, to put down a practical foundation for his
dream of a better future. It was the problem of giving an adequate answer
to the pope's peace initiative, which he wrestled with during the summer,

that set him to thinking about the larger question. At the beginning of September he wrote to House suggesting that it might be better to prepare more effectively for the process of peace. Would it not be possible to assemble a group of experts for this task? He had heard that other countries were doing the same. House replied at once. Creating a group to work behind the scenes was right up his alley.[1]

House began the organization of a body of scholars who have gone down in history under the fitting name of "The Inquiry." He assembled a large group of experts in many fields and established their headquarters in the offices of the American Geographical Society in New York. He personally kept a finger in the pie; he named the philosopher of religion, Sidney E. Mezes, who happened to be his brother-in-law, as director, and the young newspaperman, Walter Lippmann, as secretary.

It was a splendid plan. The sober enthusiasm of so many specialists ought to make an important contribution to understanding the great questions of the peace. They believed in Wilson's ideals, and set to work assiduously. In short order they produced a host of bulky reports on 101 topics. They sought information from practice as well as from books; one informant was their European colleague Thomas G. Masaryk, whose lectures were a high point of their preparatory program.[2]

The problem quickly arose how to coordinate all this expert knowledge into practical advice. The Inquiry grew much too fast, as happens with such bodies, and almost became a rival of the State Department. Internal quarrels increased the difficulties, and it was not too easy for Wilson to work with it. He took the members with him to Paris and consulted them, and he therefore surprised his colleagues in Paris by his knowledge of details. They might consider his theories too abstract, but they had to concede that his facts were accurate, Wiseman wrote.[3] This sounded fine, but in practice things did not go smoothly. Wilson was not usually a good listener, and he was too quick to put his "moral ideals" ahead of reality and believed too much, as one of his advisers, the historian James T. Shotwell remarks, "in his own ability, single-handed, to secure their acceptance"; he would ask now and then for advice, but he did not really bring his fellow commission members and his advisers into his negotiations.[4]

Meanwhile House was much more directly involved in the questions of the war by 1917. It was to some extent against his will, for his ambition had been to play a large part in the making of the eventual peace. But just as he was beginning the organization of the Inquiry, a request came from London for an American representative in the Allied war council and Wilson wanted no one other than House. The colonel was still very adept at flattering his great friend. If this war could be justified at all, House told the president, it was principally because it provided him the opportunity to do "unselfish service." Unlike the traditional great figures of history—Alexander, Caesar, and Napoleon—who had used their power for personal and national aggrandizement, Wilson could use his for "the general good of mankind." He suggested that the time had come to make a statement of general principles about the war aims. Tears came to Wilson's eyes, reported House, and he himself was equally moved: "The friendship shown me by the President and Mrs. Wilson touches me deeply. There is no subject too intimate to be discussed before me; there is nothing that can be thought of for my comfort or pleasure that is not urged upon me."[5]

House therefore had to go to London. He arrived at the beginning of November, at a critical moment in the Allied conduct of the war. Russia had been eliminated as a participant by the second revolution, and Italy was badly battered at Caporetto. This perilous situation did lead to closer collaboration and extended talks about the American help, which was so necessary. But House did not succeed in his aim, which was to persuade the Allies to accept making a joint declaration on the basis of a fair peace. Once more the colonel was not a match for the hard-boiled European realists. To be sure, he had a pleasant and very busy time. He saw everyone who was anyone; he lunched with King George V, he had broad discussions with Lloyd George and a host of ministers and generals, who impressed him with their greatness (!) and friendliness. He went to Paris, where Clemenceau had no trouble winning his confidence. But the Frenchman turned down his request point-blank, rejecting even a very cautious formulation to the effect that the war was not being waged for aggressive ends or reparations. Clemenceau, House remarked, adhered to his motto: "*Je fais la guerre*" (I am fighting a war); Lloyd George was too much under the influence of the Conservatives; the Italians held stubbornly to their demand for restoration of their *irredenta*.[6]

In December House returned to Washington empty-handed. Wilson now had to appear himself as the principal actor. This probably did not displease him too much. His mistrust of the Allies was once more confirmed, and his program could be all the clearer and freer of compromise. House's failure gave him a second impulsion, following the challenge from the Bolsheviks, to make known his own points for peace.

A third factor also moved him to action—the shaky situation of

Austria-Hungary. The Dual Monarchy, which with incredible reckless-
ness had been the first to enter the war, was no longer able to meet the
colossal demands placed upon it. The numerous peoples within its frontiers grumbled and resisted; their soldiers went over to the enemy. (It was
just at this time that the Czechs in Russia began to form a separate problem, as we shall soon see.) Finally, the government in Vienna lost its grip
on the motley Hapsburg empire. The new emperor, twenty-nine-year-old
Charles, who had succeeded the aged Francis Joseph in November, saw
the coming storm and tried by secret negotiations to save his empire and
his crown. On Christmas 1917 his minister of foreign affairs, Count Czernin, gave a very conciliatory speech, and he too spoke the language of the
moment: a fair peace without annexations or reparations was all that Vienna wanted.

Wilson now had to make clear what he had in mind. He could link
up with the general feeling, but he had to make it more precise. He believed that he could thereby get the public opinion of the exhausted
peoples of Europe behind him. As a measure of preparation, he asked
the Inquiry, which had just set about its work and still burned with idealism, to submit to him a general report with suggestions. Mezes and two
young collaborators, David Hunter Miller and Walter Lippmann, drew
it up and Wilson received it shortly before Christmas.[7] It gave a survey
of the actual situation in Europe, but also presented cautious counsel that
was in accord with Wilson's ideas and hence to his taste. Its emphasis lay
upon the great German danger, especially expansion toward Baghdad. An
ambivalent attitude was recommended toward Austria-Hungary: stimulation of the national movements but a warning against splitting the
Austrian empire into separate states. Its vision of Russia was still naïve:
it described the Russian revolution as anticapitalist and filled with "religious love of Russia," so that it formed a good counterweight against
Protestant Germany. In general, Wilson should play upon "the almost
universal feeling on the part of the common people that the old diplomacy
is bankrupt and that the armed peace must not be restored." Of course
there was nothing he wanted more; it was a report he could have written
himself. The report also included a number of practical suggestions on
territorial questions and Wilson readily made use of them.

About the turn of the year he busied himself again with the peace
program. He did not spare himself and gave the impression of extreme
fatigue, reported House anxiously.[8] But he was doing now at last what he

wanted most of all to do, he was solving his dilemma. In a long conversation two days later with Spring-Rice, he told the British ambassador what he planned to say. He wanted to go over the head of the German government and speak to the German people, as the Bolsheviks were doing. He must reply to their appeal to all peoples. He too wanted to make an end to all aggression; he too believed in self-determination, although it was a principle that could not be applied with too strict logic. In any case the whole American people stood behind him to a man.[9]

During the same day (January 4) Wilson discussed with House the basic things that he would say in his speech. Late into the evening they bent over the maps that House had brought from the Geographic Institute, and the next day they went over them again. The report by House in his diary drips with self-satisfaction; if we are to believe him, almost all the good ideas came out of his inventive mind, and with much self-assurance he spurred Wilson now and then: "As to Russia I urged him to be at his best." House believed in Wilson in his own opinionated way. The president was "the only one who measures up to the requirements of the day when the world is in such agony."[10]

What a difference from Lloyd George, thought House. He had tried to persuade the British prime minister to do something equally great, but he was "not big enough to realize the necessity for it." Now at the beginning of January, however, Lloyd George surprised House and the whole world with a peace message, as well as an appeal for a just peace without revenge and reparations, "upon the very same lines I urged upon him," maintained House, a little dazed. The wizard of Wales loved surprises; that he now, on January 5, so suddenly joined the peace chorus is to be explained by a complex of motives. He was truly concerned over the course of the war after the awful losses suffered by the British army at Ypres in the autumn. He was reacting also to events in Russia; he was not averse to coming to an agreement with the Germans for a compromise at the expense of the Bolsheviks. And he enjoyed being ahead of Wilson, that is certain. But he said apologetically that his purpose was only to win over the English workers with his progressive language.[11]

Wilson was disconcerted. Lloyd George had cut the ground from under his feet, he told House. But House reassured him that now the situation was finally cleared up and his task had become all the plainer. Wilson accepted these observations. What else could he do? He wanted to be more specific than the British prime minister. And, as usual in periods of tension, he maintained his composure by spending much time on the golf course and in the evening by reading Wordsworth.

II

Of all the impressive sermons that Wilson preached to his people and to the world, none became so famous as his "Fourteen Points" speech of January 8, 1918. It attained a breadth and depth, in space and in time, greater than that of all the others. Not that it is his finest address; there are others, such as the "peace without victory" speech of a year earlier and the declaration of war of April 1917, which are more splendid in rhetoric and wider in vision. But this time Wilson was more practical, adding as it were deed to words; he developed a practical program that was of importance for the whole world.[12]

He opened by explaining the reasons for his speech. He took as his starting point the negotiations at Brest-Litovsk, which had been suspended and which he thought had failed. He spoke with warm sympathy about the Russians as the helpless victims of "the grim power of Germany"; he praised exuberantly the Russian soul, which had not surrendered, which had expressed its conception of right and humanity with "a frankness, a largeness of view, a generosity of spirit and a universal human sympathy" that should speak to everyone. More than ever this was a war between right and wrong, freedom and compulsion. That was why the United States was taking part, for it was unsoiled and unselfish; it wanted peace for the whole world. For this peace he now expounded his program of fourteen points.

He began with five general points of principle. The beginning of the first point rang out like a trumpet blast: "Open covenants of peace openly arrived at." Henceforth there would be no more secret treaties but open negotiations. But what precisely did these words mean? That diplomats could no longer meet behind closed doors? Or only that they must make public the results of their confidential discussions? The first answer seems to have been obvious, and in Paris, where all discussions were held in secret, the press made its case for access by an appeal to this point. But Wilson wrote a half year later to Lansing that he had not intended that no more "private discussions of delicate matters" could take place, but only that no more secret treaties could be concluded.[13] The fine formula turned out to be quite ambiguous.

Fourteen Points

The second point contained the principle of the open seas. That too seemed fine, but it annoyed the British no end. What did it really mean? Would maritime hegemony in a new world order no longer be necessary? Or was there concealed behind it an American desire to dominate the seas themselves? After all, the Americans were busy constructing their own navy. The "open seas" question became a latent point of difference at the peace conference in Paris. Point three, the removal of as many economic frontiers as possible, was an old liberal principle that had been part of Wilson's New Freedom. Point four, the reduction of armaments, was pretty much merely a pious wish, and it was hardly discussed at Paris. Only the fifth point of principle, a free and honorable settlement of all colonial claims, with the interests of the populations involved weighing as heavily as those of the colonial power, was a ticklish affair during the peace negotiations, for major interests were at stake.

The next eight points were concerned with territorial questions. Not accidentally, Wilson began with Russia. He feared that the Western countries would misuse the upheavals in Russia in order to intervene. This was unacceptable and he gave the Allies a sharp warning: the way Russia was handled by her "sister nations" would be "the acid test of their good will, of their comprehension of her needs as distinguished from their own and of their intelligent and unselfish sympathy."

Point seven required the restoration of Belgium. All were in agreement on this point, but even here Wilson put stress on a supplementary moral issue: the emancipation of Belgium meant that trust in law and agreements among nations would be restored to a place of honor. Point eight concerned the evacuation of France and formulated in cautious terms the restitution of Alsace-Lorraine. Point nine established the principle that the boundaries of Italy "should be effected along clearly recognized lines of nationality." This rubbed the Italians the wrong way; their *sacro egoismo* appealed stubbornly to the secret treaty of London. Bitter confrontations in Paris over this issue would result, even when Wilson compromised more than a little on it.

The following point was too ambiguous to have much chance: Austria-Hungary must be maintained, but the peoples in the Dual Monarchy had the right to autonomous development. Point eleven applied the principle of self-determination with careless vigor to the Balkans, mentioning Romania, Serbia, and Montenegro by name; it also promised the Serbians an outlet to the sea. All this was to be achieved "along historically established lines of allegiance and nationality." The Turks came off badly; in point twelve they retained only what belonged to them on an ethnic basis, while the other nationalities in the Ottoman Empire were promised autonomous development. The Dardanelles must become an open waterway. The last territorial point concerned the restoration of Poland, to which all districts with a predominantly Polish population would belong, and it too would receive an outlet to the sea.

All in all, the Fourteen Points seemed practical and responsible. How lightly they skipped over historical problems would only become evident in Paris. But there was also a fourteenth point, a panacea for all the shortcomings now and later, a League of Nations: "A special association of nations must be formed under specific covenants for the purpose of affording mutual guarantees of political independence and territorial integrity to great and small states alike." This short sentence carried a heavy burden, too heavy as it turned out. In these few words the future world peace was settled, totally and permanently. For Wilson everything revolved around it; he did not see the difficulties and he did not want to see them, and this would in the end bring his downfall.

These points did not exhaust the issues with which he was concerned. The German problem obviously kept him very busy; it also contained the whole of his dilemma. Once more he voiced his admiration for the good Germany, so great in science and "pacific enterprise." It deserved an equal place among the nations. But he had to know which Germany he would be facing at an eventual peace conference, the Germany that had found its voice in the majority in the Reichstag (he referred here to the peace resolution of the previous summer), or the militaristic Germany that wanted to win the war. In this way Wilson attempted at this time (and he would do it again repeatedly) to make an appeal to the "other Germany." He would consider only a democratic Germany for a peace without victory (that is, one without defeat). These were words that stuck in German minds.

It is probably significant that Wilson's speech was received with much greater enthusiasm in the United States than in Europe. American politicians were very satisfied with it, the newspapers rejoiced. The *New York Tribune* spoke of a second emancipation proclamation: Lincoln had freed the slaves, Wilson freed the peoples. But the perverse Europeans wondered whether it was all as practical as it seemed. The *Times* of London remarked that some of Wilson's proposals seemed to assume that the kingdom of justice on earth was within human reach. Skepticism in France and Italy was even greater.[14]

The reaction of the Central Powers was cautious but definitely averse. The German chancellor Count von Hertling (a philosopher, he was a scholar in politics like Wilson himself, and had followed Michaelis in the chancellorship in November) and the Austrian minister Czernin replied, by coincidence, on the same day, January 24, the former harshly and the latter mildly. Both praised the general principles of the Fourteen Points, which presented no problem, but both rejected primarily those territorial points that affected their countries. A response on Wilson's part became necessary. He was now at a stage where he felt that, as the spokesman of mankind, he had to maintain the initiative as a peacemaker.

Once again he consulted House, and House, in his usual self-confident way, sought to manipulate him: "I nearly always praise at first to strengthen the President's confidence in himself which, strangely enough, is often lacking, and was particularly so of this address."[15] On February 11, Wilson gave another address to a combined meeting of Congress. He examined in detail Hertling's criticism; he made a sharp contrast between what he called the old diplomacy according to the methods of the Congress of Vienna and the new international legal order that no longer recognized any country's individual interests but sought only peace for mankind. There was, he said, a general desire for peace; the statesman now stood before the court of mankind to be judged. Didn't Hertling know that?

Wilson presented a number of new points, four in number, which essentially formed one single grand principle. It was in this speech that he used for the first time the word, "self-determination," that was to assume such very great importance. He described it as a general principle, a categorical imperative. " 'Self-determination' is not a mere phrase. It is an imperative principle of action, which statesmen will henceforth ignore at their peril." It was no longer possible to achieve peace by an agreement among a few strong states. All parties must be involved, and the general judgment of mankind would decide whether it was a true, just peace and not merely a deal between rulers.

The four points followed from this: (1) every problem must be considered on its own merits; (2) peoples and territories "are not to be bartered about from sovereignty to sovereignty as if they were mere chattels and pawns in a game, even the great game, now forever discredited, of the balance of power"; (3) every territorial settlement must be in the interest of the populations involved; (4) all national aspirations must be met as far as possible, without leading to new causes of disunity. Therefore the war was a war of total emancipation.[16]

Again a speech filled with great words and absolute truths, as complete as Judgment Day. Again Wilson's belief that there is a single great key that fits the whole of reality and will solve "every issue everywhere." But in reality the concept of self-determination was much more complicated and dangerous than it had seemed at first glance and than Wilson himself in his lofty idealism could or would even have suspected. At a later date, an English author of a long book about the Peace of Versailles, made a cogent observation: "That the principle is a disruptive, as well as a cohesive force goes without saying. The difficulty of deciding how large an area or a population must be before it has a right to self-determination seems fundamental."[17]

When he gave his address, Wilson had not yet considered this fundamental question. For him self-determination was really something like popular sovereignty, "consent of the governed," as he knew it from the tradition of the American and French revolutions. The people in their simple majesty knew what was good, and they wanted what was good. Together the peoples formed the best guarantee of peace, an idea in which there was at least a bit of Rousseau. As the historian Alfred Cobban has written: "His [Wilson's] belief in the goodness and power of world opinion, which might be termed the General Will of humanity, and in its identity with the General Will of every democratic nation, enabled him to hold that the self-determination of nations, and national sovereignty, was a possible basis, indeed the only basis, of world peace."[18]

Wilson believed that the peoples were good and also that they were peaceful, more peaceful than their governments. Again we see the resemblance to Rousseau, who said, "There is no war between men: there is war only between states."[19] Wilson echoed: "I sometimes think that it is true that no people ever went to war with one another. Governments have gone to war with one another. Peoples, so far as I remember, have not."[20]

It is very remarkable that Wilson should believe that self-determination means peace and that democracies are peaceful by their very nature. After all, as a historian he knew that the history of American democracy, a history of territorial expansion and manifest destiny, was anything but peaceful. He undoubtedly also knew the sober observations of Alexander Hamilton, whom he greatly admired, in the *Federalist Papers*. Hamilton had sharply rejected the myth that republics are more peaceful than monarchies, giving as striking examples Athens, Venice, and Holland.[21] Wilson nonetheless disregarded the bitter reality of the past; it was the future he believed in.

He was not familiar with the whole problem of European nationalism and he had never read Herder, the German thinker who upheld the notion of the European nations as organic entities. In his innocence he placed emphasis upon self-determination without recognizing that it was more likely to lead to conflict than to the brotherhood of nations.

In general Wilson's principles more and more broke loose from reality and lived their own lives. Self-determination was one such principle. During the war it became one of the major foundations of Wilson's new world order. We shall never subject another people, he had said back in 1915, "because we believe, we passionately believe, in the right of every people to choose their own allegiance and be free of masters altogether."[22]

Only very slowly, as the reality of Europe began to come closer, did he discover the dangerous consequences of the principle. In the discussion with Spring-Rice on January 3 just mentioned, he wondered whether it was in fact possible to apply it consistently. The example of the threatening dismemberment of Austria-Hungary was probably in his thoughts when he said: "Pushed to its extreme, the principle would mean the disruption of existing governments to an undefinable extent. Logic was a good and powerful thing but apart from the consideration of existing circumstances might well lead to very dangerous results."[23] The Englishman must have heard this with satisfaction, for the British Empire was not about to grant self-determination to all its peoples.

Later, in Paris, many began to realize the difficulties and dangers in this splendid principle. Lansing hit the nail on the head in a confidential memorandum, in which he wondered what self-determination would mean for the Irish, Indians, Egyptians, and South African Boers. What would happen with the Muslims in Syria and Palestine, and how did that fit in with the idea of Zionism, to which Wilson was very sympathetic. "The phrase is simply loaded with dynamite. It will raise hopes which can never be realized." It was the dream of an idealist, he said, and it is clear whom Lansing really had in mind.[24]

As Wilson himself came to see, he had to be very cautious in Paris when trying to put his great principles into practice. He acknowledged that when he had first spoken of self-determination he had not realized that there were so many peoples who would claim it as their right.[25]

III

Wilson considered his program for peace to be quite reasonable, but in the grim spring of 1918 it achieved not one success. The warring parties were quite fatigued, it is true, but they were therefore all the more determined to throw every resource into the fight. There was nothing like the general will to peace on which Wilson rested his hopes.

Germany once more showed the colossal efforts of which it was capable. It had compelled the Bolsheviks to sign the humiliating peace of Brest-Litovsk (March 3) and it was able now in consequence to shift many divisions to the Western front. Ludendorff hoped to force a final decision with them. On March 21 the German offensive began; with one fierce attack after another the Allied forces were driven back, and the German army once more approached the gates of Paris as it had done in 1914. But, as one expert remarked, the German position was brilliant but hopeless. Germany was in no condition to exploit the successes it had achieved. It was worn out, materially and also morally.

Nonetheless the Germans placed the Allies in great difficulty and their call for more American help became very pressing. Lloyd George sent one begging letter after another. "It is of paramount importance that American troops should be sent to France with the utmost speed possible and I wish you to urge this on the President," he wrote to the new British ambassador in Washington, Lord Reading.[26] Lloyd George could reasonably maintain that Wilson's procrastinations were the cause of the threatening disaster in France, Reading told Wiseman.[27] Wilson did what he could; he told Reading that 120,000 men would be sent to Europe every month.[28] But Lloyd George continued to make his demands: "There can be little doubt that victory or defeat for the Allies depends upon the arrival of the American infantry."[29]

Wilson was bewildered and dazed. He had in his ready optimism believed that the Germans no longer had the capability to make such stupendous exertions; it was, he told Wiseman, "a great shock to him," and compelled him to make "a readjustment of opinions and hopes to which he has stubbornly clung in spite of much advice to the contrary."[30]

Wilson very quickly began to see that he should speak less of his ideals and more of winning. On April 6, just a year after the declaration of war, he gave a speech in Baltimore that was much more militant than usual. To be sure, he still wanted to be just to the German people, he said. He spoke at the level of total metaphysical abstractness: "There can be no difference between peoples in the final judgment, if it is indeed to be a righteous judgment." But the German leaders had shown their true nature at Brest-Litovsk. Wouldn't they act the same way if they won in the West? The first task therefore was to win the war. He ended on a bellicose tone:

> There is, therefore, but one response possible from us: Force, Force to the utmost, Force without stint or limit, the righteous and triumphant Force which shall make Right the law of the world and cast every selfish dominion down in the dust.[31]

This was a different Wilson who was speaking; he had become a soldier in the vanguard, God's soldier. All the same his dilemma remained. Two days later he had a confidential conversation with a group of foreign journalists, and then he softened what he had said in Baltimore. He continued to hope for signs that the Germans were coming to their senses, he said; he did not want to use "knock-down and drag-out language." He did not want to march to Berlin in triumph. If that had to be, it had to be. But one day the world would still come to its senses, however mad it was at the present time. He continued to believe in peace through right.[32]

TWENTY-TWO

The eyes of the people have been opened and they see.
The hand of God is laid upon the nations.
         —*Woodrow Wilson, November 11, 1918*

PEACE
AT LAST

*I*N THE LAST YEAR OF THE WAR the right of the peoples to self-determination came to stand ever more clearly and emphatically in the center of Wilson's exalted world of ideas. He did not anticipate, however, all the surprising and incongruous implications of the principle. If the people were as good as Wilson wanted to believe and the world was as evil as it was in 1918, what was the source of this painful discrepancy? This question was a variation upon one so readily asked by all idealists, certainly in America: How does it happen that evil touches good people? And Wilson in this period more and more gave the answer that Rousseau had given: because they have evil governments; men are good, but not their governments. It was a reply of faith that gave a deeper meaning to the insane events. Mankind, good mankind, awakening at last from its nightmare, was joining together in a league of nations for a better world.

    This explanation of the meaning of the world's suffering, with its religiously tinted prospect of salvation, was at the same time a guide for political activity. Who other than Wilson himself would be in a position to lead—indeed, was called to lead—this good mankind into the phalanx of the coming new world? It was a question now of organizing good men everywhere into a "moral force" that would be irresistible. In Wilson's philosophy the tension between determinism and voluntarism is never resolved; he had to take the leadership but he also knew that this "moral force" was a force that no one could resist. The true leader is the man who understands what is really happening, he always maintained.

It was a question, he argued with House in the spring of 1918, of rallying the "liberal opinion" of the world. For in his usage, which seems somewhat old-fashioned to us today, "liberal" and "moral" meant just about the same thing. But the next question was obvious: Rallying against whom? Against the bad governments, of course! As applied to Germany, Wilson's standpoint was certainly simplicity itself: the good German people must be freed from the military autocracy under whose yoke they lived and set into action against it. An appeal must be made to the German parties that in the summer of 1917 had adopted the peace resolution. Wilson's problem, however, was that he was at least equally suspicious of the governments of the countries with which he was officially allied, even if only with the status of "associate." In France and England too, he held, the militarist and jingoist authorities had to give way to truly liberal regimes. Wilson's appeal to good men, it may therefore be said, hinted lightly of revolution.

That was only one side of the coin. The freedom of the people, it appeared at the end of 1917 and the beginning of 1918, could also be endangered because evil forces from below were seeking to dominate them. Wilson was familiar with the old theory of "mixed government," *imperium mixtum*, which equally feared monarchy and anarchy; and what was now happening in Russia was a warning against anarchy. The collaboration of the liberal forces therefore had at the same time an accent of opposition to revolution; it had to keep the liberal and socialist elements in Europe in the good camp, the moderate camp, Wilson's camp. House tells us in his diary that Wilson and he in February 1918 discussed the "trend of liberal opinion" in the world. They

> came to the conclusion that the wise thing to do was to lead the
> movement intelligently and sympathetically and not to allow the

ignoble element to run away with the situation as they had done in Russia. He [Wilson] spoke of the necessity of forming a new political party in order to achieve these ends.

Wilson was enthusiastic. With his usual self-assurance House added "that I find myself instead of leading as I always did at first, rather in the rear and holding him back." Indeed, House would wisely maintain the balance and keep the prophet in tow!¹

The president of the United States as a prophet remains a remarkable sight, one that has become incredible for us. Constantly we are compelled to ask ourselves whether he really believed it himself. It seems probable that he did. He avowed the dogma of the good peoples and the bad governments now in all his public speeches. For instance, on July 4, 1918, he spoke splendidly before a group of diplomats at Mount Vernon about the meaning of the war, the meaning of all history. The great struggle between the defenseless peoples and their cruel rulers was now, he said, in its last phase.

> The Past and the Present are in deadly grapple and the peoples of the world are being done to death between them. There can be but one issue. The settlement must be final. There can be no compromise.

And in order to give a practical touch to his stirring vision, he spoke— again in "points" of the four things that he wanted. These were exalted and vague: (1) destruction of arbitrary power anywhere that can "disturb" the peace of the world; (2) settlement of all questions by the free acceptance of any settlement by the "people immediately concerned," that is, self-determination; (3) consent of every nation to be governed in its conduct by the same "principles of honour and of respect for the common law of civilized society that govern the individual citizens"; (4) establishment of an organization to keep the peace.²

Wilson counted upon the gentle forces at whose head he stood. He knew for certain, he wrote a day later to a friend, that Europe is now governed by the same reactionary forces that until a few years ago (before he became president, he meant) also dominated this country. But he was convinced that he could reach the peoples of Europe over the heads of their governments.³

With that remarkable grandiose belief, Wilson moved forward toward the coming peace. It was steadily clearer during the summer of 1918 that the war was nearing its end, although most Western leaders dared to hope cautiously for the spring of 1919. But in the middle of June the last great offensive of the Austrians against Italy failed, and in the middle of July the final German offensive, the Peace Storm, was halted by tenacious French resistance. Now it was the turn of the Allies! In August their great counteroffensive began: *tout le monde à la bataille!* (everyone into battle!). It ended with immense success, with a breakthrough on a broad front. The morale of the German troops began to waver, and they fled or surrendered. August 8 was the German "black day." At the crown council that was held at Spa on August 13–14, Ludendorff, reporting that victory was no longer possible, offered his resignation. It was refused.

In September the German position grew still worse, in part because of an American offensive at Saint-Mihiel east of Verdun. On September 26 Marshal Foch launched three big offensives simultaneously. Three days later, September 29, the crown council met again in Spa and this time the painful decision to ask for peace could not be avoided. The German government realized that it had to take radical steps that would soften the great debacle to some extent. In the "twilight of the gods" that descended over old Germany, only a single point of light could be discerned, the peace program of the American president, and it was decided to appeal to his Fourteen Points. The Germans realized, however, that they could not go to Wilson with their old institutions still intact. In order to become democrats, in conformity with what he had repeatedly said, they undertook what has been called their "revolution from above."

It was a world gone topsy-turvy. The Supreme Army Command, which lost its nerve, itself started the revolution. It was the pressure by Ludendorff that forced Hertling, the conservative chancellor, to resign and made it possible for Prince Max of Baden, a liberally inclined idealist, to succeed him. A parliamentary system had to be established as soon as possible. With such a promise, Wilson could be approached. On October 3 a note was sent to the American president requesting peace negotiations upon the basis of the program that he had outlined in his message to Congress on January 8 and had amplified in other addresses, in particular in his speech of September 27, about a week earlier.[4]

We therefore have to backtrack seven days in our story to the speech of September 27 in which Wilson had once more summarized his whole program and amplified his Fourteen Points. He felt the approach of peace. He had received through various channels reports of the German desire for peace, and he wished to fall in with it. House had been urging him to act at once because the time was favorable. As the Allies moved toward victory, he wrote Wilson, the influence of the American president would inevitably decline. He should therefore try to commit the Allies to his program as much as was possible, all the more because victory itself made it probable that those in power—Lloyd George, Clemenceau, Sonnino, "and their kind"—would remain in office and would be hostile to the program.[5] Wilson agreed. When House visited him in September at his summer home in Magnolia, Massachusetts, he showed the colonel the draft of the speech he would make.[6]

Its specific purpose was to call upon Americans to subscribe to a new war loan. It became, however, a broad view of events, filled again with his well-known thoughts about the larger significance of the war. There were "positive and well defined purposes which we did not determine and which we cannot alter." Statesmen, if they did not wish to meet defeat, had to support these aims. "The common will of mankind has been substituted for the particular purposes of individual states." Individual statesmen had started the war, but the war itself had changed everything "in its sweeping processes of change and settlement." This had become clear once Americans were involved in the war.

Wilson spoke solemnly and poetically on September 27. Through the voices of the dead, the war itself called for taking final decisions. He defined the whole situation in a series of rhetorical questions: Should military rulers be allowed to determine in the future the fate of peoples over whom they ruled only by the right of force? Should powerful nations be allowed to "wrong" weak countries? Should people be ruled, "even in their internal affairs," by arbitrary and irresponsible force, or only by their own will and choice? "Shall there be a common standard of right and privilege for all peoples and nations?" All those who gave the proper answer to these questions would understand his points, now five in number: (1) "impartial justice" without discrimination among nations; (2) no "special or separate interest" as the basis for a peace settlement; (3) no separate alliances within "the general and common family" of the League of Nations; (4) no "special, selfish" economic combinations or boycotts; (5) all international agreements and treaties without exception must be made public.

Toward the end of his speech, he returned again to the great plan of salvation that he discerned in history. Statesmen had sought its meaning in vain, but the mass of ordinary people had discovered what it was about.

> The counsels of plain men have become on all hands more simple and straightforward and more unified than the counsels of sophisticated men of affairs, who still retain the impression that they are playing a game of power and playing for high stakes. This is why I have said that it is a people's war, not a statesmen's. Statesmen must follow the clarified common thought or be broken.[7]

Is music made by the key in which it is set? Or does Wilson's idealism sound more absolute in words than it was in reality? And was it at the same time so vague that it could be diluted in practice? For a number of years he had presented perfect and ever more beautiful visions of peace to the peoples. Now peace was suddenly almost at hand. The German note came a week after this speech. Now the great expectations he had set forth had to be made good, and his promised leadership would have to prove itself in practice.

II

The German note made clear how great Wilson's dilemma was. The idealist in him had to rejoice that his ideals, embodied in his Fourteen Points, had become the foundation of the peace. The practical politician had to be cautious, however, and sound out how honest the German desire for peace really was. Then, if he did accept the German request, could he obtain the peace he wanted? It obviously would not be a peace without victory. But would it be also without *vae victis* (woe to the defeated)? And would the Allies be willing to follow him in such a policy? There was also the very practical question whether, now that the victory had been achieved, he still had the means to compel his allies to go along with him.

He was in an awkward position, between two or three fires: from the Germans, whom he mistrusted even when they began to preach the good cause; from the Allies, who as he knew did not in the slightest share his ideals; and from the opposition in his own country. The American people, like the Allies, had become truculent; it was not for nothing that they had been swept along by Wilson's own propaganda organizations, notably his friend George Creel's Committee on Public Information. And the leaders of the Republican opposition, Roosevelt, Lodge, and all their kind, played willingly upon this mood, loudly demanding a hard policy toward Germany, "unconditional surrender," a march to Berlin, a dictated peace.

At the beginning of October the situation was extremely confused. The war was almost over, but not with certainty. No one knew exactly what the domestic situation was in Germany, although secret reports came about the chance of a revolution. With the Bolshevik threat so close, how real was the danger? Wilson was unsure with what German government he could negotiate. "Unless some sort of Gov[ernment] offers medium of communication, we might witness Bolshevikism worse than in Russia," he told his cabinet.[8]

For the time being the regime in Germany was the new government of Prince Max of Baden, about whom Wilson knew just about nothing. The president wanted to send a reply to its request for peace talks, although House and Tumulty advised him to delay or reject it. He decided to reply very cautiously with three counterquestions: (1) Did the Germans really accept the Fourteen Points as the basis of negotiations? (2) Were they ready to evacuate all occupied territories at once? (3) Did the chancellor speak in the name of the Imperial government or of the German people?[9] These "self-righteous and pedantic questions," as Golo Mann calls them, put the Germans on the spot; they had to become democratic or fear the worst. But at the same time his questions implied a chance of reconciliation.[10]

Obviously the Allies were unhappy and suspicious because Wilson had acted on his own. He wants to stay alone and superior, he is Jupiter, sneered Clemenceau. And Lloyd George, even more angered, accused Wilson of leaving the Allies out in the cold. The three prime ministers (Orlando for Italy) together sent an urgent telegram to Wilson warning that the evacuation of the occupied territories was still not an adequate guarantee for German submission. The German army might be able to regroup once back in their own country.[11]

There were also many protests within the United States. The journalist David Lawrence warned Wilson in a long letter about the growing feeling of vindictiveness and anger among the people, a feeling which was directed primarily against the German emperor. The "man in the street," he wrote, believed that Germany had not yet "been licked enough." "Mr.

President, rightly or wrongly, our people have been fed intolerance and personalities for eighteen months."[12]

Senator Henry Ashurst urged Wilson to satisfy the expectations of the American people. There was now a broad fear that the president in his notes to the German government had been giving away the advantages that the brave American soldiers have won with the sword. "If your reply should fail to come up to the American spirit, you are destroyed." Wilson's answer to Ashurst is very indicative of his lofty attitude:

> So far as my being destroyed is concerned, I am willing if I can serve the country to go into a cellar and read poetry the remainder of my life. I am thinking now only of putting the U.S. into a position of strength and justice. I am now playing for 100 years hence. . . . When Germany fully meets our terms we are through. Can it be that the people do not remember my Fourteen Points and my speeches of July 4th and September 27th?

Ashurst responded frankly. No, the people do not remember the details of these speeches.[13]

The German government in its reply of course showed its best side. Apart from tactical considerations, there was also in the liberal and Socialist circles in Germany an honest feeling of repentance and hope. The Germans wished to be converted from nationalism to internationalism. Whether that mood truly came from the heart, however, is the question. Matthias Erzberger, the strong man of the Center party, described the Fourteen Points as so vague that they gave room for every kind of interpretation. It was a correct observation, but it could also be made from the other side, as the Germans would learn at their cost.[14]

For the moment the Germans were optimistic. Their note of October 12 gave a positive reply to all Wilson's three questions. But meanwhile, under the pressure of the Allies and of public opinion in his own country, the president became somewhat more reserved. He told the cabinet he was shocked by "American Prussianism," an ironic name for intolerant hatred of Germans; he might have to become their advocate for justice.[15] He did nothing of the sort, however. In the reply that he sent to the German government on October 14, he informed them that he would do nothing without the agreement of the Allies. He demanded guarantees that the Germans would not resume the war and asked for assurance that he would be dealing with the German people themselves.[16]

The German leadership could not do anything but give in. At first the army leadership tried again to reassert itself. After his panic reaction, Ludendorff, who regained his nerve, reported on October 17 that the war was not yet lost. But his vacillations had shorn him of his influence, and the German government no longer listened to him. It agreed in its note of October 20 to a complete halt to the submarine war, and it gave a detailed account of its plans for the democratization of the German political system.[17] It was truly a capitulation, and Wilson could be satisfied.

Still he was not satisfied, far from it! As early as October 23 he reacted in a sharp third note to the German tone of reconciliation. He had to be sure that Germany would no longer be in a position to take up arms again. For that reason, he informed them, he was transmitting the whole correspondence to the Allies, who would now have to impose an armistice, a mere cessation of hostilities; only German acceptance of it would show how sincere the German desire for peace was. And the president had to add the observation that it was still not entirely clear to him from the note of October 20 whether in Germany "the principle of a government responsible to the German people has yet been fully worked out." The power of the king of Prussia (as he called the emperor) still appeared to be untouched. The time had come to speak the hard truth. The government of the United States wanted to negotiate only with the German people.

> If it must deal with the military masters and the monarchical autocrats of Germany . . . it must demand, not peace negotiations, but surrender. Nothing can be gained by leaving this essential thing unsaid.[18]

What had happened to make Wilson so harsh? Again and still, he was caught in the tight grip of his dilemma. He had to conquer the peace that he wanted from the Allies and from public opinion in his own country. Even within his own cabinet, as appeared in its meeting on October 22, the mood was very fierce; most of the members wanted stern measures, Germany must at least withdraw beyond the Rhine. Public opinion wanted unconditional surrender.[19] And public opinion was more important than ever, because midterm elections were approaching. That was, of course, an improper argument for an idealist like Wilson, and he said he did not want to have anything to do with it: "I am dealing in human lives, not politics." But he was not completely insensitive to politics. We shall shortly see how hard he played the game of politics.

But his hard language was in the first place intended to make an impression upon the Allies. He hoped to restrain them from making the armistice too harsh. He pretended therefore to be more combative than he really was; he wished to save what he could, to maintain a balance that in fact no longer existed. The reaction in Germany was of course horror and dismay. The emperor and the generals were furious; there was for them only one reply possible to this "shameless yokel" in the White House, resistance "to the bitter end." Hindenburg and Ludendorff rushed to Berlin to argue for a halt to all negotiations. The imperial chancellor, Prince Max, stood his ground; he realized that there was no turning back. He threatened to resign if the generals had their way, and the emperor responded by dismissing Ludendorff. On October 27 the German government sent a final humble note to Wilson with a pious wish that the armistice might be the first step toward a just peace. A memorandum was added that promised a whole series of constitutional reforms.[20]

It would all be in vain. The chances for a peace based on a balance of forces became constantly smaller. The Germans had accepted the Fourteen Points as a basis for peace, but the Allies as yet had not. Wilson still had to convince his friends, and he attempted this once more by sending the faithful House to Europe again. It was still another peace mission. As in the earlier missions, Wilson gave him carte blanche. The two friends parted in a mood of trust. House tells the story in his diary: The president gave him the broadest powers. "It virtually puts me in his place in Europe." When he said goodbye, Wilson told him: "I have not given you any instructions because I feel you will know what to do." How wonderful this all was, House went on to philosophize; this concerned one of the most important missions that had ever been undertaken, and yet no word of advice or consultation was necessary between them. "He knows that our minds run parallel, and he also knows that where they diverge, I will follow his bent rather than my own."[21] It would turn out that this was not entirely true.

House knew the European situation. To persuade the Allies to accept the Fourteen Points, he would first have to explain them, however, for the bare text did require some elucidations. When House reached Paris on October 16, he asked Walter Lippmann, who was now in Paris as the representative of the Inquiry, and the journalist Frank Cobb (the man to whom Wilson had given his interview shortly before the declaration of war, and who was now in Paris as the correspondent for the New York *World*) to prepare an interpretation of the Fourteen Points. They painted it as a quite liberal document: Germany would not be totally excluded from eventual colonial mandates; the reparations would be limited to actual war damage (which meant that England would not be included); Austria, if it lost its empire, would receive the option of joining Germany; and so on. It all sounded very hopeful to the Germans, who were able to put their hands on the document. They could not cite it to support their case, however. Wilson himself cabled House that he found the interpretation very fine, but that the details were "merely illustrative suggestions" that would have to be worked out further at the peace conference.[22]

House was unable to persuade the Allies, who after all remained quite skeptical about Wilson's dreams, to accept the Lippmann-Cobb interpretation. On October 29 and 30, House had long discussions with Lloyd George and Clemenceau. Remarkably, the talks essentially revolved around the first and second points of principle. The French shook their heads over Wilson's open diplomacy, and the British could not accept the open seas. Did they really mean their objections or were they using them as a lever to extract concessions in the much more important question of the armistice? What did freedom of the seas really mean, what did Wilson have in mind? The British navy minister, Sir Eric Geddes, who had recently visited Washington, had let Lloyd George know that Wilson's opinions in point two were "obviously unformed," that he spoke "in generalities."[23]

It was not remarkable that the British were so worked up; Wilson was vague indeed. But they were realists who did not yet see perfect peace ahead of them. The League of Nations seemed to them a dream and they were not willing for its sake to reduce their own maritime supremacy, on which their security depended, to the status of a bargaining chip. They were suspicious about what was happening. They asked themselves whether an American striving to push Great Britain aside and even to surpass it in order to rule the seas, lurked behind Wilson's fine words.

Furthermore the Conservatives harbored a personal dislike of Wilson. He had remained neutral for three years in order to enrich his country, they said, and now he wanted to reform the world. This distrust was strongly fed by Wilson's American enemies, with Theodore Roosevelt in the lead. The former president wrote letter after letter to his many British friends. One, which became very famous, was sent in January 1918 to the writer Rudyard Kipling, who passed it on to Lord Milner, so that it reached King George V and the cabinet. Wilson, wrote Roosevelt, was "a cold and selfish hypocrite, a clever and adroit demagogue, and wedded to the belief that rhetoric is action." His peace plans were dangerous and played into Germany's hands.[24]

Lloyd George personally shared these Conservative irritations to the full; he was probably also jealous of Wilson's leading role. House remarked that Lloyd George was full of mistrust toward what he called Wilson's secretiveness, and he was cynical about Wilson's new order. Before he would concede on point two, said the British prime minister, he wanted to see whether this League of Nations became a reality.[25]

The discussions did not go well. Taking a big gamble, House even threatened a break. Be careful, he warned, that the president doesn't decide that if the Allies do not accept his Fourteen Points, he would end the negotiations.[26] Wilson stood firmly behind his negotiator. His cablegrams displayed all his haughty naïveté. He instructed House not to make any concession, and he still appeared to be moved by the idea that the war was directed as much against British "navalism" as against Prussian militarism: "We are pledged to fight not only to do away with Prussian militarism but with militarism everywhere." And, a few days later, he instructed House to threaten that if the British did not concede, the Americans would build the strongest navy in the world.[27] But he could also threaten in a more moralistic way. There would be no real difficulty over peace terms and the interpretation of the Fourteen Points, he said, if the Entente statesmen would be "perfectly frank" with the Americans and had no selfish aims that would "alienate us from them altogether." On the one hand, Germany has accepted the Fourteen Points; on the other, England could not do without American friendship in the future. Wilson told House that if the Allied statesmen were trying to nullify his influence, they should be "boldly" forced to admit it and he would tell all the world.[28]

In Wilson's name House stood upon the walls of the holy city and proclaimed that the Fourteen Points were the basis for a better world. Finally, a compromise was reached on November 3, but in fact it contained nothing concrete. In another long discussion, House informed the negotiators how attached Wilson was to point two, and Clemenceau, more than tired of the whole business, turned to Lloyd George, saying,

"We accept the principle of freedom of the seas." But when House asked Lloyd George whether he did too, he got the reply that it would be impossible for any British prime minister to do so, although he was willing to discuss the question in the light of the new conditions created by the war. "Why do you not say so?" asked House. Replied Lloyd George: "I am perfectly willing to say that to the President and I will instruct the British ambassador in Washington to so inform the President." Thus the matter was advanced by the use of vague phrases.[29]

All the threats by Wilson and House were hollow, however. The Allies received them with evasions, and in the end House achieved nothing more than a compromise set down in an official declaration sent to the Germans on November 5; it was signed by Lansing and hence is known as the Lansing Note. The Allies promised to accept the Fourteen Points as a basis for the peace negotiations, with the proviso that they retained for themselves complete freedom of the seas and that they understood by the word "restoration" "that compensation will be made by Germany for all damage done to the civilian population of the Allies and their property by the aggression of Germany by land, by sea and from the air." This was language that opened the doors wide for a harsh peace, but once it had come this far, what could Wilson do but accept?

House had achieved another spurious success and crowed about his victory: "I consider that we have won a great diplomatic victory in getting the Allies to accept the principles laid down in your January eight speech and in your subsequent addresses."[30] It soon turned out that reality, in the first instance the armistice, was less beautiful.

In the Lansing note, the Germans were invited to send negotiators to discuss the armistice. This stern document was drawn up by the generals of the Allied Supreme War Council and had the clear purpose of making the Germans completely powerless: they must withdraw their armies behind the Rhine, deliver large quantities of weapons, artillery, airplanes, and rolling stock, and turn over their navy to their British archenemy. They had no choice but to bend and sign. On November 3 a revolt had broken out in the navy at Kiel and had spread like wildfire through the country. Everywhere workers' and soldiers' councils had been set up. But the great fear of the West that Germany too would be swamped by Bolshevism proved baseless. The forces of law and order were too strong. Here and there, as in Bavaria, a radical revolution took place, but in Berlin the majority socialists of the Social Democratic party kept the reins in their hands. They made the revolution legal. The emperor was compelled to abdicate, and he left the country. As Max Weber has observed, "To cling to the throne became worthless once he had to bow to an American professor."[31] He fled on November 9 to the Netherlands. Under the leadership of the stalwart Friedrich Ebert, a sincere democrat with an authentic German feeling for order and authority, a new government was formed. The excesses of the Left were repressed, and a pact between Hindenburg and Ebert cut off "extension of terroristic Bolshevism," in Hindenburg's words.[32]

On November 11 in the forest of Compiègne, the German delegation under the leadership of Erzberger in the name of the new German government signed the terms set down by Foch. The war was over. The winners celebrated. "Autocracy is dead," cabled House to Wilson. "Advance democracy and its immortal leader. In this great hour my heart goes out to you in pride, admiration and love."[33] And Wilson himself in an official declaration experienced a truly religious revelation:

> A supreme moment of history has come. The eyes of the people have been opened and they see. The hand of God is laid upon the nations. He will show them favour, I devoutly believe, only if they rise to the clear heights of His own justice and mercy.

He spoke to Congress on the same day, giving a detailed report of the armistice terms and concluding that the road was free for a new world order for all peoples. The victors, he asserted, had this cause not only in their minds but also in their hearts. They were unselfish; they wanted justice; their purpose was to protect the weak. Out of the chaos that had reigned, a world of respect and love must emerge. Without revenge, as the Germans too would observe:

> They will find that every pathway that is stained with the blood of their own brothers leads to the wilderness, not to the seat of their hope. . . . We must hold the light steady until they find themselves.[34]

The great moment had come at last; he could make the peace about which he had dreamed so long. In the nature of things, it could not be a "peace without victory." Such a victory assumed partners who were equal, but there were none now. Nonetheless he had attempted to salvage something of his ideal, and to that purpose he had conducted his own negotiations, for he distrusted the Allies almost as much as the Germans. In general, the historical judgment on Wilson's exchange of notes with the Germans is not unfavorable; he brought them to their senses in a respectable way and hence shortened the war.

But was he losing the peace? Had the tragedy of Versailles begun already in this last month of the war? Did he preserve the balance that a fair peace had to bring? Did he really resist the pressure of the Allies and the opposition in his own country? How much did he have to concede in order to maintain himself? It was just in this period of crisis that, as we have noted, he was driven into a corner by the midterm elections for Congress. In the United States politics always goes on, no matter what happens; the regularity of elections is fixed by the calendar even if the world is in flames. In the American political system midterm elections cannot lead to a governmental crisis. But, because they can deprive a president of his majority in Congress, they can have practical importance. They can also have a symbolic value, as a disavowal of him.

Wilson, the political scientist, of course understood this as well as anyone. He knew foreign countries would interpret a loss for his party as a personal defeat: "They would say that I had been repudiated, and such strength and power as I possess among them for the conclusion of the sort of peace that I have set my heart upon . . . would be gone."[35] This fear led him to take a decision that has been much argued over, to make an appeal to the voters to vote for his party, so that, at that critical moment, the continuation of his administration would be assured. Of course, he wrote, he did not want to accuse the Republicans of lacking patriotism, but still a strong "unified" leadership was necessary. The Republican leaders in Congress had constantly sought to undermine his position, and victory for them would be interpreted in Europe as "repudiation of my leadership."[36]

Wilson's appeal was an unusual and dangerous step. It was not really proper, his wife warned him. And, what was worse, it was counterproductive. In the grip of his idealism, Wilson wrongly believed that the voters held to the dream of a better world as strongly as he did. But they made their choices as they ordinarily did, for very different reasons; often it was the personality of the candidates as well as economic conditions, such as the sharp rise of prices caused by the war. And, to the extent that their choice was also determined by foreign policy, they certainly did not support Wilson's plan of reconciliation. There was a virulent anti-German feeling among the broad public. Men such as Roosevelt and Lodge had made skillful use of it during the campaign and called for a hard peace, in which American interests were paramount: "No peace that satisfies Germany can in any degree satisfy us. It cannot be a negotiated peace. It must be a dictated peace."[37] Wilson did not sufficiently sense the strength of American nationalism, nor was he aware that he was speaking over the heads of the people.

It may very well be that even without Wilson's appeal his party would have lost. It is even probable. Still the Republicans used his words skillfully to their own advantage. They put on a brilliant show of pained indignation over such lack of appreciation of their patriotism, and hammered all the harder on the need for reparations and revenge. Roosevelt wrote to Lodge: "I am glad Wilson has come out in the open: I fear Judas most when he can cloak his activities behind a treacherous make-believe of non-partisanship."[38] And the chairman of the Republican party, Will Hays, spoke of a common, unjust, and mendacious trick, an insult.[39] The result was in any case a bitter disappointment for Wilson. The Democratic party lost its majority in both houses. This meant that in the Senate the committee on foreign relations would come under the chairmanship of a Republican, indeed no one less than his archenemy Henry Cabot Lodge!

Wilson was deeply distressed. He told Senator Homer S. Cummings that his problems had become much greater, for the opposition could now frustrate his foreign policy.[40] And in fact the Republican leaders did not fail to explain at once to their friends in London and Paris that Wilson no longer spoke in the name of the American people. Lloyd George and Clemenceau were warned; according to the British prime minister the elections were "a humiliating defeat for the President," which notably lessened his prestige and "crippled his authority throughout the Conference."[41] Wilson lost in his own country. It had not helped him that in the later notes to Germany he had adopted a sharper tone. Of course, he did not face a parliamentary motion of nonconfidence, which is not part of the American political system (it may be recalled that as a college student he had argued for such a connection between the presidency and Congress), and he could still move to shape the peace. But he could no longer rely on a "moral majority" among his own people. It was the blind fate of popular favor! If the elections had been held not a week before the armistice, but a week afterwards, they would probably have given him a big victory!

As for Germany, it was condemned by the armistice to impotence, and how could it have been otherwise after such a defeat? As the loser, it would have peace imposed upon it. In fact Wilson's policy had failed. Only fourteen days earlier he had cabled House what he wanted, that is, an armistice "as moderate and reasonable as possible . . . because it is certain that too much success or security on the part of the Allies will make a genuine Peace settlement exceedingly difficult, if not impossible."[42] Wilson had sought to keep a balance for his fair peace.[43] Now he had lost everything. True, House had used the Fourteen Points as bargaining chips, but it is too easy to shift the blame upon him. Essentially Wilson had been trapped by his own dilemma. He could not at one and the same time be both participant and judge. The Germans of course realized this at once. There was no more bitter criticism of the scholar in the White House than that of his fellow professor, the great sociologist at Munich, Max Weber. Now that Wilson has permitted the weakening of Germany, he wrote in October, he can no longer be the honorable judge. And, in a speech on November 4, he said in even more portentous words:

> It is the peculiar destiny of the world that the first man to be its true
> ruler should be a professor. How much he is a professor we see in the
> great act of stupidity he has committed—the armistice terms. If he
> doesn't prevent Germany from entering into peace negotiations in
> a disarmed state, then his own rule will be at an end.[44]

TWENTY-THREE

For after all, nations are not conducted upon reasoned
opinion; they are conducted upon the common impulses
of the heart.
　　　—*Woodrow Wilson, March 17, 1909*

THE
LEAGUE OF
NATIONS

HE "WORLD OF YES-
terday" was no more. A world that for
a century had basked in a dream of
progress had gone under in a spasm of
senseless self-destruction. The Western
nations had sacrificed millions of their
youth on godforsaken battlefields; they had
been shattered and impoverished. Now they searched for new certainties
and if possible for a new peace. Strange new horrors tore at mankind;
hunger and poverty were old but an influenza epidemic and Bolshevism
were new. The abyss seemed to open. Where were the values that could
restore the world? And how could the peacemakers go at their task? Did
the pathway to the light of the future pass through the darkness of experience? Or was it better to hold fast to old values, to balance and good
sense? Should Woodrow Wilson when he came to France visit the battlefields and allow himself to let what had happened on them soak into
his soul?

　　He did not go to the military cemeteries, fearing precisely the feeling
of rage and despair that would overwhelm him. He wanted to be not a
player in the game but the umpire, not the historical actor but the his-

torian, even if one whose study was his own experience. He remembered how, when he was a boy of eight, he had seen the devastation wrought by Sherman on his march to the sea through Georgia; it was a memory that seared him for the rest of his life. He realized that the tragedy of every war is that peace must be made by the survivors. He thought there should be at least one person at the peace table who had not gone mad, and feared that if he went to the battlefields he too would lose his mind. If he had his way, indeed, he would have adjourned the peace conference for a year and sent everyone home to "get the bile out of their systems."[1]

Wilson did not underestimate the devastation in Europe, but he retained his nineteenth-century American optimism. His whole existence was tied up with it; he could not live without hope. He clung to the idea of a grand radical cure, to a mystical faith in the mankind of the future, who were purified by events and repented. He had to represent that mankind; he had to make a new peace.

That is why he had to go to Paris. In itself this was no small decision, for never before had an American president gone to Europe. Was it really wise to leave Washington, to expose himself to the confused world that he did not know? There were many voices opposed. House was not at all in favor—no wonder, for he saw for himself the magnificent role as the modest but powerful representative of the United States. He cabled the president from Paris that many there thought that "it would be unwise for you to sit in the Peace Conference. They fear that it would involve a loss of dignity and your commanding position." It was a clever dodge. Wilson would not participate because he was a head of state, and that would compel Clemenceau as premier to cede his place to President Poincaré. Wilson did not accept the idea, naturally. Aghast, he cabled back in great haste that he would not be bothered by the loss of dignity now that the great goal to which his life was dedicated was so close. What Clemenceau and Lloyd George and the others want "seems to me a way of pocketing me."[2] House was disappointed. "It was difficult for me to simulate a satisfaction that I did not feel, but I did the best I could."[3]

In any event, Wilson made the journey. He was overwhelmed by his mission. His Czech colleague Thomas Masaryk, who understood him well ("now, we were both professors") warned him about the European statesmen: "But he wouldn't listen, for he was too filled with his plan for a League of Nations to take obstacles into account."[4]

Obviously Wilson did not go to Paris by himself, but he placed him-

The League of Nations

self at the head of a peace delegation. It had to be very carefully assembled. The first requirement was that it had to be representative of the whole American people, for a peace treaty would have to be ratified by the Senate with a two-thirds majority. It would have been sensible for Wilson to take this into account from the beginning.

Remarkably, Wilson did not do so at all. He put together a delegation that consisted of persons who were intelligent but not independent or had any importance of their own. Obviously the Republicans had to be represented, and it would have made sense to select one or more persons with influence in their party. He might have considered President Taft, a fervent supporter of the idea of a League of Nations, or former cabinet member Elihu Root, a lawyer of great authority whom he had sent to Russia the previous year. Through persons of such prestige he would probably have been able to keep open a dialogue with the United States. But Wilson was not a man for dialogue, he lived too much within himself, he wanted no one of authority alongside him. He chose the former diplomat Henry White, who had a great deal of diplomatic experience but carried no political weight.

White was the only Republican in a delegation of five. The other four were Democrats, but even they were selected without thought of their influence or their ties within the party. Bryan's name was mentioned, but Wilson thought him too idealistic: "Mr. Bryan is soft-hearted, and the world just now is very hard-hearted."[5] How interesting an implicit judgment this was of himself, as if he were the hard-nosed realist who could stand up to the world.

Lansing had to go to Paris because of his position as secretary of state, but this did not change the difficult relationship between him and Wilson. Seldom consulted, Lansing became the fifth wheel of the delegation. He remained in House's shadow, and the bitterness between them was plain to see. Lansing was not informed at all about most of the things he needed to know, wrote House in his diary. Lansing was someone about whom he could not be enthusiastic, commented House, but still the president should have treated him with more consideration.[6] House could speak so condescendingly because he saw himself as the "Super-Secretary of State."[7] His shameless son-in-law, Gordon Auchincloss, told Josephus Daniels, the secretary of navy, who, on arriving in Paris, asked where he could find Lansing, that there was no need to see the secretary of state, no one in Paris paid any attention to him. He should go to see Colonel

House instead; he was the man whom all Paris looks to in these negotiations.[8]

It was obvious that House would be involved. He had already come to Paris, but now for the first time he received an official position as a member of the delegation. "I wish in my soul that the President had appointed me as Chairman of the Peace Delegation with McAdoo and Hoover as my associates. . . . If I could have had these two men as my associates and only these, I would have been willing to guarantee results."[9] The other delegates were not at all big enough for him, and Lansing and White were too weak to matter. Why didn't the president name a man of the caliber of Root? "He has made again one of his common mistakes."[10]

The only member of the delegation in whom House saw something worthwhile was General Tasker Bliss, "a scholarly statesmanlike soldier." But even Bliss did not count for much. In May, after five months, he told an interviewer that he had not had the slightest influence on the treaty. Since December, he said, he had not seen the president for more than twenty minutes in all.[11]

Wilson left for Paris at the first opportunity. He sailed on December 3 on the *George Washington*, the "Argosy of Peace," as it was often called. It was a fitting name for the ship and the journey. Everything depended upon his ark of salvation. That was how the world saw it, and no metaphor for it went unused. All world history could now be completed, as if the ring around the earth had finally been closed, but in the opposite direction, from west to east. "There *was* a new passage to the Indies," wrote Ray Stannard Baker, touched by emotion.[12]

Wilson felt the same way. The sea journey was good for him. He strolled on deck frequently and relaxed in the evening by watching films, for which he had developed great fondness. But somewhere on the ocean he decided, at the suggestion of William Bullitt, according to Bullitt's diary, to take the whole company that was traveling with him (principally the scholars of the Inquiry) into his confidence. He sat in the salon in their midst (sitting he seemed taller than he really was, and very impressive, wrote one of those present) and told them of his dreams and ideals, and some of them, feeling that this was a historic occasion, set down their accounts of it. It was a scene worthy of Plato! What scholar would not dream of the chance to sit in the class of the philosopher-statesman whose teaching was sharpened by hands-on practice and who would at last guide the confused world along the true paths of reason!

Wilson explained that his League of Nations would not be instituted according to a theoretical plan but would grow organically. He entered into details on many matters: reparations, colonies, and so on. He emphasized once again that America was the only disinterested country in the whole world. The Allied governments did not even represent their own peoples, which enabled the poison of Bolshevism to work so easily. He warned that the peace must be based on "the highest principles of justice," which meant the weal of mankind and not of their leaders. "If it is any other sort of peace then I shall want to run away and hide on the island of Guam or somewhere else remote, for there will follow not mere conflict but cataclysm." He ended his plea with an appeal: "Tell me what is right and I'll fight for it."[13]

He had heard, he said, that while he and his listeners were still on the high seas, Clemenceau and Lloyd George had been dividing the spoils. America was absolutely opposed to their plans to squeeze everything they could out of Germany. He remained firmly committed to "peace without victory." He proudly added that he was coming not to bargain but to stand by principles, "and once they learn that that is my purpose, I think we can come to an agreement promptly."[14]

Wilson crossed the wide sea, it seemed, filled with optimism and self-assurance. But was he truly so sure of himself? Or did there lurk beneath this shining surface of self-confidence a feeling of doubt and fear? Creel, the director of American propaganda, tells us that Wilson shared his anxieties with him during a walk on deck. The whole world, he said, looks to America for help and support because at last the peoples are tired of their tyrants. But will it be possible to remove all the old injustice all at once? "What I seem to see—with all my heart I hope that I am wrong—is a tragedy of disappointment."[15]

II

In torn, suffering, yearning Europe the American president was awaited as nothing less than a messiah. In Italy the soldiers knelt before altars on which stood his portrait. In Poland his name was the watchword of freedom whispered by students. Along the railway line from Brest to

Paris, people knelt by the tracks as the train carrying the president-liberator passed. Great crowds saw him as their succor and salvation and welcomed him as the true champion of humanity. It was all honestly meant, although it was also the work of Creel's propaganda committee, which had toiled hard in Europe. This elated acclamation came principally from Left groups, liberals, and socialists. They cheered him not only for what they thought he represented but also because he was their only reasonable alternative to the other dream of the same era, the far-out dream of Bolshevism. We have already seen that the French Socialist, Albert Thomas, made a vigorous choice for Wilson and against Lenin. On Wilson's arrival in Brest, the Socialist party and trade unions organized a great demonstration. Their newspaper, *L'Humanité*, published a special issue, to which literary lights like Anatole France, Romain Rolland, Léon Blum, and others contributed. Wilson was pictured as a combination of Marcus Aurelius and Montesquieu.

In England there were similar expectations of salvation, again chiefly on the Left among Liberals and Labor, but not only among them. On November 11, a true-born Conservative like Lord Curzon quoted in the House of Lords Shelley's adaptation of Virgil: "The world's great age begins anew,/The golden years return." And Bernard Shaw greeted Wilson as the "Man of Destiny" who embodied the "mystic force of evolution."[16]

Wilson's triumphal tour of Europe took him from Paris to London and then to Rome. Everywhere he was greeted as a savior, as the "Redeemer of Humanity" (*Redentore dell' Humanità*) and "God of Peace" (*Dio di Pace*), in the words of the Italian banners.[17] He spent weeks indulging in this pomp and circumstance, immersed in a sea of flags and songs, carried along by beautiful words that promised so much for the future. Justice! Peace! When we hear Wilson speak in these first weeks, everything is radiant. Sometimes a harsh sound breaks through, as when he replies to Poincaré, the president of France, who wants no reconciliation with the foe, that there exist "eternal principles of right and justice" which bring with them "the certainty of just punishment."[18] But for the most part his outlook is peaceful. He speaks of the peoples who form "the organized moral force of men throughout the world," of the tide of good will: "There is a great tide running in the hearts of men. The hearts of men have never beaten so singularly in unison before. Men have never been so conscious of this brotherhood."[19]

The League of Nations

In these speeches Wilson rose high, very high, above the bustle of daily life. In Manchester:

> For, after all, though we boast of the material sides of our civilization, they are merely meant to support the spiritual side. We are not men because we have skill of hand, but we are men because we have elevation of spirit. It is in the spirit that we live and not in the task of the day.[20]

And, that same evening:

> There is a great voice of humanity abroad in the world just now to which he who cannot hear is deaf. We are not obeying the mandates of parties or of politics. We are obeying the mandates of humanity.[21]

What words these are! House, who remained behind in Paris, was moved by them, but Bonsal, his secretary, heard them more skeptically. There were millions of people, he thought, who would not listen to the promises of the great crusader from over the sea, although they had welcomed him with such rejoicing a few weeks earlier.[22]

Bonsal may have felt that the tide was beginning to turn and that enthusiasm was collapsing. Alas, there was in fact no moral tide that carried all with it. There was rather a divided Europe in which the peoples were driven at least as much by muddled feelings of rage and revenge as by lofty thoughts of right and reason. Wilson himself had experienced the impact of such vindictiveness during the off-year elections in the United States, and it was at least as prevalent in Europe. Clemenceau told the Chamber of Deputies at the end of December that he disagreed with Wilson, although he had, he said, the greatest admiration for the American president's "noble candor" (which was changed in the parliamentary journal to "noble grandeur"); he thereupon won a vote of confidence by a majority of 380 to 134.[23] Lloyd George triumphed equally convincingly in elections for the House of Commons just before Christmas. His coalition of Liberals and Tories, in which the latter were dominant, ran on an electoral program of hate and revenge against Germany with slogans like "Hang the Kaiser" and "Make Germany Pay," received no less than 526 of the 707 seats. It was not Lloyd George himself but the navy minister Sir Eric Geddes who uttered the notorious words, "We shall squeeze the German lemons until the pips squeak."[24]

Wilson's moral majority therefore existed only in his poetic imagination. He was totally out of touch with reality. The Europeans did not know what to make of his fine words. They asked themselves whether he actually meant what he said. "I am one of the few people who think him honest," said Lloyd George to his friends. But he too was exasperated when the president blew his own horn loudly and gave no sign that he understood the sacrifices England had made: "Not a word of generous appreciation issued from his lips."[25] Wilson, the American, could not establish an accepted character and place in Europe. The Europeans thought he was American, with his smooth, streamlined face, showing no emotion behind his shining glasses. Those who admired him saw what they expected, like the interviewer for the *Times* of London who described him as not the "lean, long-faced, somewhat cadaverous-looking man" one saw in photographs, but friendly, with serious eyes and a smile on his lips. But someone less friendly, as for example the doughty Lady Asquith, saw him with much sharper eyes: "I examined his lanky face, egotistical, slightly sensual and charming if too frequent smile, and noted the refinement of his brow and nostrils."[26] Lloyd George described with equal dislike "his high but narrow brow, egoist."[27] Even Sir Robert Cecil, a Christian statesman and idealistic supporter of the League of Nations, confided to his diary that after days of negotiating with Wilson he did not like him: "I do not know quite what it is that repels me: a certain harshness, coupled with vanity and an eye for effect." He did not think Wilson was a true idealist; he preferred House.[28] It did not matter that Wilson had the greatest admiration for Cecil, even calling him "the greatest man he had ever met."[29]

In a word, the European leaders did not like Woodrow Wilson. From the start there was tension between them. Clemenceau, an old hand in politics, was not the man to come under the influence of Wilson's lofty words. He knew the United States; he had lived there just after the Civil War, spoke English well, and had married an American woman. He had no high opinion of American idealism, as was evident in the witticisms he made at Wilson's expense. God had needed only ten commandments, but Wilson fourteen, he jibed. That was a superficial play on numbers, but there was real bite in his jest that Wilson talked like Jesus Christ but acted like Lloyd George. Years before, in May 1916, he had been sharply critical of Wilson's speech before the League to Enforce Peace: "If the Creator needed seven days to organize a couple of creatures of which the first born instinctively tore each other apart, Mr. Wilson, in one sovereign word, is going to create men such as never have been seen, whose first need will be love and universal harmony."[30] And, in reaction to the "peace without victory" speech, he wrote: "Never before has any political assembly heard so fine a sermon on what human beings might be capable of accomplishing if only they weren't human."[31] In brief, this was classic realism confronting classic idealism. No wonder that Theodore Roosevelt admired Clemenceau, even writing to him, "Oh Lord, how I wish you were President of the United States."[32] Clemenceau believed in France and in nothing else. France must be protected against German aggression, once and for all, and that could be done only by power, not by a super-parliament such as Wilson, who did not know what Europe wanted.[33]

Wilson for his part found Clemenceau to be what he called "feminine." By this he meant that Clemenceau was too down to earth, too realistic. In Wilson's scale of values, the ability to think in generalities was proof of true manliness. Clemenceau, he said to Ray Stannard Baker, displaying his sense of humor, "is like an old dog trying to find a place to rest. He turns slowly around following his tail, before he gets down to it."[34] And, another time, he argued arrogantly that Clemenceau had the typical French trait "of standing still mentally."[35] But after a while a certain sympathy developed between the two men. In any case, both were cut from the same cloth; each stood for something and understood that the other did too.

Wilson's dislike for Lloyd George was greater, for he found him an elusive prevaricator. David Lloyd George, the magician from Wales, was in truth a nimble man who showed many sides to the world. He had begun as progressive Liberal but was tied up now in coalition government with the Tories. An intriguer who skirted issues, he practiced personal, not principled, politics. He has been praised for not having rigid principles but human warmth. He could whip up the voters, but kept his distance from such jingoes as the press magnate Northcliffe and did not lose his head in "all this welter of democracy." Finally, say his defenders, he sought a moderate peace, more so even than Wilson, and therefore could not understand idealists of the unbending American kind. Ray Stannard Baker wrote bitterly in his diary that Wilson and Northcliffe fought "for the soul of Lloyd George, who has no soul."[36]

When Wilson landed in Europe in the midst of these men, Clemenceau, Lloyd George, and the Italian Orlando, he found himself in an uncomfortable position. Richard Hofstadter, the American historian, has nicely compared his situation to that of an American reformer trying to work alongside political "bosses."[37] He was equally vulnerable. Personally he believed firmly in "scientific peace," but what did the phrase mean? He claimed it meant that he worked for peace in a scientific, impersonal, abstract way. He was in his own mind a true pragmatist. He had once written that he had no patience with "ifs and conjectural cases. My mind insists always upon waiting until something actually does happen and then discussing what is to be done about it."[38]

He annoyed his fellow negotiators beyond measure with his abstract certainties, his "sermonettes" (as Clemenceau called them) to his "dear friends," his condescension, his solemn appeals to mankind, his stereotypical repertory of little jokes, his nervous laughter. They breathed more easily in February when he made a short trip home to America. One of the English delegates, Sir James Headlam-Morley, wrote to a friend: "I think it is a good thing that Wilson has gone away; it is extraordinary to hear from those who have heard his speeches at the Conference how very strong a feeling of distrust and opposition he creates."[39] But his attitude of superiority may have been only an outward show. Desperate to achieve his goals, he tried to do everything himself, to attend every meeting, to read through every document, and even to write many of them himself. Sometimes he sat through the night in front of his typewriter. "No nervous man could stand for months the constant strain of the work which the President unnecessarily took upon himself," wrote Lloyd George. Tics in his face betrayed his exhaustion.[40]

Wilson was not the cool, haughty man he appeared to be. He was ceaselessly tortured by the thought that he bore the responsibility for all the young men he had sent into battle. Was this pain real, or was it just a poet's sensitivity? The question is a difficult one to answer. Wilson has sometimes been compared to Abraham Lincoln, the melancholy president during the Civil War.[41] But we must ask whether, like Lincoln, he was moved by pity. Or were these soldiers nothing more than abstractions, splendid examples of a lofty reality—or unreality? He repeatedly called upon the example of the soldiers who fought and died. They provided the meaning and the justification for his plans. Yet, he experienced intense fear of visiting their graves, although in December he did go to a hospital for wounded soldiers. He cast the American soldiers in a most extraordinary role. Europeans, he asserted, had believed at first that the Americans acted out of pure self-interest. But when they saw the American soldiers, they saw not ordinary men but crusaders.

> They were not like any of the other soldiers. They had a vision; they had a dream, and they were fighting in a dream; and, fighting in that dream, they turned the whole tide of battle, and it never came back.

This astonishing piece of history became a fixed part of his speeches. He seemed actually to believe it, and probably had to, to ease his conscience. When he finally set foot in a military cemetery in May, he confided his deepest feelings to his hearers. As commander-in-chief he had been responsible for these fallen men. He had sent them to France to die. Could he, would he, then, ever say anything that did not conform to the promises he made to them when they went overseas?

> There is something better, if possible, that a man can give than this life, and that is his living spirit to a service that is not easy, to resist counsels that are hard to resist, to stand against purposes that are difficult to stand against, and to say, "Here stand I, consecrated in spirit to the men who were once my comrades and who are now gone, and who have left me under eternal bonds of fidelity."[42]

Once again he followed the example of Luther, displaying the stubbornness of a man who feels himself to be at one with the dead. But what a task to live up to! It was the end of May when he stood in the cemetery in Suresnes, and how much of what he sought at the peace conference had already been lost!

III

An enormous amount has been written about the Peace of Versailles. All the documents have been published, and many analyses given—enough to fill a library. But nonetheless, or probably just for that reason, it is extremely difficult to get a clear picture of what happened. What one sees is chaos and confusion. The historian is driven to complain that it is almost impossible for him to discover its meaning and coherence. Probably he can do so if he adheres to some oversimple scheme. That is what is done, for example, by the enthusiastic chronicler Ray Stannard Baker; for him everything is white or black, good or evil. He sees America in opposition to Europe, Woodrow Wilson as Daniel in the lion's den and in the teeth of the beast. Others see the events as the future struggling with the past. In Paris in 1919 the comparison was readily made with the Congress of Vienna a hundred years earlier. Deep satisfaction was expressed at the change from the feudal era when the voice of the people was not heard at all, when diplomats in backrooms restored the old order, created the Holy Alliance, and shifted their peoples about like cattle. The Congress of Vienna danced, the Congress of Paris worked.

We ask, which was really better? Or whether we really learn from history. It was not at all simple to understand the Versailles peace conference. It was not a clear struggle between good and evil, as Wilson had told his audience aboard the *George Washington*, but, as an English historian has written, "a turbulent collision of embarrassed demagogues." Nicolson called it a fog,[43] a fog that began with its organization—or lack of it.

No one, Wilson least of all, had clearly considered beforehand how the conference should be organized. There were no clear plans, not even for when the conference should begin. True, the French did have a plan, but it was based upon the mutual promises of the Allies, an effort to escape from the Fourteen Points and therefore unacceptable to the Americans. But that makes it all the more extraordinary that the Americans, and Wilson most of all, had nothing ready, had not even considered that the Fourteen Points required a follow-up. Was Wilson too sure of himself? Or too unsure, affected by the victory of the conservatives in the elections? Yet, the longer he waited, the weaker his position became. It was the middle of January before the first meeting could be held.

There were still other questions. Who should attend the meetings? Representatives of all the belligerents? Should the big and the small countries have equal numbers of delegates? And what would be on the agenda? Nothing had been prepared. Everything was done by trial and error. Now and then a plenary session was held with delegates from all the participating countries, but it was inevitably more a forum for oratory than a body where business could be done. Out of the wartime Allied Supreme War Council arose the Council of Ten, in which the leaders of the five most important countries (France, England, the United States, Italy, and Japan) sat with their foreign ministers. After a while the body proved not to work well, and in March the leaders of the Big Four began to meet separately in secret. If "open covenants" were the goal, they were not in any case "openly arrived at."

Committees were formed in large numbers for every subject. According to the French delegate Tardieu, who counted them, there were fifty-two committees that met 1,646 times in all.[44] The most important was certainly, thanks to Wilson, the Commission for the League of Nations. He devoted extra time to it and became its chairman. It was after all the great dream that he had had for years; we have seen that he had come out in favor of the League in May 1916. As early as 1914 he had suggested the creation of an international legal order, which would have to find its support in public opinion, "the mistress of the world." It would come into existence because of "a spirit of hope which believes in the perfectibility of the law with the perfectibility of human life itself."[45]

These were certainly not Calvinist words, yet the descendant of Presbyterian Scots had not forgotten his origins. He thought up a name for the charter of his League of Nations that carried memories of both the Bible and Scottish history—Covenant. It had to be a sacred alliance such as God had concluded with his people and the Scots several times with each other.

> My ancestors were troublesome Scotchmen and among them were some of that famous group that were known as the Covenanters. Very well, there is the Covenant of the League of Nations. I am a Covenanter."[46]

Geneva, the city where Calvin had conceived covenant theology, attracted Wilson most strongly as a home for the new League.

But this admirer of Burke thought that this covenant could not be imposed ready-made upon mankind; on the contrary, it had to be a living reality that grew organically. First there had to be an agreement among the nations, and only afterwards an organization with a constitution. The core of the matter was a mutual promise of the nations that they would stand by each other in case of aggression. The practical working out could come later. It was as if Wilson, on the basis of a romantic quasi-pragmatism, recoiled before practice. Ideas were far ahead of facts. The unsuccessful lawyer feared the legal implications of an international organization. While the English government had created as early as 1916 a commission led by Lord Phillimore to work out plans for such an organization, the American president kept to the surface. Only in the summer of 1918 did House begin, at Wilson's request, to draft a charter intended to be an improved version of the draft plan submitted by the Phillimore Commission. House discussed it in correspondence with English supporters of the concept, such as Lord Robert Cecil. On June 16, 1918, he sent to Wilson a draft "Covenant of the League of Nations," an idealistic document whose starting point was the principle so dear to Wilson that "the same standards of honor and ethics should prevail internationally and in affairs of nations as in other matters."[47] Wilson revised the document in September but scrapped the plan for an international court that House had included. Wilson did not want the matter placed in a juridical context; the League of Nations had to rest upon international public opinion—that was the court he believed in.[48]

Still, Wilson was not yet ready to go public with the plan. We can say with hindsight that it would have been better if he had made his plans widely known; they had to prove themselves with public opinion, and, not to be forgotten, with the Senate whose approval would be necessary. But Wilson feared a debate over his holy objective that might descend into squabbling; he was not fond of facing objections. On the *George Washington* he had explained to his collaborators what he had in mind: a system not worked out in too much detail, consisting of "covenants, that is, agreements, pledges, etc. such as could be worked out in general form and agreed to and set in motion." It would be a vague form of organization, with a council of ambassadors in a neutral city like The Hague or Berne. Its weapon would be a simple boycott of an aggressor country; the aggressor would be outlawed. "And outlaws are not popular now."[49]

Wilson arrived in Paris with his exalted faith in the goodness of mankind, and began his great work. From the start he directed all his efforts toward one goal, on which everything else depended: a League of Nations. He saw it as an essential part of the peace treaty, the heart, the core, the guarantee of all the other agreements. If the question of the League could be settled, House observed in his diary, almost every serious difficulty would disappear of itself.[50] Wilson agreed. He wanted a document that would work in practice, not a legalistic one. He snapped peevishly at Lansing, who had put two lawyers to work (lawyers were still his bane): "Who authorized you to do this? I don't want lawyers drafting this treaty."[51] But he came strongly under the influence of the South African statesman Jan Christiaan Smuts, who had just written a pamphlet, *The League of Nations: A Practical Suggestion*, with a plan for a league in which the nations would bind themselves by more than an occasional conference of ambassadors, and he used it to modify his own draft charter.[52] He became more and more enthusiastic; it must be the foundation for a better future.

Although it was a Frenchman, the Abbé de Saint-Pierre, who had conceived a "Plan for Perpetual Peace" in 1713, there was no longer any great faith in France in such notions. The French leaders, Clemenceau at their head, had not the slightest interest in the idea of an international legal order. What they wanted was security, guarantees that France would not again be the victim of German aggression. When they realized that Wilson was not to be diverted from his ideals, they saw making his League of Nations into an effective organization with power to enforce its principles as the only solution. Moral opinion was by far not enough. The French proposal became a point of bitter disagreement in the committee assigned to draw up the charter.

The League of Nations committee met on borrowed time. Questions of the peace were handled during the day by the Commission of Ten, while the League of Nations committee met in the evening. This arrangement wore out the American president. Clemenceau and Lloyd George did not bother with the committee, but Wilson as chairman had to be always present, and of course he would not have wanted it otherwise. He was a considerate chairman, allowing everyone to speak, but he held stubbornly to his own plans and resisted French notions of a league with organs of enforcement. In that case it would be only an alliance of the victors, he thought, intended to hold down the Germans, a new Holy Alliance. The peoples must now have the say, not their greedy, conservative governments.

He spread his message far and wide. He warned the rulers that it was not they but their subjects who were in charge, and he told them to their faces in the second plenary session at which the League of Nations committee was organized: "Gentlemen, the select classes of mankind are no longer the governors of mankind. The fortunes of mankind are now in the hands of the plain people of the world." What magnificent words! For his hearers, who after all belonged to the "select classes," such words of exalted moral force must have been embarrassing. But what did they really amount to? What was the significance of the proposal for an automatic boycott of "outlaw" nations? How would it be organized? Difficult questions came up in the committee, in the first place organizational ones. Should the small nations have the same voice and weight as the big countries? Were all nations mature enough for admission? And what was "maturity"? Democracy? When could the defeated countries join the League? Would Germany become a member?

Another question of principle was how the League of Nations could achieve a solution of the colonial question. Wilson was absolutely opposed to letting the British dominions grab the German colonies. A clash resulted not only with the Australian prime minister, William Hughes, a tough realist who delighted in poking fun at Wilson's dreams, but also with Smuts, who was in many ways the same kind of idealist as Wilson. The shrewd Boer conceived a system of three kinds of mandate for countries at different levels of development, and he worked on persuading Wilson through House and Lloyd George. In exchange for their votes in favor of the League of Nations, the Australians and South Africans obtained the colonial territories they wanted. Wilson defended the new mandates given them as a humane solution; the colonizing powers, he argued, governed peoples who "were yet at a low stage of civilization," with humanitarian purposes.[53]

It remains puzzling that Wilson attached so much importance to the vague promises of the charter of the League. It was finally adopted, after ten long meetings. In his speech on the conclusion of the charter on February 14, the president spoke in words that rose far above reality. He first read out the Covenant, all twenty-six articles. There would be a League of Nations with a general assembly in which all countries would be represented, a council in which only the big countries would have permanent seats, and a secretariat in Geneva, while an international court of justice would also be established (Wilson had conceded on this issue). The principal purpose would be to oppose aggression; the members bound themselves in the famed Article X "to respect and preserve as against external aggression the territorial integrity and existing political independence of all States members of the League. In case of any such aggression the Executive Council shall advise upon the means by which this obligation shall be fulfilled." This was vague enough, although it would give rise to many disputes. The whole charter was a noble attempt to establish rules of international law, but it remained only an attempt. Probably, had conditions been more favorable, the League would have grown naturally into a living body. But circumstances became very unfavorable, precisely because so many gross compromises were concluded for the sake of the League.

The words with which Wilson accompanied the introduction of the document only made the impression of elevated vagueness worse. He asserted once again that the whole proposal rested "upon one great force, and that is the moral force of the public opinion of the world." This was the radiant light by which all sinister evil in the world would be exposed and brought down. Yes, there was also armed force, but "in the background" as a "last resort." What this meant was not clear. But the president was convinced that "a living thing is born." Fine, it was flexible, open, "general in its terms," but definite about one essential point. "It is a definite guarantee of peace. It is a definite guarantee by the word against aggression." This "guarantee by the word" was of course not enough for the French. Words satisfy none but believers.[54]

Wilson believed he was the true realist. With all the considerable arrogance of which he was capable, he turned on those who did not agree with him. A striking example is the manner in which he condemned the French delegate on the commission, Louis Bourgeois. Bourgeois was a very talkative man, but still a person of both experience and ideals; he had attended the conferences at The Hague in 1899 and 1907, and now he represented his country in the League of Nations commission. He repeatedly clashed with Wilson, for he defended the French preference for a League of Nations with machinery to enforce its decisions. Behind his back, Wilson denigrated Bourgeois to Cecil and House.

If I am correctly informed, M. Bourgeois was the leader of the talkfest at The Hague in 1899. He blazed the trail, or so his friends claim, but it ended in fog overhead and in bog underfoot. The whole business was wishy-washy—though well meant, of course. After talking for weeks, those loquacious delegates wound up with, not agreements—oh no, but with *voeux* or wishes. "Pious" wishes they were, I grant you, but they were without binding force upon those who signed, or upon those who declined to sign. Now we are met here for hard-and-fast agreements, for binding stipulations, for commitments, and it is my task to see that no nation or group of men holds out on us—those silly pawns in the murderous game of power politics! But of course I would not hurt M. Bourgeois' feelings. I respect them more than I do his plans for peace or the brains that hatch them.[55]

This is a long quotation, but how poignantly typical of Wilson. One can hardly avoid the impression that the man who spoke these words conducted himself as a nineteenth-century professor was expected to do, but that, with all his incredible arrogance, he really was ranting against himself. Was that why he was so obsessed by this opponent?

According to Lloyd George his arrogance went further. In his vivid but malicious memoirs, the prime minister tells us that Wilson is supposed to have said:

> Why . . . has Jesus Christ so far not succeeded in inducing the world to follow His teachings in these matters? It is because he taught the ideal without devising any practical means of attaining it. That is the reason why I am proposing a practical solution to carry out these aims.[56]

Wilson believed in his League of Nations as a remedy for all troubles, a miraculous cure that would work precisely because it was so entwined with the peace treaty itself. The treaty might not be perfect, he said in April, but with the League of Nations as an integral part of the treaty, there was a mechanism to improve its operation.[57]

But actually it worked the other way round, a fact that Wilson completely missed. The delegates of the Allied countries exploited his League of Nations proposal to extract concessions from him; the peace turned out very badly because he repeatedly made compromises in order to save his beloved plan, carrying it through the bustling debates to safe harbor. We will discuss all that bargaining in the next chapter, but let us conclude this chapter with the sage words of Henry White. "The fact is," wrote the deeply disappointed White in May, "that the League of Nations, in which he had been more deeply interested than anything else from the beginning, believing it to be the best if not the only means of avoiding war in the future, has been played to the limit by France and Japan in extracting concessions from him; to a certain extent by the British too, and the Treaty as it stands is the result. The Italians overshot the mark."[58]

TWENTY-FOUR

But the Bolshevists, so far as we could get any taste of
their flavor, are the most consummate sneaks in the
world. I suppose because they know they have no high
motives themselves, they do not believe that anybody else
has.

—*Woodrow Wilson*

RUSSIA

I F   W E   A R E   T O   R E D U C E   T H E
complex and opaque chaos of the past
to meaning, it is tempting, and even necessary, to turn variety into unity and
darkness into light. This holds true especially for the period of eventful confusion
during the winter of 1918–1919, on the scale
of world history the shortest of eras. Everything seemed to be bunched
together, everything entangled with everything, in mutual contrast—war
and peace, restoration and revolution, selfish interests and idealism, hope
and despair. That is how we see a hawthorn bush in the winter dunes,
stubborn and fierce, a tangle of branches, a crisscross of contradictions,
of mutual division—one can hardly believe that in the spring it will offer
itself to us in a dazzling display of white flowers.

It is an image that befits the story of Woodrow Wilson, who really
did believe that out of the winter of war would come a springtime of
blossoming peace and justice. His stubborn effort to realize his dream
gives a kind of meaning to the Peace of Versailles. The first large work
on the making of the peace, Ray Stannard Baker's *Woodrow Wilson and
World Settlement*, is built upon such a vision. For Baker the peace con-

ference was a struggle of the old against the new, of conservatism against a commitment to the future, of European pessimism against American optimism. It was a vision in Wilson's spirit: Baker, as we have seen, represented "His Master's Voice" with fervor and naïveté.

It is not easy for historians to accept such simplicities, for the past is not simple. But variations of this splendid vision have continued down to our own day. It is not very surprising that in the years after the Second World War, when the Cold War gave rise to a clear-cut dualism of East and West, there were scholars who claimed to find the same dualism at work in the final years of the First World War. Bolshevik Russia had come into existence, and they argued that the big problem in Paris was not Germany, as was first held, but Russia. The fear of the Red menace is said to have controlled the negotiations in Paris. The American historian Arno J. Mayer elaborated this vision in a book with the significant title *Politics and Diplomacy of Peacemaking: Containment and Counter Revolution at Versailles, 1918–1919.* When it was republished in a popular edition, it was given the even catchier title *Wilson versus Lenin.*[1]

It is tempting to work with a set pattern like this. Everything seems to fit in, and what doesn't fit ceases to be important. The whole history of the years 1917–1918 then becomes decisive for what follows: the Cold War, Wilson versus Lenin, evolution versus revolution, conservatism versus revolution, individualism versus social responsibility—all of it, take your pick. Then one can give meaning to the apparently abstract rhetoric of Wilson, behind which lurked a well-organized campaign against Bolshevism. By his words Wilson restrained the European working class from taking Lenin's side. We have seen that in fact French Socialists, through the mouth of Albert Thomas, very deliberately made this choice. Another American historian, N. Gordon Levin, Jr., reduced it to an even clearer pattern. Wilson, he asserts, argued for a liberal capitalist world order with its own international law, safely protected against both traditional imperialism and revolutionary socialism. Within this system America easily became dominant morally and economically.[2]

It is also tempting to force a pattern upon the complicated reality of a person, in this case the man Woodrow Wilson. Otherwise, in the dense clouds of his exalted verbiage, he defies probability. There must be some logic behind this puzzle, some concealed purpose, all the more in the case of this rational intellectual, this enlightened liberal scholar who emblazoned logic on his banner.

Russia

But the problem remains that reality does not fit the pattern, neither of the time nor of the man. To be sure, Bolshevism became one of the great issues of the ensuing half century, but it was not the only one and not the dominant one at the time; it appears so only in hindsight. Whoever reads the minutes of the endless but fascinating discussions in Paris is struck by the confused multiplicity of themes and problems. The peace was shaped not by the fear of Russia but in reality by suspicion of the new Germany. As *The New Republic* concluded a bit spitefully, the choice was made not between Wilson and Lenin; a third possibility—Clemenceau!—was the one taken.[3]

This is also true with regard to Wilson. Of course he believed in a vision that he personally thought was the summit of logic, which was a golden middle way between imperialism and Bolshevism. Levin is not wholly wrong. Wilson did favor a bourgeois, reasonable order of things, in which—as we have already seen—interests and ideals were not contradictory. But this logical vision and the accompanying rhetoric flowed from his American Enlightenment philosophy, and it was neither influenced by the new teachings from the East nor significantly changed by them. And it was, in truth, logical only in a derivative sense; it was in the end a religious force that soared above logic. It contained an irrational element, a certitude that clashed with reality. This was its greatness and the source of its downfall.

Wilson did not at all follow with regard to Bolshevism the clear and logical line of conduct that principles and propaganda might lead us to expect. Like the other Western statesmen, he had to seek his way in confrontation with the bewildering new event. He used his principles in this quest, but they were not always applicable. His principles were, of course, opposed to those of Bolshevism; this student of Burke believed in organic development, not in revolution. He had, too, the instinctive dislike of the ordinary citizen for the Communist system and even believed current twaddle about it. For instance, he told Grayson that Bolshevism would be brought to America by "Negroes" returning from abroad. Black American soldiers had been treated as equals in France, and "it has gone to their heads"! Another proof was a lady friend's experience with a black laundress who wanted bigger wages because "money is as much mine as yours."[4]

Bolshevism, he said in a talk he gave aboard the liner on the way to Europe, was a poison, a new tyranny. But the Bolsheviks should not be fought blindly; an effort should be made to understand them. "What I am present keenly interested in is in finding the interior of their minds," he wrote to Lansing in January 1919.[5] He had an eye for social conditions. Wasn't Bolshevism one of the ways in which the yearning of mankind for justice was manifested? Wasn't it an understandable protest against the excesses of capitalism? He had learned from history that it made little sense to oppose such a development by force. The Russian Revolution, like the French Revolution and even that in Mexico, had to be allowed to run its course. "My own feeling is that Russia should be left to settle her own affairs in her own way." In the long run the Russians, "great organisers in their own way, organisers of village communities," would come to their senses. But intervention would only strengthen extremism.[6] He explained his attitude to the Council of Ten in Paris:

> There was certainly a latent force behind Bolshevism which attracted as much sympathy as its more brutal aspects aroused general disgust. There was throughout the world a feeling of revolt against the large vested interests which influenced the world both in the economic and in the political sphere. The way to cure this domination was in his opinion, constant discussion and a slow process of reform.[7]

Self-determination also applied here and in its nature implied non-intervention. In the West one might hope for the acceptance of democracy everywhere, but it could not be forced upon countries. If they did not want to accept it, "that is none of my business." But the problem was that other countries, France, England, and Japan, did not want to let events take their course but were quite ready to intervene to bring the revolution to an end. Already in his Fourteen Points Wilson had warned against such interference, calling the Russian question "the acid test" for telling whether the Allies honestly believed in the principle of self-determination. He was vigorously opposed to all intervention; he did not even want to issue a declaration of opposition to the Bolsheviks. It was against the spirit of his government, he wrote, "to interfere with the form of government in any other government."[8]

Yet the war gradually entangled him in the Russian problem. As long as the war lasted, he had hoped that Russia would continue to play a role in the struggle against Germany. This left him in the grip of a nasty dilemma. Originally he had received favorable reports from Americans in Moscow about the new government. When, at the beginning of March 1918, Trotsky asked the Allies for help (but it was only a maneuver to fend off the threatening Japanese intervention in Siberia), he responded favorably. He sent a friendly message to the Soviets in which he expressed the true friendship of the American people for the Russian people and promised that it was ready to do all that it could to help restore Russia's sovereignty and independence.[9] But he had to add that at the moment the United States was unable to help.

This declaration was at the same time a warning to Japan and the other Allies. It was nonetheless received in Russia with sarcasm and answered with a blunt message to the peoples of the world who suffered under the capitalist yoke. They would soon be liberated! The Allies were not deterred from acting by their American friend. They were firmly determined to call a halt to the Bolshevik revolution. Already in March 1918, British troops landed in Murmansk, and later in Archangel as well, in the Far North, and in April a British-Japanese action began at Vladivostok. They preferred to undertake these operations with the support of the United States and began therefore to exert strong pressure upon Washington.

Wilson was uncertain what to do. Already in March he was almost ready to approve the Japanese intervention, and he drafted a declaration that the American government had confidence that the Japanese government "in putting an armed force into Siberia is doing so as an ally of Russia," that is, in order to help Russia against Germany. This was obvious sophistry and Wilson soon abandoned it after he received a fiery plea against intervention from a young official at the State Department, William Bullitt. Such a step, wrote the idealistic young man, would undermine the president's moral leadership. He should not take part and he should not accept it. "We cannot wash our hands in this matter. . . . Pontius Pilate washed his hands. The world has never forgiven him."[10]

Wilson understood such religious language. He had to preserve his purity, but the problem was, as always, how to stay both pure and responsible. The Allies continued to ply him with arguments and in the end they swayed him. The issue in the Far North, they argued, was the safeguarding of the huge stores of arms and munitions in Archangel. In the Far East it was the protection of the Czech Legion. The first argument was nonsense, for most of the materiel had long since fallen into the hands of the Bolsheviks. But the Czech Legion was a more important matter, which greatly complicated the situation. In Siberia in the spring of 1918 some 50,000 Czech troops, mostly deserters from the Austrian army, were on their way to Vladivostok, where they hoped to be sent to the Western front to continue the struggle for the freedom of their homeland. A number had already reached Vladivostok, and the remainder were scattered along the Trans-Siberian railway. They had come into conflict with the Bolsheviks, who, the Allies claimed, were using German and Austrian prisoners of war against them. To bring the Czechs back was an obvious military objective, one that gave Wilson the certainty of rectitude that he needed to act.

He wrote to House in the summer:

> I have been sweating blood over the question what is right and feasible to do in Russia. It goes to pieces like quicksilver under my touch, but I hope I see and can report some progress presently, along the double line of economic assistance, and aid to the Czecho-Slovaks.[11]

American help had to remain small, however, and it was directed at very limited goals. In the memorandum that Wilson sent to the Allies and repeated in an announcement to the press two weeks later, he declared that the aid program definitely did not involve the United States in Russian domestic affairs or invade Russian sovereignty.[12]

This sounded very good, but nonetheless the United States was poking into a wasp's nest, and became willy-nilly a party in the muddled Russian civil war. In September three American battalions arrived in Archangel, where they remained until the summer of 1919, and in the same month Americans also landed in Vladivostok, where they guarded sections of the Amur railway. Events soon went much further than Wilson had intended. The whole question became still more difficult when the American troops remained in Russia even after the war ended in November 1918.

It is not at all surprising that Wilson at this time really no longer knew what to do. An abrupt withdrawal would hurt his position when speaking to his allies in Paris about the peace and the League of Nations. In any case the Western policy toward Russia was in a muddle. Reports and analyses of every kind went the rounds. The Bolsheviks contributed their share to making the confusion even greater. Their situation was critical in the winter of 1918–1919; whole regions of Russia were in the hands of rightist generals, and the country's economic position was desperate. They therefore adopted a conciliatory policy for the moment. The diplomat Maxim Litvinov sent an emotional letter on Christmas Eve—the date was deliberate. He besought the Allies not to believe all the slander about the Bolsheviks, but to listen to the other side of the question; the Bolsheviks, he said, wanted order and peace and were ready to talk about the Russian debts. Wilson, stirred by this appeal to his emotions, sent a special delegate to Stockholm to sound out Litvinov. This diplomat, William H. Buckler (a half-brother of the member of the peace delegation, Henry White), heard the Russian preach the good cause, and he advised Wilson to reply with mildness and understanding and thus to strengthen the moderate elements among the Bolsheviks.[13]

The belief that there were such moderate elements, that things could work out, that a prudent policy would drive a wedge between Lenin and Trotsky, and other such vague fantasies, appeared to offer an answer to the problem of how to approach the new Russian rulers. It was the way Wilson wanted to go. He stubbornly resisted the plans of Foch and Clemenceau and the right-wing members of the English cabinet, with Churchill as their spokesman, to intervene in favor of the rightist generals in South Russia and Siberia. Yet he definitely did not wish to recognize the new Russian regime. He saw combatting Bolshevism by economic means as the only solution to this dilemma. With removal of the cause of dissatisfaction, the danger would disappear too.

But in fact Wilson solved nothing. Lloyd George tried to save the situation by offering to bring the various Russian parties together around one table. Clemenceau at first fiercely opposed this proposal, accepting it finally only if the meeting were not in Paris but at a safe distance. The island of Prinkipo in the Sea of Marmora was selected as a site. Wilson, instantly enthusiastic over such a democratic solution, issued a proclamation full of fine words about peace and freedom, inviting the battling parties to make the decisions for themselves.[14] But nothing came of the proposal; the Bolsheviks were willing to go to Prinkipo, but the other parties, the right-wing leaders Kolchak and Denikin, absolutely refused.

The Prinkipo scheme was a failure. It could not have been otherwise, for it was totally unrealistic. Yet liberals like Wilson and Lloyd George continued to hope for one or another peaceful solution, but without making a real effort. The conservatives, to the contrary, men such as

Clemenceau and Churchill, argued in the spring of 1919 for recognition of the regime of Admiral Kolchak in Omsk, which seemed to hold a winning hand. Churchill came specially in the middle of February to Paris to urge a vigorous joint policy against Bolshevism, but it was again Wilson who thwarted it. Intervention, he said, offered no solution. What country was ready actually to send the number of troops proposed? It would be better to establish contact with the rulers in Moscow, even if it was only to obtain more information.

When Wilson gave this reply to Churchill, it is probable that he had just heard of a new plan from House. It remains a bit puzzling just how far he supported it, and the whole affair remains controversial. The main lines amount to this: House and Lansing proposed sending a mission to Moscow, originally only with the purpose of finding out more about the situation. With the cooperation of the British (Lloyd George's secretary, Sir Philip Kerr, was involved in it, but it is unclear how much the prime minister himself knew of it), House went further and gave the mission the powers to negotiate. The American journalist and diplomat William C. Bullitt was chosen as leader of the small delegation; he was an ambitious, eloquent, and very idealistic young man of twenty-eight who had been working at the State Department as an adviser on European affairs. Bullitt chose his collaborators, among them the renowned journalist Lincoln Steffens. This group left at the end of February for Moscow, where they were met very courteously. They succeeded in concluding a provisional treaty with Lenin and Chicherin, the Soviet commissar for foreign affairs. Things seemed to be going very well. Bullitt personally was in the clouds, he met Lenin "in a thoroughly conciliatory mood," found him "a straightforward man of the quickest intelligence and a certain serenity, humor and broad-mindedness," and he concluded an agreement with nothing but reasonable and humane terms: repeal of the economic blockade, armistice and amnesty on all sides, withdrawal of the Allied troops, recognition of the war debts of the Russian governments, and a peace conference.[15] He saw a Russia, Bullitt reported, that was admittedly struggling with hunger and other great problems, but full of promise for the future; the schools were open again, the trains were running on time, and there was no prostitution. His friend Lincoln Steffens summed up this optimism in a phrase that has become classic (there are disagreements about its exact formulation and the time it was uttered): "I have seen the future and it works."[16]

Russia

The elated Bullitt returned at the end of March to Paris and turned in a glowing report with the conclusion that only a socialist government was possible in Moscow, that Lenin's wing of the Bolshevik party was the more moderate, and that there could be no peace in Europe without first making peace with the revolution.[17] But bitter disillusionment followed. The only person who even seemed to share his enthusiasm was House, who noted in his diary that he now saw a way out of "the vexatious problem," provided the prime ministers and the president wanted to support it.[18] They did not. Lloyd George, nimble as usual, received Bullitt favorably at first and permitted him to describe what he had experienced, but then was scared off by the fierce comments in the English press, in particular the articles of the very authoritative journalist H. Wickham Steed.[19] In the House of Commons Lloyd George, in a shameless lie, declared that he had indeed heard rumors of a young American who had returned from Moscow, but that President Wilson apparently did not attach the slightest importance to the reports, because he had not spoken a single word about them in the meetings in Paris. Wilson in fact did not want to have anything to do with the affair; claiming a headache, he declined to receive Bullitt when he came to see him. The young, audacious but inexperienced diplomat was left standing outside in the cold, furious and desperate. He sent Wilson a letter in which he quoted the remarks of Lloyd George and asked categorically whether they were true. He received no reply.[20]

This was not the end of the matter. Bullitt became the first young idealist to be deeply disappointed with Wilson. In May he wrote an open letter to the president, very outspoken but also quite moving in its tragic mood of offended feelings: "I was one of the millions who trusted confidently and implicitly in your leadership and believed that you would take nothing nothing less than 'a permanent peace' based upon 'unselfish and unbiased justice.'"[21] There was no reply to this letter either. Bullitt had not spoken his last word, however. He continued to pursue Wilson with his grudge. In September, testifying at the hearings Lodge had organized in the Senate on Wilson's peace treaty, Bullitt gave vent to his embitterment. Playing into the hands of the archconservative Lodge, he helped bring about the downfall of his once admired idol.

Indeed, this is not the end of the tale. About 1930 Bullitt made the acquaintance of Sigmund Freud. The famed psychoanalyst appeared to share his hatred for Wilson, considering him responsible for the downfall of old Austria. Together they decided to unmask their antihero in a psychobiography, a book that only appeared in 1967, after the death of Mrs. Wilson.[22] This is the book we discussed in chapter one. To put it mildly, it is a one-sided contribution to the understanding of the curious personality of Woodrow Wilson, the incomprehensible man whom we have seen at his most incomprehensible in his policy toward Russia. The man who was against intervention but intervened, who opposed Bolshevism but halfheartedly sought conciliation with it.

The disavowal of Bullitt's mission meant that the last chance for a modus vivendi with the new rulers in Russia went by the board. This was probably a tragic development; some historians, the authoritative George Kennan among them, have described it in such terms. A judgment in this question naturally depends upon one's vision of the viability and trustworthiness of the Soviet regime. But it was a matter about which Wilson, dependent as he was upon what he heard from right and left, could hold no firm opinion of his own.

He would have preferred to withdraw American troops from the Russian hornet's nest as soon as possible. But once in Paris he had to reckon with the Allied leaders, who favored intervention. What alternative did he offer them? They repeatedly pointed out to him with great emphasis and much exaggeration the threat of Bolshevism flooding over Europe. Especially when the Communists under the leadership of Bela Kun seized power in Hungary at the end of March, a panicky mood developed in the meeting rooms and corridors in Paris.

At the same time the presence of the Americans in Siberia had led to many complications and finally to an unsolvable dilemma. They could not be present without becoming involved in the civil war; every action that they undertook to protect the Trans-Siberian railway meant support for Kolchak. But withdrawing would enable the Japanese to gain hegemony in Eastern Siberia and Manchuria, which would run exactly counter to the American policy of the open door in the Far East. Furthermore, the Japanese had to be kept friendly as the foremost support and bulwark of the League of Nations in Asia. It was a desperate situation.

Wilson, consistent at least in his approach to the situation through his social ideals, continued to believe that assistance with food was the best solution. The threat of the Bolsheviks, he said to the liberal editor of the *Manchester Guardian*, C. P. Scott, "was mainly an invasion of ideas and you could not defeat ideas by armies."[23] Early in January he sent a cablegram to Tumulty containing a message to Congress appealing for funds for food shipments. "Food relief is now the key to the whole European situation and to the solutions of peace. Bolshevism is steadily advancing westward, has overwhelmed Poland, and is poisoning Germany. It cannot be stopped by force but it can be stopped by food."[24] Food relief was the humanitarian and effective magical solution for the whole complex of political problems. At first Wilson took advice from the special American commissioner for economic assistance, Herbert Hoover, later the president, a typical American pragmatic idealist who had earned his spurs in organizing relief for the Belgian population. Hoover gave Wilson a memorandum in which he warned about the "murderous tyranny" of the Bolsheviks and proposed establishment of a commission to alleviate hunger in Russia. Wilson himself should be its great spiritual leader and "analyze, as only you can, Bolshevism from its political, economic, humane and its criminal points of view, and while yielding its aspirations, sympathetically to show its utter foolishness as a basis for social development."[25]

But Hoover had something quite different in mind. He could not accept a compromise with the Russian leaders, with the Western powers promising to end the hostilities (so that Bullitt in the end obtained a little of what he had proposed). Hoover drew up a sharp protest, but Wilson prevented a publication of this memorandum.[26] When food relief in Russia was actually gotten under way by the famed Norwegian explorer Fridtjof Nansen, Hoover opposed it too. It was of course not a political solution; at the least it was naïve to believe that the Bolshevik government could be brought down by it. In the course of 1919 the regimes of Kolchak and Denikin, once apparently so powerful, collapsed like a house of cards, and the Bolsheviks extended their power over the whole of the Russian Empire. By this time the Czechs had left Vladivostok for their homeland, and the Western armies of invasion gradually pulled out. The last American contingent sailed home from the harbor of Vladivostok on April 1, 1920.

This brought an unsatisfactory and inevitable end to Wilson's policy toward Russia. There were too many contradictory aims in it. Wilson had to resist first German and then Japanese imperialism; he had to conduct a policy with regard to Russia that did not estrange him too much from his allies and did not clash too strongly with the rapidly growing anti-Bolshevik feelings; but he had also to remain true to his ideals of self-determination and nonintervention. He had to support the Czechs but not the right-wing Russians. It was, as the best expert in this field, the historian Betty Miller Unterberger writes, "an impossible task."[27] But that, alas, was true of all of Wilson's policies.

TWENTY-FIVE

I have fighting blood in me, and it is sometimes a delight
to let it have scope, but if it is challenged on this occasion
it will be an indulgence.
—*Woodrow Wilson*

He has a conception that he is the arbiter of the universe
and that he knows everything by intuition.
—*William Howard Taft*

FRIEND AND FOE

E WILL RECALL THAT Harold Nicolson characterized the peace conference as foggy, an event without plan, program, or even agenda. When we watch the conclusion of a peace, what do we expect to see? Classically, the victors and the defeated sitting around a table and negotiating. Negotiation, however, was usually a one-sided activity, with the victors laying down the terms for peace and the vanquished accepting them. But just because the Allies in Paris in 1919 had the example of the execrated Congress of Vienna hovering before their eyes, they took a very different course of action.

At Vienna, Talleyrand, the brilliant French diplomat, had played a positive and accepted, indeed an appreciated role, and therefore had been able to save a great deal for his defeated country. This example probably led the negotiators in Paris to agree upon peace terms among themselves first and then to present it to the enemy as an accomplished fact. In any case, from the beginning the distinction between a preliminary peace, which the Allies drew up themselves, and a definitive peace, which they would then negotiate with the defeated foe, was left vague. Unfortunately, there existed a disastrous confusion of language about this difference, leading to great crises and conflicts not only among the various Allied leaders but also between Wilson and House. No one defined exactly what a "preliminary peace" specifically would be. If it was to be a total agreement over territorial and financial terms, it would obviously come into conflict with the spirit of Wilson, his idea of a fair peace without victory. Wilson warned Lloyd George point-blank in December that the notion of a preliminary Inter-Allied Conference did not at all appeal to him. He said that the general peace conference would be a "sham" if terms were fixed beforehand and simply handed to the Germans. Yet, he added, he was ready to hold informal discussions among the Allies in Paris; their conclusions would then be presented to Germany at the peace conference. It was a distinction without a difference, but Wilson insisted upon it.[1]

What Wilson intended by an informal peace was a temporary one that was no more than an "exalted armistice," a settlement only of the most urgent questions, but still with a draft charter of a League of Nations undetachably riveted to it. He hoped that he could transform this preliminary peace into an "executive agreement" in the United States that would not need the approval of the Senate.

The fact is, however, that an "executive agreement" is one of the vaguest possibilities open to American foreign policy, "one of the mysteries of the constitutional order," in the language of Arthur Schlesinger, Jr.[2] That is why it has always been more popular with presidents than with Congress. Wilson, beginning to realize how much resistance he was going to meet in the Senate, hoped the concept would enable him to skirt this obstacle. His advisers, more practical in their thinking, with Lansing foremost among them, warned him that this would not be possible; both laws and practical difficulties stood in the way. The president, stubborn as always, held his ground. He therefore gave all his energies during the first month of the peace negotiations to the drafting of the charter and let other matters take their course.[3]

The question became critical because in February Wilson had to return for a short time to the United States. As president, he was needed at home for matters of domestic politics that had to be settled with Congress. He barely allowed himself the necessary time, leaving Brest in the middle of February and returning in the middle of March, spending only a week in Washington. The affairs of the peace conference did not really permit any delay, and too much time had already been lost. Still he was quite satisfied with what he had accomplished and he felt that he had the reins in his hands. He became confident that he would succeed in achieving his highest goal—the League of Nations as an integral part of the peace. The charter was ready, and he took it across the ocean as a valued trophy.

A trophy was all it was, however. Every other major problem remained unsolved; some had scarcely come up for discussion at all. The absence of an agenda exacted its penalty. And time pressed. Europe was in chaos, in shambles, threatened by hunger and anarchy (for Bolshevism was principally interpreted as an anarchistic movement). The greatest problem was what to do with Germany. How large was the danger of Bolshevism there? Or, on the contrary, was there danger of a right-wing coup d'etat? What punishment should be imposed upon the defeated foe? Whole armies were still kept under arms. The blockade remained in force, under the pressure of the French, as a weapon for compelling the "Herrenvolk," the "people of masters" as the Germans had liked to call themselves, to swallow the Allies' peace terms. Clemenceau's tirades against the German danger often dominated the discussions.

It was hoped that a preliminary peace settling military matters would at least put an end to this situation. With tension relieved, demobilization could be completed and trade again allowed to flow in its normal channels. Then, with the situation eased, the definitive peace could be arranged. But Wilson had to leave, and he gave to his friend House, who still had his complete trust, his scepter—or his magician's wand, or whatever we want to call his spectacular power in Paris when Wilson was not present in person. The president told the Council of Ten that he would leave with an "easy mind," provided that his plans were adopted in principle. He had full confidence in his military advisers. His absence should not delay making the preliminary peace, not even such thorny matters as territorial changes and reparations. While he was away, he told his colleagues, Colonel House would take his place.[4]

Yet it is not at all certain that he was as confident as he sounded. On the president's departure, House told him that he, House, hoped to have everything in order during the next four weeks. The president was startled, and House quickly added that it was not his purpose to bring everything "to a final conclusion," but to have everything ready for Wilson's approval. "This pleased him."[5]

Ray Stannard Baker, in his long book on the peace, has put forward a very dramatic argument: Wilson, the honorable president from the New

World, had no sooner gone off than the faithless Europeans, assisted by vain House, betrayed his whole ideal and hastily transformed the preliminary peace into a definitive treaty, with all its disgraceful territorial and financial decisions included but the League of Nations left out. When Wilson returned in the middle of March, he remarked (still according to Baker) that all had been lost, but he swiftly took the wheel and saved what could be saved.

This is a splendid example of conspiracy theory. It exonerates Wilson of responsibility for the lamentable peace that followed. But it is a theory without truth. Baker, in his report, leaves out—for convenience' sake—those few words by Wilson to the effect that he hoped the settlement of territorial and financial questions would not be delayed because of his absence. But, as Churchill later wrote, the fact was that these "awkward words" were present in the notes of the Council.[6] Wilson had uttered them. Alas, the real harm had been done by Wilson himself when he departed from Paris without giving House instructions; he had done the same thing before with similar missions. House was left free to settle matters and, as we have already seen, he thought he was himself much more sensible than the president and a much more skillful manipulator. Wilson was his idol, of course, but House considered him to be too abstract and unrealistic. House had to translate the dreams of his master into reality, and in this task it was better not to have one's master underfoot.

What a situation this was—Wilson away and House speaking! Moses went up Mount Sinai, and Aaron made a golden calf. This image is not my own; it comes from Baker in his assertion of the great betrayal, which is a "stab-in-the-back" theory applied to Wilson's diplomacy. It is not all nonsense. House was much more flexible than his master and he thought that he could handle the European realists, Clemenceau, Lloyd George, and their kind. But it may well have been they who manipulated him. Much has been written about the remarkably close relationship between Clemenceau and House. They seemed fitted to each other, and the Frenchman had nothing but praise for the cultivated colonel from wild Texas. Clemenceau told a journalist he was very fond of House. "We are almost like brothers who disagree on everything." But he liked him because they could talk frankly to each other and didn't go behind each other's back. "He doesn't always see eye to eye with the Great Mogul, Wilson, but he is intensely loyal."[7]

Wilson looked with suspicion on the friendship between House and Clemenceau. He told Grayson that the French leader was not to be trusted and that House was making a big mistake in showing such esteem for him.[8] Yet, only a few days later, he gave House a completely free hand, and House gladly went his own way. He can be sharply criticized for such conduct; Baker found him at fault afterwards, and so has the Danish historian Inga Floto in her recent book about House mercilessly unmasking the colonel until little more is left of him than a conceited nonentity.[9]

But nonetheless there is something to be said in House's defense. The needs of the situation were great. At the end of February reports of serious food shortages in Germany came in. House had no instructions but powers to act as he saw fit. And, in truth, where really was the boundary between military and territorial questions, for example in the question of the occupation of the Rhineland? And, above all, in this situation of need, was it really so urgent to spend time saving the splendid dream of the League of Nations instead of taking care of practical matters? True, House was vain. Was that so great a vice? If it was, the historian would have a rather large number of others to condemn as well. It sometimes seems as if historians become as moralistic as Wilson himself.

House wanted to make progress, and it seemed possible now that he had only Clemenceau and Lloyd George to face. They no longer handled the most important matters in the Council of Ten but behind closed doors as a trio (with Orlando they became a quartet). They became the "Big Four," who arranged everything in the following months. Progress was made, although interrupted on February 19 when Clemenceau was wounded by an anarchist. But he was soon on his feet again, and on March 7 House could record with satisfaction in his notebook:

> We did our work rapidly, and both George and Clemenceau felt
> encouraged that so much could be done so quickly. . . . We also
> decided to send for Orlando, George remarking that "We four Prime
> Ministers can quickly finish the business that is before us." When
> the President is away I never hesitate to act and to take as much
> responsibility as either of the others.[10]

We can see House beaming with happiness as he writes these lines, and also how much of himself he reveals. Mrs. Floto cites them to show how far House went.

It is true, of course, that he went further than Wilson actually wanted. He accepted much of what the French desired in the question of the Rhineland; in his opinion André Tardieu's idea of creating a provisional republic in the west of Germany was not foolish, and he came up also with a compromise over the League of Nations. He did not completely sacrifice it, but, being a visionary himself, came up with the idea of making it work more solidly. The members of the League of Nations committee should at once begin to function as an executive council and provide the conference with advice on the Italian question. It was an extraordinary proposal, but was it actually so much more unrealistic than Wilson's own idea of a League of Nations that had to be organized down to the last detail before peace could be concluded?

Wilson drew back, however, before the notion of putting his dream into practice so suddenly. He cabled House that such an accomplished fact would create problems in the Senate. This was certainly true, but his own plan for a preliminary peace would have met at least as much resistance in that redoubtable body, as House himself had warned him. But House now made Wilson's plan impossible, not because he attempted to separate the League of Nations from the peace treaty, but by arranging the settlement of so many questions, he made the whole plan for a preliminary peace impossible. But could he have done otherwise, in view of the entirely artificial distinction between a preliminary and a definitive peace which Wilson had fostered for so long?

The whole conception of a noble Wilson being undercut by a plotting House is artificial, a melodramatic distortion of reality. It was primarily Mrs. Wilson who gave this color to the tale in her memoirs. When Wilson came back to Brest, she relates, before going ashore he had a long talk with House with no one else present. It was past midnight when House left, and Mrs. Wilson, concerned at the lateness of the hour, went at once to her husband. Shocked, she saw Wilson wholly changed, pale as death, seeming to have aged ten years, his tight jaw showing how hard it was for him to control his feelings. Silently he extended his hand to her, and she took it,

crying, "What is the matter? What has happened?" He smiled bitterly. "House has given away everything I won before we left Paris. He has compromised on every side, and I have to start all over again, and this time it will be harder."

Friend and Foe

But fortunately he regained his composure, she tells us, "the light of battle was in his eyes" and he swore that he would fight harder than ever, he would win everything back, "or never look these boys I sent over here in the face again."[11]

From that moment, the myth goes on, the rift between the two friends became an accomplished fact. This too is untrue. Wilson continued to rely on House for a considerable period, selecting him as a deputy when he fell ill in April. Only afterwards, as we shall see, did the definitive estrangement, on which Mrs. Wilson had set her heart, take place. Her tearful tale must be taken with a grain of salt.

II

If we want to dramatize history, we could write a life of Wilson in which his relationship to House would be central. This has in fact occurred. The intimate but still strange friendship between the two men dominated the most important years of Wilson's life. But for the later years, the same thing could be done with the relationship between Wilson and Senator Henry Cabot Lodge of Massachusetts as the key. Their tie was certainly not one of friendship, unless one wants to see in them *feindliche Brüder* (brothers and enemies), hating each other but thrown upon each other, inseparable and irreconcilable.

This is dramatization that places the personal above the structural, and hence is only a half truth. Lodge was indeed a man of powerful character who had a personal detestation of Wilson, and the feeling was fully reciprocated. In his memoirs, Lodge might claim that he had "not the slightest personal hostility to Mr. Wilson," but the man who scornfully mocked "the natural cheapness of Mr. Wilson,"[12] who delighted in blowing up an erroneous reference by Wilson to a classical myth, so that Wilson "was not a scholar in the true sense at all,"[13] this man was certainly not objective. Furthermore, he was a snob. He was jealous of Wilson's reputation as a scholar in politics, for that is how he would liked to have been seen himself. This Bostonian, whose mother was a Cabot, which in Massachusetts was tantamount to high nobility, did not want to take a place below a Southerner. This Harvard graduate did not want a place below even a Princeton professor. His remark about the League of Nations charter, "As an English production it does not rank high, it might get by at Princeton but certainly not at Harvard," was probably meant as more than a joke.[14]

Lodge was an authentic New Englander, a cool, sharp, self-assured Yankee. He was also somewhat pompous. As a scoffer has said, he was just like the hard ground where he belonged, "naturally barren but highly cultivated." When he jested, there was always some purpose behind his words. And when he harbored personal feelings, they were always mingled with principles. When men such as Wilson and Lodge are compared, there is more than a simple contrast between a good protagonist and his Mephistopheles at work. Lodge also stood for the higher verities, perhaps even more strongly than Wilson, with whom as an idealist he had something in common. He too believed that the United States was the best country in the world; if America failed, mankind failed with it.[15]

Lodge had more against Wilson than personal antipathy, and the reverse was also true. Wilson saw in the objections that Lodge made to the League of Nations insuperable obstacles, but not just because they were bound up with "that impossible name." It was not merely two men who faced each other, but two worlds. In this clash Lodge represented the North against Wilson's South, the Republican party against Wilson's Democrats, the legislative power against Wilson's executive, and, last but not least, the tradition of realism (which is not without its own idealism) and nationalism (which is not opposed to international responsibility) against Wilson's idealism and internationalism.

Wilson and Lodge still belonged to the generation that had taken part in the Civil War (Lodge was six years older than Wilson). The antagonisms inherited from that era had not yet disappeared. For a Southerner like Wilson it made sense to say that the war was over and had given way to reconciliation, but Lodge, an heir of the victors, saw it differently: in the World War he stood for "unconditional surrender and complete victory, just as Grant stood."[16]

The clash between Wilson and Lodge was also one between the two political parties. At the time a "bipartisan foreign policy," such as came about after the Second World War, was still unthinkable. Wilson himself, as we have seen, had appealed to the people to vote Democratic during the elections in November, and in 1919 too the two leaders sought to make capital out of the conflict over the peace treaty. Lodge made use of it to restore unity in the Republican party, which had been badly battered since 1912, and to make it the majority party in the country again. The results showed that he had succeeded marvelously. He was able to unite the progressives and the conservatives, the isolationists and the internationalists, in one front against Wilson. He stood personally in a middle position; as a true New Englander, he was not against international involvement and belonged to the circle of realists around Roosevelt. To the Left (I use the term with some hesitation) there were the progressives, men such as La Follette, Norris, and Borah, extreme isolationists who believed that America must not be tainted by the evil world of Europe. To the Right stood the conservatives from the Northeast, men such as Root and Taft, who were quite in favor of an international legal order, which they had supported in the League to Enforce Peace. To keep these various streams together, Lodge had to maneuver with caution. He realized that there was a vague but warm sympathy for the League of Nations among the American people. Americans love to believe in the goodness of mankind, and they stood behind Wilson. But, as a witty newspaperman said, they stood far behind him. There were many other daily needs that were much more pressing.

Was it Lodge's plan from the beginning to torpedo Wilson's conception? Historians will never agree in their answers. It must be repeated that in Lodge personal and general motives were curiously intertwined. Furthermore, he never straightened out in his own mind how nationalism and the sense of mission, conservatism, and the belief in progress, were interconnected. He was certainly influenced by the exuberant optimism of his bosom friend Theodore Roosevelt. But he had also absorbed much of the melancholy pessimism of two other friends, the brothers Henry and Brooks Adams, scions of the famous family that began with John Adams. He did not share Wilson's cheerful belief in the future. He was not opposed to a League of Nations, but it would have to be an organization in which American interests were safeguarded. In Lodge's attitude there probably was also present a special personal feeling, grief over the death of his friend Theodore Roosevelt. This heroic orator and statesman, who during a long life had sought to dominate a feeble body with his martial spirit, died of a coronary embolism at the beginning of January 1919. Lodge was deeply affected by the death of this colorful and rambunctious man; his feeling that he must preserve Roosevelt's heritage intact certainly contributed to his implacability in the months ahead. How they had hated Wilson together! (It is nonetheless much too melodramatic to claim, as has often been done, that Roosevelt and Lodge in a kind of macabre conspiracy had planned together in the hospital the downfall of Wilson's plans.)[17]

The third element in Lodge's attitude was that he represented very consciously the legislative power in the American political system. He was a purebred politician. In 1918 he had been a senator for twenty-five years and was scrupulously proud of the Senate's prerogatives in foreign policy. For Wilson to have gone to Paris without a senator in his delegation and to have negotiated there without informing the Senate was for Lodge an unacceptable usurpation of powers. It is a fact of American history that after every war, during which the president as head of the executive power played a strongly dominant role, the Senate has tried to regain its ground. After the Civil War President Andrew Johnson was the victim of the Senate's resentment of the dead Lincoln; after the Second World War the memory of Franklin D. Roosevelt had to pay the price. When Lodge turned on Wilson, he continually appealed to the Senate's rights. What was worse, he filled the ranks of the Senate Committee on Foreign Relations, of which he became chairman after the Republican victory in 1918, with fierce opponents of Wilson and when he was criticized for doing it, he pointed out that Wilson had selected the membership of the peace delegation in just the same partisan and one-sided way.

What was unusual was that Wilson for his part took so ill-judged and prejudiced a stand against the Senate. In so doing he betrayed that he was not a politician but a schoolmaster who haughtily observes how stupid his students are. Through Wilson's whole political career there runs a red thread of arrogant disdain for the Senate. Yet he knew better, he had to. In his political writings, as we have seen, he had displayed his understanding of how necessary it was for a president to work together with the Senate. Little of it showed up in what he did. He couldn't stand the sight of the senators. When, during the Spring of 1916, Baker said to him that some senators did not think ahead, he replied, "Most of them never think at all." Two years later he told House that he despised most of them.[18]

He acted toward the Senate as if he were a porcupine, wrote Taft, who could not understand how someone with Wilson's responsibilities could take such an attitude. "When he sends for the Senators, he never confers with them at all—he just tells them what he wants. He doesn't know the meaning of conference or counsel. He has a conception that he is the arbiter of the universe and that he knows everything by intuition."[19]

The great democrat could not work democratically; he could not stand criticism and superciliously waved it aside. In his State of the Union message at the end of 1917 he turned furiously upon critics of his plans, and it was obvious that when he spoke of men who unsuccessfully resisted the calm sovereign will of the people he was speaking of the senators.

> I hear men debate peace who neither understand its nature nor the way in which we may attain it with uplifted eyes and unbroken spirits. But I know that none of these speaks for the nation. They do not touch the heart of anything. They may safely be left to strut their uneasy hour and be forgotten.[20]

What a mixture of sublimity and limitless arrogance! And again we see the familiar pattern, nicely rationalized, of evil leaders who do not understand the good people. The senators, he said in February 1919, do not know how the people think. They were just as far from the people, the common people, as he was from Mars. They had absolutely no feeling left for the thoughtful, progressive majority of mankind everywhere, and they cannot understand them.[21] With such confidence that he knew what he was doing while the representatives of the people were blind, he was digging his own grave.

Lodge represented his region, his party, and "his" Senate against Wilson. As we have seen, he also stood for a more realistic conduct of foreign policy. He realized the burden of responsibility that the United States would have to bear in a League of Nations. "It is easy to talk about a league of nations and the beauty and necessity of peace, but the hard practical demand is, Are you ready to put your soldiers and your sailors at the disposition of other nations? . . . This is the heart of the whole question."[22] And therefore he wanted to build into the international organization guarantees for the safeguarding of American interests. These were primarily three, although Lodge did not name specific points for the moment. First, a member of the League of Nations must have the right to withdraw at any time; second, matters of national importance, such as regulation of immigration or imports, would not fall under the jurisdiction of the League of Nations; third, the Monroe Doctrine remained a prerogative of the United States in the Western Hemisphere. The lines of division were beginning to be drawn.

Lodge versus Wilson—this became the great clash of 1919. Two men, two worlds that could not tolerate each other, either personally or in their principles. It became painfully obvious to the public during the short visit that Wilson paid to his homeland in February. From the start everything went wrong. Tumulty suggested that Wilson land in Boston, Lodge's home town. Wilson, though doubtful of the wisdom of the idea, did so. It was a direct challenge to the senator from Massachusetts. Although he promised Lodge and other senators that he would not bring their differences to public knowledge before they had spoken about them in private, he gave a speech in Boston defiantly proclaiming that he was wholly in the right. It was a brilliant speech, full of lofty ideas and intense resentments, in which his personal emotions were too strong. He boasted of "the delightful revenges" that he would have against those who "speak with a sort of condescension of ideals and idealists, and particularly of those separated, encloistered persons whom they choose to term academic," now that these have been proved to be in the right. Again he proclaimed that American soldiers were crusaders inspired by religious motives. Again he painted America as the country of unselfishness, the hope of the world. It would be inconceivable that it should not do what it promised. But he gave assurances:

> I have fighting blood in me, and it is sometimes a delight to let it have scope, but if it is challenged on this occasion it will be an indulgence. Think of the picture, think of the utter blackness that would fall on the world. America has failed. America made a little essay at generosity and then withdrew. America said, "We are your friends," but only for today, not for tomorrow.

And so on, in that brilliant mixture of vision and delusion that was so characteristic of him.[23]

He therefore immediately got on the wrong side of his opponents. His speech doomed the dinner that, at Colonel House's suggestion, he gave two days later at the White House for the members of the Committees on Foreign Relations of both houses of Congress for the purpose of discussing the treaty. The atmosphere was reasonably friendly, if we are to believe the press reports. Wilson assured the guests that the constitutional powers of Congress in matters of armaments and war were not in danger. But he also declared that the nation, like all other nations, would have to yield some of its sovereignty "for the good of the world." He answered questions for two hours, Lodge later wrote, but said nothing new.[24] Wilson himself did not feel satisfied. Once back in Paris, he reproached House because "your dinner" was a failure. The most furious response came from the strongly recalcitrant senator from Connecticut, Frank Brandegee: "I feel as if I had been wandering with Alice in Wonderland and had tea with the Mad Hatter."[25]

The atmosphere turned even worse. Two days later, on February 28, Lodge attacked in a long speech the "glittering and enticing generalities" and the risks they brought upon America. The same day Wilson returned tit for tat. In a speech to the Democratic National Committee, he proclaimed again how glorious his League of Nations was and called upon his party members to go to the country with this gospel. He concluded with a fierce attack upon his opponents:

> Because of all the blind and little provincial people, they are the littlest and most contemptible. It is not their character so much I have a contempt for, though that contempt is thoroughgoing, but their minds. They have not got even good working imitations of minds.

If he said what he really thought of them, his remarks would be "picturesque." "They are going to have the most conspicuously contemptible names in history." History will spit them out, the spirit of mankind will scorn them. When he came to write his memoirs, he would show them up for what they really were.[26]

Wilson's pathological hatred drove the conflict from bad to worse. The members of Congress refused to take such insults lying down, and they counterattacked. On March 4, the session of Congress ended; usually it recessed until December, when the new Congress would meet. The Republicans had no intention of giving Wilson such a long respite, wanting to keep a finger in the pie during the coming decisive summer. They filibustered to prevent passage of the current budget, so that the president would have to call Congress back to enable the government to continue to function. And in the next session, the Republicans would have the majority in Congress. The maneuver meant that they were using their heavy guns. Wilson had to reconvene Congress by May, giving the Republicans the whole summer to wage their attack upon him.

But this was not all they did. On the last day (or rather night) of the session, Senator Lodge presented in the upper house a remarkable document that has entered history with the name of Round Robin. A "round robin," according to the dictionary, is a written protest with the signatures in a circle, so that no one name stands at the top. It apparently originated in France, where it was called a *rond ruban* (literally, "round ribbon"). But Lodge, taking the lead in the assault, wanted his name at the top. The "round robin" was a declaration that the covenant of the League of Nations as it stood was not acceptable. No fewer than thirty-nine senators signed it, more than one-third of the Senate and therefore enough to prevent ratification of the treaty.

As was to be expected, the document was at once published to the whole world. The European leaders could not but hear how shaky was the foundation on which Wilson worked. It was indeed a blow for him, but it only provoked him to battle on. He was a fighter. Baker wrote in his diary:

> He is a good hater—how he does hate those obstructive Senators. He is inclined now to stand by the Covenant word for word as drawn, accepting no amendments, so that the 37 of the round robin will be utterly vanquished, will have no chance of saying, "Well, we forced the amendments, didn't we?" and being thus able to withdraw from their present ugly position.

Wilson said this to Baker in his wrath and exaggerated self-confidence, but he still realized that he would have to sail around the obstacle during the coming storm. He would not willingly concede that this was being done under the pressure of the Senate. On his return to Europe, he had to call the League of Nations commission into meeting again and propose a number of amendments, against his will but inescapably. The first thing he did, while still in the United States, was to issue a statement in which he placed the full responsibility for the delays in the work of government upon his opponents.[27]

At noon that same day he took a train to New York where he would board ship for Europe. En route he got off in Philadelphia to go to the hospital where his grandson had just been born. It was a giant of a baby, he said proudly. The child kept his eyes closed and his mouth wide open. If he stayed that way, said his grandfather, he would be a good senator.[28]

That evening he spoke at the Metropolitan Opera House in New York before an enthusiastic crowd of 5,000. The meeting was organized by the League to Enforce Peace, and Taft was Wilson's host and fellow speaker. Wilson was once more at his best. (Oh, if only the world could be made better with words!) All of Wilson's familiar themes were present in this address: America the selfless, the soldiers' crusade, the League of Nations as the only salvation, mankind that had awakened once and for all. Even statesmen, he said, were not so cynical that they too were not beginning to believe in it. Sometimes, he went on, when he tried to talk about it, "the profound emotion of the thing is too much." When he returned with the treaty, Americans would find the Covenant so much a part of it that it could not be taken out without destroying it.[29]

TWENTY-SIX

He is a very curious mixture of the politician and the idealist, reminding me more and more in his point of view of Gladstone. He is not to me very attractive.
    —Lord Robert Cecil

CRISIS

N THE MIDDLE OF MARCH, Wilson landed at Brest for the second time. Exactly three months had passed since his first arrival. Three months, and what a difference! Earlier there had been hope and jubilation, and almost eschatological expectations, now there was doubt and uncertainty about what in heaven's name the peace would bring. In those three months nothing had been brought to completion except the charter of the League of Nations, which in the United States had already been undermined and corroded by the fierce opposition of the Senate.

Wilson felt the tension very personally. Aboard ship he had said to his wife how difficult it was to satisfy people's expectations. "All these oppressed people look to me to fight for them. God knows I wish I could give them all they hope for, but only He Himself could do that."[1] We have already heard from the lips of Mrs. Wilson a melodramatic description of his first meeting with House. House himself gives a calmer account. He did not go aboard the ship, spoke to the president for the first time the next morning, and the first reproach he heard was that "your dinner" had been a failure. Furthermore, Wilson assured him that it was absolutely necessary to include the League of Nations in the peace treaty.[2]

For Wilson this was crucial. He was upset and furious over the Senate's obstruction. He insisted on saving his League of Nations in its entirety. He truculently told House and Cecil that he refused to accept the demands of the Senators and include amendments. That would only be weakness. But they listened to him calmly and hoped he would come round.[3]

Lloyd George and Clemenceau also had to confront Wilson's unrelenting attitude that very first day. He would not accept peace without the League, he informed them; everything depended on it. Still, he realized that the idea of a preliminary peace would not work and was ready for definitive agreements.

This was the beginning of a very busy period. Few things were settled; all the major questions were outstanding—the German boundaries, reparations, the Italian conflict with Yugoslavia, the Shantung question, among others. And the League of Nations committee had to meet again as well, for obviously amendments would have to be adopted, as Wilson acknowledged, providing, he stressed, it was not done to appease the Senate. Wilson again demanded much too much of himself. After long days of discussions with Lloyd George and Clemenceau in what became the regular meetings of the Big Three, he spent long evenings presiding over the League committee. This double activity embodied his dilemma. During the daytime he found himself in the world of hard reality and difficult compromises; in the evening he worked industriously on the blueprint of the great palace of the future, the peace without victory that so sadly escaped him during the day.

The German question now took the center of attention. Germany had been the principal enemy, and according to Clemenceau it still was. The extremist French leader responded angrily to any word of reconciliation spoken by Wilson or Lloyd George. Those from beyond the shores could prattle about moderation and understanding, but he knew the Germans, "a servile people which needs force to support an argument."[4]

Lloyd George adopted a position contrary to Clemenceau's. A typical representative of British insular mentality, he hoped for a balance in Europe, a Germany that would be a barrier against Bolshevism, and a moderate peace. After all, English selfish interests had been sated, the

German fleet had been turned over, and the German colonies had become English mandates. Only where real British interests were at stake, as in reparations, did Lloyd George also take an uncompromising position. But his memorandum on the peace (the so-called "Fontainebleau memorandum," which he had drawn up), dated March 25, 1919, was a model of sensible moderation, imbued with the concepts of "peace without victory." Wilson would not have been able to improve it.[5]

In March all the major problems still remained to be settled. They can be divided into three groups: the territorial questions, reparations, and, closely associated with it, war guilt. Wilson wanted to solve them as honorably as possible; he held fast to his great ideals. But he was not equally prepared on all three of these points. In the question of borders, he at least had principles, the just principles of the self-determination of the peoples. He therefore frustrated the French demand to annex the Saar district outright and to separate the Rhineland from Germany and establish it as a republic; House had gone too far in approving these proposals during his absence. He was also upset by the behavior of the French occupation troops in the Rhineland, which reminded him of the "carpet-baggers" after the Civil War.

He didn't want to hear anything about historical and strategic frontiers, he said; he continued to hold firmly to this principle too. It was logical, he said, appealing to "the sense of justice which is in the heart of the French people." The French replied with the argument that the Saar district had been French for a period in 1814. That was a hundred years ago, a long time, countered Wilson. Yes, said Clemenceau sarcastically, it is a long time in American history. He followed with a long tirade about German cruelty and untrustworthiness. He told Wilson he could never apply his principles of self-determination in a logical manner, and pointed to the Balkans.

I respect your sentiment, which is very honorable. Your role is grand. But you are moving away from our goal. You will sow hatred; but you will encounter bitterness and regrets. This is the reason why we must arrive, not at a mathematical justice, but at a justice which takes sentiment into account.

Wilson rejoined:

Crisis

I thank you for the very beautiful words which you have spoken; I am conscious of all their gravity. . . . I believe as you do that sentiment is the most powerful force which exists in the world. . . . What I seek is not to deviate from the path being followed by this great world movement towards justice. I wish to do nothing which would allow it be said of us: "They profess great principles but they admitted exceptions everywhere, wherever sentiment or national interest made them wish to deviate from the rule."[6]

Our account thus far has been taken from the notes made by the translators, Sir Maurice Hankey and Paul Mantoux. They left out the sharpest clashes, however, as we know from the testimony of others who were present. Sometimes the mood became extremely tense, as during this meeting on March 28. House tells us that Clemenceau accused Wilson of being pro-German, which the president vehemently denied.

Clemenceau then stated [House goes on] that if they did not receive the Sarre Valley, he would not sign the Treaty of Paris. To this the President replied, "Then if France does not get what she wishes, she will refuse to act with us. In that event do you want me to return home?" Clemenceau answered, "I do not wish you to go home, but I intend to do so myself," and in a moment he left the house.

At noon, Wilson told House:

I do not know whether I shall see M. Clemenceau again. I do not know whether he will return to the meeting this afternoon. In fact, I do not know whether the Peace Conference will continue.

That afternoon the two fighting cocks stood facing each other again. Wilson, on his feet, made a passionate declaration, admitting

that it would be easy enough merely to punish Germany, merely to wreak vengeance for wrongs done; that he himself had no illusions as to what Germany had done . . . but he believed they had a greater mission than the mere punishment of Germany. Germany should be made to pay for what she had done and pay to the last farthing . . . but if they should crush Germany, wreck her economically, they would assuredly turn the ultimate sympathies of the world toward

Germany; the terms laid upon Germany should be stern . . . but they should be terms which the unenraged generations of the future could read and say: "This is justice, not vengeance."

At one point, when Clemenceau seemed about to rise from his chair, Wilson snapped fiercely: "Sit down. I didn't interrupt you this morning when you were speaking." Clemenceau, abashed, took his seat again. Then, when Wilson finished talking, the Tiger, as Clemenceau was called, got to his feet, saying, "You are a good man, and a great one."[7]

Clemenceau was given to spontaneous but short-lived outbursts of feeling, but his suspiciousness was permanent. Two days later, he asked the English journalist Steed:

Talk to Wilson. How can I talk to a fellow who thinks himself the first man for two thousand years who has known anything about peace on earth. Wilson imagines that he is a second Messiah. He believes he has been sent to give peace to the world and that his preconceived notions are the only notions worth having.[8]

Wilson's fears that all his principles would be watered down with exceptions were confirmed by events. Clemenceau had been right when he said the principle of self-determination would break down in the face of European realities. Everywhere, in Danzig, Teschen, Eger, and in Transylvania, an ethnic solution to the differences clashed with historic traditions and economic and strategic interests. Everywhere the new small states showed themselves as insatiably greedy as the old, great "empires" they replaced.

Finally all this rhetoric, raging, and emotionality in general ended in major compromises. Wilson backed off from his rigid stand on principle, as he had to do if he was to get the amendments to the League charter accepted. For his Allied friends the amendments became an ideal way to swing him to their position. It was decided after much talk that no member state would be obligated to take a mandate upon itself (this had been a difficult point, for Wilson was favorable to an American mandate over Constantinople or Armenia, but the Senate was dead set against it); the domestic affairs of member states, which of course included immigration policy, did not fall under the competence of the League of Nations; the Monroe Doctrine was not affected by the terms of the Covenant;

and finally that a member could withdraw from the League with two years' notice. The French were rabid in their opposition. Now we see, wrote French newspapers, that the sacred permanent world order doesn't have to last more than twenty-four months.

The French were deeply worried. They had no interest in the League of Nations if it did not guarantee their security, which was their only goal. They insisted upon making sure that the events of 1914 did not recur, with at least military defenses along their natural frontier, the Rhine. They did not receive everything they wanted, but the Rhineland, including a broad strip of territory east of the river, was divided into three zones, occupied for five, ten, and fifteen years respectively, the whole to be demilitarized forever. How easily men make settlements for an inscrutable and fearsome future!

The French accepted this compromise only because an additional guarantee was given to them. On April 20 Wilson and Lloyd George finally agreed to a special security treaty with France promising to come to her aid if Germany attacked her. This was at the very least an extraordinary maneuver on Wilson's part; for one thing, such a promise would certainly meet fierce resistance in the Senate, and for another it was a direct violation of his principles and his dislike of bilateral agreements. Furthermore, the treaty was superfluous in view of Article X of the Covenant, the notorious article in which the signatory nations promised mutual assistance in case of aggression. The French did not put their trust in the charter for a single moment, however. Wilson defended the concession on the grounds that it was only temporary, lasting only until the League of Nations was organized and effective. He had not ceased to believe in his dream.

He held on to his principles as much as he was able, but most were lost or mangled. He did manage at least to prevent French annexation of the Saar district, which became one small victory in practice for the League. The Saar would contribute the wealth of its coal mines to the French treasury for fifteen years, but the League would oversee the plebiscite to be held then and meanwhile protect the rights of the inhabitants.

He won, at least in part, in another thorny problem, the status of Danzig and the Polish Corridor. He kept the port city, which was wholly German, from being annexed by Poland; instead it became a free city under the administration of the League of Nations. This was, to be sure, a solution that was certain to fail in the long run and even become the occasion for a new war, but if we judge Wilson not by the eternal principles that he himself proclaimed but by the practical possibilities, it was probably the least bad solution of the problem (a comparison with events after the Second World War makes us painfully aware how few were the scruples of a later generation in handling matters that Wilson did not treat lightly).

Where he could, Wilson still stood in the breach for self-determination. What do the inhabitants themselves want? was his oft-repeated and sensible question. It is obviously impossible to discuss here all the questions and differences that presented themselves then, for this is a book not about the Peace of Versailles but about Woodrow Wilson. Belgium was no exception to Wilson's discovery once in Europe that every country forgot its altruistic principles if it had a chance to expand its territory.[9] During the critical days at the end of March, Paul Hymans, the Belgian foreign minister, came before the Big Four in 1919 to seek a revision of the treaty of 1839 which acknowledged Belgium's independence from the Netherlands. Belgium wanted portions of the southern provinces of the Netherlands which had historically been part of the adjacent Belgian provinces, and proposed that the Dutch receive as compensation the mouth of the Ems River, which was German territory. Hymans put his case very arrogantly, to the annoyance of Lloyd George and Wilson. The president asked him on what grounds they could talk about Dutch territory when the Netherlands had remained neutral during the war.[10]

But most questions were not solved so simply. While all the varied territorial problems were under discussion, the no less difficult matter of reparations kept intruding. The history of the financial aspects of the peace is probably the most striking and the most controversial, indeed it could be said the most surrealistic element in the whole tale. It is probably the most written about, beginning with the famed accusatory book by John Maynard Keynes, *Economic Consequences of the Peace*, which was published in 1920. Again, we need pay attention to it here only insofar as Wilson was involved. More than a year before, in his amplification of the Fourteen Points in February 1918, he had made it emphatically clear that "there shall be no annexation, no contributions, no punitive damages." This was in accord with his principle of "peace without victory," without punishment.

Punishment implies guilt, but reparations for damage done does not do so explicitly. Germany had invaded France, causing enormous destruction during four years of war, which must be made good. This was even truer in the case of innocent Belgium. But the word "reparations" is flexible, and the French minister of finances was soon speaking of "integral" reparations. The English spoke instead of "indemnities," which could be interpreted even more broadly. What was involved was whether Germany would have to pay only for the damage that it had caused, or had to pay for the costs of the war in general, as was implied by the word "indemnities." When Lloyd George proposed a committee on "reparations and indemnities," Wilson protested, demanding that the last word be dropped.

There was no dispute that Germany would have to pay, but no one knew just how the size of the damage would be determined. In fact, the greediest claimants did not even want it to be fixed, because if the figure were left open, there was more opportunity to gain. Immediately after the armistice, as we have seen, public opinion in the Allied countries was swept by intense vindictiveness, and the most exorbitant figures were named. The Americans proposed a prudent thirty billion dollars, the British 120 billion. The British, who had not had any fighting on their own territory, feared that they would be deprived of the advantages of victory if German payments were limited to "pure reparations." They therefore wanted the formula that had been employed in the armistice, "damage done to the civilian population," interpreted as broadly as possible. It could include, for example, the pensions for wounded soldiers, widows, and orphans.

But the British government was itself divided. There were more prudent voices heard warning that Germany should not be ground down too much, lest the balance in Europe be lost, especially in view of the threat from Bolshevism. Lloyd George, who played the political game to the hilt, realized on the one hand that he had to meet part way the extreme demands of the House of Commons, but on the other that his moderate ministers were right. He therefore took the pragmatic position that it did not matter very much how high the reparations figure was set, for time would tell how much Germany could actually pay.

The Americans were utterly opposed to such a solution. Wilson was absolutely opposed to the inclusion of all war costs in the reparations payments, and rejected every effort to persuade him by Lloyd George, whose motives he suspected. For his part the president attempted to talk principle to the Welshman. What did it matter, he asked him, if the cabinet fell, so long as it happened for a just cause and then he, Lloyd George, would gain "a magnificent place in history."[11] But the wizard of Wales was not a heroic moralist but an inventive man, a matchless judge of men, and he had his men everywhere. He sent his South African friend, "slim Jannie" Smuts, to Wilson, knowing how much the president admired the Boer, like himself a liberal Christian philosopher who believed in the League of Nations. Smuts persuaded Wilson that Germany should pay pensions to innocent citizens. This meant that no figure could be set immediately but a special reparations commission was given two years to work on the problem. Later, when Smuts saw how hard the peace had become, he regretted that he had argued Wilson round, but by then it was too late.[12]

Wilson finally gave in. He was not deterred by the warnings and protests of his collaborators; it was both dangerous and dishonorable, they said, to have Germany sign a blank check that the Allies could fill in with whatever astronomical figures they wanted. It is illogical, admonished the young and acute American representative on the commission, John Foster Dulles. "Logic! I don't give a damn for logic! I am going to include pensions," exclaimed Wilson in exasperation.[13] In giving in, he as always had his eye on his magical panacea, the League of Nations. He had British support necessary for his great plans and he believed that once the League was in operation, all irregularities would be straightened out. He continued nonetheless to be anxious; his financial advisers explained to him that the German economy could not function with such an immense deficit, which meant that America would have to help, "providing in one form or another credit, and thus working capital, to Germany." Wilson passed on their explanations to Lloyd George.[14]

Germany was saddled with an enormous burden of debt, provisionally five billion dollars before May 1, 1921, and after that many billions more, to be fixed by the commission. It would be a tormenting problem for a long, long time. The reparations payments were not only a painful violation of Wilson's own idealistic intentions but were also a heavy burden it was unwise to put upon the new German republic. This was probably not primarily because the economic foundations of Germany were immediately undermined, as Keynes maintained. There has been much debate over this question, and a French economist, Etienne Mantoux (a son of Paul Mantoux, who was a translator at the peace talks), later refuted Keynes's arguments. The reparations, wrote Mantoux, were not too heavy; the burden was bearable. In the end, Hitler spent more on armaments in a few years than Germany would have put out in reparations during the whole decade of the thirties. But they were in fact more than a business settlement; they constituted a psychological burden, reminding the German people for years that the war guilt belonged to them.

For this was the official justification for the exorbitant financial demands of the Allies. In order to provide a legal basis for reparations, the notorious Article 231 was added to the peace treaty. It placed responsibility for the war squarely upon Germany and its allies. But it is questionable whether the only purpose of the article was to provide a legal justification for the reparations, which is also mentioned in Article 232. This is what the defenders of Wilson maintain.[15] Or did the article also give expression to the idea that Germany, and Germany alone, had full guilt not only for the damage done but also for the outbreak of the war, that German militarism, megalomania, and braggadocio had hurled Europe into disaster?

This is not the place to judge the correctness of such arguments, which belong to German history. But it must be said that in prewar France and Britain there was no shortage of imperialism, jingoism, arrogance, messianism, and anti-Semitism to be found—the whole complex of evil presumptions for which Germany was now made solely responsible. Since the fiery accusations of Fritz Fischer, it can no longer be denied that the Germans had a great share of responsibility for the outbreak of the war in 1914, and that they passionately pushed their war aims during the conflict. But was this true only of the Germans? Golo Mann has asked the question, I think correctly, whether there was much difference between the German lust for territorial expansion and the secret treaties in which the Allies expressed their covetous desires.

II

As a mediator, Wilson had sensed the resemblance between the belligerents, but he had not known it in detail. Indeed, he had not wanted to know it, for he preferred not to learn ugly truths. His entire conception of peace without victory had been built upon the basis of impartiality. But then he had taken part in the war, and now he was taking part in making the peace, and this dilemma continued to throw him off balance and frustrate his efforts. As a result, his attitude toward Germany during the peace talks has puzzling aspects. As we know, he favored a fair peace. But what did "fair peace" mean in the spring of 1919, when he was at last confronted with European realities? What was his position with regard to the Germans? In his speech of April 2, 1917, on the declaration of war, he had declared that America was at war with the militaristic German government, but had "no quarrel with the German people," who were not responsible for the crimes of their rulers. He strongly reaffirmed this stand many times. In August 1918, he told Wiseman that when Germany got a democratic government, it could join the League of Nations.[16]

To be sure, in personal conversations he displayed his anti-German feelings. At the very beginning of the war, he had been deeply shocked by the news of the German destruction of the Belgian city of Louvain (Leuven). House tells us in his diary that Wilson "goes even further than I in his condemnation of Germany's part in this war, and almost allows his feelings to include the German people as a whole rather than the leaders alone."[17] There are many more examples of this antipathy.

He therefore tried all the more to be fair, holding that emotions should not sway political judgments. Even after the declaration of war, he held fast to his deep conviction that the vicious cycle of war-victory-humiliation-revenge-new war must once and for all be broken. He foresaw democratization of Germany. In November 1918 he proposed to the Allies the sending of a note to the new German leader Friedrich Ebert calling for a "National Assembly" with which negotiations could be opened. The suggestion was blocked by the French, who with the boldest hypocrisy called it intervention in Germany's internal affairs.[18]

The puzzle is that once Wilson reached Europe he began to change. He seems to have forgotten that he had wanted to be an umpire among the belligerents and began to talk about guilt and punishment. He ended up with the notion that every people gets the government it deserves and must pay the penalty for it.

It is very difficult to determine when this change began, and even more difficult just why. Klaus Schwabe, who has written the fundamental study of Wilson's relationship with Germany, believes that some hardening of Wilson's attitude began to be visible in November 1918.[19] At the very time when everything was changing in that shattered land, he began to talk more and more about Germany's guilt. The November revolution in Germany had toppled the military regime like ninepins, and all its pomp and bluster had proved hollow and ineffectual. A democratic government had taken office in Berlin under the leadership of Ebert. He was a saddlemaker and a Socialist; a solid German in character, he was no radical revolutionary, such as the Allies so feared. A new Germany was coming into existence.

The new government appealed, of course, to Wilson's promises, especially to his Fourteen Points. It was a legitimate appeal, but it did not answer some difficult problems about the broken continuity of government in Germany. Were the new German leaders the heirs of their predecessors, not only juridically, so that they were obligated to pay the debts of the previous regime, but also spiritually? Wilson had promised fair treatment to a democratic Germany, but were the new leaders truly democrats? Had the advocates of reconciliation, politicians like Matthias Erzberger and Gustav Stresemann, scholars like Max Weber and Hans Delbrück, and so many others who now played a role, turned against their former conservative nationalism? The Allies, deeply distrustful of everything German, were influenced by the so-called "camouflage theory," which held that the new government in Germany was no more than a façade behind which the old military forces were temporarily concealing themselves. Now that the time for action had come, Wilson not only wanted guarantees before he would make good on his great promises, he did not want to carry them out at all for the time being. He talked now not of the guilt of the German government but of that of the German people. What it came down to was that Germany as a whole was guilty, as set forth in Article 231 of the peace treaty.

Emperor William II was singled out as the special culprit, however, to appease the simpleminded hatred of the masses in the West for the "Kaiser." Article 227 provided that Emperor William II would be tried by a special court on charges that he had violated international morality and sacred treaties. Historically it was not true that the emperor was the key figure in Germany's guilt, for he had been little more than a vain weakling whom the generals manipulated at their ease. But it was a question not of truth but of satisfying the wrath of the masses.

The problem, however, was that there was virtually no basis in international law for such a trial. The French and English argued that it was justified by emerging law and the feeling of justice embodied in common law. The Japanese had no taste for an accusation against a crowned head of state; with truly impressive prescience they recognized the danger that such a precedent might present for their own emperor. The Americans were also opposed, but on the basis of their own constitutional ban on ex post facto legislation making actions criminal prior to the legislation establishing the crime. John Foster Dulles vigorously defended this principle in the commission on the war guilt question. The issue was bitterly debated in the Council of Four, where Wilson at first followed his advisers, fearing, he said, a court of victors.[20] He also feared a judgment based on emotions. "The worst punishment will be that of public opinion," he said. "Don't count on it," Clemenceau jeered. He and Lloyd George wanted the emperor turned over by the Netherlands to the Allies. To Wilson's query about a Dutch refusal, Lloyd George replied that Holland would then be told it would not be admitted to the League of Nations.[21]

Once again Wilson and his fellow negotiators had clashed over principle. Once again he began by upholding a grand principle of justice and ended by yielding under pressure. That is the heart of the matter. He continued to maintain that only moral guilt was involved, but suddenly voted on April 8 for the formation of a court to try the German emperor. He even undertook to draw up the text of a compromise: Holland would be asked to turn over the emperor; he would be tried by a court of five judges on the charge not of violating criminal law but of "a supreme offense against international morality and the sanctity of treaties." Sentence would be according to "the highest principles of international policy."[22] On May 1, he went even further. Lloyd George proposed scrapping the words Wilson had used in his draft about not applying "the criminal law," and the idealistic American president accepted the change without turning a hair.[23] It was a painful reversal, but in the end without result, because the Dutch government, despite the continuing hopes of Clemenceau and Lloyd George and despite Wilson's belief that the Netherlands lost its right of refusal once the peace treaty was signed, did not yield to the Allied demand for extradition of the emperor.[24]

What inspired Wilson to make this bewildering shift? Rather, what lack of inspiration came over him that he abandoned so easily causes for which he had fought so hard? It may have been, as a perceptive German historian puts it, "a typical Wilsonian compromise," because he could not stand alone. "He was most uncomfortable in this isolation; like most well-reared persons, he found it difficult to make himself always disliked."[25]

Was the cause of this shift oversensitive good manners, then, or was it something quite different? Perhaps the change in his attitude was related to the state of his health, as various observers have suggested. The peace negotiations were a kind of war of attrition for all involved, but certainly most of all for Wilson, who took everything so intensely and kept colliding with pitiless reality.

A serious crisis developed. The situation at the end of March was particularly tense. The reports of worsening conditions in different parts of Europe, the hunger riots in Germany, the Bolshevik revolution in Hungary, the hopeless confusion in Russia, made the tension almost unbearable. Feelings repeatedly rose high in the meetings of the Big Four. Wilson was close to despair. "The President was at the end of the tether," wrote Baker in his diary. Things could not go on that way; a break had to come. Baker spoke to Wilson about events in Eastern Europe. He knew that, Wilson replied, but peace had to be made on the principles already laid down and accepted, or it would not be made at all. To Baker's suggestion that the time was nearing when the president would have to speak out, Wilson replied that this would break up the peace conference, and he had to do everything he could to "keep things together." "If I speak out," he said, "I should have to tell the truth and place the blame exactly where it belongs—upon the French."[26]

Wilson turned for advice to House, with whom his friendship was more or less still intact. Wilson consulted him frequently, wrote House in his diary on April 1, for the situation was difficult. House described Lloyd George as "a mischief maker who changes his mind like a weather-vane" and lacked profound knowledge of any of the questions presented. Orlando was "level-headed," but handicapped because he did not speak English. Clemenceau, a man of the old regime, was "the ablest reactionary" at the conference, but could not be dealt with except in "ways the world will no longer consider, and which we hope to make forever obsolete."

> The President is becoming stubborn and angry, and he never was a good negotiator. So there you are. I think the President is becoming unreasonable, which does not make for solutions. Nothing is being run in an orderly way.

And the next day House recorded that Wilson expressed the opinion that Mantoux, the French interpreter, could not stand him, and the president added, "I am not sure that anybody does."[27]

The German historian whom I cited above was quite right: Wilson could not abide a situation in which everyone was against him. His despair became such that he asked House to replace him again in the Council of Four. He could not go on, he was sick, literally sick, of it. The next day, April 3, he had to remain in bed; he had had what Grayson described as a sudden attack. At three o'clock he was still healthy and well; at six he had coughing attacks so severe that he could hardly breathe. He ran a high fever and suffered severe diarrhea. Grayson first thought of food poisoning but decided it was influenza, the epidemic that was taking so many victims in Europe. A wakeful night followed, but the next day he began to recover slowly.[28]

There has always been intense discussion of this illness, for it was accompanied by troubling psychological symptoms—suspicions that the French servants were spies; pointless clamor over where the furniture was placed; and hallucinations like those of a feverish child. Wilson became much more stubborn. A few days later, when he was able to dress and heard from House that Clemenceau was again making the most unreasonable demands with regard to reparations, he took a final step, ordering that the *George Washington*, the liner that had brought him to Europe, be made ready for a return trip to the United States. According to the ever-faithful Baker, this helped, for the French conceded on every point, the Rhineland, the Saar, and reparations. But Baker is wrong, for when the issues were finally settled in April, it was Wilson, not Clemenceau, who made the largest concessions. These were the painful concessions I discussed earlier.

This was probably also the moment when Wilson definitively changed his attitude toward Germany. His illness occurred in the first week of April; immediately afterwards he began to yield to the pressure of his Allied partners. The motif of guilt and punishment became central in his concerns. It is difficult to decide whether the cause was psychological, the mind affected by the body. Edwin Weinstein, the author of a medical-psychological biography of Wilson, suggests that Wilson came to his sharp condemnation of Germany as "a way of denying his own feelings of guilt and responsibility for American participation, and such denial is greatly enhanced by the presence of brain damage."[29]

The illness may not have been grippe at all but a mild stroke, as Lloyd George and others thought. "After April," the British leader told Harold Nicolson years later, "he [Wilson] fell entirely under the influence of Clemenceau."[30] Lloyd George was certainly speaking out of spite, but it is nonetheless a fact that Wilson and Clemenceau came much closer in their harsh attitudes toward Germany.

Is it necessary, however, to give a medical or psychological explanation for Wilson's change? There may also be ideological factors for his sudden rigor, a return to the Calvinist concepts of guilt and retribution in which he had been raised. This is what Baker thought. During these crisis days of April, he penned a hard-edged portrait of Wilson: "a man of consuming mind, hard, predetermined, it is fortunate that he is for right things, not wrong. He would be terrible if he were evil. In him John Knox—Calvin—on too large a scale."[31] But this is probably a false notion, expressing the amazement of a friendly, freethinking optimist with the prevalent caricature of Calvinism in his mind.

Wilson's rigorous attitude can probably be explained as well if not better on the basis of his characteristic liberal moralism. Raising the question of guilt was not at all a Calvinist quirk but rather an expression of optimism; the belief in man's goodness was the basis for enforcing the strictest standards of judgment. It was only with the spread of democracy and humanitarian ideas in the nineteenth century that war came to be condemned as aggression and the question of war guilt became relevant. Another consequence was that the customary amnesty clause was dropped from peace treaties and replaced by the demand for retribution.[32]

In an extraordinary paradox, Wilson yielded to the European realists and himself became harder, more rigid, more inflexible. This was true not only in his attitude toward Germany but also in his personal contacts, especially in his relationship with House. Before his illness he had had such great trust in the "Colonel" that he had asked him to replace him on the Council of Four. The break between them followed his illness. Wilson's worsening paranoia began to be directed more and more toward his most faithful friend. House's downfall resulted. But more was involved. Not only the president personally, but the whole American delegation became exasperated by the man's pedantry and self-importance. Lansing had not been able to stand House for some time, but then he had himself been out of things for a long time. No one bothered with him and he felt deeply the humiliation of House's really taking over his own tasks as secretary of state. Meanwhile the president had let his new dislike for House be seen "in rather a pitying way."[33] But also some of his economic advisers, like Bernard Baruch and Vance McCormick, were offended by House, whom they found too arrogant.

Doctor Grayson, who was very close to Wilson, likewise had nothing good to say about House. In his diary he has given an illuminating explanation of what was happening to House. As long as the "Colonel" had no official function and worked behind the scenes, he could give the impression of a wise sphinx who served the president well. But he received too much attention and deference in France, and he was made too much of by his windbag of a son-in-law, Gordon Auchincloss. No sooner was he involved in the peace conference than House began to bask in his delusions about himself, and he began to play up to the press as a major player. Now he was concluding compromises right and left and thereby undercutting the president. He became the "Great American Acquiescer," who gave everything away to the Allied leaders, "the champion Yes man. Yes with Lloyd George, and Yes, Yes with Clemenceau."[34]

Even Baker, who earlier had seen House as "the universal conciliator, smoother-over, connector," now found him to be only a dilettante and player of games, a supersecretary without any feeling of responsibility. Perpetually optimistic, he compromised the most sacred principles.[35]

House was brought down by his vanity. He was all too ready to give to others, including the press, a glimpse of his importance; he gloried happily in his role as "gray eminence" behind the scenes, like Richelieu's Père Joseph in the seventeenth century. But the stage curtains happened to be transparent. It was Wilson's wife who was finally delighted to catch him in his act. House seems to have become the victim of his son-in-law's tactlessness. Auchincloss thoughtlessly suggested to the famed British journalist Wickham Steed an article in which the impression was given that House had saved the peace conference when Wilson fell ill. In his article published in the *Daily Mail*, which was widely read in Paris, Steed piled it on a bit thick and ascribed the success of the conference to House's selflessness. From the *Daily Mail* it was picked up by other English and American newspapers.

Mrs. Wilson confronted House with the piece when he came to visit; he turned purple, she records in her memoirs, and Grayson later told her that he had the proof that House had inspired these pieces through his son-in-law. But Wilson himself was not yet convinced. When his wife reported her meeting with House, he said, "Oh, I am sorry you hurt House. I would as soon doubt your loyalty as his." And when she continued to accuse House of being a jellyfish, the president responded philosophically, "Well, God made jellyfish, so, as Shakespeare said about a man, therefore let him pass, and don't be too hard on House."[36]

It is not entirely clear just when the break became definitive. Grayson later recounted (but his memory was probably colored by melodrama) that Wilson had told him that it was a hard blow, "harder than death," when a friend like House, whom you have taken to your bosom is led to betray you by the flattery of others. But, as we know, around April 20 Wilson was still hesitating to condemn House.

The break was therefore not as melodramatic as Mrs. Wilson, Baker, and Grayson describe it, but it did happen nonetheless. In the months that followed, Wilson continued to use House for many contacts and saw him in the League of Nations committee, but the friendship withered away. House ceased to visit the Wilsons at their residence and no longer had the president's former trust. Soon they seldom met. Back in America, they lost all contact, and finally Wilson refused even to reply to letters from House.

Thus Wilson went again through the tragedy of a break with his best friend, as he had once done with Jack Hibben in Princeton. This proud and sensitive man in the final test knew only absolute relationships and absolute solutions.

TWENTY-SEVEN

He is the victim I am afraid of his own popularity, and
he has failed in all his greatest purposes because he
overestimated his popularity and miscalculated his own
ability to deal with shrewder and more realistic men.
　　—*Walter Lippmann, 1919*

*M. le président Wilson, le prophète inspiré d'une noble
entreprise d'idéologie dont il allait fâcheusement devenir le
prisonnier, connaissait insuffisamment cette Europe qui gisait
en morceaux devant lui.*

[President Wilson, inspired prophet of a noble ideological
enterprise whose prisoner he would sadly become, knew
too little of the Europe that lay in tatters before him.]
　　—*Georges Clemenceau*

PRINCIPLES AND INTERESTS

IT WAS ALMOST A MIRACLE, LI-
terally and physically, that Wilson was
able to hold out in Paris. He was in har-
ness without interruption; he involved
himself in everything; he was accosted by
every kind of dreamer, fanatic, visionary,
and greedy adventurer; he received advice
every day from all kinds of experts, who often contradicted one other.
Take, for example, a busy day in his datebook, as kept by Grayson: there
are eighteen engagements in succession: a Chinese delegation, another of
Assyrian-Chaldeans, still another from Dalmatia, representatives from
the Republic of San Marino, where he was made an honorary citizen,
from the Women Workers of America, the Patriarch of Constantinople,
the president of Albania, the Greek envoy to Rome, the Romanian minister Bratianu, a Portuguese politician, one from Armenia, another from
Serbia, and an editor from the *Manchester Guardian*, and so on. Every
question came before him, all in addition to the daily meetings of the Big
Four and often the evening meetings of the League of Nations committee. And, in the intervals, lunches and dinners with colorful guests who
came to have their say too: "After all this ocean of talk has rolled over me,

I feel that I would like to return to America and go back into some great forest, amid the silence, and not hear any argument or speeches for a month."[1]

He had no time for the things in which he found relaxation at home—the theater, vaudeville, films—and he did not speak the language. In the middle of April he went one evening to a performance in which some English was spoken. But it was wholly French, wrote Edith Benham, especially when the girls began to take off their clothes and jokes were made "not of the Sunday school variety." He did enjoy the "decent parts."[2] When he was really tired, he found more relaxation in a game of solitaire.

On only one occasion did he have time to play a round of golf, and Grayson persuaded him once to go for an automobile ride. What probably best enabled him to keep his balance was his ability to keep some distance from things. He could still enjoy himself among a few intimates, telling anecdotes (often the same ones) and reciting limericks. With all his seriousness and exaltation, he had a taste for humor. There were many sides to him, as does happen in great men.

Still, the daily cares were large and numerous, and Wilson's principles were always being challenged. That was true most of all for the Italian question. Italy had remained neutral in 1914, but in 1915 had sold itself to the highest bidder, the Entente, which at the moment was in the best position to pay off its debts with other people's property. The secret treaty of London gave the greedy Italians the prospect of the most extravagant territorial acquisitions: Trentino, South Tirol up to the Brenner Pass, Trieste, Gorizia and associated regions, North Dalmatia and a number of Dalmatian islands, Valona in Albania, the definitive possession of the Greek archipelago of the Dodecanese, which the Italians had occupied in 1912, and even more. The only thing that was withheld from Italy with some firmness was the port of Fiume.

The Allies in Paris were bound by this treaty, but not, of course, the United States. Wilson knew nothing about the secret treaties and his ignorance now seemed to be an advantage. He had proposed in point nine of the Fourteen Points a different solution of the Italian frontiers: "A readjustment of the frontiers of Italy should be effected along clearly recognizable lines of nationality." This was quite different from the provisions of the London treaty, which would put 225,000 Tiroleans and more than 1,200,000 Yugoslavs, not to mention Greeks and Turks, under Italian rule. Italy wanted to be paid for its commitment and its heroism; it boasted of its glory and quickly forgot its defeats. This was called *sacro egoismo*, "holy selfishness."

Rout and ruin make men humble but triumph puffs them up with pride, is a truth taught in the Bible. After the disastrous defeat of Caporetto, the Italians had displayed much understanding of developments in the Balkans. In the pact of Rome in April 1918, they had been willing to recognize the new nation of Yugoslavia. But after the victory of Vittorio Veneto at the tag end of the war, they began to make extreme demands. The Socialist Leonida Bissolati, who found the annexation of Dalmatia a bit too much to swallow, resigned from Orlando's liberal cabinet in December; the strongly nationalist minister of foreign affairs, Sidney Sonnino, became its dominant figure. Wilson was kept well informed about these developments, by reports in particular from Ray Stannard Baker. However, Baker was an optimist who painted the situation in far too rosy colors, so that the president gained the impression that his beautiful paradigm of the good people against the evil government was applicable in Italy too.[3]

Wilson's favorable impression was reinforced by his grandiose tour of triumph through Italy early in January. It was true, the Italian people adored him, they worshipped him. Hosanna! Blessed is he who comes in the name of the Lord, in the name of humanity, *Il Redentore dell'umanità*! Wilson delightedly took it all in. In Rome he had a conversation with Bissolati, who had just quit the cabinet, and he heard from him what he wanted to hear, that Italy did not have any right to Dalmatia, that the treaty of London was valid only against Austria, that Fiume must become a free city.[4]

This conversation was in fact a risky interference in Italian affairs, and protests came at once from every side. Some protesters bore resounding names: Mussolini, Marinetti, D'Annunzio. Wilson continued to hope; he wrote a letter to Orlando pointing out how much Italy had won by the war, Trentino and Trieste, and most of all, the downfall of the archenemy Austria. Italy no longer needed to fear any threats, and therefore the treaty of London was no longer valid.[5] But he doubted whether he could persuade the Italians; they lacked "a wide view of things," and for the moment he did not send the letter.

It is quite strange that Wilson, although he had been clearly forewarned, still gave much away, much too much. The Inquiry informed him that the proposed boundary on the Brenner Pass was in direct violation of the principle of self-determination, but nonetheless he voted in its favor in January. He thereby abandoned his principles and also his best weapon in the difficult continuing negotiations. It is plausible that Orlando won him over by displaying great enthusiasm for the League of Nations. But didn't Wilson see what would follow? It is true that he later regretted it. At the end of May he told Baker: "I am sorry for that decision. I was ignorant of the situation when the decision was made." He excused his compromise with an appeal to the future. It probably could not be changed now, "but those Tyrolese Germans are sturdy people—and I have no doubt they will soon be able themselves to change it." This is probably what he imagined would happen with all the ugly compromises that he made, that the common people would set them right. It was, to put it mildly, a naïve idea.[6]

The question remained a sore one. Already in April Wilson received a report from one of his best expert advisers, Archibald C. Coolidge, a professor of East European history at Harvard, who explained that bringing in strategic considerations regarding the Brenner Pass made a mockery of Wilson's principles and furthermore did not belong within his vision of the future.[7]

But by this time the Italian problem had gone from bad to worse. The Italians were far from satisfied with what had been promised them; they began to maintain that the big Slavic country on their eastern frontier constituted a new threat to them, and they insisted upon trying to get hold of most of Dalmatia and even the port of Fiume. They made great play with the argument that Bolshevism was threatening in Yugoslavia. Wilson got another warning from his experts and decided this time to cross the Italian claims. When Italian affairs again received the attention of the Big Four at a meeting in April (the Italians sulked because they had not had their turn), he raised his voice.

The people in the Inquiry had reminded him in a specially urgent letter of his promise, made aboard the *George Washington*, when they had been together on the way to Europe in December. They brought up what he had said then: "Tell me what is right and I'll fight for it. Give me a guaranteed position." Well, this was one. The Italians were demanding Fiume and part of Dalmatia as "loot," but they belonged to Yugoslavia, not to Italy.

Never in his career [they added] did the President have presented to him such an opportunity to strike a death blow to the discredited methods of old world diplomacy. To the President is given the rare privilege of going down in history as the statesman who destroyed, by a clear-cut decision against an infamous arrangement, the last vestige of the old order.[8]

This language must have spoken to Wilson, flattered him, because it echoed his own. House recommended a compromise, but the president put his foot down.

The Italians pulled out all the stops at the meeting of the Big Four. They threatened, wept, insinuated. Days were spent in this way. Even on Easter morning, pious Wilson, instead of going to church to hear a sermon, had to listen at ten o'clock in the morning to Orlando's litanies, which ended with dramatic sobbing. But Wilson blew his trumpets from the highest pinnacles of his house of cards. Peace had to be made on an "entirely new basis" and a "new order of international relations" established. Economic and strategic arguments must be brushed aside. "Military men" had been responsible for the German annexation of Alsace-Lorraine and had led Europe to "one blunder after another." You could not believe in an old and a new order at the same time, you "could not drive two horses at once. The people of the US of A would repudiate it." And so on, with the lofty arguments of the idealist colliding with the hard facts of the realists.

Sonnino shouted defiantly that the Italians had negotiated a treaty "with you" (meaning England and France). A "third party" (meaning Wilson) arrives and refuses to recognize the agreement, invoking the League of Nations. Let the League go and "put Russia in order," if it can; let it settle the affairs of the Balkans. But "he" (Wilson!) "can't change human nature that way." America had said nothing to them for five months. "Now, after having made concessions right and left to legitimate interests, she wants to recover her virginity at our expense by invoking the purity of principles."[9] Sonnino, the Italian foreign minister, who as a Jew was very familiar with his Old Testament metaphors, put it more pungently. Wilson had gone fornicating with France and England for four months, and now he was attempting to reestablish his virtue at the expense of Italy![10]

It is worth remarking that while Wilson appealed to grand principles, geopolitical, or, more precisely, ethno-political motives, also played a role. In the Council of Four he explained that the future would be decided by the peoples of Asia. Behind the Slavs there stood a reservoir of at least eight hundred million people, and it was important not to estrange them.[11]

The Italians were not persuaded. Now, in his desperation, Wilson resorted again to his familiar political mythology and appealed over the heads of the evil Italian leaders to the good Italian people. He published a "Statement on the Adriatic Question," in which he set forth the situation: Fiume must become a free port for its entire hinterland; the safety of Italy was no longer in danger; Italy had received a very great deal, its natural frontiers right up to the Alps. He spoke of the friendship of the American people for the Italian people and appealed of course most of all to his sacred principles:

> Interest is not now in question, but the rights of peoples, of states
> new and old, of liberated peoples and peoples whose rulers have
> never accounted them worthy of right; above all, the right of the
> world to peace and to such settlements of interest as shall make peace
> secure.[12]

As was to be expected, the statement had an effect contrary to that intended. A howl of rage ran through the whole Apennine peninsula. Boundless anger was directed against the moralist meddler from America. Even such a moderate Marxist as Gaetano Salvemini, later to become famous for his struggle against fascism, asked wrathfully why Wilson had compromised his principles on the colonies, on the Saar, on the Monroe Doctrine, but now deliberately took it out on Italy.[13]

The situation seemed hopeless. The French and English continued to be cautious, supporting Wilson privately but seeking compromise. Lloyd George was "as slippery as an eel," Wilson said to Grayson, "the most unsteady individual you can imagine." He asserted something different every day, and made the wildest somersaults.[14] Clemenceau watched philosophically, for France had little interest in the matter. Italy, he said, "is like a pretty woman, with whom it is better to agree."[15]

The question ran far into May, with endless debates. The Italians made themselves impossible by high demands in the rest of the Mediterranean region. The once mighty Ottoman Empire was going through its final convulsions. It had already been stripped of all its possessions outside its core in Asia Minor, but the victors were preparing now to chop up what remained. Greece was in the forefront; refighting the Persian Wars of antiquity, it claimed the coast around Smyrna, where the majority of the population was still Greek. But the other Allies wanted a piece of the loot for themselves, and none more brazenly than Italy, which since 1912 had been in possession of the Dodecanese, whose population was wholly Greek, and now in 1919 put down with brute force a resistance movement encouraged by Wilson's ideals.

Nowhere was a more flagrant mockery made of Wilson's principles than in the eastern Mediterranean. The word "self-determination" was really never heard in all these subtle arguments about agreements (which had in fact been made in secret treaties during the war), mandates, spheres of influence, interest zones (as the territory occupied by the Italians was called), and the like. All this greed wrapped up in fine words was, as we know with hindsight, a striking example of human shortsightedness, for in the end it all came to nothing. The bear's skin was divided by the treaty of Sèvres, but it turned out that the bear wasn't dead. Turkey experienced a rebirth under Mustapha Kemal Pasha, the later Atatürk; it applied with vigor the principle of self-determination, and in the Peace of Lausanne a few years later, all the foreign claims were officially abandoned.

The question of Fiume had an unsatisfactory course. In 1920 a treaty was concluded making it a free city, but in 1924 it went to Italy and remained with it until after the Second World War.

Wilson's policy toward Italy is the most classic and tragic example of the clash between his great ideals and the muddled European reality. But his position was considerably worsened because his own supporters were divided and his actions were inconsistent. He compelled the world to judge him by his own principles, and hence he could not help but fail. But what problems this confronts us with! What do principles really mean? No, this book is not an essay on the problem of ethics in politics; it is only an illustration of it, and the Italian question is an example.

The Japanese question is another. The Japanese presented to the League of Nations committee in February an amendment to make racial equality a principle in the Covenant. It was a proposal that perturbed everything and everyone. It seemed so simple and reasonable, but what would be its consequences? Did it not imply that the subjects of the member states had to be given equal treatment in every country? Did it not also mean that they might immigrate freely everywhere? This was an immense specter haunting the white inhabitants of Australia, New Zealand, and, not to be forgotten, California.

It was a proposal that had to be handled with kid gloves. After all, the Japanese were appealing to old Western ideals. House attempted to gain a compromise by using the terms of the American Declaration of Independence, "all men are created equal." Balfour, the British statesman-philosopher, objected that the equality of mankind was an outdated eighteenth-century idea. He was, he said, far from convinced that some-one from central Africa should be considered the equal of a European or an American.[16] He thought the Japanese did not mean what they said but were using it as an argument ("blackmail" was his word) in order to sup-port their claim upon Shantung.

This was only a half-truth. No doubt the Japanese were shrewd dip-lomats who played the game of pressure politics with great skill. But Westerners, and certainly the British and Americans of the beginning of the twentieth century, who were saturated with an Anglo-Saxon sense of racial superiority, did not realize what racial discrimination meant for its victims. The demand for equality arose from and was pushed by broad layers of the Japanese population, and it gained additional force precisely because Wilson preached his grand principles of equality. The Japanese therefore made their appeal to him. "If the discrimination wall is to re-main standing, then President Wilson will have spoken of peace, justice and humanity in vain, and he would have proved after all only a hypo-crite," wrote a Japanese newspaper.[17]

The Japanese really meant what they said, although they also used this question to reinforce their other demands. They wanted to take over the German rights in Shantung and they made a claim upon the German islands in the Pacific Ocean north of the equator. But they continued to press the question of racial equality; when they did not gain acceptance of their amendment in February, they returned in April with a new, more moderate formula ("equality of nations" instead of "racial equality"). There was immense excitement over the issue in Australia and the United States. Wilson fully understood that he could not consider conceding what the Japanese wanted. It was the revenge exacted by his character as an American from the South who had all the prejudices of his region (it was he who had been responsible for introducing racial segregation to Washington). All his courtesy and goodwill did not help. Even if he had been willing to do as the Japanese wanted, he dared not risk a clash with the English and their hotheaded overseas dominions. He had to put interest above principle in order to save his great principle of the League of Nations. What did he really save?

In the meeting of the League of Nations committee on April 11, a long, long evening that lasted until a quarter past one in the morning, the Japanese insisted upon a vote to include their equality proposal in the covenant. Baron Makino defended the proposal brilliantly and obtained a majority in favor, the French, Italians, Greeks, Brazilians, all the southern peoples who were not as burdened with the sense of white superiority. But noble Lord Cecil had to declare with a stumbling voice and shame in his face that he could not vote for the proposal. And noble Wilson, who presided over the meeting, in the end baffled the whole assembly by declaring that a majority of votes for the proposal, eleven for and seven against, was insufficient, because in matters of such importance unanimity was required. In other questions of importance for the United States, such as the Monroe Doctrine (in which the Japanese had supported the Americans), he had not applied his rule, but now it was enforced, arousing deep bitterness.[18]

Japan did not get its way, not at least with regard to the charter. But it did in the much more important question of Shantung, obtaining the German rights in the peninsula, although with a promise that the district would be returned to the Chinese as soon as possible. This actually happened in 1922, but in 1919 no one could foresee it. Wilson's compromise was extraordinarily unpopular in his own country. The old American feeling of sympathy for the Heavenly Empire was at stake. A violent anti-Japanese mood swept over the country, and the question of Shantung became one of the most powerful arguments in the Republican arsenal against Wilson and his League of Nations.

He was quite wretched about what had happened; he suffered from the reality with which he was confronted so harshly; he did not want to dirty his hands, and he could not sleep because they were dirty. He told Baker how difficult the decision had been. The guilt lay in "the dirty past." His sympathies lay on the Chinese side. But imagine what would happen if the Japanese quit the peace conference; the whole peace conference would break up. The Italians would go, the Belgians (who wanted a greater say in the reparations questions) threatened to follow. Would Germany still be willing to sign? Everyone would depart and begin to rearm, and in the end nothing would be gained, not even the withdrawal of the Japanese from Shantung. There was only one hope, and he gambled on it—the League of Nations. If Japan were a member alongside China, there would still be a chance. He knew that his decision would not be popular in the United States, and that he would be accused of violating his own principles. Nevertheless he *must* work for the new world order.

Baker added his own comment:

> The League of Nations is a matter of *faith*: and the President is first of all a man of *faith*. He believes in the League of Nations as an organization that will save the world. He is willing even to compromise desperately for it. Suffer the charge of inconsistency for it—he is the only *Man* here![19]

TWENTY-EIGHT

*Ik ben bitter teleurgesteld beiden met Wilson en Lloyd
George, die kleiner mannen zijn dan ik ooit zou gedacht
hebben. Maar jij oordeelt een man eerst recht in een grote
krisis, en ik moet zeggen dat dezen twee in mijn opinie maar
zwak en licht bevonden worden in de grote weegschaal.*

[I am bitterly disappointed with both Wilson and Lloyd
George, who are smaller men than I ever thought. But
you judge a man correctly for the first time only in a
great crisis, and I must say that these two in my opinion
were found weak and light in the great scale.]
—*Jan Christian Smuts*

THE PEACE SIGNED

WOODROW WILSON, AS WE know, had not wanted the war to end as earlier wars had ended. If it could not be made a war without victory, at least it could be a war without humiliation and revenge. At last the vicious circle of history would be broken and the opponents would become brothers.

Not much came of it. The terms of the peace treaty were not just and did not accord with Wilson's principles. And the defeated foe was not treated or heard as Wilson had originally intended.

At the end of April a German delegation was finally permitted to come to Versailles to conclude peace, to hear what it had been decided to do with the German fatherland. The delegates were brought on a special train, which, on its passage through the war-devastated regions of northern France, rode as slowly as possible so that they could fully see the effects of their attack. When they reached Versailles, they were told that they would be handed the peace terms on May 7, but that they could not enter into an oral discussion about them; they would be permitted only a reply in writing, and it must be ready within two weeks. It was a flagrant violation of Wilson's most sacred principles.

The head of the German delegation was a diplomat of the old school, Count Ulrich von Brockdorff-Rantzau. He served the new Socialist government with a sense of patriotic duty; he hoped to save what could still be saved, and it was his opinion that this could be done only by an emphatic appeal to Wilson's principles and promises. Indeed, he even looked forward to having a personal conversation with Wilson; if he could speak to him alone, he could probably convince him.[1] But the handicap faced by the German diplomat was that he was a man of a bygone tradition, a very haughty aristocrat. He unfortunately let this be seen all too clearly when he was received with his retinue on May 7. This famous scene has been described many times, for it was historical drama of the first order.

At precisely three o'clock in the afternoon, the German delegates were admitted into the great hall of the Hotel Trianon-Palace. They were given a special place directly facing the triumphant enemies, Clemenceau in the middle, Wilson and Lansing on his right, and Lloyd George and Bonar Law on the left. Clemenceau stood up and opened the meeting with a short, sharp address in which he informed the Germans that they could now receive the peace for which they had asked, a peace, he said, that our peoples have bought dearly and for which we are determined to receive complete indemnification. There will be no discussion; you will receive fourteen days to prepare your written objections. Thereupon the great white book containing the treaty was officially handed to the German minister.

Brockdorff-Rantzau accepted it with a stiff bow and asked to speak. And he did speak. The impression that he made was bewildering. There was not a person present who was not aghast at the proud, biting manner with which the German used his harsh language, an example of all that came to mind when one spoke of Prussian Junkers. What seemed worst of all was that he continued to sit during his speech. Was that a deliberate insult, or was it due to his weakness? According to Grayson, he trembled in every limb, and while he spoke he had to try to keep his hands from shaking.[2] But from a report by one of his fellow delegates, the Hamburg banker Max Warburg, it appears that his stance was deliberate, he did not want to stand before his enemies as a man accused, an impression that could have been given by the arrangement of the chairs.[3]

The attitude taken by Brockdorff-Rantzau was a great diplomatic blunder. Wilson even said to Lord Riddell:

> The Germans are really a stupid people. They always do the wrong thing. They always did the wrong thing during the war. That is why I am here. They don't understand human nature. This is the most tactless speech I have ever heard. It will set the whole world against them.[4]

Why really did the German diplomat conduct himself so undiplomatically? What in heaven's name inspired him to rub his enemies the wrong way? Was it in fact what his adversaries called typical German tactlessness? Or was his unyielding stance prompted by a realization that he had to appeal to Wilson's own principles? He replied not as a diplomat but as a moralist. He reminded the American president all too emphatically that he had been in the right earlier, which is seldom a wise tactic. Some of the members of the German delegation, true realists like Carl Melchior and Max Warburg, had urged for a businesslike approach without big words, an acceptance of the bitter situation that confronted them; it must be possible to do business with the French. But Brockdorff-Rantzau chose a principled, melodramatic confrontation, talked about "the force of the hatred which confronts us here," and directed his words not to businesslike considerations but to the question of war guilt, wholly in Wilson's fashion. We are powerless, he said. We have heard the passionate demand that we must pay as vanquished and be punished as guilty. We must admit that we have the sole guilt for the war, but such an admission would be a lie on my lips. We do not seek to exonerate Germany from all responsibility. The attitude of the former German government contributed to the calamity, but we emphatically reject the idea that Germany alone should be considered as guilty.

And he continued in this vein. He pointed to the prevalence of imperialism in prewar Europe; he spoke with utter bitterness of the blockade of Germany which was still being maintained half a year after the war, and which had taken many victims. Think of that when you speak of guilt and atonement! He appealed vigorously to Wilson's principles, binding for the Germans and binding for the Allies; he warned that Germany could not pay all the financial debts; he asked that his country be admitted to the League of Nations. "A peace which cannot be defended in the name of justice before the whole world, would continually call forth fresh resistance."[5]

Wilson himself could have said it, but he did not, for he had changed. Others said it, many others in the Allied camp. When the peace treaty, cooked up in secrecy, finally became known, there was a storm of alarm and indignation, and the storm increased when the German delegation two weeks later returned with very reasonable objections, which however were stated in quite strong terms. These were addressed in the first place to the unbounded reparations, but also discussed other issues, like the Saar, the German-Polish frontier, international supervision of German waterways, the exclusion of Germany from the League of Nations, and more. In melodramatic exaggeration the Germans complained: a whole people would have to sign the sentence of their outlawry, their condemnation to death! They made strong counterproposals, most of which had no chance of acceptance, pleading for instance for a plebiscite in Alsace and a German mandate over its former colonies. And naturally they asked for open negotiations, appealing in so many words to the first of the Fourteen Points: "Open covenants openly arrived at."[6] Nothing drove the German people so close together in these sorrowful days as the peace treaty; from Left to Right reechoed the raging and impotent protest against what soon was called the "*Diktatfrieden*" (dictated peace).

As I have said, it was not only Germans who protested the peace treaty. There were many among the leaders of the Allies who were furious about the botched work of the Big Four. Smuts was one of the first to protest. "The more I have studied the Peace Treaty as a whole, the more I dislike it," he wrote Wilson. "Under this treaty, Europe will know no peace," he added.[7] The American president, who had great respect for Smuts, gave the best reply he could manage. He admitted that the peace was "very severe indeed," but "I do not think that it is on the whole unjust in the circumstances, much as I should have liked to have certain features altered." And he exonerated himself with the argument that "the German State" had committed "a very great offense against civilization." It was necessary for once to make clear that such conduct would be followed by severe punishment.[8]

Smuts was not persuaded and returned to the argument in a long letter. The peace ought to have been a "Wilson peace," based upon the

Fourteen Points, a peace of "appeasement." (Smuts was one of the first to use the word in this sense, in a letter to Lloyd George at about the same time. The roots of the later ill-fated "appeasement" of the 1930s must be sought in the British sense of guilt over the Peace of Versailles.)[9] The Allies should not end the war by following Germany's example in beginning it, reaping discredit with a treaty that would be another "scrap of paper." It was "unfair" to place all responsibility upon Wilson, but the Germans had made a good case for some of their objections. "All the one-sided provisions, which exclude reciprocity or equality, and all the pinpricks with which the Treaty teems, seem to me both against the letter and the spirit of your points."[10] In personal letters to others, Smuts was much more outspoken in his anger. Wilson "has failed Democracy—the man who was to make the world safe for Democracy."[11] Lord Robert Cecil echoed these judgments: the war was in conflict with the best intentions of the combatants, especially with the Fourteen Points. Lansing, who had been excluded in every respect, agreed bitterly; he told everyone who would listen (including Bullitt, who later loudly repeated what he had said), that the peace as a whole was no good. "Hopelessly bad" was how he described it to Baker.[12] The treaty was "the worst ever drawn, a great human tragedy," said James Brown Scott, a legal expert for the American delegation. "The statesmen have but given their people what they want and cry for . . . and have made a peace that renders another war inevitable."[13]

Many younger men said it too, upset by what had become of all their fine dreams. The great disillusionment began. Almost the entire American delegation was depressed. Everyone of liberal sentiments raised his voice. Walter Lippmann wrote to Ray Stannard Baker that the situation created by the treaty was

> profoundly discouraging to those who cared most for what the
> President has been talking about. For the life of me I can't see peace
> in this document, and as the President has so frequently said, states-
> men who cannot hear the voice of mankind are sure to be broken.

In another letter, written to Raymond Fosdick, he called the treaty "a far worse job, I think, than the Treaty of Vienna a hundred years ago."[14] And William White waxed satirical: this was truly the peace that surpasses all understanding. According to the deeply disappointed historian Carl Becker, Wilson

> goes on calmly assuming that the new international order can be attained by precisely the kind of peace which he formerly said would make it impossible. I don't say he could have done differently—but I say if he was right in 1918 he is wrong in 1920. The man has no humor, no objectivity, no abiding sense of or contact with reality.[15]

That was the general tenor of criticism, directed in the first place not against the peace treaty as such, but primarily against the chasm that had opened between Wilson's lofty promises and ideals and the reality that he had helped to hatch. This was a judgment that was obviously stronger in Germany than in other countries, one not to be taken at face value because of its partiality. On the lips of many it was even a morally questionable judgment, because many German leaders listened to Wilson only when they had no other choice, and it was these same rightist circles that later called into life the legend that Germany had put its trust in Wilson and laid down its weapons too soon, the same people who upbraided the Left government for signing the peace treaty and laid down the basis of a new and cruel revanche.

But was the German judgment in itself so unfair? It was in any case puzzling that the same Wilson who had so emphatically preached reconciliation through "peace without victory," now spoke of right and punishment and hence glossed over the humiliation of Germany. This should be crammed down his throat, one German newspaper suggested:

> It is not possible that a person should so contradict himself with solemnly proclaimed principles. The enemy's peace proposal is a slap in the face for every word spoken by Wilson.

And Theodor Wolff, an outstanding liberal, wrote in words of fury:

> He is a sophist of idealism, and in order not to see the deception practiced on others, he deceives himself.

If Wilson really had contributed to this peace, wrote Theodor Heuss, another liberal who would later become famous as the first president of the German Federal Republic after the Second World War, "he must appear before the court of world history as a charlatan."[16]

The German literature on Wilson is enormous and vitriolic. The German delegation that worked feverishly at Versailles on the reply to the peace terms quoted the declarations of Wilson (and of other Allied leaders), recalling in particular how emphatically the president of the United States had declared (in a speech on October 26, 1916) that "no single fact has been the cause of the war, but in the last resort the deeper responsibility for the war is borne by the whole European system, its combination of alliances and understandings, a complicated web of intrigue and espionage which inevitably caught the whole family of peoples in its meshes," and "that the explanation of the present war is not so simple and its roots sink deeper into the dark soil of history."[17]

This was precisely what Brockdorff-Rantzau was attempting to argue, what the report of the German historians, among them Max Weber and Hans Delbrück, who he had insisted come to Versailles with him, had tried to explain. A distinction must be made between immediate causes of the war and the underlying conditions that are to be found in "the dark soil of history" but which cannot be defined by only one side.[18] But Wilson no longer wanted to hear any of this; now he spoke with a different voice, with a severe and thin sound. He now forgot his own deep insight into the general human causes of war and narrowed the war guilt question to a political problem that could easily be solved by imposing special punishment on Germany, as the English Labor leader Arthur Henderson remarked.[19] Now Wilson said to Grayson: "The terms of the treaty are particularly severe, but I have striven my level best to make them fair, and at the same time compel Germany to pay a just penalty." Now he was not concerned with understanding and reconciliation but with guilt and punishment, and wrote, as we have seen, in these terms to Smuts.[20]

He stiffened in an attitude of strict righteousness, he dug in behind a causal moralism. But this put him under immense tension, as if he were defending himself against himself. He sought the firm ground of certainty, but in the Europe that boiled and churned around him he found that he had landed in a quagmire. His exasperation was enormous. It was a hard time and he was exhausted.

On May 3, Dr. Grayson wrote in his diary that he had never seen Wilson as tired as that evening at the table, and a few weeks later Baker recorded that the president had a ghastly look about him: "The left side of his face twisted sharply, drawing down the under lid of the eye. The strain upon him is very great." He seemed unable to go on any more physically, and mentally a decline was visible. "Often recently he has had trouble in recalling at the start exactly what the Four did during the earlier part of the day."[21]

For Wilson the protracted peace conference in Paris became an atrocious war of attrition, especially because he insisted on trying to do everything himself. Lamont, a great admirer, thought Wilson's biggest mistake was not delegating anything.[22] After his illness early in April Wilson didn't seem the old Wilson any more. Medical historians have examined Wilson's health and suffering during this period down to the smallest detail. Why, they ask, did it happen that at the end of April and early in May his handwriting, which had once been so flowing, began to be jerky and scrawling? Was this perhaps the consequence of a small stroke about April 28? They have sought an answer using the whole arsenal of their arcane medical terminology, but, because they do not give precise answers, the lay reader is left with questions. Like most historians, they get no further than the simple solution that "the proof of the pudding is in the eating." Are we able to observe a diminution of intellectual force in Wilson's speeches and letters of this time? Did he become more confused, more unsure of himself? Did he lose his quick, superior grasp of events? Was his increasing rigidity a consequence of his illness?

His conduct at a dinner at the beginning of May, was odd, even according to the commentary of the expert editor of his papers. A well-known British judge, Sir Thomas Barclay, invited Wilson to dinner with a notable group of princes, statesmen, and jurists. We can see the scene before us, the magnificence and the pomp, everyone in evening dress and bemedaled. Wilson was honored with fine words, and everything was going along smoothly and decorously. He responded, however, in the most surprising way.

To play down the eulogies accorded him he told the story of a young woman who went to the circus for the first time in her life. When she saw a magician read a newspaper through a two-inch board, she suddenly got up, disturbed, and said, "This is no place for me to be with a thin calico dress on." This was only the beginning. He was in a lighthearted mood, quite out of place amid all that brilliant company. He then pulled out all the familiar stops of his oratory, the themes of peace and humanity, but with an extra social accent that insulted his distinguished audience to their face. When he thought of mankind, he said, he did not always think of well-dressed persons.

> Most persons are not well-dressed. The heart of the world is under very plain jackets. The heart of the world is at very simple firesides. The heart of the world is in very simple circumstances. And unless you know the pressure of life on the humbler classes, you know nothing of life whatsoever. . . . Those of us who can sit sometimes at leisure and read pleasant books and think of the past, the long past, that we had no part in, and project the long future—we are not specimens of mankind.[23]

He went on with these ideas, which his audience no doubt found a bewildering flight of fancy. Should we therefore conclude that he really was at sea in his thinking, that he was falling back on worn-out words and ideas, as his editor says? Is it not rather an appealing trait in Wilson's personality that he could speak such thoughts without embarrassment to such a splendid company? We have earlier seen that he was not always attentive to the kind of audience he faced. He believed he had a universally valid message. This belief in his absolute cause engaged him totally, and the more he had to spend his days compromising his principles in the realm of the limited and the conditional, the more he had to speak differently in the evenings and on his days off.

A fine example of such use of the great words and special certainties that were peculiarly his may be found in the remarks he made when he visited the cemetery at Suresnes on May 30. He spoke brilliantly, moving his audience to tears. Standing by the soldiers' graves on a bright spring day, amid flowers in profusion and sadness in abundance, he could express again his deepest feelings. He spoke of the mandate of the dead, the pain of the mothers, the grand instrument of the League of Nations that would prevent such tragedy from ever happening again. The peoples of the world had awakened and they sat in the saddle! This was the usual fare he served, tempting and delicious, but far above the real world. A poet stood there, not the negotiator who had been busy for months haggling with his allies. With his head in the sky he proclaimed quietly: "Private counsels of statesmen cannot now and cannot hereafter determine the destinies of nations." Statesmen had accepted the principle of the

League of Nations, "and that is the proof that there shall never be a war like this one again."[24]

The deeply moved Baker marveled at his greatness and thought of Lincoln at Gettysburg,[25] but House had a different judgment. Wilson's oratory no longer swayed the multitudes nearly everywhere, as he had once done. "But if he is not careful, the feeling of distrust for him will become universal."[26]

House obviously had in mind the discrepancy between Wilson's grand dreams and his everyday political activity, a divergence that only became wider. In the lengthy, twice-daily meetings of the Big Four, Wilson the dreamer had to weigh practical pros and cons. No matter how hard it was, he kept at his task and didn't let himself be put upon. The major questions seemed to have been settled, but there was still much business to be done. And often what was involved could not be solved by the principles for which he stood. How poignant it was, for example, that pogroms took place on a large scale in the very nations of Eastern Europe that became free in that tumultuous, promising, and treacherous spring of 1919. It was the fault of the Jews themselves, who took a provocative attitude, maintained the Polish pianist Paderewski who became the leader of the new nation.[27] Wilson proposed international agreements for the protection of minorities, but the countries involved would hear nothing of such a violation of their sovereignty. Wilson was powerless in his brave new world!

His attitude was humane, honorable, and impressive, but obviously all too self-contradictory. What would the right of self-determination mean if the great powers continued to maintain a right of supervision over the newly free nations? And what about the idea that everything would come out right if only power came into the hands of the people, the good people? Did he himself feel the paradox? His ardent but not uncritical admirer Baker did feel it, writing in his diary, "Again it appears that the world in future is not to be governed by a democratic society of equal nations, but dominated by a powerful group of great powers with benevolent intentions!"[28]

II

There were a hundred and one complicated questions to handle, but the discussions within the Big Four always came back to the German problem. Once the Germans had presented their objections, the question became how far to meet them. As was to be expected, Clemenceau wanted no concessions whatever, but now Wilson joined him. Not only had Wilson become harder, more rigid and irreconcilable, but he also tried to hold firmly to what had been decided and so emerge with some success. Too much time had been lost already; he wanted to conclude the conference. He still had before him a hard battle with the Senate in the United States, which he would liked to have avoided but which he was sure was coming.

But, in the spring of 1919, everything in Europe was uncertain and different from what it appeared to be. Lloyd George, of all people, adopted Wilson's standpoint; he certainly did so also for political reasons, however, because public opinion in England had shifted, and the call for a temperate peace had become stronger. The roles were being exchanged. Now the mildness that Wilson had argued for in March was preached by Lloyd George and the earlier British severity was now characteristic of the American position.[29] The British prime minister appealed to the Fourteen Points, the right of self-determination; he proposed at the beginning of June to hold a plebiscite in Silesia, to limit drastically the occupation of the Rhineland, and to admit Germany into the League of Nations in the near future. "I am doing nothing other than abiding by your Fourteen Points," he told Wilson in one of the heated discussions that now arose again in the Council of Four. "I am only demanding a settlement upon the principles of self-determination which I learned from you."[30] The Allied leaders lived in fear that at the last moment Germany would refuse to sign. What would happen then? Weeks passed in long discussions of plans for a continued occupation of Germany, which were worked out by Marshal Foch. But that was an extreme option that no one desired, and Lloyd George argued skillfully and strongly for reconciliation.

Still Wilson did not want to allow his position to be determined by circumstances; he sought to stay at the level of principle. He was disgusted by the British attitude; it was opportunism, and there was nothing more foreign to him. Lloyd George became his bête noire, and he found him arrogant and insufferable. "The President said he had a hard time keeping his temper: from telling the British premier exactly what he thought of him." He compared Lloyd George to Theodore Roosevelt, who was similarly a superficial politician, out for applause, also a quasi-reformer, changeable as quicksilver.[31] On June 3 he called a plenary meeting of the American delegation, which he had not previously done, in order to discuss the new problems. He went through all the questions with his advisers, was willing to make a few adjustments here and there, but nonetheless came to the conclusion that little should be changed, that the Germans had not brought forward a single decisive argument in all their objections. "Where have they shown that the arrangements of the treaty are essentially unjust?" Of course they were severe, but that is what they deserved.

> And I think it is profitable that a nation learns once and for all what an unjust war means in itself. I have no desire to soften the treaty, but I have a very sincere desire to alter the portions of it that are shown to be unjust, or which are shown to be contrary to the principles, which we ourselves have laid down.[32]

Wilson, who had not wanted or waged war against the German people, now wanted them punished. Germany had to expiate what it had done, and it should not become a member of the League of Nations. Once he had argued that the League should not become a coalition of the victors. "Nothing is clearer to me from reading the President's speeches," wrote Walter Lippmann, "than that he intended that Germany democratized should become a member of the League."[33] Now it had to remain outside. Indeed, it was worse, for the League became a kind of guardian over Germany, a schoolmaster whose task it was "to see whether the Germans are behaving as they ought to. They must first prove that they are worthy of being admitted and that they know how disadvantageous it is for them if they are not admitted."[34]

The president maintained this stern attitude without a break. He explained it in detail in an interview on May 17 with the Dutch journalist Salomon van Oss, the founder and editor-in-chief of the *Haagsche Post*, a Dutch weekly journal of liberal opinion something like *The Nation* in the United States. Van Oss obtained the interview because of his friendship with Bernard Baruch, whose influence upon Wilson became very strong after the departure of Colonel House. Wilson indicated he was not talking for direct quotation, but expected the Dutch reporter to use his discretion in giving his impressions.

Van Oss paints an attractive picture of Wilson. He appears as a tall, amiable man, "with features that the whole world knows, from illustrations and caricatures: the long, rather thin face, narrowing somewhat to the large, broad chin; the resolute mouth, the large keen grey eyes behind his glasses, the regular features, the thin, rather grey hair above a broad, high forehead." His complexion, "like that of so many of his countrymen of his years, is pale." In his smile, which "lights up the strong features from time to time . . . seriousness and dignity are tempered with something very friendly and winning."

The president, van Oss continued, "translates all the peace problems —often unconsciously perhaps—into terms of the League of Nations and of opposition to war. . . . [He] is confident that sound understanding will bring mankind to complete the work energetically and in unison. A realist, like all idealists who wish to accomplish something, the President has been obliged to yield here and there, in order to accomplish for the fundamental idea what it has not been possible to accomplish in practice."

When the Dutch journalist told him frankly that the peace had left an unfavorable impression in the Netherlands, Wilson explained "the necessity of righting wrongs," since "nations are responsible, and . . . in the future they shall be held responsible for all that their governments may do. They shall no longer be able to avoid the consequences of the crimes of their governments by saying that the latter acted without their approval." He faulted the peoples even in democratic Europe for lack of "a continual and timely interest in what their governments are doing day by day." They had to be raised to a higher sense of their political responsibility. Using a metaphor familiar to the seafaring nation of Holland, "the will of the people must continually function as the rudder of the Ship of State, and it is not sufficient to elect from time to time a captain and crew for that ship."[35] As we see, Wilson gave his Dutch visitor an excellent survey of his ideas, in which his lofty naïveté and stern self-assurance both emerge.

Later, in September, during his tragic trip through the American West from Columbus to Los Angeles, he returned constantly to his moral judgment in defending his attitude. In Paris, he said, the statesmen had tried to be just. They had recognized that Germany was a great nation and they had no intention of crushing the German people, "but they did think it ought to be burned into the consciousness of men forever that no people ought to permit its government to do what the German Government did."[36] He seems to have forgotten the division between evil governments and good peoples which had been so essential in his vision of

1917–1918; now a people paid the price for its government. And thus Wilson turned his Old Testament wrath upon the Weimar Republic.

The reply of the Allied leaders to the German objections was a grim one. By the middle of June they came to an agreement about its text after endless discussions, during which the "chameleon" Lloyd George made Wilson's blood boil.[37] They made few concessions, accepting a plebiscite in Silesia and the prospect of a limit to reparations. But they restated emphatically Germany's guilt for the war, the greatest crime ever committed against humanity. "Germany, under the inspiration of Prussia, has been the champion of force and violence, deception, intrigue and cruelty in the conduct of international affairs." It could not be accepted immediately into the fraternity of nations but had first to prove itself by good behavior. True, there had been a revolution in Germany but only at the last moment when all was lost. The Germans were quite wrong in appealing to Wilson's words of reconciliation; they used them in a one-sided way, and the Allies countered with quite other quotations from the rich oratorical past of the president, such as his appeal to justice as a condition for peace and his demand that the German people had first to change in character.[38] It was a hard reply, as Wilson wanted. He told faithful Grayson that he did not want to make any more concessions even if it meant the Germans would refuse to sign. It was all their own fault! Clemenceau, Grayson adds, was glad to hear him say it.[39]

Germany, under the heaviest pressure, signed the peace treaty. The threat of an Allied march to the Weser, with an even tighter blockade (which Wilson opposed), left the Germans no choice. Nonetheless the cabinet's acceptance of the treaty brought it down. The Socialist chancellor Philipp Scheidemann refused point-blank: "The treaty cannot be tolerated or fulfilled. Anyone who put himself and ourselves in such shackles would see his hand dry up."[40] Half the members of the government, including Brockdorff-Rantzau, resigned. A new cabinet, led by another Socialist, Gustav Adolf Bauer, persuaded the Reichstag to accept the treaty; again it was the Catholic leader Erzberger who played a crucial role in the decision. It included one reservation—a request that the paragraph on Germany's exclusive war guilt be dropped. The victors were not ready to do it, however. They had been made more implacable by the events in Scapa Flow, the sound off the north coast of Scotland where Britain's most important naval base was located. The German war fleet had sailed there in accordance with the peace treaty terms to be turned over to the British; instead the ships, which lay at anchor, were suddenly scuttled. This happened during the same weekend when the treaty was to be signed, and the wrath of the Allied leaders was understandable. Yet, even if the mass sinking was a violation of the peace treaty, no one knew exactly what could be done about it. It did not make much difference to Wilson; he stood by his hard position that no more concessions should be made to Germany. He was ready for an absolute ultimatum, he said.

On June 28, exactly five years after the assassinations in Serajevo, the war which they had sparked came to a formal end. Two German ministers, Hermann Müller and Johannes Bell, appeared at Versailles to put their signatures on the peace treaty in the presence of the Allied leaders in the Hall of Mirrors of the palace. It was the place where the German Empire, the Second Reich, had been proclaimed forty-eight years earlier. The ceremony was deliberately designed to humiliate the Germans; it was also another demonstration that the dream of a "peace without victory" had been too beautiful for the real world. Wilson whose dream it had been, sat in the front row of the victors. There exist no photographs of the ceremony, as unbefitting so solemn an occasion; a painting was acceptable, however, and there is one by an English artist, William Orpen. After the treaty had been signed, the Big Three walked out onto the terrace of the palace, where the crowd greeted them with loud cheers.

The peace was made, and Wilson could return to the United States to discuss the treaty with the Senate. Debate over its ratification would be the next and final act of the grotesque drama. Wilson left the same day by train for Brest. At the station he said farewell to his colleagues and collaborators. Among them was House, who had a last, brief conversation with Wilson. Even now the Colonel gave the president a piece of sensible advice, to approach the Senate with the same spirit of reconciliation with which he had approached his Allied colleagues in Paris; then he would have no trouble. Wilson was no longer in any mood to listen to House's wisdom. He bitingly told him, in what amounted to a reprimand, "House, I have found one can never get anything in this life that is worth while without fighting for it." House, sure of himself as always, continued to press him with historical examples, but Wilson probably did not even hear him. Coldly he said, "Good-bye, House." They would never see each other again.[41]

III

The history of the Versailles peace has called forth a welter of difficult questions. Was it too harsh, a *Diktatfrieden* that automatically elicited a reaction of revanche? Or was it, on the contrary, too mild a settlement, enabling the old forces in Germany to continue? In any case, is there a direct causal link between 1919 and 1933? Does the guilt for the disastrous consequences lie with the men who, in Paris, laid down the rules for the future? These are all questions that in their nature cannot be given a conclusive or logically satisfactory answer. But they are also questions that cannot be evaded. If this peace were not accepted, Wilson said many times on his swing through the West in the fall, there would be another war in twenty years.

> The next time will come; it will come while this generation is living, and the children that crowd about our car as we move from station to station will be sacrificed upon the altar of that war.[42]

How horribly right he proved to be! What he predicted came about just as he said. But was he himself guiltless? Hadn't he written the whole scenario for that future? The defeat was a humiliation, not intended as such by him in his noble naïveté, but nonetheless felt as such by the vanquished. Humiliation led to dreams of revenge; the seeds of a new war were put into the soil. Of course, they would only grow when the climate was favorable, when events, primarily the Great Depression that began in 1929, permitted. But beyond question the seeds were planted by the peace of Versailles. Obviously, too, we must add at once that the world of 1919 was far too frightful in its confusion to be straightened out by talks between four heads of state. The problems were overwhelming and the failure of the Big Four was almost inevitable.

The German historian Klaus Schwabe rejects the accusation against Wilson that he betrayed the Germans. Wilson, he writes, held on to his principles, but he did "come down a bit from some of his goals—most of all those which concerned the economy, least those which concerned territorial questions—and on some he gave way altogether." But doesn't this amount in the end to betrayal of his principles, although a sublimated betrayal, just as he sublimated everything else? Schwabe, furthermore, seeks a solution by a distinction among Wilson's aims when they are judged within different time scales. In the short term, he says, Wilson sought a soft solution, as in his negotiations regarding the armistice; in the middle term, in the working out of the peace treaty, his wish to punish Germany was more strongly expressed; but there is also a long term, and Wilson hoped that in the end Germany would be integrated into Europe.[43]

Historians, in their quest for consistency, have to fit Wilson into some pattern, if need be, one that takes time into account. This provides a way out: in the long run, in the future (but with what a frightful inter-mezzo!), Wilson would be right. This is the way Arthur Link, Wilson's outstanding biographer, approaches the question. For him, Wilson's vision might seem foolish at first sight, because it clashed with reality, but there is in fact a "higher realism." This adds a wider dimension to the problem of Wilson; his deeds then must be judged within the perspective of the future. In it his deeds accord with his words; if they were failures in the short run, all is reconciled in the perspective of a better future. It is a quite Wilsonian idea, paralleling the way Wilson himself saw the League of Nations as the panacea for all temporary compromises.

But is it possible to separate today and tomorrow from each other in this way? Is this how the relationship between realism and idealism actually works? What is the value of a prophet in politics? These are the questions we constantly encounter. There is a deep tragedy within them. Let me repeat: Wilson himself saw and warned that if there was not a just peace, there would be war again in twenty years. Does it follow from this that he personally shared in the responsibility for the horrors that would break out two decades later? Link's reply is that he did not. At Versailles there was the familiar tension between the ideal and reality, but it is inherent in all human striving. One can only ask why Wilson failed. There are more than enough reasons. After the armistice he had no means to compel France and England; he had been weakened in his own country by the elections; he had formidable opponents in Clemenceau, Lloyd George, Orlando, and Sonnino; his ideal of "open covenants" was frustrated. And yet, Link maintains, he gained a reasonable peace that worked and created a new international order. He snaps at the critics:

> It is time to stop perpetuating the myth that the Paris settlement
> made inevitable the rise to power of Mussolini, the Japanese militarists,

and Hitler, and hence the Second World War. That war was primarily the result of the Great Depression.[44]

All the same, questions persist. If the war that came in twenty years was not the consequence of a bad peace, or if it wasn't such a bad peace after all, was Wilson's forecast just a stab in the dark? But then why reproach the others who opposed him? They too made predictions, and none probably so accurately as Senator Charles Thomas of Colorado. In the debates over ratification in the U.S. Senate, he argued that the harsh peace was quite understandable, for what Germany had done to the world could hardly be made good. He went on:

> But the Germans are human beings, possessed of human attributes, influenced by human motives, and inspired by human impulses.
> . . . Our treaty with her will be respected and its covenants performed so long as the allied powers can so dictate. It will be repudiated whenever that power shall disappear, and this whether Germany be within or without the league of nations. The aspiration of Germany will be the coming of that hour. She will prepare for it, within the limitations of the treaty if she must, but she will prepare for it nevertheless.

We can proclaim now, he went on, that there is no more threat of war, but Germany will go ahead. "For it is the everlasting truth that no peace of force has ever outlived the force which imposed it." And the irony of history, Thomas continued, is that Wilson himself by his principle of self-determination undermined his own internationalism. "The spirit of nationalism was never more assertive than it is now. President Wilson's announcement of the right of self-determination was like deep calling unto deep. The response greeting it was universal."[45]

Other critics, particularly from the right, echoed this realistic vision. One was the French historian Jacques Bainville, who warned that Germany would bow its head for fifteen years and then resume its rights; the first victims would be the allies of the victors in the East, Poland and Czechoslovakia. The peace, as Bainville put it, was too mild for its hard terms.[46]

An inescapable question remains: What did the rise of Hitler have to do with the peace of Versailles? Wasn't it the bad peace that made it possible for him to arouse the worst moods among the German people, precisely that nationalism of which Senator Thomas spoke? As Golo Mann has written, "This mass of falsehoods hung about the neck of the new German republic like a millstone."[47]

There were other forecasts made during those years of 1919 and 1920. In Germany Max Weber issued a prognosis: If German territory was seized and the reparations imposed, then, "after a period of timid pacifism due to exhaustion, every worker who felt that way would become a chauvinist." And Walter Simons, the secretary of the German peace delegation, warned of a new nationalist movement in Germany if the peace treaty were *not* signed; it would be led by "a hitherto undiscovered leader, who would place himself at the head of a great popular uprising."[48]

But Germany did sign the peace treaty, and it made little difference for the future. The *Führer* came, fourteen years later, when the Depression gave him his chance, but riding on a wave of disillusionment and anger over the *Diktatfrieden* of Versailles. Grisly lines of connection run between 1919 and 1933, which were seen by the intelligent banker Max Warburg when he refused to accept an official position in the German delegation to Versailles. A Jew cannot do it, he said, "anti-Semitism would in any case be the result."[49]

TWENTY-NINE

*M. Wilson ne connaissait pas l'Europe, et sa résistance
obstinée aux insignifiantes concessions qui lui étaient
demandées à Washington, montre que l'Amérique elle-même
ne lui était pas suffisamment connue. C'était un doctrinaire
au meilleur sens du mot. Un homme d'intentions excellentes,
mais d'émotions cristallisées.*

[Mr. Wilson did not know Europe, and his obstinate
resistance to insignificant concessions asked of him in
Washington shows that he did not know America well
enough either. He was a doctrinaire in the best sense of
the word. A man of excellent intentions but crystallized
emotions.]
— *Georges Clemenceau*

ARTICLE X

WE COME TO THE FINAL act of what we may truly call a drama, complete with a fated dénouement—but without the catharsis. Wilson's life remained, at least within the span of years granted to him, a life unreconciled. All later interpretations, as we saw at the end of the previous chapter, have sought to give it unity and meaning by placing it in a historical perspective. This book too must probably conclude in such an epilogue, lest it become a *Sinngebung des Sinnlosen*, an explanation of the inexplicable. But for the present we still stand on the threshold of the dramatic last struggle, the Armageddon—to use the apocalyptic terminology of which Americans are so fond—of Wilson's life.

He had finally came home, for good, to his immense country. He came as swiftly as he could. On June 28 the peace was signed in the Hall of Mirrors at Versailles; on June 29 his ship sailed from Brest; on July 8 he was in New York. En route he had celebrated the Fourth of July, and of course he gave a speech to the soldiers and sailors going home on the same ship. The great moralist spoke the familiar words and truths, America as the representative of humanity, in the service of mankind, America as the land of true freedom, freedom to do good, not wrong.[1] As soon as he landed in New York, he spoke again, briefly and solemnly: Americans would continue to stand by the world, would remain true to "the vision which they saw at their birth."[2]

He was keeping his powder dry for the speech he would give in the Senate two days later. There he officially presented his peace treaty—with the Covenant an indissoluble part of it—in order to receive, in the language of the Constitution, the "advice and consent" of the senators, the two-thirds majority necessary for ratification. The last big battle had to begin, and he went into it full of confidence. His lengthy address was tranquil, with muted eloquence, although it repeated the familiar themes of a selfless America, the crusade of the noble soldiers, the general will, in Europe too, to bring a new world order into being, in which the common interest would prevail over self-interest, the League of Nations as the true safeguard of the future, and finally an end to the vicious circle of war and vengeance. Mankind had a new task and hope. "Shall we or any other free people hesitate to accept this great duty? Dare we reject it and break the heart of the world?" Admittedly, the treaty was not perfect; it had come into existence with "minor compromises," but these at no point touched the heart of the principles involved. America must therefore stand by the treaty and thus demonstrate its adulthood. Was it not just twenty-one years (the age of maturity in law) earlier that the country had begun its role in international politics (with the war against Spain)?

Wilson spoke to the point and with self-command. But he could not fail to conclude with a highly emotional plea. Again God, again the predestined course of history, again America's obligation and vocation, again the metaphor of the heavenly light upon the path.

> The stage is set, the destiny disclosed. It has come about by no plan of our conceiving, but by the hand of God who led us into this way. We cannot turn back. We can only go forward, with lifted eyes and freshened spirit, to follow the vision. It was of this that we dreamed at our birth. America shall in truth show the way. The light streams upon the path ahead, and nowhere else.[3]

To listen to Wilson, even through the medium and the barrier of print, is a bizarre pleasure. There is something bewitching in his rhetoric;

it is so otherworldly, so unreal. If one listens to it for any time, one begins to believe that it is the center about which the world turns, that America in that long, hot summer of 1919 was defined and stamped by the question of the peace treaty, that the whole American people was mesmerized by this single burning question of war and peace, that it yearned to devote itself to the service of all humanity. Then it seems that all attention is concentrated on the one great drama that was being played out in the Senate in Washington.

But this is a grave distortion of reality. America was anything but totally engrossed in the dream of its president. There were many other immensely difficult problems that demanded attention. The huge army called up in haste, part of which was in Europe, had to be demobilized and all the discharged soldiers given jobs again. This was particularly difficult in an economy that itself had to be converted to peacetime needs, but which was harassed by inflation and big strikes in the coal mines and steel industry. And the American public, which during the war had been kept in a state of artificial excitement by Creel's propaganda committee, was still preoccupied by the so-called threat of Bolshevism; the "Red scare" was another artificial state of excitement fostered and exploited by the authorities, in particular Attorney General Palmer, in order to keep order and put a spoke in the wheels of the labor unions. Everywhere uncertainty and fear reigned. During the summer the country was startled by immense race riots, bloody clashes between blacks and whites in various big cities, such as Washington, Chicago, and Omaha.

The Americans were like people who waken from a strange dream and cannot believe what they see in the varied everyday reality about them. They had to restore their sensation-filled society to its orderly ways, but they seemed unable to live any more without artificial stimulants. They whirled from one problem to the other. In this same year of 1919, after much emotional debate, they were also adopting two new amendments to the Constitution, the eighteenth, which prohibited the manufacture and sale of alcoholic beverages, and the nineteenth, which gave women the vote.

No, the Americans had other things on their minds than the problems of far-off Europe. But in the Senate the game had to go on, according to the fixed rules of the Constitution: a two-thirds majority for ratification of the treaty, but with inclusion of possible amendments by a simple majority plus one, that is, forty-nine out of a possible ninety-six votes. The first question of importance was how possible and how wise it was to adopt amendments to the treaty. They would in any case require new negotiations with the Allies, for an international treaty cannot be changed by one of the parties to it. On the advice of elder statesman Elihu Root, a man of great authority in the Republican party, the opposition decided to set forth its grievances in "reservations." In any event, the United States should reserve to itself specific rights on various points. Whether this required revision of the treaty itself remained unclear for a while. These points were primarily the articles of the Covenant; there was hardly any discussion of the terms of the peace treaty itself, with a few exceptions, in particular the Shantung question.

When Wilson had come ashore on July 8, the fuel for the fires of controversy was already piled up. The battle could break out at once in full fury; everyone was ready. In March Senator Lodge had thrown down the gauntlet with his "round robin." In May, Congress convened again, and by July a number of proposals were introduced which ran directly counter to Wilson's intentions. But the majority was still certainly favorable to him. This was also true of public opinion during the spring; it seemed improbable that Wilson's magnificent plans would flounder and fail so painfully. It was only the delay and the long, drawn out debate that harmed them so greatly. The people wanted to go along, but as time went on the ideal lost its force. This was well understood by Wilson's foes, which was why they deliberately stalled the conduct of business. They played the game according to the cumbersome procedures of the Senate, like workers who protest by working by the rule book.

Wilson's foes were undoubtedly motivated not only by political but also by personal antagonisms. But it remains one of the most difficult historical problems to decide how heavily human passions and vanities weighed in the bitter clash that dominated American politics in the summer of 1919. A conclusive answer is obviously impossible. By his own fault Wilson had drawn upon himself the hatred of many senators. It is almost beyond belief that so experienced a politician could so systematically estrange the men with whom, under the Constitution, he had to work—and no one knew that better than Wilson himself, the theoretician of politics! Worse, he insulted them to their face, as during his brief stay in the United States in March. He had sown the wind—could he expect not to reap the storm?

More than personal animosities were involved, however. An indescribably motley coalition came together during the summer in opposition to the great idealist in the White House. It was an unnatural alliance of a rare kind, with conflicting motives and muddled values. Idealism and conservatism, progressivism and provincialism, blind hatred and naïve pedantry, all were jumbled together and directed against a man who himself was progressive, idealistic, principled, and capable of the most intense hatred.

Disillusioned idealism on the Left allied itself with embittered chauvinism on the Right. Wilson was shown up as a hypocrite by journals that had once supported him, such as *The Nation* and *The New Republic*. Did he ever believe in his own oratory? wondered Oswald Garrison Villard, the editor-in-chief of *The Nation*. The peace treaty was "an inhuman monster," wrote Croly in anger. The cynics were right about Wilson; those who had believed in him had been betrayed.[4] Wilson was attacked at least as fiercely in the right-wing press; William Randolph Hearst led in raging condemnation of Wilson's "hysterical devotion to other nations."[5] As in Europe, the war was followed in America by an upsurge of triumphant and vindictive nationalism; even in his own country Wilson proved wrong, for there was no decisive "moral force" for reconciliation. On the contrary, the gentle forces that he was certain would win were overwhelmed by the wrath of Wilson's enemies and the desire of the American people for revenge, or at least by their indifference. As the year advanced, the people turned away from Wilson's dream. Back to the everyday pleasures of ordinary life, back to what during the next decade would be called "normalcy"! Its appeal proved stronger than all the visions of a better future.

Anti-Wilson feelings were further strengthened by the huge propaganda campaign of Wilson's fiercest adversaries. It was paid for, it may be noted, by the money of a few big capitalists, such as Henry Clay Frick and Andrew Mellon, the same men who became famous for their magnificent art collections. The foremost organizer of the whole action was none other than George Harvey, Wilson's old friend who had pushed him for the presidency in 1906 but was now his outspoken foe. Thus Wilson was fought on every side, with capitalist and anticapitalist means and arguments, by big industrialists and Populists out in the West.

Wilson's opponents in the Senate, building on this hostility, succeeded in making the conflict one between political parties. Before this, not all Democrats had been for Wilson's plans and not all Republicans against them. To be sure, the bulk of Wilson's party stood behind him, accepting his tight leadership, although with increasing recalcitrance. But the Republicans had been divided. In 1912, crippled by the Bull Moose split, they had lost. In 1916, their wounds not yet fully healed, they had lost again. Only in the off-year elections of 1918 had they met with reasonable success. Now they had every interest in maintaining their regained unity. The party leaders considered the whole affair from this point of view; with the elections of 1920 in mind, they maneuvered cautiously so as not to forfeit the prize again.

They were still divided; the old line of separation between progressives and conservatives, which partly corresponded to the opposition of East and West, was still visible. But foreign policy caused even more division. In the Senate there were three clear streams among the Republicans. In the first place a group of about twelve senators were very much in favor of the League of Nations. They were ready to be satisfied with "mild reservations" in the peace treaty, and hence were called "mild reservationists." Former President Taft, although not himself a senator, was their intellectual leader; one of their best-known representatives was Senator Frank B. Kellogg of Minnesota (later to became even better known as one of the coauthors of the Kellogg-Briand Pact).

Next to them was a somewhat larger group that had much stronger criticism of the treaty, called the "strong reservationists." Their leader was Henry Cabot Lodge, a wholehearted party man. His paramount purpose was to prevent a repetition of the Republican debacle of 1912. He sought to forge a policy that would hold the advocates and the opponents of the League together, one that would neither throw the "mild reservationists" into the arms of the Democrats nor estrange those who were out-and-out foes of the League.

The third group were totally and implacably opposed to any permanent American involvement in an international order. They were called "Irreconcilables" or "Bitter-Enders." Because they were such picturesque and outspoken persons, they have drawn most attention in history. Most were outlandish examples of an incredibly provincial American political culture. They were driven by very diverse motives. Some were old Progressives from the Midwest and the Far West suspicious of anything that came out of Washington, not to speak of the rest of the evil world. Among them were attractive if naïve figures such as Senator George Norris of Nebraska, who honestly believed that Wilson's policy was a capitalist conspiracy and described Wilson's trip to Europe as royalist megalomania:

> He went to Europe in a splendor and a gorgeousness never equaled
> in the history of the world. While his fellow citizens were sacrificing
> in every possible way, he used the money that came from millions
> of honest toilers in a display of wealth and pomp never equaled by
> any king, monarch, or potentate.[6]

But most of the Irreconcilables were not as naïve as this "gentle knight of democracy," as Norris was later called when he became the spear and shield of Franklin Roosevelt. The leader of the group was William Borah of Idaho, one of the most colorful, self-willed characters who ever sat in the Senate. Borah is a story in himself, too long to be told here and too good to be left out. He came from a mountainous state in the Far West which had as yet contributed not one notable figure to the country. Its scanty electorate were proud of their tribune, who suddenly brought fame to their forgotten state. They reelected him every six years, six times in all, and he sat in the Senate from 1907 to 1940.

Borah was the supreme individualist. He was so much at odds with everyone else that Calvin Coolidge, with his dry humor, expressed surprise when he saw Borah horseback riding along the Potomac because man and beast were going in the same direction. Borah was always alone, always against, and always at center stage; Lippmann acutely called him "a deeply protestant mind."[7] A loud and pompous speaker, he was a politician at once admired and feared by friend and foe because he was utterly honest, although burdened with very simple provincial principles. He believed that everything was better in America, that things had been better in the past than they were in the present, that the wisdom of the Founding Fathers would never be equaled, that capitalism and imperialism (especially British imperialism, and indeed all internationalism) constituted a threat for the innocent United States. It is difficult to take the man seriously; one gains the impression that he was in a state of constant excitement for the sake of the excitement itself. "His passion," wrote Lippmann, "is to expose, to ventilate, to protest, to prevent and to destroy." A mocking observer compared him to a self-winding clock: "Borah was always winding himself up, but never quite struck twelve."[8] He was rabidly opposed to the League of Nations; even if the Savior himself came to earth to argue for it, he said, he would still be against it.[9]

Borah was the soul of the resistance. But alongside him stood other very strong willed and influential men, each deserving a sketch if there were enough room here. One was Philander Knox, who as a cabinet member under Taft had practiced "dollar diplomacy," a realist par excellence, cool and keen-witted, and therefore called the "brains" of the group. Frank Brandegee of Connecticut was the "tongue" of the Irreconcilables, a brilliant, cynical, and deeply troubled mind (he later committed suicide). Hiram Johnson of California, a former Progressive who had been the candidate for vice-president with Roosevelt in 1912 and had won popularity because of his struggle against the railroads in California, was a loud demagogue, the "noise" of the group. In all, the Irreconcilables were a variegated group of dreamers and cynics, populists and men who held the people in contempt, joined together only by their antipathy to Wilson.

They were conspicuous, but it is a question how important they were. All told, they came to at most nineteen men (including a single Democrat). This meant that only a fifth of the Senate was opposed to all international ties. All the other Senators were in favor of some involvement. Yet the League of Nations plan failed, the whole plan failed.

Whose fault, in the end, was it? Does it even make sense to ask the question? We probably learn little more from history than human inadequacy, the *maxima culpa*. "What theme had Homer but original sin?" Yeats asked. But how do we distribute this guilt? In the drama that was enacted in 1919 in Washington there are more than enough guilty parties to be found, and it is also possible to speak of a general madness. In the long run, however, we come back to the two main actors, Wilson and Lodge. There are few historians who have not pointed them out, singly or both, as the principal suspects in the case. With Wilson it was idealistic stubbornness, to which we constantly return. With Lodge, who was trying to hold together the three groups of his Republican party, it was sly partisanship. He succeeded by the use of the trickiest tactics. He has been reproached by historians for placing party interest ahead of the country's needs, playing the game of politics as if nothing mattered but winning.[10]

It is difficult to judge this issue. It is possible to maintain that Lodge really did have principles, that his priority was the interests of the United States, not those of his party. When he began to see that no accommodation was possible, that his own nationalism could never be in accord with Wilson's internationalism, he became more implacable. At the deepest level, what was involved was a difference in mentality. Lodge could not believe in what he called "the beautiful scheme of making mankind suddenly virtuous by a statute or a written constitution." Probably at work too was that he was growing older. In his growing pessimism he felt himself closer and closer to the Adams brothers; he wrote to Brooks Adams in September 1917 that he was no longer under the spell of nineteenth-century doctrines that "we were in continual evolution, always moving on to something better with perfection as the goal."[11]

It is probable that in a clash of spirits, the cynic will come out ahead of the idealist. Wilson believed in mankind but not in men (and certainly not in Lodge), but did not recognize this paradox. From the vantage point of his abstract position, he saw everything in black and white and would always lose. Lodge, however, would make an estimate of the mental attitude of his opponent, and hence he won. In his memoirs he described this clash of minds with much perception but also much malice. He was, he wrote,

> convinced that President Wilson would prevent the acceptance of the treaty with reservations if he possibly could. I based this opinion on the knowledge which I had acquired as to Mr. Wilson's temperament, intentions and purposes. I had learned from a careful study of the President's acts and utterances during those trying days—and it was as important for me to understand him as it was for his closest friends—that the key to all he did was that he thought of everything in terms of Wilson. In other words, Mr. Wilson in dealing with every great question thought first of himself. . . . Mr. Wilson was devoured by the desire for power.[12]

This was certainly a partisan judgment and does no justice to Wilson's high purposes. But it contained enough truth to work. Lodge saw all too well his adversary's weaknesses. Lodge operated with nagging slowness, trying Wilson's patience until it bled. He arranged to begin by holding hearings of the Senate Committee on Foreign Affairs, but did not open them until the end of July. The first two weeks were devoted to the complete reading of the text of the peace treaty, all 268 pages of it; it was a meaningless performance with only a secretary present, but it ate up time. Then came the witnesses, a long, colorful array, some sixty in all, whose testimony was industriously recorded, although much of it was quite irrelevant, and finally printed in a report of almost 1,300 pages. All the wisdom and all the absurdity that could be brought to bear on the treaty were heard. Enemies of Wilson came to explain how the Irish groaned under the English yoke without any right of self-determination, how the city of Fiume was Italian to the core, how the colored peoples were deprived of their rights by a charter of the League of Nations that did not guarantee race equality, and so on; everyone vented his wrath at the hearings. Especially strong was anti-British feeling; it was a scandal that the British Empire through its dominions had six seats in the Council of the League and the great United States only one. The whole show reminds one of the biblical tale of David and those in trouble in Adullam cave: "And every one that was in distress, and everyone that was in debt, and every one that was discontented, gathered themselves unto him" (1 Sam. 22:2).

More important was the testimony of Wilson's collaborators, Baruch, Miller, Lansing, Bullitt and, on behalf of the treaty, Wilson himself. Lansing testified twice and made a painful, pitiful impression. It turned out that he was not well informed about essential matters, from which he had been excluded. Everything had gone wrong, he declared; Wilson should never have gone to Europe, the Europeans had been too sly for him, the League of Nations would not work with such partners. These were the helpless pronouncements of an embittered man, heard with delight by the bloodhounds on the committee, like Knox and Brandegee.

Much more disturbing than Lansing's testimony was that of William Bullitt, the young man who had traveled to Russia in the beginning of the year with such overwrought expectations and then had been so casually disavowed by Lloyd George and Wilson. Bullitt, young, brusque, and full of anger, presented to the eager committee members the original draft of the charter of the League, written by Wilson; it had come into his hands through House. He maintained that no one in the American commission had felt much in its favor. And he revealed that Lansing in particular had attacked it sharply. In a revelation that came like a bombshell, he quoted Lansing word for word:

> I believe [Lansing had told him] that if the Senate could only understand what this treaty really means, and if the American people could really understand it, it would unquestionably be defeated, but I wonder if they will ever understand what it lets them in for.[13]

It was a glaring break of confidence, and the dismay was great. Bullitt himself was apparently the principal victim; the press unanimously denounced him for his betrayal, and his career seemed at an end. (Later, under Franklin D. Roosevelt, he returned to diplomatic service, becoming the first ambassador of the United States to the Soviet Union in 1933.) Lansing, who had always protected Bullitt, was exposed before the whole country and was unable to defend himself. Wilson was furious; his own secretary of state had opposed him! He told Tumulty:

> Think of it. This from the man whom I raised from the level of a subordinate to the great office of Secretary of State of the United States! My God! I did not think it was possible for Lansing to act in this way.[14]

Not for one moment did it enter Wilson's righteous soul that it was he himself who was principally at fault; that for five long years he had never taken Lansing into his confidence on a single important question. Not surprisingly, Lodge and his friends rubbed their hands in glee. Bullitt's testimony was welcome dynamite to put under Wilson's treaty.

II

As one plunges deeper into all this talk, all these debates, all these mutual reproaches and allegations, all the passions of that strange year 1919, one sometimes has the feeling that one is watching a surrealist play about the meaninglessness of human existence. The very language and logic employed seem totally absurd. The disastrous confusion of the moment has been continued in the debates of historians, for the key question in our reflections is always whether there were really any differences among the parties, whether it would have made much difference if Lodge's "reservations" had been accepted, whether, indeed, it might not have served Wilson's purposes better if they had been.

An absurd play, "full of sound and fury, signifying nothing," a conversation on the boards with so many meanings that the spectator's brain reels. There is no more striking example of this confusion than the discussion that Wilson had with the committee. He was invited to give his vision of the disputed problems, and he therefore invited the committee members to come to the White House. It would be a good opportunity to explain to them what was as plain as day to him. He received his guests in the stately East Room of the White House. As was his manner, he was courteous, although he knew full well how hostile were some of the men facing him. For his archenemies—it is not too strong to call them that—were there, men such as Borah, Brandegee, Knox, Johnson, and of course Lodge himself, the chairman of the committee. They asked many questions, many more than the Democratic members of the committee who were present, Wilson's faithful supporters such as Gilbert Hitchcock of Nebraska, John S. Williams of Mississippi, and Key Pittman of Nevada.

For three hours they talked at him and he at them, naturally without reaching any result. Wilson might believe in the reasonable system of democracy, but he was not good at practicing it, and the same was true for his interlocutors. Both sides had long since taken their stands. Wilson began with a short statement of his ideas. The matter was urgent, he said, for many great problems could not be settled so long as the peace treaty was not signed. All the objections that had been brought by the committee in March had been met: The Monroe Doctrine was recognized, control of domestic problems safeguarded, the right of withdrawal expressly guaranteed, and the constitutional powers of Congress in matters of war and peace assured. As for the big stumbling block, Article X of the Covenant, it was not really as ambiguous within the framework of the whole treaty as had been said. It was a moral, not a legal obligation, leaving Congress free to interpret from case to case. And it was truly "the very backbone of the whole covenant. Without it the League would be hardly more than an influential debating society!"

Article X was the heart of the matter, the pivot around which world peace would revolve, at least in Wilson's eyes. It was the article of faith upon which the world would stand or fall, *articulus stantis et cadentis mundi*, to vary a term in theology! The moral foundation of the new humanity!

Did Article X really mean very much? Did it obligate the United States, as Lodge put it, "on the appeal of any member of the League not only to respect but to preserve its independence and its boundaries"? Did this derogate from the sovereignty of the United States? This is how he explained it in a major speech that he gave to the Senate on August 12.[15] It is probably worthwhile to quote the text of Article X again:

> The Members of the League undertake to respect and preserve as against external aggression the territorial integrity and existing political independence of all Members of the League. In case of any

such aggression or in case of any threat or danger of such aggression the Council shall advise upon the means by which this obligation shall be fulfilled.

I repeat, what did this mean? In what way were the member states of the League bound not merely to respect but also to preserve each other's territorial integrity and political independence? The second sentence of the article states that the Council of the League would "advise upon the means." Were economic sanctions intended? Or military sanctions? And, most of all, how binding would its recommendation be? It was all very vaguely formulated. Was this the penalty for Wilson's inability and even his refusal to think in legal terms? For him an international order was a question of mentality, of moral commitment. But this really ran against the tradition of American political thought. American politics is practiced by lawyers, who make up more than half the membership of Congress. Americans have always sought legalistic solutions to their problems. There inheres in this attitude an element of idealism, to be sure, but a more cautious one, better provided with guarantees and escape clauses. The leading Republican politicians desired an international order as much as Wilson did, but they wanted it to be formulated more precisely. For Taft, the former president and able lawyer who would later become Chief Justice of the United States, Article X was acceptable if need be, but not without certain reservations. For Root, an authority in the field of international law and a conservative, it was a dangerous formula. It would make existing power relations perpetual, he said. Therefore it was necessary to add an amendment setting a time limit, for example of five years.[16]

Article X became the principal subject in the long debate of the president with the senators. As has been said, it was an utterly strange conversation, so absurd because it at one and the same time clarified and covered up the problem. It was as if it were impossible for them really to understand each other, as if, as Wilson said, they were even speaking different tongues. Although he meant his remark more technically, it hit the nail on the head: "You see, we are speaking of two different fields, and therefore the language does not fit."

The language did not fit, and the discussion became very strange. Senator Borah was the first to bring up the notorious Article X. He said it was his impression that the president intended Article X to be primarily a moral obligation, and asked if that was right. Wilson said it was. Borah went on to ask whether it was not also a "legal obligation." No, said the great idealist, it was "an attitude of comradeship and protection among the members of the League, which in its very nature is moral and not legal." The fat was in the fire. Was the article binding if it was not "legal"? Wilson was asked. It was "an absolutely compelling moral obligation," he replied. America was not bound by it, but it was morally bound—a very curious concept, which drew comment from Senator Warren G. Harding of Ohio. Harding was not a man of great vision or leadership; although he would follow Wilson as president in 1921, he was not a success in that high post. But Harding did have the sound understanding of a lawyer, and he wanted to probe Wilson's casuistry. In so doing, he brought the president to even stranger utterances. Harding asked what use were Articles X and XI if they were nothing more than a moral obligation. This was directly contrary to Wilson's noble convictions, and he responded haughtily with a sententious platitude, "Why Senator, it is surprising that that question should be asked. If we undertake an obligation we are bound in the most solemn way to carry it out." But brave Harding was not to be driven from the field by such moral artillery. If it was just a moral obligation, he replied, then any nation could interpret it for itself. No, said Wilson, there is "a national good conscience in such a matter," which was "one of the most serious things that could possibly happen." (Wilson, we see, believed in such beautiful curiosities as this!) He went on to explain the difference between a "moral" and a "legal obligation." A moral obligation, he began, was superior to a legal obligation, "and if I may so so, has a greater binding force"; but in the moral obligation there was an element of individual judgment. A "legal obligation" was automatically binding, but "in every moral obligation there is an element of judgment. In a legal obligation there is no element of judgment." Wilson's use of such private terminology led to a confusing discussion over whether an obligation that went into effect automatically, or one in which the individual made a judgment, was more binding.

Wilson was asked whether the separate guarantee that Wilson and Lloyd George had given to France was a moral obligation. At first he said yes, but had to admit at once that it was a "legal obligation," as was proper in an international treaty, but with "a moral sanction" added. But that applies to every treaty, Borah rejoined.

That was the way it went, all misunderstanding and failure of understanding. Brandegee thought the whole Covenant vague and unclear, and Wilson defended "the plain writing of the treaty." In your opinion, said Brandegee. And Wilson in turn: "No sir, it is a question of being confident what language means, not confident of an opinion." What a characteristic reply for a poet! This was now the whole question. Wilson did not speak the language of the lawyers who faced him. America, he explained, is morally bound to "the general moral judgment of the world," which was self-evident. It was still unthinkable for Wilson to assume that this would be the end of the matter; he could not imagine that a disastrous time would come in which the judgment of the American people would conflict with that of the rest of the world.

It was magnificent, and it was unreal. Wilson's subtle sophistry turned a sharp juridical mind like Root's to fury. Such a difference between "moral and legal obligations," he wrote, "is false, demoralizing and dishonest."[17] This was indeed a strong judgment, but still Wilson's approach to the whole problem remains puzzling. Was it in fact only his inadequate legal learning that played him a nasty trick? How did he come to this ambivalent theory of obligation? Did there lurk behind it some hesitation (which would not be expected of him) to go into international obligations? Some historians have so interpreted it. Walter Lippmann, in a book of 1943 about American foreign policy, thought he had observed this ambivalence in Wilson as well as in Taft; as idealists they wanted to accept great obligations, but at the same time they were too pacifist to add force to them.[18] And Roland Stromberg, in his book on collective security and American foreign policy, makes a similar observation: "What men wanted to do was both to accept and to qualify an international obligation." Wilson and his associates, Stromberg continues, must have known that the League of Nations would not receive any real power, and therefore they preferred to use the word "obligation" for its psychological effect. Stromberg then quotes Lansing's comment: "It may be noble thinking but it is not true thinking."[19] American politics, we may add, is always marked by noble thoughts. Whether it should be called pacifism, as Lippmann does, is the question; it is, it seems to me, more a general American inclination to remain free of commitments, a thoughtless belief that with fine promises one can settle the problems of the world for all time.

Wilson, as we well know, excelled in noble thoughts and preferred not to see the ugly side of things. This probably explains why he became so confused during the hearing (for the senators' visit to the White House became more and more a hearing) when asked if he had known of the existence of secret treaties among the Allies. Borah was the first to press him. When had Wilson first heard that there were "secret treaties"? Was it just after he arrived in Paris? Yes, certainly, declared Wilson, "the whole series of understandings were to me disclosed for the first time then." Johnson returned to the question. Did he know anything of these secret treaties before the conference in Paris? "No sir. I can confidently answer that 'No' in regard to myself." Johnson then asked whether his Fourteen Points were not a reaction to the secret treaties. Not at all, Wilson exclaimed, he had never known about them at all!

We must ask ourselves again, what in God's name inspired the president to such an obvious lie? His medical-psychological biographer Weinstein says that his guilt and anger made him relatively inarticulate.[20] Perhaps he had actually blocked out unpleasant facts. Did he in his first reaction lie honestly and then, when trapped like a schoolboy, become caught in the net of his own denials? It was and remains a curious question. Walter Lippmann, who had once so admired him, was disillusioned and wrote in *The New Republic*: "Only a dunce could have been ignorant of the secret treaties." The correspondence of the Fourteen Points with the treaty was an "almost miraculous coincidence."[21]

Wilson's conversation with the Senate committee obviously was fruitless. Neither the president nor his adversaries persuaded the other side that they were wrong. Meanwhile time ran on and with its characteristic appetite consumed the sympathy that the people had had for Wilson's plans. Fall approached, and the Senate hearings were concluded; they had not produced much besides sad and sordid revelations, culminating on September 12 in William Bullitt's shocking allegations. The dirty laundry of the White House was hung out for all to see.[22]

Wilson felt his peace slipping away from him. He could no longer accept a compromise, he decided; he had done his utter best, he had sought in vain to persuade the stubborn Republicans, individually and together. They were beyond persuading. Already on August 1 one of their leaders, Senator James E. Watson, had warned him that he would be defeated if he did not accept Lodge's program. Wilson replied that in that case he would appeal to the people. It was too late for that, said Watson. Wilson was like a man caught in quicksand; the harder he struggles, the deeper he sinks.[23] But Wilson felt that he still could do something to turn the tide, something grandiose, for he would not do anything mean, political, or practical. In accordance with his principles, he would make an appeal to the people. He decided to make a tour of the country to persuade ordinary people of the supreme importance of his cause. The senators were too small for him; the people, the great, good American people, would understand him and they would want what he wanted.

THIRTY

The heart of this people is pure. The heart of this people is true. This great people loves liberty. It loves justice. It would rather have liberty and justice than wealth and power.

—*Woodrow Wilson*

THE FINAL DEFEAT

ILSON'S PLAN TO AP-peal to the people was a grand gesture, but an empty one. It was meaningless in practice, for there was no political mechanism through which it could operate. This was expressed in short and succinct fashion by a senator who had asked Wilson whether the United States could conclude a separate peace treaty with Germany, to which the president replied solemnly that the people would never permit it. "There is no way," replied the senator, "by which the people can vote on it."[1] This was exactly right. How would it help if the whole American nation stood behind Wilson as one man? It was the Senate, not the people, which voted on ratification of treaties. To be sure, the senators were also dependent upon public opinion, for in the last analysis they too were representatives of the people. But they were elected for six-year terms, so that most of them had no reason to be concerned about an election campaign, and they did not need to be much worried about what the people thought.

But Wilson did not act according to rational judgment, weighing the pros and cons. He had to move, and nothing would hold him back.

He had to work off his emotions; he was unable to remain courteous forever, as he had been on that agonizing day with the senators, smiling at men he held in deep scorn. He had to accuse them, to nail them to the pillory as traitors to America, traitors to mankind. He yearned for the redeeming battle.

It was a dangerous undertaking. At sixty-two he was no longer young, and he had demanded much too much of himself in Paris. He had paid the price with a serious decline in his health. Dr. Grayson warned him sharply, but he seemed to be seeking martyrdom. The young men who were sent overseas did not refuse because they faced danger. To Tumulty, who also expressed objections, he said, "Even though, in my condition, it might mean the giving up of my life, I will gladly make the sacrifice to save the Treaty."[2]

In any event, he was unwilling to spare himself. His itinerary was too heavy. A special train (trains were still the general means of reaching people with political messages; what radio or television would have done for Wilson!) would carry him through the Midwest and the West, through the regions where isolationism and progressivism were both strong, where he had won in almost every state in 1916. The Northeast was too Republican and opposed to him to warrant the effort, the South was too Democratic for him to need to go there. The journey would last three weeks, during which he would make some forty speeches before crowds that varied from a few thousand to some tens of thousands. It was a grueling program that would have felled a stronger man, all the more because he had to spend many nights in the jolting train in order to cover the enormous distances. America is much too large a country, it is a miracle that it holds together, it is in any case much too large to grasp, direct, or convince in a single action, as the twenty-eighth president would find out for himself.

Forty speeches in twenty-two days was far too many. Naturally they were not all polished and inspired pieces, for he barely had time to prepare them. He lived on the edge during this journey; he tried to prepare his speeches quickly and often repeated himself. He endeavored to speak the language of the people, to give the impression that he was a very realistic person: "If you do not want me to be too altruistic, let me be very practical."[3] He explained at length why the peace treaty was so outstanding, "the great humane document of all time."[4] Admittedly, there were some blemishes on it, but at least everything in it would be discussed publicly so that everything bad would be brought to light and eliminated. "Nothing is going to keep the world fit to live in like exposing in public debate every crooked thing that is going on."[5]

The whole course of world history, he told his audiences, had been changed. The ideas of freedom and equality, which had been proclaimed for the first time in the American Revolution of 1776, were now heard all over the world. "This treaty is nothing less than the organization of liberty and mercy for the whole world."[6] In all previous treaties the winners had divided the booty among themselves, but now for the first time the opposite happened: "This is an absolute renunciation of spoils, even with regard to the helpless peoples of the world." Even the poor peoples of Africa now stood, through the mechanism of mandates, under the supervision of the League of Nations, "the greatest humane arrangement that has ever been adopted."[7]

It was no miracle, however, for, as he continued to maintain, the parties in Paris, his partners in Paris, had all been well-intentioned: "The hearts of men like Clemenceau and Lloyd George and Orlando beat with the people of the world as well as with the people of their own countries."[8]

How are we to explain such an improbable conception of the facts? Had he forgotten all the misery, the quarrels, the intrigues, the anger? Was he indulging in this propaganda with full awareness of what he was saying? Was he carried along by the flood of his own exalted language, in which everything that wasn't true became true?

He continued at his task for weeks at a time, day after day. There are historians who shrug off the oratory of this last tour, saying that he was no longer himself, that he spoke "tired words, not Wilson's: they were patched-up street phrases."[9] This is once more the Wilson who was in the grip of illness, the rigid Wilson. The explanation remains hypothethetical. It seems to me rather that on this tour, on the borderline between hope and despair, he became himself more than ever. Every theme, every dream of his life returned in great abundance and variety. Was he rigid? Certainly, in his ultimate, challenging, relentless self-assurance, without doubt or subtlety.

And in his nineteenth-century, Victorian, poetic soul, everything had a finer and fairer look than in the harsh reality around him. He did want to be a realist. He tried to explain the situation in the Shantung peninsula, especially in the cities on the West Coast, where Japanese affairs held much interest. He also wanted to wade into his enemies; he appealed once more to his combative Scottish ancestors, and he fought with dishonest arguments. He dared to suggest that pro-German feelings were to be found among his adversaries, or he described the peace as the best barrier to Bolshevism.

Yet, when he spoke about his eternal visions, when he shamelessly twisted history from his American point of view and confidently provided assurances for the future with his League of Nations, he was at his best. As an American, he said, he could not help but be an idealist, for "America is the only idealistic nation in the world."[10] The heart of this people was pure and true; this great people loved liberty and justice more than riches and power![11] That was why the American people did not look backward, as so many other nations did, but ahead, "its eyes lifted to the distances of history, to the great events which are slowly culminating, in the Providence of God, in the lifting of civilization to new levels and new achievements."[12]

The American army had saved the world. It was an achievement greater than the discovery of the Holy Grail, than the liberation of the Holy Sepulcher, than the struggle "fought under that visionary and wonderful girl, Joan of Arc." It was greater than what the armies had done in the American Revolution or the Civil War. "As their fathers saved the Union, they saved the world."[13] The United States was still the best country in the world. "America is great because she has seen visions that other nations have not seen."[14]

Which Wilson was it that dared to speak in this way? Was it the historian, who like so many other American historians knew little of the history of Europe? Or was it the Romantic poet of Wordsworth's school? He shared Wordsworth's vision of purifying nature that lifts men up morally. This is how he described in San Francisco the train ride that he had made through the magnificent mountains of the Northwest.

> As I came through that wonderful country to the north of us it
> occurred to me one day that the aspiring lines of those wonderful
> mountains must lead people's eyes to be drawn upward and to look
> into the blue serene and see things apart from the confusions of
> affairs, to see the real, pure vision of the interests of humanity.

The true spirit of America rose above "the entangling interests of everyday life."[15] This was the real Wilson speaking, who excelled in the ability to look above and beyond the confusion of ordinary life. His image came from Psalm 121 ("I will lift up mine eyes unto the hills"), but its spirit was more that of the optimism of Wordsworth.

Wilson did more than lift up his eyes. His visions were grandiose and beautiful, but there was also another, deeper impelling force in his oratory during this journey. It was his feeling of guilt over the war, of which we have spoken already. This too was a central theme in his poetic soul. He felt the madness and the pain of the war. The pity he felt was deep and real, and he returned again and again during his journey to the horror of the war and to its costs, not just economically but most of all in human terms. He always brought himself in, for it was he who had sent all those young men into combat. He spoke of this in words that moved his hearers, like himself, to tears. He warned and called for vigilance:

> Everywhere we go, the train, when it stops, is surrounded with little children, and I look to them almost with tears in my eyes, because I feel my mission is to save them. These glad youngsters with flags in their hands—I pray God that they may never have to carry that flag upon the battlefield.[16]

It is remarkable that a man could be so deeply and truly troubled by the madness of the world of human beings, and at the same time could believe so easily, with such optimism, in a simple means to ban these horrors from the world for all time. It is miraculous that a man could be at once so profound and so lighthearted, that his tears could so easily turn into rejoicing. For he had a perfect means, a sanctifying method, which was Article X, complemented by Article XI (in which it was laid down that every member of the League had the right to call attention to any problem that might threaten peace). He repeated a hundred times that Article X was the heart of the Covenant, "cutting at the heart of all wars." It was a "moral obligation." "Is any man, any proud American, afraid that America will resist the duress of duty? I am intensely conscious of the conscience of this great nation."[17] For so magnificent a vision, "reservations" were an insult and unacceptable!

Wilson did really speak a different language than his opponents. But did he speak the language of the American people, whom he wanted to reach? It is difficult to measure the success of his speeches. He could draw huge crowds, which usually met in sports stadiums: there were 15,000 in Kansas City, 25,000 in Tacoma. When he spoke to 30,000 in San Francisco, he had to use a public address system, an innovation that hampered his delivery. For the most part the crowds cheered loudly, and sometimes their excitement could hardly be calmed. From this point of view the trip was a great success, and he received a vast amount of publicity. But some historians have wondered whether the president spoke in too elevated tones. Did he assume too great unselfishness on the part of the people? Shouldn't he have taken his chances with the normal concerns of the people and spoken of the advantages of the peace treaty for the United States? They are probably right, but in the end it did not matter much. The senators in Washington, especially those who represented the very states that he had been most concerned to visit, such bitter antagonists as James Reed of Missouri, the only Democrat among the Irreconcilables, or Borah of Idaho and Johnson of California, were not moved by Wilson's speeches. They continued to assail him and all were reelected.

The trip had been for naught, but the personal consequences were disastrous. His doctor had been right; the exertion had been too great and the journey ended in a tragedy. While traveling, the president constantly complained of severe headaches, but had almost no time for rest. Between speeches, there were meetings, receptions, obligations, and parades, always people, always excitement, always noise. Each day brought news from Washington: the nagging of the Senate Foreign Affairs Committee, with its climax in mid-September in the report of Bullitt's testimony, which deeply shocked Wilson.

Here and there en route there were brief rests, meetings with family members and friends. Mrs. Peck came to see him in Los Angeles. Mrs. Wilson invited her to lunch to show that she had not been affected by the talk about Wilson's earlier relations with the lady, who had become elderly and worn out. It was a sad scene of nostalgia for a past forever gone. When she said goodbye, Mrs. Peck drew upon poetry: "With all my will, but much against my heart, we two now part."[18]

Gradually the torment of his headaches began to overshadow everything else. Edith Wilson and Dr. Grayson warned him to be calmer. He refused. "No, I have caught the imagination of the people. . . . I should fail in my duty if I disappointed them. . . . This will soon be over, and when we get back to Washington, I promise you I will take a holiday."[19]

He went on as before until the bitter end came at last. On September

25, he gave a speech in Pueblo, Colorado. He was exhausted but while he was speaking the old spirit returned, recharged. He spoke with great animation and his listeners were deeply moved. He returned to all his old themes and ended with an apotheosis very characteristic of his myth of a political Last Judgment:

> I believe that men will see the truth, eye to eye and face to face.
> There is one thing that the American people always rise and extend
> their hand to, and that is the truth of justice and of liberty and of
> peace. We have accepted that truth and we are going to be led by it,
> and it is going to lead us, and through us the world, out into pastures
> of quietness and peace such as the world never dreamed of before.[20]

Psalm 23 for the whole world! These were not tired words and scrambled phrases, as the historian Ferrell calls them, they were Wilson himself, through and through, as he really was.

That evening his headache returned worse than ever before. On the train Dr. Grayson thought that it might be good for his patient to take a walk in the cool evening air, and the train was stopped in the middle of the prairie. The little group—Wilson, his wife, and Dr. Grayson—strolled a bit in the twilight. A farmer driving by in a car stopped and offered them a cabbage and apples for their supper. After an hour, they went back aboard the train and resumed the journey.

The crisis came that very night. About half past twelve Edith Wilson heard her husband call to her. She found him sitting on the edge of his bed, his head resting on the arm of a chair: he could not sleep because of the pain, he said, and thought Grayson should be called. He hurried in, concluded that his patient was deathly ill, and that they must return to Washington as fast as possible. All the remaining speeches—some four or five—had to be cancelled. Wilson protested at first that it was his duty to go on, then gave way. "I don't seem to realize it, but I seem to have gone to pieces. The doctor is right. I am not in a condition to go on."[21]

This was the sorrowful ending of his tour. The train returned directly to Washington, arriving two days later. He seemed to be a bit better at first, although the headaches would not go away. But a severe attack followed five days later, on October 2. Early in the morning, when his wife came to him, he complained about the loss of strength in his left hand. She helped him to stand up to go to the bathroom and left him

The Final Defeat

there for a moment to call the doctor on the telephone. When she returned, she found him half-conscious on the floor. Together with Grayson she helped him to bed. Grayson found a complete paralysis of his left side. The president had ceased to function.

A president between death and life was an ambiguous situation not foreseen in the Constitution. It provided (Article II, section 1, par. 6) that in the event of the death or "inability" of the president to govern, the vice-president should succeed him. But the problem was that "inability" was not defined. Who decided when it had occurred, and who would then act and take the helm of government into his hands? The vice-president? If he acted too quickly, he would be accused of usurpation. The cabinet? There was much to be said for their taking the responsibility, since government had to continue. Or, the third possibility, the Congress? All these alternatives were discussed in the ensuing crisis. But no decision was taken, because the situation remained unclear.

In consequence, Mrs. Wilson, a sturdy personality, took command. She was later greatly criticized for her firm action. In her memoirs she justified what she had done. She would have considered her husband's resignation, but the medical specialists whom she consulted advised her not to take from the patient his most important incentive for recovery. His mind remained crystal clear, they said, and he should have a chance. She therefore decided to act, not with the intention of keeping the country's government going, but to save her husband's life.

This explanation of her conduct by Wilson's caring wife has often been questioned. Did competent specialists really think that the gravely ill president would ever be able to govern again?[22] Or did Edith Wilson make the decision herself, not, as some accused her of doing, out of a lust for power, but because she wanted to protect her husband and believed that resignation would be too great a shock for him? There is no certain answer, only that she took upon herself with great assurance the role of regent, like a queen-mother in hereditary monarchies who governs for a king not yet of age to rule in person. Tumulty and Grayson supported her, and they rejected indignantly a sensible proposal by Lansing, who as secretary of state was the senior member of the cabinet, to allow the vice-president to govern temporarily.

Thus, it has been said, a woman became in effect president of the United States. This meant that the national government almost came to a halt. For three months the president remained in almost complete isolation, seeing no one but his wife and his doctors and nurses. He was very ill, for a time unable even to stand or walk; his sight was seriously impaired and he had to have papers read to him. He could do very little work, because he could concentrate for no more than five minutes. His tendency to overlook subtleties was heightened, and he judged every matter by absolute standards. He experienced everything with intense emotionality, and he burst into tears on the most trifling occasions.

Edith Wilson therefore governed the country. All important state documents first went through her hands and she consulted with Grayson to decide whether the president was in a condition to learn about them without excessive reaction.

> I, myself, never made a single decision regarding the disposition of public affairs. The only decision that was mine was what was important and what was not, and the *very* important decision of when to present matters to my husband.[23]

It is virtually certain that she did what Wilson himself wanted. His indomitable will remained active. From the beginning he had believed that he would get back on his feet; he would not allow the control of affairs to be taken from his hands. In the very first week after his return, he heard with annoyance the news that Lansing had called a meeting of the cabinet. Yet it had been an entirely reasonable decision, for the members had to know what their situation was. They asked Grayson and Tumulty for more information about Wilson's illness, and the doctor told them that Wilson's mind was sound, but that he had had a "nervous breakdown from indigestion and a depleted system." He could not say more than that, he added, but could only ask on behalf of the president by what authority they had met when he was in Washington and had not called them into session.[24]

Wilson held firm. He had been struck down but stood upon his dignity and remained inflexible. He had no plans to yield to the Senate on the peace treaty, although the hour of truth was approaching fast. While Wilson had been traveling through the West, Lodge had seen to it that he got a sufficient number of senators behind him. The hearings had been concluded in the middle of September. The formal debate on the floor then began and lasted for weeks. The august members made it

The Final Defeat

plain that the Senate was stubborn in its intention to maintain its important role. All amendments failed because of the opposition of a coalition
of Democrats and "mild reservationists." The fact of the matter was that
there was still a clear majority for an internationally oriented course.
Events might well have gone otherwise if Wilson had not gone off to
storm castles in the sky, if he had not dreamed of a "moral force" but had
remained in Washington to form a coalition with moderate Republicans
by compromise. True, there would not have been even then a two-thirds
majority, but there would have been a chance of a breakthrough for acceptance. Now there was none, for he drove the moderates into the arms
of the "strong reservationists" around Lodge, who welcomed them with
open arms.

It is true, we must add, that he was willing to make some small
concessions behind the scenes, halfheartedly and in secret. He had prepared several reservations on his own, and had typed them out before he
left on his tour. He gave them to his faithful helper, Senator Hitchcock,
with orders not to reveal their origin no matter what happened, and to
introduce them only if strictly necessary. They concerned the issues already raised, the Monroe Doctrine, the right of withdrawal, control of
domestic affairs, and the right of Congress to declare war. Hitchcock
changed them a little, but they were still doomed to failure.

At the beginning of November, Lodge presented his reservations in
final form. They were fourteen in number, which some saw as a sly thrust
at Wilson's Fourteen Points and proof of the senator's hostility. Lodge
became more truculent. His proposals were presented for a vote one by
one, and easily obtained a majority. The mild reservationists voted for
them; they did not see them as impairing the treaty, as Wilson asserted.

In hindsight, this appears to have been true. The reservations were
for the most part merely somewhat sharpened repetitions of the same
matters that had been discussed all along: the right of withdrawal, the
Monroe Doctrine, freedom to reject mandates, and, most important, the
second reservation, directed against Article X; it provided that the United
States would not be obligated to give support to other countries "unless
Congress should so provide." In brief, not much that was new, but expressed in a somewhat critical tone. Wilson saw the reservations as a betrayal of those who had fallen in the war, and would not hear of their
acceptance.

The question remains: Were the differences really large? A comparison of Lodge's reservation concerning Article X and Hitchcock's is instructive. Lodge wrote:

> The United States assumes no obligation to preserve the territorial integrity or political independence of any other country, unless in any particular case the Congress, which under the Constitution, has the sole power to declare war or authorize the employment of the military or naval forces of the United States, shall by act or joint resolution so provide.

Hitchcock (which means Wilson) wrote:

> It [the government of the United States] understands that the advice of the Council of the League with regard to the employment of armed force contemplated in Article TEN of the Covenant is to be regarded only as advice and leaves each member State free to exercise its own judgment as to whether it is wise or practicable to act upon that advice or not.

In both cases there is a reservation, the final freedom of action. In the first case it is formulated more broadly, more precisely, and more juridically, a legal obligation with an explicit constitutional limitation. In the second case, there is a different kind of freedom of action, a moral obligation with the limitation that if the Council's advice were not wise—which for Wilson meant not "moral"—the United States could refrain from acting upon it. A difference, to be sure, but not one on which the whole affair had to founder. If only there had been just one man of stature in that whole welter of politicians intent on having their own way, a man wise, detached, and authoritative enough to be able to mediate and to dispel the confusion! There was not one, however. Not on the Republican side, where Taft, the sagacious former president, was still too easygoing to come out against party fanatics like Lodge, and even the sharp-witted former cabinet member Elihu Root was himself too much a party man. Not on the Democratic side, where Wilson was strong enough to maintain party discipline with an iron hand. Hitchcock, the Democratic leader in the Senate, was too much a good-natured yes-man to resist him, although himself ready for compromise. He told Stephen Bonsal that he was personally in favor of a ratification of the treaty "in almost any form," but "those in control at the White House prevent me from receiving instructions direct." He only heard that "the President will not budge an inch. His honor is at stake. He feels he will be dishonored if he failed to live up to the pledges he made to his fellow delegates at Paris."[25]

Hitchcock found great difficulty in getting to see his chief, but managed two brief meetings before the final vote in the Senate. He was shocked when he saw Wilson. The once self-assured and elegant gentleman had become an ailing old man with a white beard lying in bed, but still clearheaded and as stubborn as ever. When Hitchcock told him that without the reservations, the treaty would not receive even a simple majority, not to mention the necessary two-thirds, he groaned, "Is it possible? Is it possible?" Hitchcock had been instructed by Mrs. Wilson not to get into an argument, lest her husband become too excited. But at one moment Hitchcock remarked, "Mr. President, it might be wise to compromise with Lodge on this point." "Let Lodge compromise," was the terse reply. Hitchcock of course agreed, "he must compromise also, but we might as well hold out the olive branch." And again the reply like a shot from a gun: "Let Lodge hold out the olive branch."[26]

No conciliation seemed possible. A year earlier there had seemed a chance that Colonel House might manage to come between Wilson and Lodge. He had remained in France over the summer and returned to the United States in October. He was in bad health, suffering from gallstones. But he felt himself called upon to seek a breakthrough in the dreary stalemate that had arisen and thought he was the man to do the job. He sent young Stephen Bonsal, who had worked for Wilson in Paris as a translator but also knew Lodge well, to the senator from Massachusetts to see if there was any way out of the impasse. Lodge received Bonsal in friendly fashion and seemed inclined to give way to some extent. They went through the treaty together, Bonsal tells us in his memoirs, and Lodge made somewhat conciliatory changes here and there in the text. Bonsal brought these to House, who in his usual way became delighted and sent the document with an accompanying letter to the president. But no reply came. It is probable that Mrs. Wilson held back the materials. She had never liked House and thought reminding her husband of him would be too heavy an emotional burden.[27]

No one was left who could mediate between the two embattled leaders. The ship of state, en route to its destination of a treaty formally ending the war, seemed to be steering relentlessly toward the rocks. Men who had worked with Wilson in Paris, such as Herbert Hoover, Bernard Baruch, and Thomas Lamont, wrote urgent letters to him but received no replies. Even Edith Wilson, according to her memoirs, finally pleaded with her husband in desperation, "For my sake, won't you accept these reservations and get this awful thing settled?" His reaction was melodramatic. "He turned his head on the pillow and stretching out his hand to take mine answered in a voice I shall never forget: Little girl, don't you desert me; that I cannot stand." At stake was the country's honor, he said, and his eyes lit up. It is a thousand times better to go down fighting "than to dip your colours to dishonourable compromise." Edith Wilson felt herself trapped. Suddenly she saw everything clearly, she told Hitchcock, who very soon afterwards received a letter from the president.[28]

On November 19 the ax was ready to fall, as the Senate moved to vote on ratification. Hitchcock read Wilson's letter with its final advice: Do not vote for the treaty with the Lodge reservations, which meant its nullification. The debate went on for another whole day, and the vote on the first reading came after midday. First there was a ballot on the treaty with Lodge's reservations. It was rejected by a vote of thirty-nine for and fifty-five against; almost all the Democrats voted in the negative, and were joined by the Irreconcilables, who wanted no treaty whatsoever. Then came a vote on the treaty as Wilson wanted it, without any amendments. The Democrats of course voted for it, but the Irreconcilables moved over to the opposite side to join the other Republicans. The result was a vote of thirty-eight for and fifty-three against. In other words, as Senator Hitchcock had foreseen, there was no majority for the treaty in any form, neither two-thirds nor even an ordinary majority.

The end had come, the dismal end. The United States would not sign the peace treaty and it would not become a member of the League of Nations. For a brief tumultuous moment the country had been joined to the strange outer world; now it turned away from it, not because that is what it wanted to do but because it did not know what it wanted to do. There was no real majority for a return to isolation, only impotence and then bewilderment. Of course, there were shortsighted people on either side who thought they had won or lost and correspondingly rejoiced or lamented. It was, exclaimed Borah, "the second winning of the independence of America, the greatest victory since Appomatox." A Democratic newspaper called it "the greatest tragedy since the crucifixion of the Saviour of Mankind."[29] America is the land of boundless superlatives.

Senator Brandegee concluded with deep satisfaction a conversation with Lodge: "We can always depend on Mr. Wilson. He has never failed us. He has used all his powers to defeat the peace Treaty, because we would not want to ratify it in just the form which he desired," and Lodge replied, "That is quite true. Without his efforts the Treaty would have been accepted by the Senate today."[30]

The rejection of the treaty was a powerful shock, an incredible fact, a surprise that many could not accept. At once floods of protests began, desperate attempts to do something even at the eleventh hour, indeed even after twelve o'clock. Letters, telegrams, campaigns, demonstrations, everything. In Europe there was confusion and perplexity; the Allies were taken utterly aback by the incomprehensible political game of the Americans.

The English were so bewildered that they decided to send a special ambassador to the United States, one of their most important statesmen, former Foreign Secretary Sir Edward Grey, who had been elevated to the peerage as Lord Grey of Fallodon. During Grey's contacts with House before American entry into the war, his sagacity and moderation and the great prestige he held in America as well as in his own country had been evident. No publicity was given to his mission, although he actually traveled with special instructions; its cover was a trip to the United States for an operation on his eyes. He arrived in New York at the end of September and went to Washington where he met most of the political leaders, including Lodge. He was not received by Wilson, however. Just why has never been made fully clear. It may have been that Wilson feared any mediation; it may also have been that he was angry because Grey had met Lodge and, according to what Houston heard, had spoken in very friendly terms about Lodge's actions in the Senate.[31] It may have been that he was annoyed that Grey, by a very understandable error, attempted to approach him through House. Or was Mrs. Wilson behind the decision, fearing her husband would become overwrought? Or was it a personal question for her, the presence in Grey's party of one Major Stuart, who she heard had made improper jests about her marriage?[32] The White House had become a fortress and Grey could only wait in diplomatic patience, meanwhile writing long letters home to defend his conduct against the new foreign secretary, Lord Curzon, who, like Lloyd George, was very suspicious of the reservations and more generally of American policy, which was in British eyes inherently unreliable.[33]

After three months Grey had had enough and returned home without having accomplished anything. At the end of January 1920 he published a long letter in the *Times* of London, analyzing the situation in the United States in fundamental but prudent terms. He called attention to the revival of the isolationist tradition and perceived the conflict between the executive and the legislative powers. Most striking, however, was his assertion that the reservations mattered little; they did not prevent the countries of Europe from working together, he concluded, and did not essentially weaken the League of Nations.

This meant that the Americans heard from an outsider that Wilson's assertion that the amendments constituted a nullification of the League of Nations was not true. Grey's letter had an enormous impact in the United States. Newspapers made a big to-do over it and the debate revived. Why couldn't the treaty still be ratified? it was asked. What Grey had done, in effect, was to go over the head of the American government to the American people. Wilson was receiving a dose of the same medicine he had been giving to others, and, as was to be expected, the hermit in the White House was indignant and insulted. He issued a statement that Grey had acted without consulting him, which was true enough but not the whole truth, which was too painful for Wilson to admit. He even dictated an angry letter to his wife, saying that Grey had very improperly attempted to influence the Senate and the president, in which case he should be recalled. But Grey had already gone home, and fortunately there was still enough good sense in the White House not to publish the letter. In any case the British were very disillusioned. "America had been offered the leadership of the world," wrote Lloyd George maliciously, "but the Senate had tossed the Sceptre into the sea."[34]

Wilson was ill and inaccessible. The question whether he was really still able to govern came up in the Senate, which decided to find out what the situation really was. Whatever the pretext, it would be a painful task. Two senators, Hitchcock for the Democrats and Albert B. Fall of New Mexico for the Republicans, were sent to the White House ostensibly to discuss the critical situation in Mexico, where an American consul had been kidnapped, but actually to see how much the president was in command of his mental powers (*compos mentis*, in the language of lawyers). Hitchcock and Fall went on December 5 to the White House and found Wilson in bed, a pale figure with a white beard, but fully alert and quick-witted. When Fall sanctimoniously said that everyone had been praying for him, Wilson replied, "Which way, Senator?"[35]

Wilson knew very well what he did not want, but it was not clear even to him just what he did want. Tossing about in his bed, he came up with a most improbable plan: Let all the senators who had voted against the treaty resign and run for reelection with the issue the League of Nations. If they were reelected, the president and vice-president would resign instead, and a new Republican secretary of state would become president. This notion accorded with the familiar Wilson pattern of an appeal to the people, but it was also the wildest fantasy. Lodge, Borah, and the other unbending opponents of the treaty disdained the proposal.

As always, Wilson put his trust in the people. In a letter that he addressed to his own party, he gave voice to this reliance in a different way. At the beginning of January the traditional party banquet in honor of Andrew Jackson was held in Washington. Wilson naturally was unable to come, but he sent his supporters a clear message in a letter that was read by the chairman, Homer Cummings. America had to give leadership in the future without compromises or objections. If there was uncertainty about what the American people wanted, it was easy to ask them; in that case the coming presidential election in November 1920 would take the form of "a great and solemn referendum."

The letter had a strong impact upon the assembled diners, but it also aroused immediate resistance, which came in fact from Wilson's old rival and collaborator, William Jennings Bryan, who still had a great deal of influence in the Democratic party. Bryan protested that a presidential election should not be a referendum; it would be more democratic to solve the question of the treaty by a compromise. Bryan's remarks created an instant tumult. Disunity in the party resulted. It was also quite surprising that Wilson, who had always insisted upon haste, should now be satisfied to delay a decision until November.

There was wide agreement with Bryan that a political compromise was necessary. A way had to be found out of the situation. A matter of such importance, wrote Taft in great anger, should not be wrecked upon the enmity of two individuals, who, wrote Taft in great anger, "exalt their personal prestige and the saving of their ugly faces above the welfare of the country and the world." The Senate should come to its senses.[36]

In January it appeared that a compromise would be reached. A group of Republican and Democratic senators put their heads together to find a solution; even Lodge joined them. They faced strong opposition, however. Wilson sent a letter to the Democrats in the Senate insisting that no concession be made, and on the other side Borah pressed Lodge, even threatening a break with the Republican party. The result was that the compromise effort collapsed.

Wilson, by making the achievement of his own ideals impossible, made himself impossible as well. He now lacked everything necessary for success in politics: prudence, flexibility, and tact. He was increasingly isolated. He not only wanted to take the helm of state into his own hands again, but even more to get his revenge upon those who had lost his favor. In February it was Lansing against whom he took action. Although he knew the answer, he wrote the secretary of state to ask whether it was true that during the president's illness he had repeatedly convened meetings of the cabinet. Lansing replied that he had indeed done so, considering them necessary and expedient. If Wilson did not agree with what he had done, he would submit his resignation. All Wilson's rancor accumulated over the years broke through in a highly offensive letter accepting Lansing's offer. He named one Bainbridge Colby, a New York lawyer who was a very faithful supporter but had no experience whatsoever in foreign affairs, as the new secretary of state.

Lansing's dismissal had a very bad press. The letters, made public on Wilson's instructions, displayed the president's coldest side. Lansing was seen as a martyr whose sense of duty and conciliatory attitude had made him the victim of Wilson's arrogance and pettiness. Public opinion turned more and more against the president, and protests streamed in.

Wilson did not seem to care. Entrenched within the White House, he was impregnable in his self-righteousness and imprisoned within his own certainties. That is at least how it appears, for we actually know very little about Wilson at this stage; he ceased to have contact with the world outside through visitors or correspondence. Occasionally an edict would issue from the White House, that was all.

At the end of February he sent out word that he would not sign the treaty if it was adopted with the reservations. Hitchcock asked several moderate senators to speak to him about a compromise, but to no avail; Wilson would not even receive them. In the middle of March, when the treaty was about to be voted upon after a second reading, he wrote another letter to Hitchcock reminding his fellow Democrats of their duty. Again

Article X was the key question. Without turning a hair, he claimed that the article meant that the great powers were renouncing their old pretensions of political conquest and territorial aggrandizement. Everything depended now upon a choice between democracy and imperialism. The reservation about Article X meant preserving the old order. Did anyone really want that? he asked.[37]

Wilson's mind had become rigid to the point of absurdity; he lost all feeling for nuance or reality. It became impossible for him to accept any compromise. The only question that remained, therefore, was whether even his faithful supporters in the Democratic party, beginning to see what was happening to their leader, would accept any longer the strict discipline he imposed upon them.

On March 19, ratification of the treaty came up for the vote on second reading. This time several Democrats went over to the other side and voted for the treaty with the Lodge reservations, the only question before them. Better half a loaf than none at all, they no doubt thought. The roll call became tense as Democratic senators voted in favor when their names were called. But there were not enough of them to carry the day. It was principally the senators from the Southern states who remained loyal to Wilson and succeeded, in combination with the Irreconcilables, in defeating the treaty. This time there was a majority for it, forty-nine to thirty-five, but still not the required two-thirds. The fanatics of right and left, swept along by Wilson and Borah in brotherly misguidance, remained true to their dreams of purity: all or nothing! It was nothing. For the second time, nothing.

Wilson was defeated but not broken. Deeply convinced of the sacredness of his cause, he saw himself as a martyr with a clear conscience. On the eve of that second and final vote, he discussed what was coming with Grayson. Doctor, he said, "the devil is a busy man." Then he read to him a passage from the Bible, 2 Corinthians 4:8–9: "We are troubled on every side, yet not distressed; we are perplexed, but not in despair; persecuted, but not forsaken; cast down, but not destroyed."[38]

THIRTY-ONE

When thou passest through the waters, I will be with
thee: and through the rivers, they shall not overflow thee:
when thou walkest through the fire, thou shall not be
burned; neither shall the flame kindle upon thee.
—*Isaiah 43:2*

THE END

FAITH IS THE SUB-
stance of things hoped for and
the evidence of things not
seen—that is how the writer of the Epistle
to the Hebrews begins his famous eleventh
chapter, which sings of the transcendent
greatness of the proofs of faith in every age.
Does Wilson belong in this array of proofs? Should we say something
like this, that, through faith, Woodrow Wilson scorned the realities of this
world as naught, that, seeing what the eyes cannot see, he continued to
look ahead to a future of peace and righteousness? Or should we say that
in the case of a statesman such greatness of soul comes to look like re-
fractory stubbornness and lack of realism?

The answer in both cases is "no." We cannot explore here the eternally unanswerable question of how faith and reality touch and even affect each other. We can only go into the fact that Wilson continued to
believe, hoping when hope was gone, when every chance for the realization of his ideals had been wrecked.

It was an incredible spectacle, grandiose and absurd at the same
time, like faith itself. We seldom meet it in a statesman. He stood firm,

literally and especially spiritually. This is a strange metaphor for a man who lay flat on his back in bed and for a time could not stand at all and then when he got back on his feet could only shuffle. He was sick almost to death. Yet he refused to resign but remained at his post in the White House.

It is not that he never doubted his decision. In the spring of 1920, when he had lost out on every issue and the Senate had smashed his dream once and for all, he did think of stepping down. With characteristic self-knowledge he told Grayson:

> My personal pride must not be allowed to stand in the way of my
> duty to the country. If I am only half efficient I shall turn the office
> over to the Vice-President. If it is going to take much time for me to
> recover my health and strength, the country cannot afford to wait
> for me.

The good doctor encouraged him to stay and suggested he hold a trial meeting of the cabinet to see what he could do. Wilson reluctantly accepted, complaining that he had met nothing but discouragement from those who agreed with him in principle and therefore ought to be supporting him and working with him.[1]

On April 13 the cabinet met with the president. It was a short and painful session. Faithful David Houston, who had become secretary of the treasury, described in his memoirs how badly the great man had declined:

> The President looked old, worn, and haggard. It was enough to make
> me weep to look at him. One of his arms was useless. In repose his
> face looked very much as usual, but, when he tried to speak, there
> were marked evidences of his trouble. His jaw tended to drop on one
> side, or seemed to do so. His voice was very weak and strained.

But he held himself upright and began the meeting as he usually did with a joke. But he could not go on much longer, and his attention wandered from the business at hand. Dr. Grayson kept looking in to see how things were going. The spectacle continued for not quite an hour, and then Mrs. Wilson came in and at her suggestion the meeting was ended.[2]

Wilson took only one initiative. He presented to the Senate on May 24 a proposal that the United States accept a mandate over Armenia from the League of Nations. It had no chance of adoption and was rejected by a vote of fifty-two to twenty-three. Why did Wilson even present it? Perhaps he wanted to play the part of a martyr. Perhaps he wished to work upon the conscience of the country.

Much more surprising than this utterly hopeless initiative was his atttitude toward the presidential elections to be held in November. Despite everything, he hoped for a Democratic victory. Indeed, he appears even to have dreamed of becoming a candidate again for a third term! What brought that idea into his sick brain? Was it that Dr. Grayson did not have the courage to tell him that he was incurably ill? The doctor shrank from speaking the truth, but did his utter best to prevent this disaster of Wilson's nomination. He asked Senator Carter Glass, a very loyal supporter of Wilson's who was going to the Democratic convention in San Francisco, to make sure it didn't happen. An election campaign would kill Wilson, he said.

Wilson himself bubbled with confidence. He did not present his candidacy for the nomination officially, but he believed that there was no other obvious good candidate. He hoped that the convention would deadlock and at the last moment call upon him. He would accept, of course.[3] He went so far as to invite a newspaperman to the White House for an interview. The journalist, a gullible chap, reported that the president was again in tip-top condition. He made strong decisions and wrote his signature with a firm hand, although he limped a little—but nowhere near as much as General Wood, one of those running for the Republican nomination! The reporter took a photograph showing the president at his best, from his good right side, behind his desk, pen in hand and ready to sign documents being placed before him by Mrs. Wilson. The symbolism may have been intentional.

Wilson sent his brand-new secretary of state, Bainbridge Colby, who no longer had much to do abroad, to the convention to nominate him if the opportunity arose. On his arrival Colby, self-deluded, telegraphed Wilson that there was "unanimity and fervor of feeling for you."[4]

The most extraordinary part of this whole amazing business was that Edith Wilson, who guarded her husband as faithfully as a watchdog, allowed him to go as far as he did. She must have realized how disastrous his plans would be for him. Yet, when Tumulty asked her desperately to restrain Colby, she refused sharply. Was she too hoping for the impossible? Surprisingly, she says nothing about the whole affair in her memoirs.

The End

In any event the matter was brought to a halt in San Francisco. The responsible Democratic leaders knew very well how things actually stood. They warned Colby off and went ahead with the nominations. After considerable discussion they turned down the two leading candidates, both members of Wilson's cabinet, William McAdoo, whom the president had opposed although he was his son-in-law, and A. Mitchell Palmer, notorious as the organizer of the "red scare" against radicals and pacifists. Instead they gave the nomination for the presidency to James M. Cox, the governor of Ohio and a virtual unknown nationally; his running mate was Franklin Delano Roosevelt, a young politician from New York State.

According to an eyewitness, when Wilson heard the news, he burst out in a flood of curses and invectives.[5] It was a rare loss of self-control, and soon over. His illness and his heightened emotionality were probably at fault.

The Republicans for their part smelled victory in the air. Lodge, the man who had kept his party tightly united, gave the keynote speech to the Republican convention. He called upon the delegates to settle accounts with Wilson. "Mr. Wilson and his dynasty, his heirs and assigns, or anybody that is his, anybody who with bent knees served his purposes, must be driven from control."[6]

He was appealing to the popular mood. The American people had had their fill of the idealism, the noble exaltation, and the sacrifices that Wilson had urged upon them and exacted from them. In the words of Senator Warren G. Harding, the little man who became the Republican candidate, they wanted to go "back to normalcy." Harding was the very model of mediocrity. He was a back-slapping common politician, shrewd enough in ordinary matters but utterly without vision, strength, or power of will. He was called a "wooden Indian," as lifeless as the painted statues in front of American cigar stores. "Back to normalcy" meant that there would be no more fuss over the ideals of America, no involvement in an international political order, no membership in a hazily defined League of Nations (although a number of leading Republicans, including Root, Hughes, Hoover, and Stimson, forecast that he would bring the United States into the League with a "modified" membership—which never happened).

The campaign was fought hard. Cox and Roosevelt presented themselves as Wilson's spiritual heirs. They went to the White House to get his blessing and promised him that they would do battle for the League of Nations. He welcomed them happily, still seeing in the coming elections a great referendum on his ideals. He was confident that his party would win, for he knew the American people and they would stand behind him. On Election Day, November 2, 1920, he met with the cabinet and told them, "The American people will not turn Cox down. A great moral issue is involved."[7]

But the American people had very different things on their mind. The outcome was not at all a confirmation of Wilson's dreams but the greatest defeat the Democrats had ever suffered. Harding won in a landslide, receiving sixteen million votes against Cox's nine million. Only the Southern states, which had been traditionally Democratic since the Civil War, remained loyal to the party; the rest of the country went for Harding, the ordinary man whom nobody knew much about because there wasn't much to know. He became one of the least prepossessing of American presidents, notorious for the corruption and scandals in his government.

Wilson had badly misread the mood of the American people. He thought that he and he alone understood and represented them, but they turned their backs on him. He was living in a political vacuum. Reality had escaped him. The great, noble nation envisioned as serving mankind flung itself into the chaotic orgy of pleasures called the Roaring Twenties.

This indictment may be a little too strong, however. Although Harding became a president who was Wilson's opposite in every respect, there were some Republicans who sought on an individual basis to improve matters on the world scene. Charles Evans Hughes, whom Wilson had defeated in a nip-and-tuck battle for the presidency in 1916 and who became secretary of state under Harding organized a conference in 1922 to bring some order into international relations in the Pacific. His successor under Coolidge, Frank B. Kellogg, picked up some threads of Wilson's dreams in Europe and concluded a pact with Aristide Briand, the French foreign minister, providing for outlawing war. These were at least attempts to do something, although they were too legalistic, too unrelated to hard reality, and lacked the necessary binding force.

In December 1920, not long before Wilson's term of office ended, he was given the consolation of the Nobel Peace Prize. It was balm for his wounds. Yet he resented the simultaneous award of the prize for 1919 to Léon Bourgeois, the French activist on behalf of the League of Nations, whom Wilson had scorned in Paris as an empty prattler. In any

The End

event, Wilson was in no condition to go to Oslo, and the prize was accepted on his behalf by the American ambassador.

On March 4, 1921, Wilson's second term of office ended. In accordance with tradition, he rode with his successor from the White House to the Capitol, where he signed a few last bills into law. He did not remain for Harding's inaugural address; there were too many steps for him to climb, and he made his way out almost unnoticed. He was driven to the new home his wife had chosen, a stately mansion on S Street in a fashionable quarter in northwest Washington. The eight long years of great successes and greater defeats now lay behind him.

II

He had almost three years still to go, three quiet years after all the pomp and circumstance of the presidency. There was not much he could do any more. He did what he could, even opening a law practice in partnership with his friend Colby. Hard work was beyond him, however, and it existed more in name than in reality. It was just another idle dream. He tried to keep up too with the affairs of the Democratic party, maintaining fairly close contact with its new chairman, Cordell Hull.[8] But he no longer exerted any real influence. His health slowly declined; he had to follow a prudent regimen, avoiding exertions, worries, and emotional strain. He would often break into tears without any reason.

Life became pleasantly indolent, always under the strict eye of his watchful wife. His principal relaxation was to go for a ride every day in the car through the beautiful environs, for S Street was still on the edge of the city. There was also reading, which now meant being read to, not reading to others as he used to do. His fare was light, Dickens and detective stories. On Saturday nights he went very regularly to a nearby vaudeville theater to see the show. He had a regular seat in the back of the orchestra, which he could reach easily.

Now and then there were visitors, old friends and even onetime allies from Europe. Clemenceau, eighty-one years old but still hale and hearty, came in 1922, and Lloyd George in 1923. They exchanged friendly reminiscences, forgetting the painful parts, as old men do.

Wilson was caught up in the tragedy of Franklin Roosevelt, who had served him as under secretary of navy. Roosevelt, aged only thirty-nine, came down with polio in August 1921, and their shared health problems brought him and Wilson closer together. When Wilson heard that Roosevelt was recovering, he wrote to express his delight. He even joked that he was envious and wondered which of them would be the first to play another round of golf.[9] He was spared the painful knowledge that Roosevelt would be crippled for the rest of his life, or the healing knowledge that he would overcome his handicap to become president.

Unpleasantness of another kind crept in too. Another loyal friend, Joe Tumulty, who had been his secretary since the days of the governorship in New Jersey, was suddenly dismissed. Mrs. Wilson was behind the blow. Her sudden rise in life had gone to her head, and she looked haughtily down on Bryan, Lansing, and House, always with a pose of great indignation and disdain for their supposed lack of good manners. Now came Tumulty's turn. The specific issue was the merest trifle: Tumulty declared that Wilson had given a message to send to a Democratic meeting in New York, and Wilson denied he had done so. Edith Wilson called him a "cheap political hack" who had climbed above his station. In her memoirs she devoted long, unpleasant pages to proving her case against him. Yet Tumulty had served his president long and faithfully, and in this same year he published an admiring book about his boss, *Woodrow Wilson As I Know Him*.[10]

Publishers plied Wilson with invitations to resume writing. One offered $150,000 for a history of the peace conference, and another proposed a biography of Jesus Christ! He turned them all down. Even a long-planned book on the philosophy of government got no further than a heartfelt dedication to Edith Bolling Wilson, who had taught him "the full meaning of life," because she was so honest and wise and wholly herself.[11]

In 1923 he finally managed to produce an article. It took great effort, for, even though it ran only a few pages, he had to dictate it by bits and pieces. Its theme was a large one, "The Road Away from Revolution." The revolution in the title was the Russian, and it was, he said, a danger that could not be met by pure capitalism but only by a conversion in "the spirit of Christ." The piece lacked any trace of Wilson's once splendid prose style. It was eventually placed in *The Atlantic Monthly*, and he was paid $200 for it.

Wilson did address himself to the people again, but not in writing. A friend, believing that Wilson might enjoy the experience of speaking over the new medium of radio, persuaded him to give a radio talk on the eve of Armistice Day, November 11, 1923. The equipment was brought into his house. He refused to sit before the microphone, however; he had to speak on his feet. The effort was hard for him and he had to be very brief. He spoke of the great sacrifices of the people and of "the shameful fact" that America had withdrawn "into a sulken and selfish isolation, which is deeply ignoble because manifestly cowardly and dishonorable." Only by turning its back on self-interest could America restore its true tradition.[12]

He was not particularly pleased with this experiment of oratory by machine, but it nonetheless made an impression on his still loyal followers. The next day, thousands streamed to S Street to pay tribute to him. It was noon on Sunday and Wilson came to the door to greet them. Senator Glass gave a brief speech about the hope that does not die. Wilson replied equally briefly, but his emotions made the words stick in his throat. A band then played an English hymn, "How Firm a Foundation," that had become popular in America. Based on Isaiah 43, it spoke of God's solace to man in pain:

> When through the deep waters I call thee to go,
> The rivers of woe shall not thee overflow.
> For I will be with thee, thy troubles to bless,
> And sanctify to thee thy deepest distress.

It was probably these familiar words that made Wilson decide to stop the band and say something more. Now, as if recalled to life and full strength, he spoke clearly, firmly, without tears, and with the deepest self-assurance:

> Just one word more. I cannot refrain from saying it. I am not one of those that have the least anxiety about the triumph of the principles I have stood for. I have seen fools resist Providence before, and I have seen their destruction, as will come upon these again, utter destruction and contempt. That we shall prevail is as sure as that God reigns. Thank you.[13]

It was the last speech made by a man who had learned nothing from life but was as proud and vindictive and true to his complete faith as he had ever been. He was a grand figure, a prophet with the fire of Isaiah. Not long afterwards, in January—he was by then very weak and had only fourteen days to live—he had a visit from Raymond Fosdick, a young diplomat whom he had designated to be the U.S. representative in the Council of the League of Nations. Weak as he was, he confessed again to his visitor his deep belief in the people. Critics might call the League an overidealistic conception, but, he said, "The world is run by its ideals." The tears ran down his cheeks, and Fosdick was deeply moved. He described the conversation in an article not long afterwards in the *New York World*. It ended:

> My last impression of him was of a grim, determined jaw, a tear-stained face, and a faint voice whispering "God bless you." With his white hair, and gray, lined face he seemed like the reincarnation of Isayah [sic] crying to his country: "Awake, Awake, Oh Zion. Put on thy beautiful garments, Oh Jerusalem. Oh Jerusalem, Thou that stonest the prophets!"[14]

Isaiah, who had been purified by fire! The dying man drew from his prophetic certitude a reconciliation with his tragic fate. To him it had not really been tragic. To another visitor, an old friend from student days, he explained that it was better that the American people develop slowly toward the right decision. He told his oldest daughter that what had happened had really been for the best: if America had joined the League, it would have been a personal triumph for him, but now the people would first have to come to its own understanding. "Perhaps God knew better than I did after all."[15]

At the end of January his condition became very bad. Dr. Grayson, who had just left for a vacation in the South, rushed back to Washington to find his patient near death. Wilson lived for several more days, and met death calmly. When several medical specialists came to his bedside, he joked. "Be careful, too many cooks spoil the broth." Then, a few moments later, peacefully, "I am ready."

He died on Sunday morning, February 3, 1924, a cold, sunny day. In the distance the bells were ringing, and in the street friends and admirers had crowded in, alarmed by the bleak bulletins of the last few days. They kneeled in the street to pray for him. At last Grayson came out with the final bulletin: "Mr. Wilson died at eleven-fifteen this morning. His heart action became feebler and feebler and the heart muscle was so fatigued that it refused to act any longer. The end came peacefully."[16]

A few days later he was buried in the huge, almost completed National Cathedral on the north side of Washington. It was a great solemn ceremony in the presence of all the notables, led by President Calvin Coolidge (Harding had died of a heart attack in 1923). Absent was only Senator Henry Cabot Lodge. He had been selected to be a member of the official delegation from Congress, but had received at once a letter from Edith Wilson. She coolly told him that his presence would be painful for himself and unwelcome for her. He replied courteously that he would do as she wished and not appear.[17] Not all things are reconciled in death.

THIRTY-TWO

For we are saved by hope: but hope that is seen is not hope: for what a man seeth, why doth he yet hope for?
—*Paul to the Romans, 8:24*

EPILOGUE

IS IT HISTORY'S PURPOSE, INdeed its task, to pass judgment? The tale is told. Do we need an epilogue to sum it up? If we say that the hero of this tale failed, are we drawing a moral conclusion? We must say that Woodrow Wilson failed if he is measured by by the standards that he himself set and by the expectations that he himself aroused. We must say too that America failed if we measure the country by the preamble of its Declaration of Independence.

If we go this far, we must go further, to say that Woodrow Wilson was the example, the very embodiment, of America's naïve optimism. We must go even beyond this, to say that this failure encompassed the failure of all nineteenth-century liberalism and belief in progress. In Wilson, we would then maintain, the nineteenth century with its simple Victorian rules of conduct failed, and before it also the Enlightenment's belief in Locke's "state of nature." Neither was adequate for the catastrophes of the twentieth century. There was another failure too, that of the rational Christianity that is confident that God's will can be done on earth, that heaven and earth are bound up with each other, and that—to use a term from contemporary theology—"politics is everything."

Wilson was then a typical nineteenth-century man who found himself in the disastrous twentieth century. His failure was unavoidable, especially because he was a poet and because the language he used, the language of Romanticism, could not cope with the future. A Dutch poet, Martinus Nijhoff, has sung:

> *Men kan niet, als geheel een vorige eeuw*
> *puinhopen zien en zingen van mooi weer.*

> [We cannot, like the whole century before us,
> See the wreckage and still sing of good weather.]

More than ever it is evident that eternity and time are incommensurable and that purity and responsibility are incompatible.

Would it have been better if Wilson had not known the dilemma of the poet in the real world? In the words of Winston Churchill: "If Wilson had been either simply an idealist or a caucus politician he might have succeeded."[1] But what would his success have amounted to? He might have been able to preserve the immaculacy of his dream in a wicked world, or he might have achieved a number of temporary political victories. Neither was his purpose. His poetic vision could never be satisfied with imperfection, and so he failed.

When peace came—the peace that proved to be an interval between wars—the Americans refought the war of 1917–1919 with words, as they do after every war. Characteristically, America blamed itself for the great misadventure. Revisionist historians and politicians singled out Wilson as the accomplice—as it worked out, the clumsy accomplice—of capitalism and the arms industry, as the president who bound his country to the Allies with golden chains. Especially during the decade of the thirties, the country returned to its self-satisfied isolationism, so that Franklin D. Roosevelt had to repeat the whole process of 1914–1918.

During the Second World War, the ideals for which Wilson had struggled were again at stake, and again he became a model for his country. The mistakes of 1919 would not be repeated. The picture of the gallant president who had gone down fighting was evoked in a host of books and articles and even in a major film.[2] This time his ideals were realized, at least in part: a new league of nations was formed with the name of the United Nations; and the United States, which had finally learned its lesson, did not crawl back into its shell but instead played the leading role in the world that Wilson had envisioned. In 1956, during the celebration of his hundredth birthday, many kind things were spoken and written about him. At last the prophet had been proved right.

This period of Wilsonian euphoria did not last long. As America became more and more involved in its international responsibilities in a world that bore little resemblance to what Wilson had had in mind, the criticism of his dreams was resumed. Revisionists belonging to the New Left saw him once again as the man who had promoted capitalism under the cloak of liberal ideals. Opposing them, a new school of realists rejected his prophetic style as harmful to the national interest. George Kennan had Isaiah's vision of the kingdom of peace in mind when, in 1951, in his famed book *American Diplomacy 1900–1950*, he wrote about Wilson's peace that "this was the sort of peace you got when you allowed war hysteria and impractical idealism to lie down together in your mind, like the lion and the lamb."[3]

But nowadays both revisionism and realism are somewhat out of date again, and Wilson has found new defenders. None is so vigorous as Arthur S. Link, the Princeton historian who has ventured upon the publication of a biography in many volumes; the fifth, coming down to 1917, is the last at the time of this writing. He has also undertaken the publication of all letters and documents by and about Wilson, in some sixty volumes. With these works, the great man has been made accessible to a new generation of historians. Link, as his work has progressed, has become more and more an apologist for his hero. He judges Wilson not by the standards of his own time but by those of eternity. For him, Wilson did not just fail in 1919, but also, and more fundamentally, "guided by the Holy Spirit," he showed the way to the future. His was a Christian "higher realism."[4] Wilson as a prophet probably remains an accepted picture of the man. The sage old Republican statesman Henry Stimson said much the same thing, although in more muffled tones, in his memoirs: "In the errors of Woodrow Wilson there was always a certain prophetic grandeur. Even if he was wrong . . . he was wrong in the right direction."[5]

Every judgment about Wilson remains dependent upon the outlook of the beholder. In history no definitive conclusion is possible. Must we condemn Wilson as a hypocrite, reject him as a dreamer, admire him as a prophet? Whichever we do, there is still something to be said for the notion that the meaning of history lies in its dramatic force. This means that a great man is one whose life and work speak to the imagination. It remains not only part of our present, but also an example to us. It constantly acquires new meaning and therefore is not meaninglesss. Is this because it was so pulled and torn by the tension between good and evil? Because Wilson was the great moralist? Or because he articulated moral problems so admirably? Because Wilson was the poet as orator? Or because his problems became ours? Because Wilson was a prophet?

He was great not because he succeeded but because he dared. It is no little thing when a man with superb self-overestimation believes that he can change the whole world! Whose faith grows stronger the older he gets! "I find myself, as I grow older, instead of growing more cooler [sic], growing hotter, taking the world more seriously, feeling more and more as if it were my particular function to straighten it out."[6] How absurd that sounds, and how awe-inspiring!

Wilson will probably live on as the man who embodied "the principle of hope" in its boundlessness, a utopian in politics, one who was great in his failure. He described his own immortality in the address to the Sons of St. Patrick in New York, from which I have just quoted. As always he spoke of spiritual values and therefore, as always, of himself. He asked his distinguished listeners how they would like to be remembered. As excellent lawyers or merchants or engineers?

> When you are dead you will wish a certain aroma of sweeter flavor
> than that to permeate the air of your birthday. You will wish men to
> look back to you as a man whose eyes were lifted to the horizon, who
> led great companies of his fellow-men in their struggle up the steep
> and difficult ways which lead to the elevation and exaltation of
> nations.

Such a man, he assured them, would go down in history as noble.

> There is no patent of nobility in a free country except this patent of
> spiritual and intellectual distinction, which makes a man who is great
> a member of no generation, but one of that select company of
> immortals the roll of whose names is the book of our hope.[7]

ABBREVIATIONS

JOURNALS

AHR	*American Historical Review*
DH	*Diplomatic History*
HJ	*The Historical Journal*
HZ	*Historische Zeitschrift*
JAH	*Journal of American History*
JAS	*Journal of American Studies*
JCH	*Journal of Contemporary History*
JMH	*Journal of Modern History*
MVHR	*Mississippi Valley Historical Review*
PAH	*Perspectives in American History*
PSQ	*Presidential Studies Quarterly*
TH	*The Historian*
WPQ	*Western Political Quarterly*

BOOKS

Cronon	Wilson, *Political Thought*
Fried	Wilson, *A Day of Dedication*
House	House, *Intimate Papers*
Link *W*	Link, *Wilson*
LL	Baker, *Wilson: Life and Letters*
PP	Wilson, *Public Papers*
PWW	Wilson, *Papers*
PR	*Papers Relating to . . . The Paris Peace Conference*

NOTES

CHAPTER 1: FATHER AND MOTHER

1. Sigmund Freud and William C. Bullitt, *Thomas Woodrow Wilson* (Boston, 1967).

2. Woodrow Wilson to Ellen Axson, Oct. 12, 1884, PWW, 3: 349–350.

3. John M. Mulder, *Woodrow Wilson: The Years of Preparation* (Princeton, 1978), 19.

4. Edwin A. Weinstein, *Woodrow Wilson: A Medical and Psychological Biography* (Princeton, 1981), 14–18.

5. Joseph Wilson to Woodrow Wilson, Jan. 25, 1878, PWW, 1: 345–346.

6. Woodrow to Joseph Wilson, Dec. 16, 1888, PWW, 6: 154–155.

7. Joseph to Woodrow Wilson, Oct. 5, 1889, PWW, 6: 400–401.

8. Joseph to Woodrow Wilson, March 12, 1887, PWW, 5: 467.

9. William Allen White, *Woodrow Wilson: The Man, His Time and His Task* (Cambridge, Mass., 1926), 59.

CHAPTER 2: AN EXCEPTIONAL YOUNG MAN

1. Aug. 25, 1873, PWW, 1: 24.

2. Nov. 6, 1873, PWW, 1: 33–35; Mulder, 39.

3. May 3, 1874, PWW, 6: 693; July 5, 1873, PWW, 1: 22–23.

4. Over Carlyle, PWW, 1: 271, 279–281, 288, 401; over Macaulay, PWW, 1: 135, 237; Henry W. Bragdon, *Woodrow Wilson: The Academic Years* (Cambridge, Mass., 1967), 56.

5. PWW, 1: 373–374, 385–386.

6. Wilson to Ellen Axson, Oct. 30, 1883, PWW, 2: 500.

7. Wilson to Charles Talcott, Dec. 31, 1879, PWW, 1: 591–593; to Robert Bridges, Nov. 7, 1879, PWW, 1: 380–383.

8. Wilson to R. Bridges, April 29, 1883, PWW, 2: 343.

9. Bragdon, 76.

10. Bragdon, 82.

11. "Congressional Government," Oct. 1, 1879, PWW, 1: 548–574.

12. "Mr. Gladstone, A Character Sketch," April 1880, PWW, 1: 624–42.

13. Wilson to Charles Talcott, May 20, 1880, PWW, 1: 655.

14. Wilson to R. H. Dabney, May 11, 1883, PWW, 2: 350–354.

15. Wilson to Ellen Axson, Feb. 24, 1885, PWW, 4: 287.

16. F. J. Turner to C. MacSherwood, Feb. 13, 1889, PWW, 6: 88.

CHAPTER 3: HUSBAND AND FATHER

1. Earl Latham, ed., *The Philosophies and Policies of Woodrow Wilson* (Chicago, 1958), 34–35; interview, March 3, 1908, PWW, 18: 3–4.

2. Wilson to Ellen Axson, Oct. 1, 1884, PWW, 3: 389.

3. Eleanor Wilson McAdoo, *The Woodrow Wilsons* (New York, 1937), 50.

4. Wilson to Harriet Woodrow, Sept. 25, 1881, PWW, 2: 84; cf. George L. Osborn, *Woodrow Wilson: The Early Years* (Baton Rouge, 1968), 80–82.

5. Osborn, 86–88.

6. Wilson to Ellen Axson, Oct. 11, 1883, PWW, 2: 465–469.

7. Wilson to Ellen Axson, Nov. 1, 1884, PWW, 3: 393–394.

8. Wilson to Ellen Axson, July 16, 1883, PWW, 2: 388–389.

9. Ellen Axson to Wilson, Dec. 20, 1884, PWW, 3: 562.

10. McAdoo, 167.

11. Wilson to Ellen Wilson, Feb. 19, 1894, PWW, 8: 468.

12. Wilson to Ellen Wilson, March 9, 1892, PWW, 7: 461–462.

13. Wilson to Ellen Wilson, PWW, 7: 462–466.

14. Wilson to Ellen Wilson, June 19, 1898, PWW, 1: 564–565; cf. Wilson to Ellen Wilson, March 10, 1892, PWW, 7: 483–485.

15. Wilson to Ellen Wilson, Feb. 14, 1896, PWW, 9: 424.

16. McAdoo, 50.

17. Wilson to Ellen Wilson, Feb. 4, 1908, PWW, 17: 612.

18. Wilson to Edith Galt, Sept. 19, 1915, PWW, 34: 491.

19. Wilson to Edith Galt, PWW, 34: 496–497.

20. Mulder, 262.

21. McAdoo, 161.

CHAPTER 4: PROFESSOR AND SCHOLAR

1. "Confidential Journal," Dec. 18, 1889, PWW, 6: 462.
2. Wilson to Ellen Axson, Jan. 21, 1885, PWW, 3: 627.
3. Wilson to Ellen Axson, Nov. 27, 1883, PWW, 2: 552.
4. Bragdon, 109.
5. Bragdon, 110.
6. Wilson to Ellen Wilson, Nov. 17, 1884, PWW, 3: 490.
7. Wilson to Ellen Wilson, Oct. 8, 1887, PWW, 5: 612–613.
8. Bragdon, 152–153.
9. Wilson to Caleb Thomas Winchester, May 29, 1893, PWW, 8: 220.
10. *Princeton in the Nation's Service*, Oct. 21, 1896, PWW, 10: 220.
11. *Princeton's Plan of Study*, Aug. 29, 1904, PWW, 15: 457–458; *The Meaning of College Education*, Nov. 12, 1908, PWW, 18: 497.
12. *Princeton in the Nation's Service*, Oct. 21, 1896, PWW, 10: 31.
13. Wilson to Jenny Davidson Hibben and John Grier Hibben, Nov. 27, 1902, PWW, 14: 224, and Dec. 23, 1903, PWW, 15: 110; cf. Mulder, 184, and Bragdon, 220.
14. Mulder, 145.
15. Mulder, 132.

CHAPTER 5: HISTORIAN AND NATIONALIST

1. McAdoo, 20.
2. Wilson to Ellen Wilson, Jan. 20, 1885, PWW, 3: 623.
3. *On the Writing of History*, PWW, 9: 193–305.
4. John A. Garraty, *Woodrow Wilson: A Great Life in Brief* (New York, 1956), 11ff.
5. Mulder, 106–109.
6. *A Calendar of Great Americans*, ca. Sept. 15, 1893, PWW, 8: 368–381.
7. Wilson (1896); cf. Bragdon, 244.
8. Wilson to R. W. Glider, Jan. 28, 1901, PWW, 12: 84.
9. *The Making of a Nation*, PWW, 10: 217–236.
10. "The Course of American History," PWW, 9: 257–274.
11. "A Memorandum: What Ought We to Do?" PWW, 10: 574–576.

12. Nov. 2, 1898, PWW, 11: 62–66.

13. Dec. 14, 1898, PWW, 11: 299.

14. "Democracy and Efficiency," Oct. 1, 1900, PWW, 12: 11.

15. "The Ideals of America," Dec. 26, 1901, PWW, 12: 215.

16. Dec. 22, 1900, PWW, 12: 57.

17. "Democracy and Efficiency," Oct. 1, 1900, PWW, 12: 18.

18. "Speech to the Pilgrims of the United States," Jan. 30, 1904, PWW, 15: 149.

19. "The Ideals of America," Dec. 26, 1901, PWW, 12: 208–227.

20. Jan. 28, 1904, PWW, 15: 143.

21. "Democracy and Efficiency," Oct. 1, 1900, PWW, 12: 12.

22. "Princeton for the Nation's Service," PWW, 14: 184; "Address at Montclair," Jan. 28, 1904, PWW, 15: 143.

23. Arthur S. Link, *Woodrow Wilson: Revolution, War and Peace* (Arlington Heights, Ill., 1979), 7.

24. "Remarks to the Gridiron Club," Dec. 11, 1915, PWW, 35: 343.

25. "On Patriotism," Feb. 23, 1903, PWW, 14: 367.

26. April 22, 1903, PWW, 14: 419–421.

27. "The Ideals of America," Dec. 26, 1901, PWW, 12: 227.

28. "Address to the Commercial Club of Chicago," Nov. 29, 1902, PWW, 14: 239.

CHAPTER 6: CHRISTIAN AND STATESMAN

1. Garraty, *Wilson*, 16, 46.

2. John Maynard Keynes, *The Economic Consequences of the Peace* (New York, 1920), 38; Harold Nicolson, *Peacemaking 1919* (London, 1934), 198.

3. Osborn, 12; William A. Williams, *The Tragedy of American Diplomacy* (New York, 1962), 64–65.

4. J. J. Huthmacher and W. Susman, *Wilson's Diplomacy: An International Symposium* (Cambridge, Mass., 1973), 8–10, 80–81.

5. Sidney E. Mead, *The Old Religion in the Brave New World: Reflections on the Relation Between Christendom and the Republic* (Berkeley, 1977).

6. March 30, 1906, PWW, 16: 350.

7. Joseph Tumulty, *Woodrow Wilson as I Know Him* (London, 1922), 335–336.

8. Dec. 28, 1889, PWW, 6: 462.

9. Wilson to Ellen Axson, Oct. 9, 1887, PWW, 5: 614–615.

10. June 11, 1876, PWW, 1: 138.

11. Mulder, 34.

12. Ellen Axson to Wilson, April 15, 1885, PWW, 4: 490; Wilson to Ellen Axson, April 17, 1885, PWW, 4: 495.

13. Link *W*, 1: 94.

14. "When a Man Comes to Himself," Nov. 1, 1899, PWW, 11: 270.

15. Mulder, 274.

16. Nov. 1, 1899, PWW, 11: 273.

17. "The True University Spirit," Nov. 7, 1902, PWW, 14: 201–202.

18. "Baccalaureate Address," June 9, 1907, PWW, 17: 195 (Wilson did not quote exactly, because he changed "disturbs me" to "disturbs us," probably with his audience in mind).

19. Wilson to Ellen Axson, Dec. 22, 1884, PWW, 3: 570.

20. "Religion and Patriotism," July 4, 1902, PWW, 12: 477.

21. Nov. 20, 1905, PWW, 12: 477.

22. "An Address on the Bible," May 7, 1911, PWW, 23: 12–20.

23. Nov. 20, 1905, PWW, 16: 229.

CHAPTER 7: POET AND SPEAKER

1. Wilson to Ellen Axson, Oct. 30, 1883, PWW, 2: 50.

2. Wilson to Ellen Axson, Feb. 13, 1895, PWW, 9: 107–109.

3. Wilson to Ellen Axson, Oct. 30, 1883, PWW, 2: 500.

4. Latham, 31.

5. April 1880, PWW, 1: 636.

6. Wilson to Ellen Axson Wilson, April 22, 1903, PWW, 14: 421; March 21, 1904, PWW, 15: 201.

7. Norman Graebner, *Ideas and Diplomacy: Readings in the Intellectual Tradition of American Foreign Policy* (New York, 1964), 476–477; Link *W*, 2: 150–51.

8. McAdoo, 12.

9. Bragdon, 230.

10. "Adam Smith," Feb. 1887, PWW, 5: 445.

11. June 17, 1893, PWW, 8: 238–252.

12. Wilson to Ellen Axson, Feb. 13, 1885, PWW, 4: 245.

13. Dec. 7, 1887, PWW, 5: 637–638.

14. PWW, 5: 635.

15. June 17, 1890, PWW, 6: 744–771.

16. Nov. 5, 1903, PWW, 15: 33–46.

17. Elizabeth Bowen, *The Mulberry Tree: The Writings of Elizabeth Bowen* (London, 1986), 64–65.

CHAPTER 8: PRESIDENT OF PRINCETON

1. June 14, 1902, PWW, 12: 420–422.

2. "New Plans for Princeton," June 24, 1905, PWW, 16: 146–149.

3. Edith Gittings Reid, *Woodrow Wilson: The Caricature, the Myth and the Man* (London, 1934), 107–109.

4. Wilson to A. C. Imbrie, July 29, 1907, PWW, 17: 299–301.

5. James Kerney, *The Political Education of Woodrow Wilson* (New York and London, 1926), 9–10.

6. M. T. Pyne to J. B. Shea, Jan. 15, 1910, PWW, 20: 19–20.

7. Wilson to C. H. Dodge, Feb. 7, 1910, PWW, 20: 83.

8. Wilson to H. B. Brougham, Feb. 1, 1910, PWW, 20: 69–71; editorial, *New York Times*, Feb. 3, 1910, PWW, 20: 74–76.

9. "Two News Reports of an Address in Pittsburgh," April 17, 1910, PWW, 20: 363–368; the remarks about "fields of blood" is absent from the version approved by Wilson, PWW, 20: 375–376.

10. Wilson to the editor of the New York *Evening Post*, April 21, 1910, PWW, 20: 378.

11. Wilson to E. W. Sheldon, May 15, 1910, PWW, 20: 456–457.

12. A. F. West to M. T. Pyne, May 22, 1910, PWW, 20: 465–466.

13. Wilson to Mary Peck, Feb. 12, 1911, PWW, 22: 424–427.

CHAPTER 9: CONGRESS AND PRESIDENT

1. Wilson to C. A. Talcott, Nov. 14, 1886, PWW, 5: 389.

2. Wilson to Ellen Axson, Jan. 1, 1884, PWW, 2: 641–644.

3. *Congressional Government*, PWW, 4: 19.

4. PWW, 36: 149–151.

5. PWW, 36: 140.

6. PWW, 36: 155.

7. "A Lecture on Walter Bagehot," July 20, 1889, PWW, 6: 333–354.

8. "Edmund Burke, The Man and His Times," Aug. 31, 1893, PWW, 8: 313–343; cf. Weinstein, 122.

9. PWW, 8: 316.

10. "Civic Problems," March 9, 1909, PWW, 19: 83–85.

11. "The True American Spirit," Oct. 27, 1892, PWW, 8: 37–40.

12. *Constitutional Government*, PWW, 18: 69–216.

13. PWW, 18: 109.

14. PWW, 18: 112.

15. Marcus Cunliffe, *American Presidents and the Presidency* (New York, 1972), 93.

16. *Constitutional Government*, PWW, 18: 116.

17. PWW, 18: 114.

18. PWW, 18: 161.

CHAPTER 10: GOVERNOR AND PRESIDENT

1. J. Presser, *Amerika, Van kolonie tot wereldmacht: De geschiedenis van de Verenigde Staten* (Amsterdam and Brussels, 1949), 168–169.

2. *Pollock* v. *Farmer's Loan and Trust Company* (157 U.S. 429, 159 U.S. 601).

3. Charles A. Beard, *An Economic Interpretation of the Constitution of the United States* (New York, 1913); Richard Hofstadter, *The Progressive Historians: Turner, Beard, Parrington* (New York, 1968), 192ff.

4. Theodore Roosevelt, *The Writings of Theodore Roosevelt*, ed. William H. Harbaugh (Indianapolis and New York, 1967), 318–319, 330.

5. Oct. 3, 1912, PWW, 25: 324.

6. Nov. 30, 1904, PWW, 15: 547–548.

7. Feb. 3, 1906, PWW, 16: 299–301.

8. G. Harvey to Wilson, Dec. 17, 1906, PWW, 16: 531–533.

9. Aug. 6, 1907, PWW, 17: 335–338.

10. *Jersey Journal*, March 10, 1908, in Link *W*, 1: 118.

11. Wilson to Mary Peck, Nov. 2, 1908, PWW, 17: 480.

12. Wilson to Mary Peck, Nov. 2, 1909, PWW, 19: 338.

13. Link *W*, 1: 194.

14. Sept. 16, 1910, PWW, 21: 99.

15. Nov. 5, 1910, PWW, 21: 575–576.

16. Wilson to Mary Peck, Jan. 3, April 22, May 1, 1911, PWW, 22: 293, 583, 598.

17. Wilson to Mary Peck, March 13, 1911, PWW, 22: 501.

18. Wilson to Mary Peck, PWW, 23: 590.

19. Wilson to Mary Peck, June 17, 1912, PWW, 24: 481–482.

20. Wilson to Mary Hulbert (Peck), July 14, 1912, PWW, 24: 550–552.

21. Wilson to Mary Hulbert (Peck), Aug. 25, 1912, PWW, 25: 55–56.

22. Link W, 1: 476.

23. Robert Wiebe, *The Search for Order, 1877–1920* (New York, 1967), 217–218.

24. Woodrow Wilson, *The New Freedom*, ed. William E. Leuchtenburg (Englewood Cliffs, N.J., 1961), 36.

25. "Two Interviews," PWW, 23: 610.

26. Wilson, *New Freedom*, 63

27. Wilson, *New Freedom*, 62.

CHAPTER 11: THE PRESIDENT AS REFORMER

1. Mulder, 229.

2. McAdoo, 196.

3. House, "Diary," Dec. 22, 1913, PWW, 29: 56.

4. March 4, 1913, PWW, 27: 56.

5. Dec. 17, 1912, PWW, 25: 599.

6. David Lawrence, *The True Story of Woodrow Wilson* (London, 1924), 82–84.

7. Wilson to Mary Hulbert (Peck), Sept. 28, 1913, PWW, 28: 336–337.

8. May 26, 1913, PWW, 27: 473.

9. Dec. 17, 1912, PWW, 25: 602.

10. Wilson to C. Glass, May 12, 1914, PWW, 30: 24.

11. Arthur S. Link, *Woodrow Wilson and the Progressive Era, 1913–1917* (New York, 1954), 226–227.

12. Villard, "Diary," Aug. 14, 1912, PWW, 25: 24–26.

13. August Meier, *Negro Thought in America, 1880–1915* (Ann Arbor, 1963), 187–188.

14. Daniels, "Diary," April 11, 1913, PWW, 27: 290–292.

15. O. G. Villard to Wilson, July 21, Wilson to Villard, July 23, T. Dixon to Wilson, July 27, Wilson to Dixon, July 29, 1913, PWW, 28: 60–61, 65, 88, 94.

16. Wilson to H. A. Bridgman, Sept. 8, to Villard, Aug. 29, 1913, PWW, 28: 245–246, 265–266.

17. Nov. 12, 1914, PWW, 31: 298–309; Stephen R. Fox, *The Guardian of the Peace: William Monroe Trotter* New York, 1970), 179–187.

CHAPTER 12: FOREIGN POLICY

1. David F. Houston, *Eight Years with Wilson's Cabinet*, 1913–1920 (London, 1926), 1: 44.

2. Walter Lippmann, *Drift and Mastery*, ed. W. Leuchtenburg (Englewood Cliffs, N.J., 1961), 81.

3. H. L. Stoddard, *As I Know Them: Presidents and Politics from Grant to Coolidge* (New York, 1927), 285.

4. Paolo E. Coletta, *William Jennings Bryan*, 3 vols. (Lincoln, Nebr., 1964–1970), 2: 117.

5. Wilson to C. Eliot, Sept. 17, 1913, PWW, 28: 280.

6. Link *W*, 2: 100–101; Ross Gregory, *Walter Hines Page, Ambassador to the Court of Saint James's* (Lexington, Ky., 1970), 31.

7. Coletta, 2: 247.

8. Oct. 24, 1914, PWW, 31: 226.

9. Georges Clemenceau, *Grandeurs et misères d'une victoire* (Paris, 1930), 114.

10. Bailey (1944), 88–89; Edward House, *The Intimate Papers of Colonel House*, ed. Charles Seymour, 4 vols. (Boston and New York, 1926–1928), 4: 361.

11. Inga Floto, *Colonel House in Paris: A Study of American Policy at the Paris Peace Conference, 1919* (Princeton, 1973), 28; Robert C. Bannister, Jr., *Ray Stannard Baker: The Mind and Thought of a Progressive* (New Haven and London, 1966), 211.

12. Alexander L. and Juliette L. George, *Woodrow Wilson and Colonel House: A Personality Study* (New York, 1964), 92–93.

13. House, 1: 114.

14. Link *W*, 2: 94.

15. House, 1: 116.

16. House to Wilson, Jan. 29, 1915, PWW, 32: 162.

17. House to Wilson, Oct. 27, 1917, PWW, 44: 454–455.

18. Garraty, 74; John Milton Cooper, Jr., *The Warrior and the Priest: Woodrow Wilson and Theodore Roosevelt* (Cambridge, Mass., 1983), 293–297; Floto, passim.

19. George, 113.

20. Ronald Steel, *Walter Lippmann and the American Century* (Boston and Toronto, 1980), 108.

21. Wilson to Edith Bolling Galt, Aug. 13, 1915, PWW, 34: 190.

22. Edith Bolling Galt to Wilson, Aug. 27, 1915, PWW, 34: 338.

23. Wilson to Edith Bolling Galt, 28 Aug., 1915, PWW, 34: 352–353.

CHAPTER 13: TWO REVOLUTIONS

1. Paul A. Varg, *The Making of a Myth: The United States and China, 1897–1912* (East Lansing, 1968).

2. James C. Thomson, Jr., et al., *Sentimental Imperialists: The American Experience in East Asia* (New York, 1981), 103.

3. Tien-Yi Li, *Woodrow Wilson's China Policy, 1913–1917* (New York, 1969), 48 n.1.

4. Warren I. Cohen, *America's Response to China: An Interpretative History of Sino-American Relations* (New York, 1971), 83.

5. March 18, 1913, PWW, 27: 192–194.

6. John Mott to Wilson, March 1, 1913, PWW, 27: 144–145.

7. Daniels, Diary, April 18, 1913, PWW, 27: 328–330.

8. House, 1: 105.

9. "Remarks to the Potomac Presbytery," April 21, 1915, PWW, 33: 49–51.

10. *Papers Relating to the Foreign Policy of the United States: The Lansing Papers, 1914–1920*, 2 vols. (Washington, 1939–1940), 2: 445.

11. "An Address on Latin-American Policy in Mobile, Alabama," Oct. 27., 1913, PWW, 28: 448–453.

12. House, 1: 209–210; cf. PWW, 31: 468–471.

13. "An Address to the Pan-American Scientific Congress," Jan. 6, 1916, PWW, 35: 441–446.

14. Link *W*, 2: 328 n.30.

15. Lansing to Wilson, Nov. 24, 1915, PWW, 35: 247.

16. Link *W*, 1: 335.

17. John Mason Hart, *Revolutionary Mexico: The Coming and Process of the Mexican Revolution* (Berkeley, 1987).

18. Kenneth J. Grieb, *The United States and Huerta* (Lincoln, Nebr., 1969), 20–21; Charles C. Cumberland, *Mexican Revolution: Genesis under Madero* (Austin and London, 1952), 240.

19. March 12, 1913, PWW, 27: 172–173.

20. C. W. Thompson to C. A. Bull, May 22, 1913, PWW, 27: 465.

21. Peter Calvert, *The Mexican Revolution 1910–1914. The Diplomacy of Anglo-American Conflict* (Cambridge, 1968), 246.

22. W. B. Hale to Wilson, July 9, 1913, PWW, 28: 27–34.

23. Walter Hines Page, *The Life and Letters of Walter Hines Page*, ed. B. J. Hendrick, 3 vols. (London, 1923–1925) 1: 204.

24. Link *W*, 2: 383.

25. Wilson to Mary Hulbert, Aug. 24, 1913, PWW, 28: 217; cf. Wilson to Mary Hulbert, Feb. 1, 1914, PWW, 29: 211.

26. Lind to Bryan, Dec. 5, 1913, March 10, 1914, 14–19; to Wilson, Jan. 10, 1914, PWW, 29: 14–19, 18–27, 328–331.

27. Alan Knight, *The Mexican Revolution*, 2 vols. (Cambridge, 1986) 2: 140.

28. July 4, 1914, PWW, 30: 251.

29. "The Record of a Conversation with President Wilson," by Samuel G. Blythe, April 27, 1914, PWW, 29: 516–524.

30. Spring-Rice to Tyrell, Feb. 7, 1914, Stephen Gwynn, ed., *The Letters and Friendships of Sir Cecil Spring Rice: A Record*, 2 vols. (London, 1929) 2: 202; Link *W*, 3: 234, 239–240.

31. Dec. 8, 1915, PWW, 35: 315.

32. "Annual Message on the State of the Union," Dec. 7, 1915, PWW, 35: 295.

CHAPTER 14: 1914

1. Houston, 1: 119–120.

2. Graebner, 407.

3. William E. Leuchtenburg, *The Perils of Prosperity, 1914–1932* (Chicago, 1958), 13.

4. Leuchtenburg, 121.

5. J. A. Thompson, *Reformers and War: American Progressive Publicists and the First World War* (Cambridge, 1987), 121.

6. Link, *Wilson: Revolution*, 2–4.

7. House, Diary, Sept. 28, 1914, PWW, 31: 95.

8. Edward H. Buehrig, *Wilson's Foreign Policy in Perspective* (Bloomington, Ind., 1957), 37.

9. Wilson to House, Aug. 25, 1914, PWW, 30: 450.

10. Wilson to Walter H. Page, Oct. 28, 1914, PWW, 31: 242.

11. Spring-Rice to Grey, Sept. 3, 1914, George Macaulay Trevelyan, *Grey of Fallodon: Being the Life of Sir Edward Grey Afterwards Viscount Gray of Fallodon* (London, 1937), 313; Spring-Rice to Grey, Dec. 8, 1914, PWW, 31: 14.

12. House, Diary, Aug. 30, 1914, PWW, 30: 462.

13. "Address on Robert E. Lee," Jan. 19, 1909, PWW, 18: 631–645, especially p. 645; cf. "A Message to Democratic Rallies," Nov. 2, 1912, PWW, 25: 502–503.

14. "An Appeal to the American People," Aug. 18, 1914, PWW, 30: 393–394.

15. House, Diary, Aug. 30, 1914, PWW, 30: 461–462.

16. Arthur P. Dudden, ed., *Woodrow Wilson and the World of Today* (Philadelphia, 1957), 39.

17. Wilson to W. J. Bryan, Sept. 4, 1914, PWW, 30: 478.

18. Gwynn, 2: 240–241.

19. Wilson to Mary Hulbert, June 7, 1914, PWW, 30: 158.

20. Wilson to E. P. Davis, July 28, 1914, PWW, 30: 12.

21. Wilson to Mary Hulbert, Aug. 7, 1914, PWW, 30: 357; M. E. Hoyt to Wilson, Aug. 11, 1914, PWW, 30: 375; cf. Wilson to Mary Hulbert, Aug. 23, 1914, PWW, 30: 437.

22. House, Diary, Aug. 30, 1914, PWW, 30: 464–465.

23. Wilson to Mary Hulbert, Nov. 22, 1914, PWW, 31: 343–345.

24. House, Diary, in Link *W*, 4: 7.

25. Wilson to Edith Wilson, June 4, 6, 1915, PWW, 33: 340, 348.

CHAPTER 15: WAR AT SEA

1. Viscount Grey of Fallodon, *Twenty-Five Years, 1892–1916*, 2 vols. (London, 1929), 2: 103.

2. Page to Wilson, July 20, 1913, PWW, 28: 52–54.

3. Wilson to Page, Sept. 11, 1913, PWW, 28: 274.

4. Page to Wilson, Sept. 6, 1914, PWW, 31: 6–8.

5. Grey, 2: 106.

6. Page to House, Oct. 22, 1914, Walter Hines Page, *The Life and Letters of Walter Hines Page*, 3: 380–384.

7. House, Diary, Sept. 30, 1914, PWW, 31: 108–109.

8. Link *W*, 3: 626.

9. Wilson to J. H. Schiff, Dec. 8, 1914, PWW, 31: 425.

10. Link *W*, 3: 626.

11. Indianapolis, Jan. 8, 1915, PWW, 32: 39.

12. PWW, 32: 41.

13. Wilson to Nancy Saunders Toy, Jan. 31, Feb. 4, 1915, PWW, 32: 165–166, 190–191.

14. Lodge to T. Roosevelt, March 1, 1915, Link *W*, 3: 158.

15. Wilson to House, July 23, 1916, PWW, 37: 466–467.

16. Feb. 10, 1915, PWW, 32: 207–210.

17. W. J. Bryan to Wilson, May 9, 1915, PWW, 33: 134–135.

18. Bryan to Wilson, April 23, 1915, PWW, 33: 67.

19. Wilson to Bryan, April 22, 1915, PWW, 33: 62.

20. House, 1: 432.

21. Link *W*, 3: 378.

22. Link *W*, 3: 379–380.

23. Wilson to Edith Bolling Galt, May 5, 1915, PWW, 33: 112.

24. Wilson to Edith Bolling Galt, May 7, 1915, PWW, 33: 125.

25. Edith Bolling Galt to Wilson, May 7, 1915, PWW, 33: 127–128.

26. House to Wilson, May 9, 1915, PWW, 33: 134.

27. Bryan to Wilson, May 9, 1915, PWW, 33: 134–135.

28. May 10, 1916, PWW, 33: 138.

29. "An Address in Philadelphia to Newly Naturalized Citizens," May 10, 1915, ibid., 147–150.

30. Tumulty, 232.

31. Cooper, 305.

32. "Remarks to the Associated Press in New York," April 20, 1915, PWW, 32: 32–37.

33. House, Diary, June 24, 1915, PWW, 33: 449; cf. House, Diary, May 7, 1916, PWW, 36: 267.

34. Wilson to Bryan, June 7, 1915, PWW, 36: 349.

35. House, Diary, Dec. 3, 1914, PWW, 31: 385; Wilson to Edith Galt, June 9, 1915, PWW, 30: 377.

36. Wilson to Edith Galt, Aug. 13, 1915, PWW, 34: 192.

37. Wilson (1939), 64; Edith Bolling Wilson, *My Memoirs* (Indianapolis and New York, 1939), 64.

38. House to Wilson, June 16, 1915, PWW, 33: 409.

39. House, Diary, June 24, 1915, PWW, 33: 449.

40. PWW, 33: 397.

41. Ray Stannard Baker, *Woodrow Wilson and World Settlement*, 3 vols. (London, 1923), 1: xxx.

42. House, Diary, March 28, 1917, PWW, 41: 497, April 26, 1917, PWW, 42: 142, Aug. 15, 1917, PWW, 43: 485–486.

43. Link *W*, 2: 67–68.

44. Link *W*, 3: 46–47.

45. Robert Lansing, *War Memoirs* (London, 1935), 18–26; cf. Daniel M. Smith, *Robert Lansing and American Neutrality, 1914–1917* (Berkeley, 1958), 19.

46. Lansing, *Memoirs*, 128–129.

47. Cooper, 292.

48. Patrick Devlin, *Too Proud to Fight: Woodrow Wilson's Neutrality* (London, 1974), 304–305.

49. George Kennan, *The Decision to Intervene: Soviet-American Relations, 1917–1920*. Vol. 2 (London, 1958), 30–31.

50. PWW, 33: 355–360.

51. Wilson to House, Aug. 21, 1915, PWW, 34: 271–272.

52. House to Wilson, Aug. 23, 1915, ibid., 298–299.

53. German note, Feb. 4, 1916, PWW, 36: 128.

54. Link *W*, 4: 257.

55. James W. Gerard, *My Four Years in Germany* (London, 1917), 234–250; Grey, 1: 221–241.

CHAPTER 16: MEDIATION

1. House, 1: 240.

2. House, 1: 240–241.

3. House, 1: 246.

4. House, 1: 251; House to Wilson, May 29, 1914, PWW, 30: 108–109.

5. House to Wilson, May 29, 1914, PWW, 30: 109.

6. House, 1: 260.

7. House, 1: 261.

8. Wilson to House, June 16, 1914, PWW, 30: 108–109.

9. Wilson to House, July 9, 1914, PWW, 30: 264.

10. House, 1: 280–281.

11. Hans Kohn, *American Nationalism: An Interpretative Essay* (New York, 1961), 25.

12. "Ideals of Public Life," Nov. 16, 1907, PWW, 17: 198.

13. "A Fourth of July Address," July 4, 1914, PWW, 30: 254.

14. C. Huisman, *Neerlands Israel* (Dordrecht, 1983), 60.

15. "A Campaign Address in Elizabeth, N.J.," Oct. 28, 1910, PWW, 21: 462.

16. "Address at the Unveiling of the State to the Memory of Commodore John Barry," Washington, D.C., May 16, 1914, PWW, 30: 34–36.

17. "Annual Message," Dec. 8, 1914, PWW, 31: 421.

18. "Remarks to the Associated Press," New York, April 20, 1915, PWW, 33: 37–41.

19. "Address to the Daughters of the American Revolution," Oct. 11, 1915, PWW, 35: 51; "Address on Memorial Day at Arlington," May 30, 1916, PWW, 37: 123–128; "Address to the Graduating Class of the U.S. Military Academy," June 13, 1916, PWW, 37: 213–214; "Final Campaign Address," Nov. 4, 1916, PWW, 38: 614.

20. "A Memorandum by Herbert Bruce Brougham, of Interview with the President," Dec. 14, 1914, PWW, 31: 458–460.

21. LL, 5: 74.

22. Bryan to Wilson, Dec. 1, 1914, PWW, 31: 378–379; cf. Bryan to Wilson, Sept. 19, 1914, PWW, 31: 56–57.

23. House, Diary, Dec. 3, 1914, PWW, 31: 384–387.

24. House, Diary, Jan. 13, 1915, PWW, 32: 65.

25. House to Wilson, Sept. 18, 1914, PWW, 31: 468–469.

26. House, Diary, Sept. 28, 1914, PWW, 31: 93.

27. Link *W*, 3: 204 n.40.

28. House, 1: 339–340; House, Diary, Dec. 16, 1914, PWW, 31: 468–469.

29. Wilson to House, Jan. 29, 1915, PWW, 32: 157–159.

30. House, Diary, Jan. 25, 1915, PWW, 32: 121.

31. House to Wilson, Feb. 15, 1915, House, 1: 374.

32. House, 1: 368.

33. Grey, 2: 120.

34. House, 1: 364.

35. Wilson to House, Feb. 20, 1915, PWW, 32: 265.

36. House to Wilson, Feb. 23, 1915, PWW, 32: 276–278.

37. House to Wilson, March 15, 1915, PWW, 32: 372–375.

38. Ernest W. May, *The World War and American Isolation* (Cambridge, Mass., 1959), 108.

39. House to Wilson, March 22, 26, 27, 1915, PWW, 32: 411–412, 438–443.

40. House to Wilson, March 29, 1915, PWW, 32: 455–456.

41. Link *W*, 3: 230; Grey to House, April 24, 1915, House, 1: 425.

42. Robert Lansing, *War Memoirs* (London, 1935), 37–40.

43. House to Wilson, April 12, 1915, PWW, 32: 513–514.

44. Wilson to House, April 1, 1915, PWW, 32: 462.

45. House to Wilson, April 30, 1915, PWW, 33: 88–89.

46. Link *W*, 3: 231.

47. Link *W*, 3: 223.

48. Bernstorff to Bethmann Hollweg, May 29, June 2, 1915, PWW, 33: 279–282, 316–318. A Dutchman was involved in this effort at mediation, which remained fairly secret. Frans van Gheel Gildemeester arrived in Washington in May with German terms and probably accompanied Bernstorff on his visit to the White House. See also A. C. Miller to Bryan, June 3, 1915, PWW, 33: 332–333, Sir Cecil Spring-Rice to Sir Edward Grey, June 6, 1915, PWW, 33: 347–348; and F. van Gheel Gildemeester to Wilson, June 7, 1915, PWW, 33: 361–362.

49. Wilson to House, Aug. 21, 1915, PWW, 34: 271.

50. Grey to House, Aug. 10, 1915, House, 2: 87.

51. House, 2: 84–85.

52. "Address to the Chamber of Commerce of Columbus, Ohio," Dec. 10, 1915, PWW, 35: 327.

53. House to Sir Edward Grey, Oct. 17, 1915, PWW, 35: 81–82.

54. House to Wilson, Nov. 10, 1915, PWW, 35: 186.

55. House, "Diary," Dec. 15, 1915, PWW, 35: 356.

56. Wilson to House, Dec. 24, 1915, PWW, 35: 387–388.

57. House to Wilson, Jan. 13, 1916, PWW, 35: 471–473.

58. "Notes of the American Embassy Secretary Irwin Laughlin," Jan. 12, 1916, PWW, 35: 474.

59. House to Wilson, Jan. 13, 1916, PWW, 35: 483–486.

60. House to Wilson, Feb. 3, 1916, PWW, 36: 122–124; cf. Link W, 19–22.

61. House to Wilson, Feb. 3, 1916, with the notes of Cambon, PWW, 36: 124–126.

62. House to Wilson, Feb. 9, 1916, with again the text of Cambon for comparison, PWW, 36: 147–151.

63. Page, 3: 281–282.

64. House, Diary, Feb. 14, 1916, Link W, 3: 133.

65. Devlin, 435.

66. Grey, 2: 122–123.

67. PWW, 36: 180.

68. Link W, 4: 139 n. 106.

69. House, Diary, March 7, 1916, PWW, 36: 262–263.

70. House, March 26, 1916, PWW, 36: 379; cf. entry of March 30, 1916, PWW, 36: 388.

71. Egerton (1979), 30–31; J. F. Niermeyer, "Ideaal en Werkelÿkheid in de buitenlandse politiek van Woodrow Wilson," *De Gids* 102 (1938): 167–168.

72. Devlin, 459–471.

73. David Lloyd George, *The Truth About the War*, 2 vols. (London, 1938), 1: 245–246.

74. David Lloyd George, *War Memoirs*, 8 vols. (London, 1933–1936), 2: 689–690.

75. Grey, 2: 131–132.

CHAPTER 17: 1916

1. Theodore Roosevelt to Rudyard Kipling, Nov. 4, 1914, in R. E. Osgood, *Ideals and Self-Interest in America's Foreign Relations: The Great Transformation of the Twentieth Century* (Chicago, 1953), 137.

2. Friedrich von Bernhardi, *Deutschland und der nächste Krieg* (Stuttgart and Berlin, 1913); cf. Osgood, who incorrectly reports that the book sold poorly in Germany.

3. House, 1: 298–300.

4. "Annual Message," Dec. 8, 1914, PWW, 31: 414–424.

5. Thompson, *Reformers*, 138.

6. House, 2: 19–20.

7. "An Address on Preparedness to the Manhattan Club," Nov. 4, 1915, PWW, 35: 167–173; "Annual Message," Dec. 7, 1915, PWW, 35: 293–310.

8. Robert Lansing to Wilson, Wilson to Lansing, Sept. 1, 1915, PWW, 34: 379–399; Aletta Jacobs to Jane Addams, Sept. 15, 1919, PWW, 34: 473; Aletta Jacobs, *Herinneringen* (Amsterdam, 1924), 164–168.

9. Link *W*, 4: 107.

10. Link *W*, 4: 30–33.

11. Link *W*, 4: 25–26; Wilson to Seth Low, Nov. 8, 1915, PWW, 35: 180–181.

12. Henry Cabot Lodge to T. Roosevelt, Dec. 20, 1915, in Link *W*, 4: 42.

13. Speech in Cleveland, Jan. 29, in Milwaukee, Jan. 31, 1916, PWW, 36: 43, 58.

14. Speeches in Cleveland, Jan. 29; in Pittsburgh, Jan. 29; in Milwaukee, Jan. 31; in Chicago, Jan. 31, 1916, PWW, 34: 38, 47, 57, 66.

15. Speech in Des Moines, Feb. 1, 1916, PWW, 36: 85.

16. Speech in St. Louis, Feb. 3, 1916, PWW, 36: 119–120.

17. Theodore Roosevelt, "Address before the Nobel Prize Committee at Christiania," May 5, 1910, Theodore Roosevelt, *The Works of Theodore Roosevelt*, ed. Herman Hagedorn, 24 vols. (New York, 1923–1926), 18: 410–415.

18. Henry Cabot Lodge, *War Addresses, 1915–1917* (Boston and New York, 1917), 21–43.

19. David Mervin, "Henry Cabot Lodge and the League of Nations," *JAH* 4 (1970): 201–214.

20. Wilson to House, May 18, 1916, PWW, 37: 68.

21. House to Wilson, May 21, 1916, PWW, 37: 88–91.

22. Lansing to Wilson, May 25, 1916, PWW, 37: 106–108.

23. "An Address to the League to Enforce Peace," May 27, 1916, PWW, 37: 113–116.

24. Spring-Rice to Grey, May 20, 30, 1916, Gwynn, 2: 268–271, 334–336.

25. "A Memorial Day Address," May 30, 1916, PWW, 37: 123–128.

26. Steel, 97–99; Link *W*, 5: 26.

27. Gwynn, 2: 347.

28. Link *W*, 4: 42–48.

29. Sept. 2, 1916, PWW, 38: 131; cf. Sept. 30, 1916, PWW, 38: 304–305.

30. "A Campaign Address," Oct. 7, 1916, PWW, 38: 365–366.

31. Jeremiah O'Leary to Wilson (telegram), Sept. 29, Wilson to O'Leary, Sept. 29, 1916, PWW, 38: 285–286.

32. "An Address in Omaha," Oct. 4, 1916, PWW, 38: 347.

33. Link *W*, 5: 141–142; William C. Widenor, *Henry Cabot Lodge and the Search for an American Foreign Policy* (Berkeley, 1980), 243–245.

34. Theodore Roosevelt to Sir Horace Plunkett, July 9, 1916, Link *W*, 5: 142; to A. H. Lee, June 7, 1916, Theodore Roosevelt, *The Letters of Theodore Roosevelt*, ed. E. E. Morison et al., 8 vols. (Cambridge, Mass., 1954), 8: 1055.

35. Link *W*, 5: 145–147; John A. Garraty, *Henry Cabot Lodge: A Biography* (New York, 1953), 329–331.

36. Tumulty, 217–218.

37. LL, 5: 160.

CHAPTER 18: THE FINAL MEDIATION

1. Devlin, 543.

2. Siegfried Sassoon, *Collected Poems* (London, 1947), 84–85.

3. Devlin, 551–553.

4. Martin Gilbert, ed., *Lloyd George* (Englewood Cliffs, N.J., 1968), 94.

5. Frank Owen, *Tempestuous Journey: Lloyd George in His Life and Times* (London, 1954), 327.

6. Link *W*, 5: 179–180.

7. Link *W*, 5: 200.

8. Niermeyer, 102 (1938): 325.

9. House, Diary, Nov. 14, 1916, PWW, 38: 646.

10. House, 2: 391.

11. Nov. 25, 1916, PWW, 40: 67–70; cf. Link, *Wilson: Revolution*, 21–46.

12. Link, *Wilson: Revolution*, 70–74.

13. House, 2: 393–395.

14. House to Wilson, Dec. 4, 1916, PWW, 40: 137–140.

15. House to Lloyd George, Dec. 7, 1916, PWW, 40: 186.

16. Klaus Hildebrand, *Bethmann Hollweg: Der Kanzler ohne Eigenschaften?* (Düsseldorf, 1970).

17. Grey, 1: 255.

18. Fritz Fischer, *Griff nach der Weltmacht: Die Kriegszielpolitik des kaiserlichen Deutschland, 1914–1918* (Düsseldorf, 1967), 247.

19. Von Jagow to Bernstorff, June 7, 1916, in Karl E. Birnbaum, *Peace Moves and U-Boat Warfare: A Study of Imperial Germany's Policy toward the United States, April 18, 1916–January 9, 1917* (Stockholm, 1958), 106 n. 8.

20. Lynar, 45.

21. "An Appeal for a Statement of War Aims," Dec. 18, 1916, PWW, 40: 273–276.

22. Lansing, *Memoirs*, 186–187.

23. Link W, 5: 224; Link, *Wilson: Revolution*, 57; Devlin, 581–583.

24. House, Diary, Dec. 20, 1916, in House, 2: 405 (but Seymour, the editor, drops precisely this sentence!); PWW, 40: 304–305.

25. House, 2: 406–407; Page, 2: 207.

26. Graf Johann Heinrich von Bernstorff, *Deutschland und Amerika: Erinnerungen aus dem fünfjährigen Kriege* (Berlin, 1920), 412.

27. Weber, *Max Weber*, 579.

28. House, Diary, Jan. 3, 1917, House, 2: 414–415.

29. Bernstorff, *Deutschland*, 327–328.

30. House to Wilson, Jan. 15, 16, 17, 18, 1917, PWW, 40: 477–478, 493–494, 508, 516–517.

31. House to Wilson, Jan. 20, 1917, PWW, 40: 526–528.

32. Link, *Wilson: Revolution*, 59.

33. Sebastian Haffner, *Die Sieben Todesünden des deutschen Reiches im ersten Weltkrieg* (Bergisch Gladbach, 1981), 55–67.

34. Steel, 109; David W. Levy, *Herbert Croly of the New Republic: The Life and Thought of an American Progressive* (Princeton, 1985), 231–232.

35. "An Address to the Senate," Jan. 22, 1917, PWW, 40: 533ff.

36. Lansing, *Memoirs*, 193.

37. Page to Wilson, Jan. 20, 1917, PWW, 40: 531–532; cf. Page, 3: 317–318, and Lansing, *Memoirs*, 195.

38. Link *W*, 5: 268.

39. Mitchell Pirie Briggs, *George D. Herron and the European Settlement* (Stanford, 1932), 25.

40. Charles Forcey, *The Crossroads of Liberalism: Croly, Weyl, Lippmann and the Progressive Era, 1900–1925* (New York, 1961), 267–268.

41. Cooper, 315. The quotation is from the Song of Deborah.

42. Lodge, *Addresses*, 247–279; cf. Widenor, 258.

43. Link *W*, 5: 274.

44. Bernstorff, 372–375.

45. House, Diary, Jan. 4, 1917, in Arthur S. Link, "That Cobb Interview," *JAH* 72 (1985): 9.

46. Lansing, *Memoirs*, 212–213.

47. Houston, 1: 229.

48. Bernstorff, *Deutschland*, 370–371.

CHAPTER 19: WAR

1. Feb. 12, 1917, Theodore Roosevelt and Henry Cabot Lodge, *Selections from the Correspondence of Theodore Roosevelt and Henry Cabot Lodge, 1884–1918*, 2 vols. (New York and London, 1925) 2: 494–495.

2. Lodge to Roosevelt, Feb. 13, 1917, Link *W*, 5: 303.

3. PWW, 41: 315.

4. Franklin K. Lane to G. W. Lane, Feb. 25, 1917, PWW, 41: 282–283.

5. Wilson to House, Feb. 12, 1917, PWW, 41: 201.

6. House to Wilson, Feb. 10, 1917, PWW, 41: 190–191; C. Smit, *Tien Studiën betreffende Nederland in de Eerste Wereldoorlog* (Groningen, 1975), 46–49.

7. PWW, 41: 283–287.

8. "A Statement," March 4, 1917, PWW, 41: 318–320.

9. Joseph C. Grew, *Turbulent Era: A Diplomatic Record of Forty Years, 1904–1945*, 2 vols. (London, 1953), 1: 220.

10. Page, 3: 333; the German text, 345.

11. Page, 3: 361.

12. Lansing, "Memorandum," PWW, 41: 321–327.

13. Lansing, *Memoirs*, 228; cf. Samuel R. Spencer, Jr., *Decision for War 1917: The Laconia Sinking and the Zimmermann Telegram as Key Factors in the Public Reaction Against Germany* (Rindge, N.H., 1953).

14. "Second Inaugural Address," March 5, 1917, PWW, 41: 332–336.

15. House, Diary, March 5, PWW, 41: 340–341.

16. March 13, 1917, Roosevelt and Lodge, 2: 503.

17. *Papers Relating to the Foreign Relations of the United States: The Lansing Papers, 1914–1920.* 2 vols. (Washington, 1939–1940), 1: 626–628.

18. D. Higginbotham, "The American Revolution in a Wider World," in J. P. Greene, ed., *The American Revolution: Its Character and Limits* (New York, 1987), 163.

19. J. H. Moorhead, *American Apocalpyse: Yankee Protestants and the Civil War, 1860–1869* (New Haven and London, 1978).

20. "A Memorial Address," May 11, 1914, PWW, 30: 13–15.

21. "A Campaign Address in Omaha," Oct. 5, 1916, PWW, 38: 348.

22. Link, "Cobb," 7–17.

23. John L. Heaton, ed., *Cobb of "The World": A Leader in Liberalism* (New York, 1971), 267–270.

24. Link, *Wilson and Progressive Era*, 275.

25. Walter Lippmann, *Men of Destiny* (New York, 1927), 122–125, 137–138.

26. Dec. 7, 1911, PWW, 33: 585–587.

27. Houston, 1: 244.

28. Lansing, "Memorandum," PWW, 41: 437–444.

29. PWW, 41: 444–445.

30. House, Diary, March 27, 28, 1917, PWW, 41: 482–484, 496–498.

31. April 1, 1917, PWW, 41: 519–527.

32. Link *W*, 5: 426.

33. PWW, 41: 536–541.

34. Cooper, 321–322.

35. Tumulty, 258–259.

36. Devlin, 689.

37. Cooper, 322–323.

38. Link, "Cobb," 16–17.

39. Devlin, 686.

40. Golo Mann, *Deutsche Geschichte des 19. und 20. Jahrhunderts* (Frankfurt, 1966), 627.

41. Huthmacher, 93.

42. Lodge, Sept. 20, 1917, in Widenor, 264; Roosevelt to H. White, Aug. 3, 1917, in Osgood, 271–272.

43. David W. Noble, *The Paradox of Progressive Thought* (Minneapolis, 1958), 48; also Thompson, *Reformers*, 173–175.

44. Thompson, *Reformers*, 158.

45. Osgood, 260.

CHAPTER 20: PATRIOTISM AND BOLSHEVISM

1. "Message to the Soldiers of the National Army, Sept. 4, 1917," PWW, 44: 142; cf. Edward M. Coffman, *The War to End All Wars: The American Military Experience in World War I* (Madison, Wis., 1986), 76–77, and Robert H. Ferrell, *Woodrow Wilson and World War I, 1917–1921* (New York, 1985), 117.

2. "A Draft of a Proclamation," ca. May 1, 1917, PWW, 42: 180–182.

3. Leuchtenburg, 46.

4. Steel, 124.

5. LL, 7: 242; cf. Thompson, *Reformers*, 184.

6. Wilson to House, June 15, 1917, PWW, 42:, 520–521; Sir William Wiseman, "Memorandum," July 13, 1917, PWW, 43: 172–174; cf. interview with William Howard Taft, Dec. 12, 1917, PWW, 45: 272–273.

7. House to Wilson, April 22, 1917, PWW, 42: 120.

8. Spring-Rice to Lloyd George, April 26, 1917, PWW, 42: 140–141.

9. House, Diary, April 28, 1917, PWW, 42: 155–158.

10. House, Diary, April 30, 1917, PWW, 42: 168–173.

11. PWW, 42: 327–328.

12. Wilson to House, July 21, 1917, PWW, 43: 237–238.

13. Balfour to Wilson, Jan. 30, 1918, House, 3: 50–51.

14. Link, *Wilson: Revolution*, 78–79.

15. April 30, 1917, PWW, 42: 173–175.

16. Henry Cabot Lodge, *The Senate and the League of Nations* (New York and London, 1925), 80.

17. "Address on Flag Day," June 14, 1917, PWW, 42: 498–504.

18. "Address to the Officers of the Atlantic Fleet," Aug. 11, 1917, PWW, 43: 427–431.

19. "An Address in Buffalo to the American Federation of Labor," Nov. 12, 1917, PWW, 45: 11–17.

20. "Annual Message," Dec. 4, 1917, PWW, 45: 197.

21. Warren I. Cohen, *The American Revisionists: The Lessons of Intervention in World War I* (Chicago and London, 1967), 58.

22. Arno J. Mayer, *Political Origins of the New Diplomacy, 1917–1918* (New Haven, 1959).

23. Fischer, 341–344.

24. Text in letter of W. H. Page to R. Lansing, Aug. 13, 1917, PWW, 43: 482–485.

25. House to Wilson, Aug 17, 1917, PWW, 43: 508–509; cf. House to Wilson, Aug. 15, PWW, 43: 471–472.

26. House, Diary, Aug. 15, 1917, PWW, 43: 485–487.

27. PWW, 44: 33–36, 57–59.

28. Morris Hillquit to R. Lansing, May 10, 1917, PWW, 42: 268–269; Wilson to Lansing, May 11, 1917, PWW, 42: 274.

29. Mayer, *Origins*, 226.

30. George Kennan, *Russia Leaves the War: Soviet-American Relations, 1917–1920*, 2 vols. (London, 1956), 1: 17.

31. Kennan, *Russia Leaves the War*, 1: 32–49.

32. May 22, 1917, PWW, 42: 365–367.

33. Justin Kaplan, *Lincoln Steffens: A Biography* (New York, 1974), 223; Lincoln Steffens, *Autobiography* (New York, 1931), 748.

34. Kaplan, 223–224.

35. Steffens, 770–772.

36. Beatrice Farnsworth, *William C. Bullitt and the Soviet Union* (Bloomington, Ind., and London, 1967), 12–13.

37. Kaplan, 219.

38. Christopher Lasch, *The American Liberals and the Russian Revolution* (New York and London, 1962), 73.

39. Edward H. Carr, *A History of Soviet Russia: The Bolshevik*

Revolution, 3 vols. (London, 1950–1953), 3: 9–11; text in George Kennan, *Soviet Foreign Policy, 1917–1941* (Princeton, 1960), 116–119; cf. also George Kennan, *Russia and the West under Lenin and Stalin* (Boston, 1961), 29–35.

40. "A Statement by Robert Lansing," Dec. 4, 1917, PWW, 45: 205–207.

41. "Memorandum of Sir William Wiseman, Notes on Interview with the President," Jan. 23, 1918, PWW, 46: 85–88.

42. Kennan, *Russia Leaves the War*, 46ff.; Lasch, 69.

43. Lasch, 78.

44. Steel, 137.

45. Farnsworth, 17.

46. Lincoln Colcord to Wilson, Dec. 3, 1917, PWW, 43: 191–193.

47. David Francis to R. Lansing, Nov. 24, 1917, PWW, 45: 119–120; Daniels, Diary, Nov. 27, 1917, PWW, 45: 147.

48. Lansing to Wilson, Dec. 10, 1917, PWW, 45: 263–265.

49. Dec. 4, 1917, PWW, 45: 199.

50. Daniels, Diary, Jan. 4, 1918, PWW, 45: 474.

51. Carr, 3: 26–27.

52. David Francis to Robert Lansing, Dec. 31, 1917, PWW, 45: 411–414.

53. David Francis to Wilson, Jan. 3, 1918, PWW, 45: 433–435.

54. "Memorandum of W. B. Thompson," Jan. 3, 1918, PWW, 45: 443–447; cf. Kennan, *Russia Leaves the War*, 245.

55. Lasch, 153; Mayer, *Origins*, 391–393.

56. Lasch, 150.

57. B. W. Schaper, *Albert Thomas: Dertig Jaar Sociaal Reformisme* (Leiden, 1953), 176.

58. Arthur S. Link, *Woodrow Wilson and a Revolutionary World, 1913–1921* (Chapel Hill, 1982), 197–198.

CHAPTER 21: FOURTEEN POINTS

1. Wilson to House, Sept. 7, 1917, PWW, 44: 120–121; House to Wilson, Sept. 4, 1917, PWW, 44: 149–150.

2. James T. Shotwell, *At the Paris Peace Conference* (New York, 1937), 10–11.

3. "Memorandum on the Inquiry," July 5, 1928, House, 3: 170–172.

4. Shotwell, 24–25.

5. House, Diary, Oct. 24, 1917, PWW, 44: 439.

6. House, 3: 278–284.

7. PWW, 45: 459–474.

8. House, Diary, Dec. 30, 1917, PWW, 45: 399.

9. Spring-Rice to Balfour, Jan. 4, 1918, PWW, 45: 454–457.

10. House, Diary, Jan. 9, 1918, PWW, 45: 550–559.

11. David R. Woodward, "The Origins and Intent of David Lloyd George's January 5 War Aims Speech," TH 34 (1971): 22–39.

12. PWW, 45: 534–539.

13. June 12, 1918, Baker, 1: 46; cf. the memorandum of Lippmann and Cobb of October, 1918, with the same explanation, House, 4: 192–193; Winston S. Churchill, The World Crisis: The Aftermath (London, 1929), 137–138.

14. House, 3: 344–347.

15. House, "Diary," Feb. 8, 1918, PWW, 46: 290–291.

16. "Address," Feb. 11, 1918, PWW, 46: 318–324.

17. H. W. Temperley, A History of the Peace Conference of Paris, 6 vols. (London, 1920–1924), 6: 558.

18. Alfred Cobban, National Self-Determination (Oxford, 1944), 19–21.

19. J. J. Rousseau, Oeuvres complètes III: Du Contrat Social: Ecrits Politiques (Paris, 1964), 601–602.

20. "Address on Preparedness," Milwaukee, Jan. 32, 1916, PWW, 36: 58.

21. The Federalist, ed. Jacob E. Cooke (Middletown, Conn., 1961), no. 6, 31–33.

22. "Address on Preparedness to the Manhattan Club," Nov. 4, 1915, PWW, 35: 168.

23. Spring-Rice to Balfour, Jan. 4, 1918, PWW, 45: 454–457.

24. N. Gordon Levin, Jr., Woodrow Wilson and World Politics: America's Response to War and Revolution (New York, 1968), 247–248.

25. Temperley, 4: 429.

26. March 28, 1918, PWW, 47: 181–183; cf. March 29, 1918, PWW, 47: 203–205.

27. House, Diary, March 29, 1918, PWW, 47: 213.

28. Reading to Lloyd George, March 30, 1918, PWW, 47: 213.

29. April 2, 14, 1918, PWW, 47: 229, 338–341.

30. Wiseman to Foreign Office, ca. March 28, 1918, PWW, 47: 184–185.

31. "An Address," Baltimore, April 6, 1918, PWW, 47: 267–270.

32. "Remarks to Foreign Correspondents," April 8, 1918, PWW, 47: 284–289.

CHAPTER 22: PEACE AT LAST

1. House, Diary, Feb. 24, 1918, in Link, *Wilson and a Revolutionary World*, 132.

2. "An Address at Mount Vernon," July 4, 1918, PWW, 48: 515–556.

3. Wilson to Oscar F. Cushing, July 5, 1918, in Lawrence W. Martin, *Peace Without Victory: Woodrow Wilson and the British Liberals* (New Haven, 1958), 179; cf. Arthur Walworth, *Wilson and His Peacemakers: American Diplomacy at the Paris Peace Conference, 1919* (New York, 1977), 138.

4. PWW, 51: 253.

5. House, "Diary," Sept. 3, 1918, PWW, 49: 428–29.

6. House, "Diary," Sept. 24, 1918, PWW, 51: 275.

7. "An Address in the Metropolitan Opera House," Sept. 27, 1918, PWW, 51: 127–133.

8. Daniels, "Diary," Oct. 8, 1918, PWW, 51: 275.

9. PWW, 51: 268–269.

10. Mann, 646.

11. Arthur Walworth, *Woodrow Wilson*, 2 vols. (New York and London, 1977), 21–22.

12. Oct. 13, 1918, PWW, 51: 320–324.

13. Henry Ashurst, Diary, Oct. 14, 1918, PWW, 51: 338–340.

14. Klaus Schwabe, *Woodrow Wilson, Revolutionary Germany, and Peacemaking, 1918–1919: Missionary Diplomacy and the Relations of Power* (Chapel Hill and London, 1985), 47.

15. Daniels, "Diary," Oct. 16, 1918, PWW, 51: 347.

16. PWW, 51: 333–334.

17. PWW, 51: 402 n.1.

18. PWW, 51: 416–418.

19. PWW, 51: 413–415; Houston, 1: 380.

20. PWW, 51: 518–520.

21. House, Diary, Oct. 15, 1918, PWW, 51: 340–342.

22. Wilson to House, Oct. 30, 1918, PWW, 51: 511.

23. John L. Snell, "Wilson's Peace Program and German Social-ism, January–March 1918," *MVHR* 38 (1951): 368.

24. Edward B. Parsons, "Some International Implications of the 1918 Roosevelt-Lodge Campaign Against Wilson and a Democratic Congress," *PSQ* 19 (1989): 142–143.

25. Arthur Willert, *The Road to Safety: A Study in Anglo-American Relations* (London, 1952), 160–161.

26. House to Wilson, Oct. 30, 1918, PWW, 51: 511–513.

27. Wilson to House, Oct. 30, Nov. 4, 1918, PWW, 51: 513, 575.

28. Wilson to House, Oct. 29, 1918, PWW, 51: 505.

29. House to Wilson, Nov. 3, 1918, PWW, 51: 569–570.

30. House to Wilson, Nov. 5, 1918, PWW, 51: 594; cf. House, Diary, Nov. 4, 1918, in Walworth, 72; David Hunter Miller, *My Diary at the Conference of Paris*, 2 vols. (New York, 1924), 1: 6.

31. Max Weber to Hans Delbrück, Oct. 6, 1918, Max Weber, *Schriften und Reden*, ed. W. J. Mommsen (Tübingen, 1984), 288.

32. Mann, 652.

33. Nov. 11, 1918, PWW, 53: 34.

34. "A Statement," Nov. 11, 1918, PWW, 53: 34; "An Address to a Joint Session of Congress," Nov. 11, 1918, PWW, 53: 35–43.

35. "A Memorandum of a Conversation with Thomas P. Lamont," Oct. 4, 1918, PWW, 51: 225.

36. PWW, 51: 317–318, 343–344, 381–382.

37. Arno J. Mayer, *Politics and Diplomacy of Peacemaking: Containment and Counterrevolution at Versailles, 1918–1919* (London, 1967), 55; Seward W. Livermore, *Politics Is Adjourned: Woodrow Wilson and the War Congress* (Middletown, Conn., 1966), 211–212.

38. Roosevelt and Lodge, 2: 452.

39. Will H. Hays, *The Memoirs of Will H. Hays* (Garden City, N.Y., 1955), 169–177.

40. "Memorandum by Homer S. Cummings," Nov. 8 or 9, 1918, PWW, 51: 646–647.

41. David Lloyd George, *The Truth About the Peace Treaties*, 2 vols. (London, 1938), 1: 160.

42. Oct. 28, 1918, PWW, 51: 473.

43. Schwabe, 88, and Walworth, 43, speak in this connection of Wilson's surprising policy of balance, but the paradox is really that this was not Wilson's actual purpose, for balance was only a means to achieve an honorable peace, nothing more.

44. Marianne Weber, 638–639; cf. Mann, 646. The original German of Weber's remarks: "Das eigentümliche Schicksal der Welt is, dass der erste wirkliche Weltherrscher ein Professor ist. Wie sehr er Professor ist, sieht man an der grossen Dummheit, die er gemacht had: den Waffenstillstandsbedingungen. Verhindert er nicht, dass Deutschland waffenlos in die Friedensverhandlungen eintritt, so ist es mit seiner eigenen Herrschaft zu Ende."

CHAPTER 23: THE LEAGUE OF NATIONS

1. Lawrence, 258–259.

2. House to Wilson, Nov. 14, Wilson to House, Nov. 16, 1918, PWW, 53: 71–72, 96–97.

3. Floto, 73.

4. Karel Capek, *Gespräche mit T. G. Masaryk* (Munich, 1969), 172.

5. PR, 1: 159–160.

6. House, Diary, Dec. 16, 1918, PWW, 53: 401.

7. House, Diary, Dec. 14, 1918, PWW, 53: 390.

8. Josephus Daniels, *The Wilson Era*, 2 vols. (Chapel Hill, 1946), 2: 392.

9. Floto, 82.

10. Floto, 82.

11. House, Diary, Dec. 16, 1918, PWW, 53: 401–402; Floto, 216.

12. Baker, 1: 1–17.

13. PWW, 53: 350–357; Lawrence E. Gelfand, *The Inquiry: American Preparations for Peace, 1917–1919* (New Haven and London, 1963), 171–175; E. M. House and Charles Seymour, *What Really Happened at Paris: The Story of the Peace Conference, 1918–1919, by American Delegates* (New York, 1921), 280–283.

14. Grayson, "Diary," Dec. 8, 1918, PWW, 53: 336–337.

15. George Creel, *The War, the World and Wilson* (New York, 1920), 163.

16. A. Lentin, *Lloyd George, Woodrow Wilson and the Guilt of Germany: An Essay in the Pre-history of Appeasement* (Leicester, 1984), 8.

17. Grayson, Diary, PWW, 53: 614.

18. "A Reply to President Poincaré," Dec. 14, 1918, PWW, 53: 386–387.

19. "An Address at the University of Paris," Dec. 21, 1918, PWW, 53: 461–463; "After-Dinner Remarks at Buckingham Palace," Dec. 27, 1918, PWW, 53: 522–524.

20. "A Luncheon Address at Manchester, Dec. 30, 1918, PWW, 53: 548–549.

21. "An Address in Free Trade Hall," Dec. 30, 1918, PWW, 53: 549–552.

22. Stephen Bonsal, *Unfinished Business* (Garden City, N.Y., 1944), 15–16.

23. PWW, 53, 544–545 n.1; Shotwell, 100; Charles Seymour, *Letters from the Paris Peace Conference* (New Haven and London, 1965), 85.

24. Owen, 501–502; Martin Pugh, *Lloyd George* (London and New York 1988), 26–28.

25. George Riddell, *Lord Riddell's Intimate Diary of the Paris Peace Conference and After, 1918–1923* (London, 1933), 57; Lloyd George, *Truth*, 1: 156–57.

26. "A News Report of an Interview," Dec. 18, 1918, PWW, 53: 422–430; Daphne Bennett, *Margot: A Life of the Countess of Oxford and Asquith* (London, 1986), 301.

27. Lloyd George, *Truth*, 1, 233; cf. 230–231.

28. Cecil, Diary, Feb. 6, 1919, PWW, 54: 514.

29. Sir James Headlam-Morley, *A Memoir of the Paris Peace Conference 1919* (London, 1972), 16.

30. Link *W*, 5: 27.

31. Huthmacher and Susman, 19–44.

32. March 22, 1919, Roosevelt, *Letters*, 8: 1302–1303.

33. Clemenceau, 128.

34. Garraty, *Wilson*, 146.

35. Edith Benham, Diary, Jan. 21, 1919, PWW, 54: 198.

36. R. S. Baker, Diary, April 9, 1919, PWW, 57: 148; A. J. P. Taylor, *Lloyd George: Rise and Fall* (Cambridge, 1961), 33–34; Lentin, 51.

37. Richard Hofstadter, *The Age of Reform* (New York, 1955), 278.

38. Wilson to Edith B. Galt, Aug. 18, 1915, PWW, 34: 241.

39. Feb. 15, 1919, Headlam-Morley, 31.

40. Lloyd George, *Truth*, 1: 282.

41. Lloyd George, *Truth*, 1: 232–233.

42. "Remarks at Suresne Cemetery on Memorial Day," May 30, 1919, PWW, 59: 606–610.

43. Lentin, 118; Nicolson, 85–90.

44. House-Seymour, 26.

45. "Remarks to the American Bar Association," Oct. 20, 1914, PWW, 31: 184–186.

46. "Address in Kansas City," Sept. 6, 1919, PP, 6: 13; cf. speech in Portland, Oregon, Sept. 15, 1919, PP, 6: 200–201.

47. House, 4: 28–36.

48. Sept. 7, 1918, PWW, 49: 469–471; cf. House, 4: 49.

49. PWW, 53: 350–356.

50. House, Diary, Dec. 14, 27, 1918, PWW, 53: 389–391, 525; cf. House, Diary, Jan. 31, 1919, PWW, 54: 407.

51. Lansing, "Memorandum," Jan. 11, 1919, PWW, 54: 3–4.

52. George Curry, "Woodrow Wilson, Jan Smuts and the Versailles Settlement," *AHR* 66 (1961): 969–977.

53. "Address to the Peace Conference," Feb. 14, 1919, PWW, 55: 177.

54. "An Address to the Third Plenary Session of the Peace Conference," Feb. 14, 1919, PWW, 55: 164–188.

55. Bonsal, 152.

56. David Lloyd George, *Truth*, 1: 225.

57. Bonsal, 206.

58. Floto, 84.

CHAPTER 24: RUSSIA

1. Arno J. Mayer, *Politics and Diplomacy of Peacemaking: Containment and Counterrevolution at Versailles, 1918–1919* (London, 1968); cf. Floto, 247–260.

2. Levin, vii.

3. Thompson, *Reformers*, 238.

4. Grayson, Diary, March 10, 1919, PWW, 55: 471.

5. Wilson to Lansing, Jan. 10, 1919, PWW, 53: 709.

6. "Statements," Dec. 28, 1918, PWW, 53: 574–575.

7. "Meeting of the Council of Ten," Jan. 16, 1919, PWW, 54: 102.

8. Wilson to Tumulty, Feb. 23, 1918, PWW, 46: 422.

9. "To the Fourth All-Russia Congress of Soviets," Jan. 16, 1919, PWW, 46: 598; cf. Kennan, *Decision*, 510–513.

10. Bullitt to Frank Polk, March 2, 1918, PWW, 46: 5110–5113.

11. Wilson to House, July 8, 1918, PWW, 48: 549–550.

12. "Memorandums," July 6, 17, 1918, PWW, 48: 542–543, 640–643; press statement, Aug. 3, 1918, PWW, 49: 170–172.

13. Litvinov to Wilson, Dec. 24, 1918, PWW, 53: 492–494; W. H. Buckler to Lansing, Jan. 18, 1919, PWW, 54: 135–137; report of Buckler, PWW, 54: 180–181; cf. Thompson, *Reformers*, 86–92.

14. Jan. 22, 1919, PWW, 54: 204–206; cf. Thompson, *Reformers*, 86–92.

15. Report of Bullitt, March 16, 1919, PWW, 55: 540–555; cf. William C. Bullitt, *The Bullitt Mission to Russia: Testimony Before the Committee on Foreign Relations U.S. Senate* (New York, 1919) and Farnsworth, passim.

16. Kaplan, 250.

17. Bullitt, "Memorandum," ca. March 18, 1919, PWW, 56: 387–391.

18. House, Diary, March 25, 1919, PWW, 56: 387–391.

19. Henry Wickham Steed, *Through Thirty Years 1892–1922*, 2 vols. (London, 1924), 1: 301–307.

20. Bullitt to Wilson, April 18, 1919, PWW, 57: 459–460; cf. Thompson, *Reformers*, 237–245.

21. Bullitt to Wilson, May 17, 1919, PWW, 57: 232–233.

22. J. Hofman and A. Stam, "De psychoanalyse in dienst van een diplomaat, Freud als co-auteur van W. C. Bullitt," *Tijdschrift voor Psychiatrie* 24 (1982): 125–134.

23. Betty M. Unterberger, "Woodrow Wilson and the Bolsheviks: The 'Acid Test' of Soviet-American Relations," *DH* 11 (1987): 89.

24. Jan. 10, 1919, PWW, 53: 709.

25. March 18, 1919, PWW, 56: 375–378.

26. F. Nansen to Lenin, April 17, 1919, PWW, 57: 438–440; House, Diary, April 19, 1919, PWW, 57: 503–505.

27. Link, *Wilson and a Revolutionary World*, 88.

1. "Imperial War Cabinet Minutes," Dec. 30, 1918, PWW, 53: 564.

2. Arthur M. Schlesinger, Jr., *The Imperial Presidency* (London, 1974), 85.

3. "Meetings of the Council of Ten," Feb. 12, 1919, PWW, 55: 106–107.

4. "Meetings of the Council of Ten," Feb. 12, 1919, PWW, 55: 106–107.

5. House, Diary, Feb. 14, 1919, PWW, 55: 193.

6. Churchill, 186–187.

7. Walworth, 148 n.13.

8. Grayson, Diary, Feb. 8, 1919, PWW, 55: 3.

9. Floto, 123, 129, 154.

10. Floto, 154.

11. Edith Bolling Wilson, *My Memoir* (Indianapolis and New York, 1939), 245–246.

12. Lodge to Theodore Roosevelt, Jan. 15, 1915, Link *W*, 3: 146.

13. Lodge, *Senate*, 220–221.

14. Bonsal, 275.

15. Speech to the Senate, Aug. 12, 1919, Lodge, *Senate*, 408–409.

16. Ruhl J. Bartlett, *The League to Enforce Peace* (Chapel Hill, 1944), 100.

17. Widenor, 310–311; Parsons, 155.

18. "Memorandum of a conversation of Ray Stannard Baker with Woodrow Wilson," May 12, 1916, PWW, 37: 34; House, Diary, May 17, 1918, PWW, 48: 51.

19. Henry F. Pringle, *The Life and Times of William Howard Taft: A Biography*, 2 vols. (New York and Toronto, 1939), 2: 912.

20. Dec. 4, 1917, PWW, 45: 195.

21. Bonsal, 48.

22. Denna Frank Fleming, *The United States and the League of Nations, 1918–1920* (New York and London, 1932), 79.

23. "An Address in Boston," Feb. 14, 1919, PWW, 55: 238–245.

24. Lodge, *Senate*, 99–100.

25. Thomas Bailey, *Woodrow Wilson and the Lost Peace* (New York, 1944), 198–199.

26. "Remarks to Members of the Democratic National Committee," Feb. 18, 1919, PWW, 55: 322–323.

27. "A Statement," March 4, 1919, PWW, 55: 408–409.

28. Grayson, Diary, March 4, 1919, PWW, 55: 410.

29. "An Address at the Metropolitan Opera House," March 4, 1919, PWW, 55: 413–421.

CHAPTER 26: CRISIS

1. Edith Wilson, 245.

2. House, Diary, March 14, 1919, PWW, 55: 499.

3. House, "Diary," March 16, 1919, PWW, 55: 538; Cecil, Diary, PWW, 55: 539.

4. March 27, 1919, Paul Mantoux, *Les délibérations du Conseil des Quatre, 24 mars–28 juin 1919*, 2 vols. (Paris, 1955), 1: 41–45.

5. Baker, 3: 449–457.

6. "Notes of Meetings of the Council of Four," March 28, 1919, PWW, 56: 365–371.

7. House, Diary, March 28, 1919, PWW, 56: 349–350; Lansing, "Memorandum," March 28, 1919, PWW, 56: 351; Walworth, 268–269.

8. Steed, 2: 310.

9. Grayson, Diary, May 6, 1919, PWW, 58: 461–463.

10. "Meetings of the Council of Four," March 31, 1919, PWW, 66: 456–458; April 16, 1919, PWW, 57: 393–397.

11. Grayson, Diary, March 26, 1919, PWW, 56: 285.

12. Curry, "Woodrow Wilson," 983–984; Jan Smuts, *Selections from the Smuts Papers*, ed. W. K. Hancock (Cambridge, 1966), 4: 93–98; W. K. Hancock, *Smuts: The Sanguine Years, 1870–1919* (Cambridge, 1962), 539–542.

13. Lamont, "Reparations," in House and Seymour, 259–290; Walworth, 279–281.

14. Wilson to Lloyd George, May 5, 1919, PWW, 58: 446–448.

15. Link, *Wilson: Revolution*, 91; cf. Marc Trachtenberg, "Versailles after Sixty Years," *JCH* 17 (1982): 505 n.43.

16. Wiseman to Lord Reading, Aug. 16, 1918, PWW, 49: 273–274.

17. House, Diary, Aug. 30, 1914, PWW, 30: 462.

18. Schwabe, 22–26.

19. Schwabe, 249; Weinstein, 342–344.

20. April 2, 1919, PWW, 56: 533.

21. April 2, 8, 1919, Mantoux, 1: 120–124, 184–192; PWW, 57: 120–130.

22. April 9, 1919, PWW, 57: 149–150.

23. "Notes of a Meeting of the Council of Four," May 1, 1919, PWW, 58: 277–278.

24. June 25–26, 1919, Mantoux, 2: 518–519, 524.

25. Fritz Dickmann, "Die Kriegsschuldfrage auf der Friedenskonferenz von Paris 1919," *HZ* 173 (1963): 40–41.

26. E. Benham, Diary, April 2, 1919, PWW, 56: 540–541; Floto, 188.

27. House, Diary, April 1, 2, 1919, PWW, 56: 517–518, 539–540.

28. Grayson to Tumulty, April 10, 1919, PWW, 57: 235.

29. Weinstein, esp. 345; PWW, 58: 633.

30. Nicolson, 43.

31. April 11, 1919, PWW, 57: 241.

32. Trachtenberg, 494–495.

33. E. Benham, Diary, April 8, 1919, PWW, 57: 140–141.

34. Grayson, "Diary," April 7, 10, 1919, PWW, 57: 66, 235.

35. Baker, Diary, March 27, April 3, PWW, 36: 338, 577–578.

36. Edith B. Wilson, 250–253.

CHAPTER 27: PRINCIPLES AND INTERESTS

1. Grayson, Diary, April 17, 1919, PWW, 57: 426–430.

2. E. Benham, Diary, April 19, 1919, PWW, 57: 502–503.

3. Baker to Wilson, Dec. 18, 1918, PWW, 53: 433–434.

4. Jan. 7, 1919, PWW, 53: 641–644; cf. Floto, 88–94.

5. Wilson to Orlando, Jan. 13, 1919, PWW, 54: 50–51.

6. Baker, Diary, May 28, 1919, PWW, 59: 574–575; cf. PWW, 61: 387–388.

7. A. C. Coolidge to the American Commissioners, April 7, 1919, PWW, 57: 95–97.

8. From Isaiah Bowman and others, April 17, 1919, PWW, 57: 432–433.

9. Council of Four, April 19, 20, 21, 1919, PWW, 57: 479–486, 512–521, 536–542.

10. G. L. Beer, Diary, May 17, 1919, PWW, 59: 244–245.

11. Council of Four, April 23, 1919, PWW, 58: 18.

12. Council of Four, April 23, 1919, PWW, 58: 5–8.

13. Mayer, *Politics*, 704.

14. Grayson, Diary, April 23, May 2, 1919, PWW, 58: 3–5, 330–333.

15. May 26, 1919, Mantoux, 2: 208.

16. Bonsal, 33.

17. Paul Gordon Lauren, "Human Rights in History: Diplomacy and Racial Equality at the Paris Peace Conference," *DH* 3 (1978): 261.

18. April 11, 1919, PWW, 57: 247–266.

19. Baker, Diary, April 30, 1919, PWW, 58: 270–271.

CHAPTER 28: THE PEACE SIGNED

1. Interview with Brockdorff-Rantzau, April 28, 1919, PWW, 58: 307.

2. Grayson, "Diary," May 7, 1919, PWW, 58: 499–504; Sir Robert Borden to Sir Thomas White, May 7, 1919, PWW, 58: 517–520.

3. Dickmann, 78–79 n.3; Peter Krüger, *Versailles: Deutsche Aussenpolitik zwischen Revisionismus und Friedensicherung* (Munich, 1986), 22.

4. Riddell, 74; Baker, Diary, May 7, 1919, PWW, 58: 529–530.

5. PWW, 58: 514–517; Krüger, 21–22.

6. Brockdorff-Rantzau to Clemenceau, May 29, 1919, PWW, 59: 579–584.

7. May 14, 1919, PWW, 59: 149–150; Smuts, 157–158.

8. May 16, 1919, PWW, 59: 187–188.

9. Hancock, 512.

10. Smuts to Wilson, May 30, 1919, PWW, 59: 616–618; Smuts, 208–209; cf. Smuts, 226–231.

11. Smuts, 263; cf. 171, 178.

12. Baker, Diary, May 19, 1919, PWW, 59: 285.

13. Walworth, 394–395.

14. Lippmann, *Letters*, May 15, Aug. 15, 1914, 114, 126–128.

15. Becker to W. Dodd, Spring 1920, Lippmann, *Letters*, 69–70.

16. Peter Berg, *Deutschland und Amerika 1918–1929: Über das deutsche Amerikabild der zwanziger Jahre* (Lübeck and Hamburg, 1963), 25–33.

17. "Observations of the German Delegation on the Conditions of

the Peace," PR, 4: 809; "A Luncheon Address to Women in Cincinnati," Oct. 26, 1916, PWW, 36: 526–33.

18. Report of historians, PR, 4: 781–94.

19. Martin, 205.

20. Grayson, Diary, May 2, 1919, PWW, 58: 332.

21. Grayson, Diary, May 3, 1919, PWW, 58: 367; Baker, Diary, May 28, 1919, PWW, 59: 574–575.

22. House and Seymour, 273.

23. "After-Dinner Remarks," May 9, 1919, PWW, 59: 598–600.

24. "Remarks at Suresnes Cemetery," May 30, 1919, PWW, 59: 606–610.

25. Baker, Diary, May 30, 1919, PWW, 59: 621–623; Edith Benham, Diary, PWW, 59: 620–621.

26. House, Diary, May 31, 1919, PWW, 59: 644–645.

27. Paderewski to Wilson, May 31, 1919, PWW, 59: 638–639.

28. Baker, Diary, May 31, 1919, PWW, 59: 645–647.

29. Grayson, Diary, June 3, 1919, PWW, 60: 43.

30. R. S. Baker, Diary, June 3, 1919, PWW, 60: 80; "Meeting of the Council of Four," PWW, 60: 88.

31. Baker, Diary, June 3, 1919, PWW, 60: 80; Grayson, Diary, June 15, 1919, PWW, 60: 569–570.

32. "Discussion with American Delegation," June 3, 1919, PWW, 60: 67.

33. Lippmann, *Letters*, June 9, 1919, 117–119.

34. June 27, 1919, Mantoux, 2: 546.

35. *Haaagsche Post*, June 7, 1919, 664–665; the text of the translation here was made at the time by Wilson's staff, and is reprinted in PWW, 60: 250–255; cf. PWW, 59: 245, PWW, 60: 566.

36. Speech in Columbus, Ohio, Sept. 4, 1919, PP, 5: 591.

37. Baker, Diary, June 13, 1919, PWW, 60: 532–533.

38. June 12, 1919, PWW, 60: 442–459.

39. Grayson, Diary, June 13, 1919, PWW, 60: 488.

40. Hagen Schulze, *Weimar: Deutschland 1917–1933* (Berlin, 1982), 196.

41. House, Diary, June 29, 1919, PWW, 61: 354–355.

42. Sept. 2, 1919, PP, 6: 380.

43. Schwabe, 56–58.

44. Link, *Wilson: Revolution*, 100–103.

45. July 29, 1919, *Congressional Record*, 66 Cong., 1 Sess., 3316–3320.

46. Mayer, *Politics*, 774.

47. Mann, 674.

48. Weber, *Schriften*, 306; Schwabe, 51.

49. Krüger, 44.

CHAPTER 29: ARTICLE X

1. PWW, 61: 378–382.

2. PWW, 61: 401–404.

3. PWW, 61: 426–436.

4. Osgood, 299; Levy, 266.

5. Selig Adler, *The Isolationist Impulse: The Twentieth Century Reaction* (New York, 1961), 43–44.

6. George Norris, *George Norris, Fighting Liberal: Autobiography* (New York and London, 1966), 213.

7. Lippmann, *Men of Destiny* (New York, 1927), 142.

8. Lippmann, *Men of Destiny*, 244; Toth, 557–558.

9. Fleming, 94–95.

10. David Mervin, "Henry Cabot Lodge and the League of Nations," *JAH* 4 (1970): 209.

11. Widenor, 351–352.

12. Lodge, *Senate*, 212–213.

13. Farnsworth, 62.

14. Tumulty, 442.

15. Lodge, *Senate*, 388.

16. Philip C. Jessup, *Elihu Root*, 2 vols. (New York, 1939), 2: 392–393; Henry L. Stimson and McGeorge Bundy, *On Active Service in Peace and War* (New York, 1948), 103.

17. Lloyd E. Ambrosius, *Woodrow Wilson and the American Diplomatic Tradition: The Treaty Fight in Perspective* (Cambridge, 1987), 180.

18. Walter Lippmann, *U. S. Foreign Policy: Shield of the Republic* (Boston, 1943), 31.

19. Ronald Stromberg, *Collective Security and American Foreign Policy, from the League of Nations to NATO* (New York, 1963), 37–38.

20. Weinstein, 351–352.

21. Steel, 163.

22. Complete text of the White House Conference in Lodge, *Senate*, 297–379.

23. Kurt Wimer, "Woodrow Wilson Tries Conciliation: An Effort that Failed," *TH* 25 (1963): 427.

CHAPTER 30: THE FINAL DEFEAT

1. Lippmann, *Selected Letters*, ed. J. M. Blum (New York, 1956), 182.

2. Tumulty, 435.

3. St. Louis, Sept. 5, 1919, PP, 6: 640.

4. Minneapolis, Sept. 9, 1919, PP, 6: 74.

5. Spokane, Sept. 12, 1919, PP, 6: 160–161.

6. Oakland, Sept. 18, 1919, PP, 6: 272.

7. Salt Lake City, Sept. 23, 1919, PP, 6: 358.

8. San Francisco, Sept. 18, 1919, PP, 6: 252.

9. Ferrell, 169.

10. Sioux Falls, Sept. 8, PP, 6: 52.

11. Omaha, Sept. 8, PP, 6: 42.

12. St. Paul, Sept. 9., PP, 6: 78.

13. Spokane, Sept. 12, PP, 6: 162.

14. Los Angeles, Sept. 20, PP, 6: 323.

15. San Francisco, Sept. 17, PP, 6: 231.

16. Link, *Wilson: Revolution*, 117–118.

17. Salt Lake City, Sept. 23, PP, 6: 351.

18. Gene Smith, *When the Cheering Stopped* (London, 1964), 78.

19. Edith Wilson, 283.

20. Pueblo, Sept. 25, PP, 6: 415–416.

21. Ferrell, 169.

22. Weinstein, 260.

23. Edith Wilson, 289.

24. Houston, 2: 37–39.

25. Bonsal, 272–275, 285–286.

26. Thomas Bailey, *Woodrow Wilson and the Great Betrayal* (New York, 1945), 178.

27. Bonsal, 272–275, 285–286.

28. Edith Wilson, 296–297.

29. Bailey, *Betrayal*, 193.

30. Lodge, *Senate*, 212–214.

31. Houston, 2: 49.

32. George W. Egerton, "The Lloyd George Government and the Creation of the League of Nations," *AHR* 79 (1978): 899–900; Ferrell, 278–279.

33. Egerton, passim.

34. Egerton, 911.

35. Bailey, *Betrayal*, 211.

36. Henry F. Pringle, *The Life and Times of William Howard Taft: A Biography*, 2 vols. (New York and Toronto, 1939), 2: 949.

37. David Cronon, ed., *The Political Thought of Woodrow Wilson* (Indianapolis and New York, 1965), 540–545.

38. Grayson, 106.

CHAPTER 31: THE END

1. Grayson, 112–113.

2. Houston, 2: 70.

3. Grayson, 116.

4. Gene Smith, 163.

5. Gene Smith, 164.

6. Bailey, *Betrayal*, 300.

7. Bailey, *Betrayal*, 344.

8. Cordell Hull, *Memoirs*, 2 vols. (New York, 1948) 1: 117–121.

9. Gene Smith, 216.

10. Edith Wilson, 332–339.

11. Edith Wilson, 309.

12. PP, 6: 540–541.

13. Gene Smith, 232.

14. Raymond B. Fosdick, *Letters on the League of Nations* (Princeton, 1966), 143–144.

15. Edith Wilson, 344; Reid, 236.

16. Gene Smith, 244.

17. Gene Smith, 249–250.

1. Churchill, 128.

2. Thomas J. Knock, "History with Lightning: The Forgotten Film Wilson," in Peter C. Rollins, ed., *Hollywood as Historian* (Lexington, Ky., 1983).

3. George Kennan, *American Diplomacy, 1900–1950* (Chicago, 1951), 69.

4. Arthur S. Link, *The Higher Realism of Woodrow Wilson and Other Essays* (Nashville, 1971), 138–139.

5. Stimson, 107.

6. "After-Dinner Remarks in New York to the Friendly Sons of St. Patrick," March 17, 1909, PWW, 19: 102–108.

7. "After-Dinner Remarks," March 17, 1909, PWW, 19: 108.

BIBLIOGRAPHY

COLLECTIONS AND WORKS BY CONTEMPORARIES

Baker, Ray Stannard. *Woodrow Wilson and World Settlement.* 3 vols. London, 1923.

—————. *Woodrow Wilson: Life and Letters.* 8 vols. London, 1927–1939.

Becker, Carl L. *"What is the Good of History?" Selected Letters 1900–1945.* Ed. M. Kammen. Ithaca and London, 1973.

Bernhardi, Friedrich von. *Deutschland und der nächste Krieg.* Stuttgart and Berlin, 1913.

Bernstorff, Graf Johann Heinrich von. *Deutschland und Amerika: Erinnerungen aus dem fünfjährigen Kriege.* Berlin, 1920.

—————. *Erinnerungen und Briefe.* Zurich, 1936.

Bonsal, Stephen. *Unfinished Business.* Garden City, N.Y., 1944.

Bullitt, William C. *The Bullitt Mission to Russia: Testimony Before the Committee on Foreign Relations U.S. Senate.* New York, 1919.

Capek, Karel. *Gespräche mit T. G. Masaryk.* Munich, 1969.

Churchill, Winston C. *The World Crisis: The Aftermath.* London, 1929.

Clemenceau, Georges. *Grandeurs et misères d'une victoire.* Paris, 1930.

Creel, George. *The War, the World and Wilson.* New York, 1920.

Croly, Herbert. *The Promise of American Life.* Ed. J. W. Ward. Indianapolis, 1965.

Daniels, Josephus. *The Wilson Era.* 2 vols. Chapel Hill, 1946.

Fosdick, Raymond B. *Letters on the League of Nations.* Princeton, 1966.

Freud, Sigmund, and William C. Bullitt. *Thomas Woodrow Wilson.* Boston, 1967.

Gerard, James W. *My Four Years in Germany.* London, 1917.

Grayson, Cary T. *An Intimate Memoir*. New York, 1960.

Grew, Joseph C. *Turbulent Era: A Diplomatic Record of Forty Years, 1904–1945*. 2 vols. London, 1929.

Grey, Viscount, of Fallodon, K.G. *Twenty-Five Years, 1892–1916*. 2 vols. London, 1953.

Gwynn, Stephen, ed. *The Letters and Friendships of Sir Cecil Spring-Rice: A Record*. 2 vols. London, 1929.

Hancock, W. K., ed. *Selections from the Smuts Papers*. Cambridge, 1966.

Hays, Will H. *The Memoirs of Will H. Hays*. Garden City, N.Y., 1955.

Headlam-Morley, Sir James. *A Memoir of the Paris Peace Conference 1919*. London, 1972.

Heaton, John L., ed. *Cobb of "The World": A Leader in Liberalism*. New York, 1924.

Hoover, Herbert. *The Ordeal of Woodrow Wilson*. New York, 1958.

House, Edward M. *The Intimate Papers of Colonel House*. Ed. Charles Seymour. 4 vols. Boston and New York, 1926–1928.

House, Edward M., and Charles Seymour. *What Really Happened at Paris: The Story of the Peace Conference, 1918–1919, by American Delegates*. New York, 1921.

Houston, David F. *Eight Years with Wilson's Cabinet, 1913–1920*. London, 1926.

Hull, Cordell. *Memoirs*. 2 vols. New York, 1948.

Jacobs, Aletta. *Herinneringen*. Amsterdam, 1924.

Kerney, James. *The Political Education of Woodrow Wilson*. New York and London, 1926.

Keynes, John Maynard. *The Economic Consequences of the Peace*. New York, 1920.

Lansing, Robert. *The Peace Conference: A Personal Narrative*. London, 1921.

———. *The Big Four and Others at the Paris Peace Conference*. London, 1922.

————. *War Memoirs*. London, 1935.

Lawrence, David. *The True Story of Woodrow Wilson*. London, 1924.

Lippmann, Walter. *Men of Destiny*. New York, 1927.

————. *U.S. Foreign Policy: Shield of the Republic*. Boston, 1943.

————. *Drift and Mastery*. Ed. W. Leuchtenburg. Englewood Cliffs, N.J., 1961.

————. *Walter Lippmann, Public Philosopher: Selected Letters*. Ed. J. M. Blum. New York, 1985.

Lloyd George, David. *War Memoirs*. 8 vols. London, 1933–1936.

————. *The Truth About the Peace Treaties*. 2 vols. London, 1938.

Lodge, Henry Cabot. *War Addresses 1915–1917*. Boston and New York, 1917.

————. *The Senate and the League of Nations*. New York and London, 1925.

McAdoo, Eleanor Wilson. *The Woodrow Wilsons*. New York, 1937.

McCombs, William. *Making the President*. New York, 1921.

Mantoux, Paul. *Les délibérations du Conseil des Quatre, 24 Mars–28 Juin 1919*. 2 vols. Paris, 1955.

Miller, David Hunter. *My Diary at the Conference at Paris*. 2 vols. New York, 1924.

Myers, William Star, ed. *Woodrow Wilson: Some Princeton Memories*. Princeton, 1946.

Nicolson, Harold. *Peacemaking 1919*. London, 1934.

Norris, George. *George Norris, Fighting Liberal: Autobiography*. New York and London, 1966.

Page, Walter Hines. *The Life and Letters of Walter Hines Page*. Ed. B. J. Hendrick. 3 vols. London, 1923–1925.

Papers Relating to the Foreign Relations of the United States: The Lansing Papers, 1914–1920. 2 vols. Washington, 1939–1940.

Papers Relating to the Foreign Relations of the United States 1919: The Paris Peace Conference. 13 vols. Washington, 1942–1947.

Reid, Edith Gittings. *Woodrow Wilson, the Caricature, the Myth and the Man.* London, 1934.

Riddell, George. *Lord Riddell's Intimate Diary of the Paris Peace Conference and After, 1918–1923.* London, 1933.

Roosevelt, Theodore. *The Works of Theodore Roosevelt.* Ed. Herman Hagedorn. 24 vols. New York, 1923–1926.

———. *The Letters of Theodore Roosevelt.* Ed. E. E. Morison et al. 8 vols. Cambridge, Mass., 1954.

———. *The Writings of Theodore Roosevelt.* Ed. William H. Harbaugh. Indianapolis and New York, 1967.

Roosevelt, Theodore, and Henry Cabot Lodge. *Selections from the Correspondence of Theodore Roosevelt and Henry Cabot Lodge, 1884–1918.* 2 vols. New York and London, 1925.

Sassoon, Siegfried. *Collected Poems.* London, 1947.

Seymour, Charles. *Letters from the Paris Peace Conference.* New Haven and London, 1965.

Shotwell, James T. *At the Paris Peace Conference.* New York, 1937.

Steed, Henry Wickham. *Through Thirty Years 1892–1922: A Personal Narrative.* 2 vols. London, 1924.

Steffens, Lincoln. *Autobiography.* New York, 1931.

Stimson, Henry L., and McGeorge Bundy. *On Active Service in Peace and War.* New York, 1948.

Stoddard, H. L. *As I Know Them: Presidents and Politics from Grant to Coolidge.* New York, 1927.

Tardieu, André. *La Paix.* Paris, 1921.

Temperley, H. W. *A History of the Peace Conference of Paris.* 6 vols. London, 1920–1924.

Tumulty, Joseph P. *Woodrow Wilson as I Know Him.* London, 1922.

Weber, Max. *Schriften und Reden, 1914–1918*. Ed. W. J. Mommsen. Tübingen, 1984.

White, William Allen. *Woodrow Wilson: The Man, His Time and His Task*. Cambridge, Mass., 1926.

Wilson, Edith Bolling. *My Memoir*. Indianapolis and New York, 1939.

Wilson, Woodrow. *The Public Papers of Woodrow Wilson*. 6 vols. New York and London, 1922–1927.

———. *The New Freedom*. Ed. William E. Leuchtenburg. Englewood Cliffs, N.J., 1951.

———. *A Day of Dedication: The Essential Writings and Speeches of Woodrow Wilson*. Ed. Albert Fried. New York and London, 1963.

———. *The Political Thought of Woodrow Wilson*. Ed. David Cronon. Indianapolis and New York, 1965.

———. *The Papers of Woodrow Wilson*. Ed. A. S. Link et al. Princeton, 1966. 61 vols. published as of 1989.

WORKS OF LATER WRITERS

Adler, Selig. *The Isolationist Impulse: The Twentieth Century Reaction*. New York, 1961.

Ambrosius, Lloyd E. "The Orthodoxy of Revisionism: Woodrow Wilson and the New Left." *Diplomatic History* 3 (1977): 199–214.

———. *Woodrow Wilson and the American Diplomatic Tradition: The Treaty Fight in Perspective*. Cambridge, 1987.

Bailey, Thomas. *Woodrow Wilson and the Great Betrayal*. New York, 1945.

———. *Woodrow Wilson and the Lost Peace*. Chicago, 1963.

Bannister, Robert C., Jr. *Ray Stannard Baker: The Mind and Thought of a Progressive*. New Haven and London, 1966.

Bartlett, Ruhl J. *The League to Enforce Peace*. Chapel Hill, 1944.

Beard, Charles A. *An Economic Interpretation of the Constitution of the United States*. New York, 1913.

Bennett, Daphne. *Margot: A Life of the Countess of Oxford and Asquith*. London, 1986.

Berg, Peter. *Deutschland und Amerika 1918–1929: Über das deutsche Amerikabild der zwanziger Jahre*. Lübeck and Hamburg, 1963.

Binkley, Robert C. "Ten Years of Peace Conference History." *Journal of Modern History* 1 (1929): 607–629.

Birnbaum, Karl E. *Peace Moves and U-Boat Warfare: A Study of Imperial Germany's Policy toward the United States, April 18, 1916–January 9, 1917*. Stockholm, 1958.

Bowen, Elizabeth. *The Mulberry Tree: The Writings of Elizabeth Bowen*. London, 1986.

Bragdon, Henry W. *Woodrow Wilson: The Academic Years*. Cambridge, Mass., 1967.

Briggs, Mitchell Pirie. *George D. Herron and the European Settlement*. Stanford, 1932.

Buehrig, Edward H. *Woodrow Wilson and the Balance of Power*. Bloomington, Ind., 1955.

———. *Wilson's Foreign Policy in Perspective*. Bloomington, Ind., 1957.

Calvert, Peter. *The Mexican Revolution 1910–1914: The Diplomacy of Anglo-American Conflict*. Cambridge, 1968.

Carr, Edward H. *A History of Soviet Russia: The Bolshevik Revolution, 1917–1923*. 3 vols. London, 1950–1953.

Clements, Kendrick A. *Woodrow Wilson, World Statesman*. Boston, 1987.

Cobban, Alfred. *National Self-Determination*. Oxford, 1944.

Coffman, Edward M. *The War to End All Wars: The American Military Experience in World War I*. Madison, Wis., 1986.

Cohen, Warren I. *The American Revisionists: The Lessons of Intervention in World War I*. Chicago and London, 1967.

————. *America's Response to China: An Interpretative History of Sino-American Relations*. New York, 1971.

Coletta, Paolo E. *William Jennings Bryan*. 3 vols. Lincoln, Nebr., 1964–1970.

Cooke, Jacob E., ed. *The Federalist*. Middletown, Conn., 1961.

Cooper, John Milton, Jr. *The Warrior and the Priest: Woodrow Wilson and Theodore Roosevelt*. Cambridge, Mass., 1983.

Cumberland, Charles C. *Mexican Revolution: Genesis under Madero*. Austin and London, 1952.

Cunliffe, Marcus. *American Presidents and the Presidency*. New York, 1972.

Curry, George. "Woodrow Wilson, Jan Smuts and the Versailles Settlement." *American Historical Review* 66 (1961): 968–986.

Curry, Roy Watson. *Woodrow Wilson and Far Eastern Policy 1913–1921*. New York, 1957.

Devlin, Patrick. *Too Proud to Fight: Woodrow Wilson's Neutrality*. London, 1974.

Dickmann, Fritz. "Die Kriegsschuldfrage auf der Friedenskonferenz von Paris 1919." *Historische Zeitschrift* (1963): 1–101.

Dudden, Arthur P., ed. *Woodrow Wilson and the World of Today*. Philadelphia, 1957.

Egerton, George W. "The Lloyd George Government and the Creation of the League of Nations." *American Historical Review* 79 (1974): 419–444.

————. "Britain and 'The Great Betrayal': Anglo-American Relations and the Struggle for United States Ratification of the Treaty of Versailles, 1919–1920." *The Historical Journal* 21 (1978): 885–911.

Farnsworth, Beatrice. *William C. Bullitt and the Soviet Union*. Bloomington and London, 1967.

Ferrell, Robert H. *Woodrow Wilson and World War I, 1917–1921*. New York, 1985.

Fischer, Fritz. *Griff nach der Weltmacht: Die Kriegszielpolitik des kaiserlichen Deutschland, 1914–1918*. Düsseldorf, 1984.

Fleming, Denna Frank. *The United States and the League of Nations, 1918–1920*. New York and London, 1932.

Floto, Inga. *Colonel House in Paris: A Study of American Policy at the Paris Peace Conference, 1919*. Princeton, 1973.

Forcey, Charles. *The Crossroads of Liberalism: Croly, Weyl, Lippmann and the Progressive Era, 1900–1925*. New York, 1961.

Fowler, William B. *British-American Relations, 1917–1918: The Role of Sir William Wiseman*. Princeton, 1969.

Fox, Stephen R. *The Guardian of Peace: William Monroe Trotter*. New York, 1970.

Garraty, John A. *Henry Cabot Lodge: A Biography*. New York, 1953.

———. *Woodrow Wilson: A Great Life in Brief*. New York, 1956.

Gelfand, Lawrence E. *The Inquiry: American Preparations for Peace, 1917–1919*. New Haven and London, 1963.

George, Alexander L., and Juliette L. George. *Woodrow Wilson and Colonel House: A Personality Study*. New York, 1964.

Gerson, Louis L. *Woodrow Wilson and the Rebirth of Poland, 1914–1920: A Study of the Influence on American Policy of Minority Groups of Foreign Origin*. New Haven, 1953.

Gilbert, Martin, ed. *Lloyd George*. Englewood Cliffs, N.J., 1968.

Graebner, Norman A. *Ideas and Diplomacy: Readings in the Intellectual Tradition of American Foreign Policy*. New York, 1964.

Gregory, Ross. *Walter Hines Page, Ambassador to the Court of St. James's*. Lexington, Ky., 1970.

Grieb, Kenneth J. *The United States and Huerta*. Lincoln, Nebr., 1969.

Haffner, Sebastian. *Die Sieben Todesünden des deutschen Reiches im ersten Weltkrieg*. Bergisch Gladbach, 1981.

Hale, William Bayard. *Woodrow Wilson: The Story of His Life*. Garden City, N.Y., 1913.

————. *The Story of a Style*. New York, 1920.

Hancock, W. K. *Smuts: The Sanguine Years, 1870–1919*. Cambridge, 1962.

Hart, John Mason. *Revolutionary Mexico: The Coming and Process of the Mexican Revolution*. Berkeley, 1967.

Higginbotham, D. "The American Revolution in a Wider World." In J. P. Greene, ed., *The American Revolution: Its Character and Limits*. New York, 1987.

Hildebrand, Klaus. *Bethmann Hollweg, Der Kanzler ohne Eigenschaften?* Düsseldorf, 1970.

Hofman, J., and A. Stam. "De psychoanalyse in dienst van een diplomaat, Freud als co-auteur van W. C. Bullitt." *Tijdschrift voor Psychiatrie* 24 (1982): 125–134.

Hofstadter, Richard. *The Age of Reform*. New York, 1955.

————. *The Progressive Historians, Turner, Beard, Parrington*. New York, 1968.

Huisman, C. *Neerlands Israel*. Dordrecht, 1983.

Huthmacher, J. J., and W. I. Susman, eds. *Wilson's Diplomacy: An International Symposium*. Cambridge, Mass., 1973.

Jäger, Wolfgang. *Historische Forschung und politische Kultur in Deutschland: Die Debatte 1914–1989 über den Ausbruch des ersten Weltkrieges*. Göttingen, 1984.

Jessup, Philip C. *Elihu Root*. 2 vols. New York, 1938.

Kaplan, Justin. *Lincoln Steffens: A Biography*. New York, 1974.

Kennan, George. *American Diplomacy, 1900–1950*. Chicago, 1951.

————. *Russia Leaves the War: Soviet-American Relations, 1917–1920*. Vol. 1. London, 1956.

————. *The Decision to Intervene: Soviet-American Relations, 1917–1920*. Vol. 2. London, 1958.

————. *Soviet Foreign Policy, 1917–1941*. Princeton, 1960.

———. *Russia and the West under Lenin and Stalin*. Boston, 1961.

———. "Soviet Historiography and America's Role in the Intervention." In John Keep, ed., *Contemporary History in the Soviet Mirror*, 286–305. London, 1964.

Knight, Alan. *The Mexican Revolution*. 2 vols. Cambridge, 1986.

Knock, Thomas J. "History with Lightning: The Forgotten Film Wilson." In Peter C. Rollins, ed., *Hollywood as Historian*, 88–108. Lexington, Ky., 1983.

Kohn, Hans. *American Nationalism: An Interpretative Essay*. New York, 1961.

Krüger, Peter. *Versailles: Deutsche Aussenpolitik zwischen Revisionismus und Friedensicherung*. Munich, 1986.

Lasch, Christopher. *The American Liberals and the Russian Revolution*. New York and London, 1962.

Latham, Earl, ed. *The Philosophies and Policies of Woodrow Wilson*. Chicago, 1958.

Lauren, Paul Gordon. "Human Rights in History: Diplomacy and Racial Equality at the Paris Peace Conference." *Diplomatic History* 3 (1978): 257–278.

Lazo, Dimitri D. "A Question of Loyalty: Robert Lansing and the Treaty of Versailles." *Diplomatic History* 1 (1985): 35–53.

Lentin, A. *Lloyd George, Woodrow Wilson and the Guilt of Germany: An Essay in the Pre-history of Appeasement*. Leicester, 1984.

Leuchtenburg, William E. *The Perils of Prosperity, 1914–1932*. Chicago, 1958.

Levin, N. Gordon, Jr. *Woodrow Wilson and World Politics: America's Response to War and Revolution*. New York, 1968.

Levy, David W. *Herbert Croly of the New Republic: The Life and Thought of an American Progressive*. Princeton, 1985.

Li, Tien-Yi. *Woodrow Wilson's China Policy, 1913–1917*. New York, 1969.

Link, Arthur S. *Wilson*. 5 vols. Princeton, 1947–1965.

————. *Woodrow Wilson and the Progressive Era, 1910–1917*. New York, 1954.

————, ed. *Woodrow Wilson: A Profile*. New York, 1968.

————, ed. *The Impact of World War I*. New York, 1969.

————. *The Higher Realism of Woodrow Wilson and Other Essays*. Nashville, 1971.

————. *Woodrow Wilson: Revolution, War and Peace*. Arlington Heights, Ill., 1979.

————, ed. *Woodrow Wilson and a Revolutionary World, 1913–1921*. Chapel Hill, 1982.

————. "That Cobb Interview." *Journal of American History* 72 (1985): 7–17.

Livermore, Seward W. *Politics Is Adjourned: Woodrow Wilson and the War Congress, 1916–1918*. Middletown, Conn., 1966.

Lynar, Ernst Wilhelm Graf, ed. *Deutsche Kriegsziele 1914–1918: Eine Diskussion*. Frankfurt and Berlin, 1964.

Maddox, Robert J. *William E. Borah and American Foreign Policy*. Baton Rouge, 1969.

Mann, Golo. *Deutsche Geschichte des 19. und 20. Jahrhunderts*. Frankfurt, 1966.

Marston, F. S. *The Peace Conference of 1919: Organization and Procedure*. Oxford, 1944.

Martin, Lawrence W. *Peace Without Victory: Woodrow Wilson and the British Liberals*. New Haven, 1958.

May, Ernest W. *The World War and American Isolation, 1914–1917*. Cambridge, Mass., 1959.

Mayer, Arno J. *Political Origins of the New Diplomacy, 1917–1918*. New Haven, 1959.

————. *Politics and Diplomacy of Peacemaking: Containment and Counterrevolution at Versailles, 1918–1919*. London, 1968.

Mead, Sidney E. *The Old Religion in the Brave New World: Reflections* on the Relation Between Christendom and the Republic. Berkeley, 1977.

Meaney, Neville K. "Arthur S. Link and Thomas Woodrow Wilson." *Journal of American History* 1 (1967): 119–126.

Meier, August. *Negro Thought in America, 1880–1915*. Ann Arbor, 1963.

Mervin, David. "Henry Cabot Lodge and the League of Nations." *Journal of American Studies* 4 (1970): 201–214.

Millis, Walter. *Road to War: America, 1914–1917*. Boston, 1935.

Moorhead, J. H. *American Apocalypse: Yankee Protestants and the Civil War, 1860–1869*. New Haven and London, 1978.

Mowry, George E. *The Progressive Era, 1900–1920: The Reform Persuasion* (American Historical Association Pamphlet 212). Washington, 1972.

Mulder, John M. *Woodrow Wilson: The Years of Preparation*. Princeton, 1978.

Nicholas, H. G. "Wilson's Diplomacy." In J. J. Huthmacher and W. I. Susman, eds., *Wilson's Diplomacy: An International Symposium*, 79–102. Cambridge, Mass., 1973.

Niermeyer, J. F. "Ideaal en Werkelijkheid in de buitenlandse politiek van Woodrow Wilson." *De Gids* 102 (1938): 188–207, 314–39; 103 (1938): 84–99, 163–84.

Noble, David W. *The Paradox of Progressive Thought*. Minneapolis, 1958.

Osborn, George L. *Woodrow Wilson: The Early Years*. Baton Rouge, 1968.

Osgood, R. E. *Ideals and Self-Interest in America's Foreign Relations: The Great Transformation of the Twentieth Century*. Chicago, 1953.

Owen, Frank. *Tempestuous Journey: Lloyd George in His Life and Times*. London, 1954.

Parsons, Edward B. "Some International Implications of the 1918 Roosevelt-Lodge Campaign Against Wilson and a Democratic Congress." *Presidential Studies Quarterly* 19 (1989): 141–157.

Presser, J. *Amerika, Van kolonie tot wereldmacht: De geschiedenis van de Verenigde Staten*. Amsterdam and Brussels, 1949.

Pringle, Henry F. *The Life and Times of William Howard Taft: A Biography*. 2 vols. New York and Toronto, 1939.

Pugh, Martin. *Lloyd George*. London and New York, 1988.

Ross, Dorothy. "Woodrow Wilson and the Case for Psychohistory." *Journal of American History* 69 (1982): 659–668.

Rousseau, J. J. *Oeuvres complètes III: Du Contrat Social, Ecrits Politiques*. Paris, 1964.

Ruiz, George W. "The Ideological Convergence of Theodore Roosevelt and Woodrow Wilson." *Presidential Studies Quarterly* 19 (1989): 159–177.

Saunders, Frances W. "Love and Guilt: Woodrow Wilson and Mary Hulbert." *American Heritage* 30–3 (April–May, 1979): 68–77.

Schaper, B. W. *Albert Thomas: Dertig Jaar Sociaal Reformisme*. Leiden, 1953.

Schlesinger, Arthur M., Jr. *The Coming of the New Deal*. Boston, 1959.

————. *The Imperial Presidency*. London, 1974.

Schulz, Gerhard. *Revolutionen und Friedensschlüsse, 1917–1920*. Munich, 1980.

Schulze, Hagen. *Weimar: Deutschland 1917–1933*. Berlin, 1982.

Schwabe, Klaus. *Woodrow Wilson, Revolutionary Germany, and Peacemaking, 1918–1919: Missionary Diplomacy and the Relations of Power*. Chapel Hill and London, 1985.

Smit, C. *Tien Studiën betreffende Nederland in de Eerste Wereldoorlog*. Groningen, 1975.

Smith, Daniel M. *Robert Lansing and American Neutrality, 1914–1917*. Berkeley, 1958.

————. *The Great Departure: The United States and World War I, 1914–1920*. New York, 1965.

————. "National Interest and American Intervention 1917: An

Historiographical Appraisal." *Journal of American History* 52 (1965–1966): 5–24.

Smith, Gene. *When the Cheering Stopped*. London, 1964.

Snell, John L. "Wilson's Peace Program and German Socialism, January–March 1918." *Mississippi Valley Historical Review* 38 (1951): 187–214.

———. "Wilson on Germany and the Fourteen Points." *Journal of Modern History* 26 (1954): 364–369.

Spencer, Samuel R., Jr. *Decision for War 1917: The Laconia Sinking and the Zimmermann Telegram as Key Factors in the Public Reaction Against Germany*. Rindge, N.H., 1953.

Spindler, Arno. *Wie es zu dem Entschluss zum uneingeschränkten U-Bootskrieg gekommen ist*. Göttingen, n.d.

Steel, Ronald. *Walter Lippmann and the American Century*. Boston and Toronto, 1980.

Stone, Ralph. *The Irreconcilables: The Fight Against the League of Nations*. Lexington, Ky., 1970.

Stromberg, Ronald. *Collective Security and American Foreign Policy, From the League of Nations to NATO*. New York, 1963.

Taylor, A. J. P. *Lloyd George: Rise and Fall*. Cambridge, 1961.

Thompson, John A. "Woodrow Wilson and World War I: A Reappraisal." *Journal of American Studies* 19 (1985): 325–348.

———. *Reformers and War: American Progressive Publicists and the First World War*. Cambridge, 1987.

Thompson, John M. "Allied and American Intervention in Russia, 1918–1921." In C. E. Black, ed., *Rewriting Russian History: Soviet Interpretations of Russia's Past*, 334–400. New York, 1956.

———. *Russia, Bolshevism and the Versailles Peace*. Princeton, 1966.

Thomson, James C., Jr., Peter W. Stanley, and John Curtis Perry. *Sentimental Imperialists: The American Experience in East Asia*. New York, 1981.

Tillman, Seth P. *Anglo-American Relations at the Paris Peace Conference of 1919.* Princeton, 1961.

Toth, Charles W. "Isolationism and the Emergence of Borah: An Appeal to American Tradition." *Western Political Quarterly* 14 (1961): 555–568.

Trachtenberg, Marc. "Versailles After Sixty Years." *Journal of Contemporary History* 17 (1982): 487–506.

Trask, David F. *Victory Without Peace: American Foreign Relations in the Twentieth Century.* New York, 1968.

Trevelyan, George Macaulay. *Grey of Fallodon: Being the Life of Sir Edward Grey Afterwards Viscount Grey of Fallodon.* London, 1937.

Unterberger, Betty M., ed. *American Intervention in the Russian Civil War.* Lexington, Mass., 1969.

————. "Woodrow Wilson and the Bolsheviks: The 'Acid Test' of Soviet-American Relations." *Diplomatic History* 11 (1987): 71–90.

Varg, Paul A. *The Making of a Myth: The United States and China, 1897–1912.* East Lansing, 1968.

Vinson, John Charles. *William Borah and the Outlawry of War.* Athens, Ga., 1957.

Walworth, Arthur. *Woodrow Wilson.* 2 vols. New York and London, 1958.

————. *Wilson and His Peacemakers: American Diplomacy at the Paris Peace Conference, 1919.* New York, 1977.

Watson, Richard L., Jr. "Woodrow Wilson and His Interpreters, 1947–1957." *Mississippi Valley Historical Review* 44 (1957): 207–236.

Weber, Marianne. *Max Weber: Ein Lebensbild.* Tübingen, 1926.

Weinstein, Edwin A. *Woodrow Wilson: A Medical and Psychological Biography.* Princeton, 1981.

Wells, Samuel F., Jr. "New Perspectives on Wilsonian Diplomacy: The

Secular Evangelism of American Political Economy." *Perspectives in American History* 6 (1972): 389–419.

Widenor, William C. *Henry Cabot Lodge and the Search for an American Foreign Policy*. Berkeley, 1980.

Wiebe, Robert. *The Search for Order, 1877–1920*. New York, 1967.

Willert, Arthur. *The Road to Safety: A Study in Anglo-American Relations*. London, 1952.

Williams, William A. *The Tragedy of American Diplomacy*. New York, 1962.

Wimer, Kurt. "Woodrow Wilson's Plans to Enter the League of Nations through an Executive Agreement." *Western Political Quarterly* 112 (1961): 800–812.

————. "Woodrow Wilson Tries Conciliation: An Effort That Failed." *The Historian* 25 (1963): 419–438.

Woodward, David R. "The Origins and Intent of David Lloyd George's January 5 War Aims Speech." *The Historian* 34 (1971): 22–39.

INDEX

355, 360–361, 367; and prevention of Wilson's candidacy for third term, 410; on trial cabinet meeting, 409; warning to Wilson regarding tour, 391, 395, 396; Edith Wilson's actions supported by, 397, 398

Great Britain, 121, 135. *See also* England

"Great Cause" campaign, 53

Greene, John Richard, 13

Grew, Joseph C., 203

Grey, Edward, 133, 134, 141, 160, 172, 177, 403–404; House and, 166–167, 168, 169, 170, 174, 203; Lodge and, 403; on mediation, 170

Hague Conferences (1899, 1907), 103, 297

Haiti, 118

Hale, William Bayard, 122, 123

Hall, William Reginald, 220

Hamilton, Alexander, *The Federalist Papers*, 261

Hankey, Maurice, 198, 329

Harding, Warren G., 386, 411, 412, 413, 417

Harper, George McLean, 28

Harper, Samuel N., 226

Harrison, Benjamin, 154

Hart, Albert Bushnell, 33

Hart, John Mason, 120

Harvey, George, 55, 81, 82–83, 106, 377

Hay, John, 35, 103, 110

Headlam-Morley, James, 290

Hearst, William Randolph, 86, 377

Henderson, Arthur, 360

Herder, Johann G., 261

Heroes, Roosevelt's proposal regarding, 233

Heroism, cult of, 35

Herron, George D., 211

Hertling, Count von, 259, 267

Heuss, Theodor, 359–360

Hibben, Jessie, 28, 56, 59

Hibben, John (Jack) Grier, 28, 56, 57, 59, 65, 343

Hindenburg, Paul von, 197, 198, 273, 277

Hitchcock, Gilbert, 384, 399, 400, 401, 404, 406

Hitler, Adolf, 4, 371–372

Hofstadter, Richard, 162, 290

Holtzendorff, Henning von, 158

Hoover, Herbert, 309, 402

House, Edward Mandell, 116, 117, 133; in Allied war council, 252–253; Baker

on, 314; Bonsal and, 401; Clemenceau and, 105, 274, 314, 339; Devlin on, 176; as diplomat, 104–105, 159–161, 164–169; Edith Wilson and, 139, 401; establishment of "The Inquiry" group by, 252; in Europe, 160–161, 166–169, 172–176; Europeans on, 105; Grayson on, 342; Grey and, 166–167, 168, 169, 170, 174, 203; health of, 401; involvement in European conflicts, 159–162; Lansing and, 154, 283–284, 341; Lloyd George and, 203, 253, 255, 274, 339, 342; on mediation, 187, 200; and peace conference, 282, 284, 313–317, 342; peace talks with Allies, 272–276; personality of, 105, 106–107, 176, 255, 266; *Philip Dru, Administrator*, 105; on preparedness for war, 180–181; Wilson and, 171, 205–206, 253, 255, 368; Wilson's friendship with, 93, 104–105, 106–108, 166, 171, 205–206, 221–222, 253, 313, 314–317, 342–343, 368; on Wilson's reaction to wife's death, 137, 138;

Designer:	Seventeenth Street Studios
Compositor:	Wilsted & Taylor
Text:	11/13 Granjon
Display:	Granjon
Printer:	Edwards Bros. Inc.
Binder:	Edwards Bros. Inc.